Atlantic History in the Nineteenth Century

Niels Eichhorn

Atlantic History in the Nineteenth Century

Migration, Trade, Conflict, and Ideas

Niels Eichhorn
Middle Georgia State University
Macon, GA, USA

ISBN 978-3-030-27639-3   ISBN 978-3-030-27640-9 (eBook)
https://doi.org/10.1007/978-3-030-27640-9

© The Editor(s) (if applicable) and The Author(s), under exclusive license to Springer Nature Switzerland AG 2019
This work is subject to copyright. All rights are solely and exclusively licensed by the Publisher, whether the whole or part of the material is concerned, specifically the rights of translation, reprinting, reuse of illustrations, recitation, broadcasting, reproduction on microfilms or in any other physical way, and transmission or information storage and retrieval, electronic adaptation, computer software, or by similar or dissimilar methodology now known or hereafter developed.
The use of general descriptive names, registered names, trademarks, service marks, etc. in this publication does not imply, even in the absence of a specific statement, that such names are exempt from the relevant protective laws and regulations and therefore free for general use.
The publisher, the authors and the editors are safe to assume that the advice and information in this book are believed to be true and accurate at the date of publication. Neither the publisher nor the authors or the editors give a warranty, expressed or implied, with respect to the material contained herein or for any errors or omissions that may have been made. The publisher remains neutral with regard to jurisdictional claims in published maps and institutional affiliations.

This Palgrave Macmillan imprint is published by the registered company Springer Nature Switzerland AG
The registered company address is: Gewerbestrasse 11, 6330 Cham, Switzerland

For
Stephanie

Preface

This project started when I worked on my dissertation and needed to figure out the conceptual framework for my project comparing events in 1848 and the US Civil War. Especially, David Armitage's concept of three Atlantic worlds interested me. The idea of a comparative Atlantic study seemed to fit rather well with my transnational project. However, I eventually turned to the transnational methodology recently embraced by Civil War historians Paul Quigley and Andre Fleche that was more appropriate for what I was doing. Nevertheless, I remained interested in nineteenth-century Atlantic history. I was troubled that Atlantic historians had decided to end their narratives in 1825. Despite abandoning Atlantic history's methodology for the dissertation, I decided to put some of my thought regarding the existence of a nineteenth-century Atlantic world on paper.

When I first started, I envisioned an article-length essay pointing out some comparisons. My goal was primarily to put secondary literatures into conversation with each other, which remains an essential goal of the book. As I worked on the article project, I took the methodological ideas and examples to a graduate student conference, where an established Latin American historian in the audience commented on my presentation that what I had done was not new and had already been done before. Humorously, less than an hour later a panel, which the same historian was part of, noted that nineteenth-century Atlantic history was an unwritten page and needed attention. He raised no opposition.

While confusing, I felt confirmed to continue. I finally had the article project completed, but it had turned into a dense and lengthy 50 pages.

It was too long for an article, so I kept researching and reading and broke the various sections up to revise the project into a book-length manuscript. It was initially just over a hundred pages suggesting a new narrative. I asked for feedback from some Atlantic historians, but their busy schedules did not allow them to provide me detailed comments. Sadly, I had to put the manuscript aside as I finished the revision to my dissertation and first book manuscript. However, I kept reading and researching during the period where the manuscript sat idle. Recently, I decided to finally revisit the project, make additions, and revise the manuscript to finally tell some of the stories of the Atlantic world during the nineteenth century.

What follows is not and cannot be an all-encompassing history of the Atlantic world during the nineteenth century. This work focuses on the exchange of people, goods, money, and ideas, the formation of nation-states and constitutional governments, and the movement of imperial frontier around the Atlantic world. Therefore, there are many stories I am unable to tell. Unfortunately, I was unable to integrate many women stories, their work as missionaries, as social reformers, and travelers. Similarly, indigenous people are not given the due attention they deserve. Reading culture and the intellectual exchange of literature and art might be another worthwhile pursuit for future historians. Similarly, urban historians might find that Haussmann Paris had a much larger influence on the urban centers of the Atlantic world. I hope that some of the shortcomings of this work will stimulate others to continue where I left off or my narrative focus was too narrowly conceived and point in the coming years to other aspects that illustrate the vibrancy of the nineteenth-century Atlantic world. I hope this work encourages my colleagues to think in Atlantic terms.

In the process of writing this book, I had the help of many library staffers at the University of Arkansas and Middle Georgia States who helped to locate sometimes obscure titles. The participants at Florida International University's History Graduate Student conference provided an enlightening perspective on Atlantic history and its workings. I also wish to thank my many professional friends and colleagues, David Armitage, Wim Klooster, David Schieffler, Scott Lloyd, Aaron Moulton,

Pat Kelly, whose conversations and suggestions were extremely helpful in putting this manuscript together. Most importantly, my thanks go to my wonderful wife Stephanie who patiently accepted the looming deadline for this book.

Macon, USA   Niels Eichhorn

Contents

1	Introduction	1
2	Migration	15
3	Trade Relations	35
4	National Revolutions	53
5	Constitutional Revolutions	73
6	Garibaldi's Revolutionary Atlantic	95
7	Slave Trade and the Return to Africa	103
8	Emancipation	121
9	Conquest of Frontiers	141
10	Imperial Projects and Expansion	159
11	Henry Sylvester Williams's Black Atlantic	179

12	Conservative Revolutions	185
13	Atlantic Tourism	215
14	Atlantic Financial Entanglements	237
15	Industrial Reform, Progressivism, and Socialism	249
16	A New Atlantic World	267
Index		275

List of Tables

Table 2.1	Migrates leaving from Bremen	21
Table 2.2	Migrates leaving from Hamburg	22
Table 2.3	Migrates leaving from Great Britain	24
Table 3.1	Imports of Bremen by value	43
Table 3.2	Export of Bremen by value	44
Table 3.3	Export of France by value in million Francs	45
Table 3.4	Import of France by value in million Francs	46
Table 3.5	Export of the United Kingdom by value in Pound	47
Table 3.6	Imports of the United Kingdom by value in Pound	48
Table 3.7	Export of the United States by value in Dollar	49
Table 3.8	Imports of the United States by value in Dollar	50

CHAPTER 1

Introduction

On April 30, 1849, the Hamburg native, Georg Laué Julius Bendixen, sailed through the Golden Gate into San Francisco. Unlike many of the passengers and crew, who quickly disembarked for the goldfields in the interior, Bendixen came to San Francisco to work for Cross, Hobson, and Company, a merchant firm. Bendixen was just one of over 300,000 migrants who arrived in California between 1849 and 1854, and one among millions who crisscrossed the Atlantic Ocean during those years. Bendixen started his journey with his father only two years earlier when the two departed their native Hamburg for Valparaiso, Chile. Born on November 19, 1828, in Apenrade, Schleswig, Bendixen grew up with his father away captaining a sailing vessel.[1] Coming from a family of mariners, Bendixen represented the nineteenth-century Atlantic world's population of seafarers, merchants, and migrants.

Bendixen had no interest to follow in his father's footstep and suffer the hardships of an ocean-going profession; instead, he embraced a merchant career with an apprenticeship in a local spice store. In the fall of

---

[1] Andreas Beckmann, "Justus Ruperti und Georg Laué Julius Bendixen: Hamburger Kaufleute und ihre Beteiligung am kalifornischen Goldrausch, 1849–1852," in *Die hanseatisch-amerikanischen Beziehungen seit 1790*, eds. Rolf Hammel-Kiesow, Heiko Herold, and Claudis Schurmann (Trier, Germany: Porto Alba Verlag, 2017), 217, 219; James Quay, "Beyond Dreams and Disappointments: Defining California Through Culture," in *A Companion to California History*, eds. William Francis Deverell and David Igler (Chichester, UK: Wiley-Blackwell, 2008), 6.

© The Author(s) 2019
N. Eichhorn, *Atlantic History in the Nineteenth Century*,
https://doi.org/10.1007/978-3-030-27640-9_1

1847, he joined his father on a trip to Valparaiso, Chile. Bendixen's luck held; with the growing trade interest of Hamburg's merchant houses in South America, an employment opportunity arose. Two merchants, who had only recently opened a branch office for Hochgreve und Vorwerk, hired the young Bendixen. The contact with people from his home region and their expansive trade network had offered Bendixen employment.[2] He, like so many, benefitted from these nineteenth-century Atlantic merchant communities and networks that spanned the region.

In Valparaiso, Bendixen and his father encountered a merchants group from the bustling port of San Francisco. His father hired on as captain for a copper shipment to Hamburg. When the ship ran aground and the owners auctioned the vessel off to the San Francisco-based Cross, Hobson, and Company, Alexander Cross, a Scottish immigrant, used the opportunity to establish a branch office for his company in Valparaiso and hired Bendixen's father to bring the refloated vessel to San Francisco. As a result of this business interaction, Georg Bendixen received a job offer in Cross's business in San Francisco.[3]

Once in San Francisco, Bendixen assisted Cross, Hobson, and Company with the massive amount of commodities they purchased and sold. These goods arrived from numerous parts of the world. As a respected member of San Francisco society and deeply familiar with the ordered and orderly society of Hamburg, San Francisco struck Bendixen as a lawless place. He joined the local Vigilance Comité, carrying a revolver, and working police duties.[4] Bendixen had a conservative outlook; he desired to bring order, law, and government to this frontier environment, not dissimilar from hundreds of others in the Atlantic world during the nineteenth century. For Bendixen, California was not the global crossroad that Chinese miners and railroad works as well as Australian miners made it, but the very edge or last frontier of the Atlantic world of the nineteenth century.

Bendixen did not stay in Cross's service for long, wishing to establish his own company. He relied on the many connections he made in Hamburg, Valparaiso, and San Francisco, as well as the personal interactions with young individuals from his home region scattered around

---

[2] Beckmann, "Justus Ruperti und Georg Laué Julius Bendixen," 218.
[3] Ibid.
[4] Ibid., 220.

the world. For the next, almost ten years and despite setbacks as a result of major fires in San Francisco, Bendixen gained respectability and an income as a merchant. Like many of his countrymen, Bendixen sought a position in an auction house. He eventually married Amalie Fischer, from a German family, and in 1865 left San Francisco to return to Hamburg.[5] Bendixen continued to rely on his personal relations for his business successes in the competitive Atlantic world environment.

Bendixen represents the nineteenth-century Atlantic world. He left his home in the German states for the economic opportunities offered in the Americas, just like thousands had done previously, stretching as far back as the Colonial era. Bendixen relied on the intricate and long-established trade networks and linkages when he searched for jobs, but also when he tried his own business luck. He faced the difficulties of political, social, and national transformations as he tried to bring his idea of law and order to the California frontier. Nevertheless, he was like many, not a stationary character. He embodied the traveler, who moved about, but at heart remained loyal to his home country. Many stories like his remain unrecognized as scholars continue to restrain themselves in the nineteenth-century nation-state narratives, avoiding application of a transnational or Atlantic approach to the Atlantic world of this era.

Historians usually do not consider Bendixen's Atlantic world of the 1850s and 1860s as part of the Atlantic world narrative. This work seeks to challenge previously held chronological assumptions about the Atlantic world and especially the claim that the Atlantic world transformed into part of a global narrative after 1825. Importantly, Atlantic history, in the words of Philip Morgan and Jack Greene, represents an "analytic construct."[6] Historians dissatisfied with the limitation of nation-state narratives, influenced by Fernand Braudel's work on the Mediterranean, and the overlapping colonial experiences during the age of exploration and colonization, embraced the broader narrative opportunities offered by Atlantic history, which allowed them to not only study one empire, colony, or region, but to place their works in a broader international framework. However, as some critics have pointed out, Atlantic history may be imperial history by another name, and that

[5] Ibid., 221–223, 227–228.
[6] Philip Morgan and Jack Greene, *Atlantic History: A Critical Appraisal* (New York: Oxford University Press, 2009), 3.

the Atlantic lacks the same cohesion as the Mediterranean.[7] However, as David Eltis convincingly shows, "The end result [of Atlantic histories] was, if not a single Atlantic society, a set of societies fundamentally different from what they would have been without participation in the new transatlantic network."[8] This work sees the Atlantic world in similar terms. The Atlantic world encompasses people who shared similar experiences in different parts of the Atlantic region and some who transferred ideas and experiences in person around the Atlantic basin.

At the same time, the Atlantic world was never a self-contained unit.[9] After all, the early Atlantic world was a highway to the riches of Asia. The Viceroyalty of New Spain transsshipped Chinese silk from the Manila Galleon onto Spain-bound vessels.[10] Furthermore, the British East India Company, the Vereenigde Oost-Indische Compagnie, and the Compagnie des Indes Orientales all relied on stopping points in the Atlantic basin to bring home the massive profits of the East India trade and replenish their vessels.[11] Historians have quarreled about the delineation between Atlantic history and Global history. In the Atlantic world, all regions developed differently because of the interactions between the various parts which contrasted from the Indian Ocean world where Europeans joined long-established trade systems as junior partners. Some historians have argued that for example "contract labor and capital flows to Asia were a nineteenth century phenomena."[12] This work begs to differ. Asia certainly grew in importance during the nineteenth century, but did not gain the same significance that the Atlantic trade network had. This work will illustrate that people continued to think in Atlantic and not global terms during the nineteenth century.

Similarly, considering the origins of Atlantic history in the era of the early Cold War and the emergence of NATO, there is a level of regionalism.[13] Technically, there were two Atlantic worlds, North and South Atlantic. Where Brazilian plantations received slaves from the

---

[7] Ibid., 5–6.

[8] David Eltis, "Atlantic History in Global Perspective," *Itinerario* 23 (July 1999), 141.

[9] Morgan and Greene, *Atlantic History*, 6.

[10] John H. Parry, *The Age of Reconnaissance: Discovery, Exploration and Settlement 1450 to 1650* (Berkeley: University of California Press, 1981), 195.

[11] Parry, *The Age of Reconnaissance*, 199–200.

[12] Eltis, "Atlantic History in Global Perspective," 142.

[13] Donna Gabaccia, "A Long Atlantic in a Wider World," *Atlantic Studies* 1 (2004), 3.

Portuguese trade partners in Congo and Angola, the North Atlantic system witnessed a diverse interaction between imperial metropoles, Africa slave ports, and the American colonies.[14] Whereas the colonial era systems operated often autonomous of each other, after 1800, migration into South American from Europe increased and Brazil made efforts for closer ties with Europe. During the nineteenth century, the North and South Atlantic systems grew closer together and transformed into something more akin to one Atlantic world, even if a significant focus remained on the North Atlantic system.

Keeping in mind that the Atlantic world is an "analytic construct," the chronological framework is a similarly arbitrary construct. The vast majority of works have adopted an endpoint around the independence of the Spanish American colonies, c.1825. They argue that with the end of the colonial empires, the Atlantic world disappeared as a cohesive unit. The foremost Atlantic history theorist and founder of the International Seminar on the History of the Atlantic World, Bernard Bailyn has defined the chronological boundaries of Atlantic history in *Atlantic History: Concept and Contours* as the period "from the first encounters of Europeans with the Western Hemisphere through the Revolutionary era." In other words, he proposed a chronology from 1492 to c.1825. He, like many others, claims that after the Age of Revolution, trends were global and no longer Atlantic.[15] Bailyn argues that once the colonies in the Americas, from New Hampshire to Chile, gained their independence, Atlantic connections dissolved. However, Canada, Cuba, and Puerto Rico remained colonies for most of the nineteenth century. Some Caribbean islands remain European colonies, controlled by the Dutch, the British, and the French, to this day. Along with trade, intellectual and political ties remain strong between the former colonies and their metropoles as individuals traveled from the Americas and Africa to Europe for education. The claim of an end of the Atlantic world with the end of the European empires is problematic.

---

[14] Kerry Bystrom and Joseph R. Slaughter, *The Global South Atlantic* (New York: Fordham University Press, 2018); Roquinaldo A. Ferreira, *Cross-Cultural Exchange in the Atlantic World Angola and Brazil During the Era of the Slave Trade* (Cambridge, UK: Cambridge University Press, 2014).

[15] Bernard Bailyn, *Atlantic History Concept and Contours* (Cambridge, MA: Harvard University Press, 2009), 3.

Dissatisfied with such an imperial-looking chronology, recent scholarship by Thomas Benjamin and the authors of *The Atlantic World* textbook have suggested a different chronological endpoint. To the authors of *The Atlantic World*, the abolition of slavery "diminished [the] coherence of the Atlantic as a self-contained unit of analysis."[16] Similarly, Benjamin sees slavery as the final of the "fundamental structures that connected and defined the Atlantic World," whose collapse meant the region no longer existed as a cohesive unit and was submerged in growing global trends.[17] However, in both cases closing in 1888 or 1900 still has a rather imperial perspective of the Atlantic World and more importantly, the focus on abolition in the Americas frequently devolves into case studies rather than an integrated and encompassing Atlantic narrative. Even more, the narrative tends to focus on the Americas at the expense of especially Africa.

Where the arbitrary endpoints in c.1825 and c.1888 are deeply ingrained in Atlantic world scholarship, some ethnic-based studies have adopted a different ending. In divergence, Jace Weaver ends his presentation of a Native American-Red Atlantic with a Native delegation to the League of Nations and Inuit contributions to an Arctic exploration, placing the end in 1924.[18] In contrast, Paul Gilroy looks at a smaller number of individuals of African descent and their contribution to an intellectual, Atlantic community that stretched well into the twentieth century. His narrative illustrates that the exchanges of ideas and intellectual developments created a shared culture within the Black Atlantic.[19] Whether looking at the Atlantic as red, black, or white, chronological endpoints are difficult to define.

Whereas many proponents of Atlantic history continued to see a history predominated by white members, i.e., a white Atlantic, or by black individuals, i.e., a black Atlantic, there are other narratives available to discuss intellectual movements within the Atlantic world. In contrast to

---

[16] Douglas R. Egerton, et al. *The Atlantic World: A History, 1400–1888* (Wheeling, IL: Harlan Davidson, 2007), 2.

[17] Thomas Benjamin, *The Atlantic World: Europeans, Africans, Indians and Their Shared History, 1400–1900* (New York: Cambridge University Press, 2013), 661.

[18] Jace Weaver, *The Red Atlantic: American Indigenes and the Making of the Modern World, 1000–1927* (Chapel Hill: The University of North Carolina Press, 2014), xii.

[19] Paul Gilroy, *The Black Atlantic: Modernity and Double Consciousness* (Cambridge, MA: Harvard University Press, 1993).

Weaver's Native America-Red Atlantic, Donna Gabaccia defines the Red Atlantic instead as one of "working-class solidarity." Ironically, the proponents of the labor Red Atlantic end their studies around 1830, when many nation-state-focused working-class studies claim a working class had barely emerged. More importantly, especially by the second half of the nineteenth century, this Red Atlantic provides a possible framing devise for the emerging industrial societies around the Atlantic.[20] The framing devises of a white, red, and black Atlantic can provide a better understanding not only of the traditional Atlantic history chronology, but also of the Atlantic world during the nineteenth century.

This study will abandon the usual endpoints of 1825 and 1888 to illustrate the existence of a vibrant Atlantic community during the nineteenth century. Since this work presents an era of transformation and change, the most natural starting point is the moment that changed the Atlantic world forever, the French Revolution in 1789.[21] This all-encompassing event, with its political, social, and national challenges to the established order, laid the foundation for the decolonization of the Americas, raised the specter of nation-state development, and the demand for constitutional government. At the same time, the endpoint for this study is the next moment of massive transformation, the beginning of the Great War in 1914 when national and imperial ambitions collided, and the new trade and communication networks dropped the state system of Europe into carnage. The world globalized with the Great War as Japan grew in importance rising as an international power. These chronological boundaries are rather Euro-centric. Nevertheless, pivotal events in Europe had an impact on the Atlantic world. Especially, the starting point in 1789 was, due to the imperial connections, transformative for the entire region. At the same time, the nineteenth-century Atlantic world was not only about the exchange of ideas, people, and commodities, many states experienced similar events, revolutions, and challenges, which invites comparative analysis.

This book will utilize a few different approaches to Atlantic history. David Armitage has provided three different methodologically approaches to understand the Atlantic world. The most frequently used way to do Atlantic history is cis-Atlantic, where historians study a

---

[20] Gabaccia, "A Long Atlantic in a Wider World," 4–5.

[21] This study uses the idea of transformation based on Aaron S. Fogleman, "The Transformation of the Atlantic World, 1776–1867," *Atlantic Studies* 6 (2009), 5–28.

community or region from a microscale perspective with an eye to the larger trends of the Atlantic world that shaped the locations and experiences. A more complex method involves the comparative presentation of communities in a trans-Atlantic presentation. The most multifaceted way to understand the Atlantic world comes from what Armitage defines as circum-Atlantic, "the history of the Atlantic as a particular zone of exchange and interchange, circulation and transmission," an all-encompassing narrative.[22] For the most part, this study embraces Armitage's trans-Atlantic approach to provide certain examples of how a nineteenth-century Atlantic world operated, which however will not be all-inclusive. Using comparative history to illustrate the shared experience of states and people around the Atlantic, will illustrate the interconnectedness of the region, especially when lacking personal narratives to showcase those ties.

Atlantic world narratives are about people, their experiences, and how their actions transformed their communities and the course of history. This study will rely heavily on personal experiences and narratives. However, *Atlantic History in the Nineteenth Century* is not, and cannot be, the final word on the Atlantic world during this century. What this book will present is "an" Atlantic history, not "the" Atlantic history. Unfortunately, some groups and individuals, especially women like Margaret Fuller, or movements, like realist art, are absent. Their absence will hopefully encourage other works to consider what the female or the artistic nineteenth-century Atlantic world looked like. The narrative that follows centers on the exchange of people, ideas, and commodities as they transformed politics, states, and frontiers.

Underlying much of the massive transformation experienced by states and communities around the Atlantic world during the nineteenth century was the continued and growing exchange of goods, commodities, and people. Millions of people crisscrossed the Atlantic during this era; some came to stay in a new home, while others came for leisure purposes. Attracted by a vast literature, migrants favored location within the Atlantic basin where they could join established communities and find economic opportunities to their liking. As Chapter 2 will illustrate, not everybody crossed voluntarily or in luxurious style, the migration

---

[22] David Armitage, "Three Concepts in Atlantic History," in *The British Atlantic World, 1500–1800*, eds. David Armitage and Michael J. Braddick (Basingstoke, UK: Palgrave Macmillan, 2009), 17–25.

experiences remained fraught with danger, even in the age of steamships. Nevertheless, sailing vessels remained the main transportation mechanism for much of the century, especially the transportation of commodities. Merchant communities and trade networks connected every part of the Atlantic world as Chapter 3 showcases. However, greater trade ties meant the desire for faster communication as transportation increased. Merchants and bankers needed reliable and speedy information in order to make transactions. Banking houses used the improved communications to extend their financial holdings, placing loans and bonds on the European markets. A system of trust developed where houses like Rothschild and Baring Brothers relied on their agents to accurately report on financial opportunities as Chapter 14 explains. While migrants, trade, and money tied the Atlantic world together and forever altered business relations, the improvement in the movement of goods and people across the ocean was largely due to the emergence of steamships. These vessels gave rise to new companies like Cunard, the Norddeutscher Lloyd, and others who focused primarily on the transport of mail and passengers. Some of these passenger-carrying companies found ways to make travel extremely luxurious catering to wealthy tourists as Chapter 13 eludes to. The movement of people and goods helped in the dramatic transformation of the Atlantic world during the nineteenth century.

These changes in communication and transportation also allowed ideas to freely travel. Preceding the French Revolution, the Atlantic world was already engaged in the Age of Revolutions, which had started with the secession of the Thirteen Colonies from Great Britain. The revolutions that followed in the footsteps of the French, be that the events in Spanish America, Ireland, Italy, Greece, or Poland, voiced demands usually twofold in nature. Chapter 4 argues that the occupation by French revolutionary troops caused a national awakening; people desired unification in states with people who shared the same culture, spoke the same language, and held the same belief systems. However, nation-states were not always embracing unification; many nations felt oppressed and desired freedom by separating from a larger state entity. The creation of nation-states was not the only demand people around the Atlantic world had, there was also the other legacy of the French Revolution where people demanded accountability from their rulers and constitutional governments that treated ruled and ruler the same as Chapter 5 presents. The perception that the lack of a constitution, of the right to elect representatives, and of a responsive legislative caused oppression spread in the Atlantic world in the aftermath of the French Revolution. However, demands for political reform fell on deaf ears and powerholders rarely surrendered their privileges. While the French Revolution, independence struggles in Spanish America, and the Revolutions in 1830 and 1848 desired to create constitutional nation-states, political reformers failed to achieve their goals. Nevertheless, conservative forces realized that constitutional governments were the future as Chapter 12 demonstrates. The Conte di Cavour, Otto von Bismarck, Porfirio Díaz, and Abraham Lincoln accomplished the goals of creating nation-states with constitutional governments in the course of the 1860s and 1870s. The fragmented state system of the early modern period with its allegiance to the king and lord ended by 1900 when people identified with their nationality in a state governed by constitutions and elected rulers.

Unfortunately, the freedom revolutionaries demanded with constitutional governments and nation-states was limited and excluded people of color. While millions crossed the Atlantic voluntarily in their search for economic opportunities, hundreds of thousands suffered in the holds of slave ships on their journey from freedom in Africa to the dehumanizing experience of slavery in the New World. Chapter 7 illustrates the long struggle to finally end the Atlantic slave trade. During the nineteenth century, about one-third of all the slaves brought to the Americas arrived, increasing the need to deal a final blow to the trade which finally happened by mid-century. However, as thousands crossed on slave ships, some desired to return to Africa to escape oppression in the Americas. The attempts to colonize freed people in Africa had limited success and by the end of the century members of the Tuskegee Institute went to the German colony of Togo to help with the growing of cotton. After states had started the process of outlawing the trade in human beings, the focus shifted to the end of slavery itself as Chapter 8 illustrates. Setting the stage, the slave rebellion in Saint-Domingue was fraught with violence and created arguments that emancipation, violence, race wars, and economic destruction were closely related. However, Great Britain soon changed that dynamic with the gradual and compensated emancipation of the empire's slave population. Slave societies followed this example, but challenges emerged as the Atlantic abolition movement demanded an end of gradualism and an immediate end of slavery. The rebellion of the southern states changed all of this when the Abraham Lincoln government determined to end slavery without compensation. With the end of slavery in the United States, the Brazilian and Spanish empires soon followed suit. However, the end of slavery in the Americas did not spell the termination of the institution in the Atlantic. In Africa, slavery still prospered; in its recently acquired colonies, the British Empire continued to allow slavery. The humanism that underlay the revolutionary upheavals also caused the demise of slavery to bring freedom to people.

Freedom, a relatively new concept in the Atlantic world and slow to come to people, did not include everybody. Since the inception of the Atlantic world by explorers, a hazy frontier existed between the civilized settlements along the coast and the indigenous interiors. Even by 1800, as Chapter 9 will show, many parts of the interiors remained unknown while explorers and adventurers attempted to cartograph and bring to attention those regions. They followed rivers and met a vast array of indigenous people. In their footsteps followed settlers who sought to put the land under the plow, pushed on by the propaganda literature suggesting the unlimited opportunities available in the interiors. Although the indigenous people were not ready to surrender their land without a fight, the result were brutal conflicts along the frontiers. This imperial push into the interiors had a concurrent outward push into new imperial project as Chapter 10 illustrates. The start of the nineteenth century witnessed the demise of empire in the Americas, with few exceptions. However, states not only had to fight for independence but continue to fight to maintain their freedom. Neighbors preyed on each other in the Caribbean, especially the increasingly powerful United States which had designs on a variety of Caribbean and Central American states. By 1900, the United States replaced Spain as the hegemon in the Americas, wrestling the final two colonies from the Spanish Empire. With Spain in imperial decline, France and Great Britain looked to new opportunities to expand their colonial empires in Africa. What the Americas were to European empires in the early modern era became the African continent in 1900. Empires remained the defining state of organization within the Atlantic world during the nineteenth century.

The emergence of industry, the mass movement of commodities, and the expansion of empires came together to bring new resources and markets into existence, and the dislocation of a working-class society brought about new questions in the second half of the century as Chapter 15 highlights. Where people could identify with a nation-state, they also grew increasingly class conscious and desired to improve their lot. A wide variety of social, economic, and political solutions emerged on the political left. What Saint-Domingue represented for slave societies in the first half of the century, the Paris Commune represented for industrial societies in the second half. There were fears of working-class unrest that required addressing. Reform movements emerged that called for social reform, welfare measures, and a new urban landscape. At the same time, the various new ideologies dispersed into the Atlantic world along the trade and communication lines in the minds and baggage of migrants. The Atlantic world remained deeply interconnected as people struggled to make sense of the modern environments brought by industrialization.

The Atlantic world in 1914 was a vastly different place, and the region dramatically transformed during the last 125 years. When the French Revolution started, the Americas, except for the newly independent United States, were controlled by European imperial powers and Africa remained largely unknown to Europeans. By 1914, few colonies remained in the Americas, but Africa had transformed into an imperially divided continent. Similarly, in 1789, Africa provided a vast number of slaves to the plantation economies of the Americas where they toiled in desolate conditions. By the end of the century, the slave trade had ended long ago and slavery was eradicated in the Americas. However, where Africans no longer had to fear their forceful removal into slavery and hardship on a Caribbean sugar plantation, the search for the exotic placed them in cages in zoological gardens in Europe. Furthermore, monarchical government with absolute powers prevailed at the time of the French Revolution. A century in the future, a diverse set of new governments had sprung into existence, ranging from constitutional monarchies to democratic republics and revolutionary Marxist communes, constitutional government was the mainstay around the Atlantic world. Finally where an ocean crossing around 1800 could take over a month followed by stagecoaches traversing bad road on a cumbersome journey to a spa or tourist site, by 1900, migrants and tourists could travel in style on massive and luxurious ocean-going vessels with railroads providing smooth and easy connections to the final destination, where hotels readymade for tourist's tastes awaited their clientele. The nineteenth century had witnessed a massive transformation of the way people thought about other places, economic matters, industry, trade, politics, and their place in society. The interconnected nature of the Atlantic world had made much of this possible allowing for a free exchange of ideas, goods, money, and people who reshaped the states around the Atlantic.

Bibliography

Armitage, David, and Michael J. Braddick, eds. *The British Atlantic World, 1500–1800*. Basingstoke, UK: Palgrave Macmillan, 2009.

Bailyn, Bernard. *Atlantic History Concept and Contours*. Cambridge, MA: Harvard University Press, 2009.

Beckmann, Andreas. "Justus Ruperti und Georg Laué Julius Bendixen: Hamburger Kaufleute und ihre Beteiligung am kalifornischen Goldrausch, 1849–1852." In *Die hanseatisch-amerikanischen Beziehungen seit 1790*. Edited by Rolf Hammel-Kiesow, Heiko Herold, and Claudis Schurmann. Trier, Germany: Porto Alba Verlag, 2017.

Benjamin, Thomas. *The Atlantic World: Europeans, Africans, Indians and Their Shared History, 1400–1900*. New York: Cambridge University Press, 2013.

Bystrom, Kerry, and Joseph R. Slaughter. *The Global South Atlantic*. New York: Fordham University Press, 2018.

Deverell, William Francis, and David Igler, eds. *A Companion to California History*. Chichester, UK: Wiley-Blackwell, 2008.

Egerton, Douglas R., et.al. *The Atlantic World: A History, 1400–1888*. Wheeling, IL: Harlan Davidson, 2007.

Eltis, David. "Atlantic History in Global Perspective." *Itinerario* 23 (July 1999): 141–161.

Ferreira, Roquinaldo A. *Cross-Cultural Exchange in the Atlantic World Angola and Brazil During the Era of the Slave Trade*. Cambridge, UK: Cambridge University Press, 2014.

Fogleman, Aaron S. "The Transformation of the Atlantic World, 1776–1867." *Atlantic Studies* 6 (2009): 5–28.

Gabaccia, Donna. "A Long Atlantic in a Wider World." *Atlantic Studies* 1 (2004): 1–27.

Gilroy, Paul. *The Black Atlantic: Modernity and Double Consciousness*. Cambridge, MA: Harvard University Press, 1993.

Morgan, Philip, and Jack Greene. *Atlantic History: A Critical Appraisal*. New York: Oxford University Press, 2009.

Parry, John H. *The Age of Reconnaissance: Discovery, Exploration and Settlement 1450 to 1650*. Berkeley: University of California Press, 1981.

Weaver, Jace. *The Red Atlantic: American Indigenes and the Making of the Modern World, 1000–1927*. Chapel Hill: The University of North Carolina Press, 2014.

CHAPTER 2

Migration

Grabaung first gave an account of the passage from Africa to Havana. On board the vessel there was a large number of men, but the women and children were far the most numerous. They were fastened together in couples by the wrists and legs, and kept in that situation day and night. Here Grabaung and another of the Africans named Kimbo, lay down upon the floor to show the painful position in which they were obliged to sleep. By day it was no better. The space between decks was so small,—according to their account not exceeding four feet,—that they were obliged, if they attempted to stand, to keep a crouching posture. The decks, fore and aft, were crowded to overflowing. They suffered (Grabaung said) terribly. They had rice enough to eat, but had very little to drink. If they left any of the rice that was given to them uneaten, either from sickness or any other cause, they were whipped. It was a common thing for them to be forced to eat so much as to vomit. Many of the men, women, and children, died on the passage.[1]

From the very start of the Atlantic world, the Americas promised migrants a vast array of opportunities. However, not all people arrived in the Americas voluntarily. Even so, some historians have claimed that by 1800 global trends replaced Atlantic ones, migration continued within an Atlantic context. The open lands and vast economic opportunities of the Americas attracted people who within the confined and socially

[1] "Narrative of the Africans," *New York Journal of Commerce* 10 (October 1839).

stratified Europe never had an opportunity to rise beyond their class status. The passage Europeans faced across the ocean was arduously long, but the level of danger decreased in the course of the century and for some even turned luxurious. While Europeans sought opportunities, Africans continued to arrive in the Americas against their will, brought to the Americas on desolate slave vessels as the above story by Grabaung indicates. Nevertheless, some Africans eventually departed the racism of the Americas for their former homelands. This chapter will illustrate that migration remained an Atlantic phenomenon. Due to the limitations of statistical material on migration and the national origins of migrants, states often did not keep records until the end of the century; therefore, this chapter can only make suggestions regarding migration patterns. Great Britain and the Hanseatic City of Bremen in northern Germany provide some rudimentary indications with regard to these patterns. When migrants departed Europe, they were frequently not native to the place where they boarded their vessel. With an abundance of ports along the North Sea and Atlantic Coast in the German states, Belgium, the Netherland, France, Great Britain, and Ireland, migrants could easily find passage to another part of the world. Migration was a transnational experience from the very outset and the Atlantic continued to be a crossroads with migrants seeking a better life as they move back and forth in the region.

Involuntary migration remained the primary experience for Africans as they traversed the Atlantic during the first six decades of the nineteenth century. Grabaung's powerful retelling of the nineteenth-century version of the transatlantic slave trade appeared in the newspapers in October 1839 and was part of the *La Amistad* case. *La Amistad* was a Cuban coastal slave trader, which carried 53 Mende from Havana to an outlying plantation. The Mende had recently arrived in Cuba from Africa on board the Portuguese slave trader *Tecora* and were on their way to a Cuban sugar plantation. Lead by Sengbe Pieh (later known as Joseph Cinqué), the slaves rebelled and took over the ship, forcing the two surviving crewmembers to take them back home to Africa. Instead, the two sailors navigated northward at night and the ship route eventually ended along the US coast. A two-year court battle ensued to determine whether the slaves on board had been illegally transported to the Americas and therefore deserved their freedom. The Supreme Court eventually, in 1841, ruled in favor of the slaves, allowing them to return to their home.[2] The *Tecora* slaves were not the only ones brought to the Americas against their will during the nineteenth century.

By the time of the *La Amistad* case, the BritishEmpire and the United States had outlawed the transatlantic slave trade for three decades. Despite British ships and those of other maritime powers patrolling the seaways against oceanic slave traders, the trade was not on the decline. The experiences of slaves aboard the *Tecora*, as recounted by Grabaung in the Connecticut courtroom, were shared by millions of slaves during the Middle Passage. In contrast, Europeans voluntarily departed the crowded continent with few chances for personal advancement, for a continent with an abundance of land and opportunities. Conditions on ships transporting people were dismal. At the same time, there was, just like in colonial times, a constant back and forth of people crisscrossing the Atlantic world in every imaginable direction for a multitude of reasons. The Atlantic remained a crossroads for migrants. State agents worked hard to attract new settlers and ensure the passage went smoothly.

Migration agent, Washington Finlay, who sold trips to the United States in the mid-nineteenth century, offered passages from Mainz, Grand Duchy of Hesse and by Rhine, Germany, along the Rhine River or overland to Antwerp, Belgium, and Le Havre, France, where the migrants boarded their vessels for the United States. The trip from Mainz or the Rhineland area to the North Sea and Channel ports was relatively inexpensive as long as the migrant used water-based transport. In contrast, a railroad passage from Paris to Le Havre was more expansive. Finlay recruited dozens of additional agents to promote the United States and was able to broker passages for some 14,000 German migrants in 1849 alone.[3] Finlay's work was common during the nineteenth century.

Throughout the nineteenth century, Bremen, Germany, Le Havre, and Liverpool, Great Britain were important ports for migrants departing for the Americas. In 1851, 19,000 migrants departed the German Weser port for New York alone. In contrast, 32,000 migrants departed the French Channel port for the United States. The two ports combined

---

[2] Marcus Rediker, *The Amistad Rebellion: An Atlantic Odyssey of Slavery and Freedom* (New York: Penguin Books, 2013).

[3] James M. Berquist, *Daily Life in Immigrant America, 1820–1870* (Westport, CT: Greenwood Press, 2008), 67.

represented only about a third of the migrants who departed Liverpool for New York that year. By the 1850s, the British port of the Mersey had developed into one of the largest migration ports in Europe. Liverpool had numerous advantages for migrants and travelers. Liverpool's location offered easy access to the Atlantic Ocean through the Irish Sea. In addition, as one of Great Britain's most important ports, Liverpool offered ships and connections to virtually every part of the world. After 1818, the port city benefitted from the establishment of so-called packet services, ships operating on a regular schedule. The predictable schedule and competition reduced prices and allowed migrants to leave Liverpool in a timely fashion without having to wait for months for a ship to their desired destination. Furthermore, with the abundance of North Sea travel, migrants could relatively easily reach Great Britain. In Liverpool, they could furthermore obtain passage beyond, for example, New York into the interior of the United States or another country.[4]

Finding a ship to the Americas was easy, but the passage remained the most dangerous aspect of migration even in the middle decades of the nineteenth century. The story of Grabaung gives a glimpse into the slave's transition across the Atlantic; white migrants suffered dangerous conditions on their journey as well. A journey from Great Britain to the east coast ports of the United States could take as little as 25 days on a fast sailing vessel but could be as long as 100 days. Since most migrants, especially in the 1820s and 1830s, traveled abroad cargo vessels, the space for passengers was limited and uncomfortable. These poor conditions often spread disease and required migrants to supply their own food. They were told to bring food for twelve weeks. Combined with the limited space, migrants could only bring a small amount of their belonging. Conditions on board migrant vessels were cramped, dirty, and disease-ridden.[5]

The 1850s brought technological advances with the arrival of steam vessels and migrants benefitted from these changes. In part, the increased speed and safety of ocean-going vessels explains the increasing number of people crossing the ocean. The arrival of steamships cut the average trip across the Atlantic down to about 10 days. The superiority of steam-powered vessels soon drew the interests of packet lines and within

---

[4] Ibid., 12–13.
[5] Ibid., 13, 64.

a decade Cunard, the Hamburg Amerikanische Paketfahrt Aktien-Gesellschaft (HAPAG), and the Norddeutscher Lloyd, among others, emerged to provide transatlantic steamship service. They offered speedy, safe, and reliable ocean crossings, monopolizing the market, and never allowing US-owned shipping businesses to thrive. European-owned companies dominated the Atlantic shipping traffic. Despite the emergence of steamships, passengers continued to travel in steerage, down in the lower parts of a vessel, but the passage was significantly shorter.[6]

Since shipping companies and ports increasingly valued passengers and especially migrants as customers, bad publicity such as individuals dying during passage or ships sinking after accidents was undesirable. Amid the various maritime trade-oriented countries came a growing realization that regulation was necessary. In 1832, Bremen addressed these issues with a series of regulations. The authorities inspected the houses where migrants resided before they boarded a vessel. Officials checked ships to insure their seaworthiness and if they carried enough food and supplies. In the 1850s, the city hired agents and provided them with promotional information before dispatching them to the likely points where migrants would board a train or riverboat on their way to Bremen. Once agents met migrants, they helped make important decisions about the migration process. The officials provided sanctioned information and did not seek personal gain and wealth at the expanse of desperate migrants. To avoid profiteering, Bremen established an Emigrant House where migrants could stay at affordable prices. The concern for the welfare of passengers in Bremen was unique and only later in the century did other shipping operators and cities follow the cities example. Bremen's good reputation diverted many immigrants through the German port city.[7]

Once migrants reached their port of departure, they usually boarded a sailing vessel. Most of the vessels involved in this transatlantic trade were sturdily built. They carried various cargos to Europe, but preferred the more lucrative migrants on the return to the Americas. The iconic and fast clipper ships, which dominated the East India and China trade, were ill-suited for the rough and bulky cargos of the transatlantic trade. While vessels from the United States carried mostly migrants

[6] Ibid., 14.
[7] Ibid., 68–69.

bound to the United States, migrants to other parts of the Americas relied on European cargo-carrying ships to provide passage. Over time, owners and yards redesigned ships to accommodate migrants, rather than to fill a hull exclusively with cargo. The passage became more comfortable. Because prices for ocean crossings were five to six times higher on a steam vessel, few migrants could afford the luxurious, fast trip and continued to travel on board sailing vessels that slowly reshaped to fit their passengers.[8]

Traveling in a ship's steerage was an uncomfortable experience. The crowded conditions on board and the lack of hygiene caused disease to spread quickly. Washing was impossible since ships carried limited water and passengers needed it for cooking and drinking. With little ventilation, the steerage turned into a horrid place during heavy seas when passengers remained confined to the bowls of the vessel. Many passengers struggled with the boredom during the long passage. Some, especially on Bremen's ships, had a strict discipline that involved cleaning and adhering to established mealtimes. Regulations made the passenger experience more bearable.[9] After an arduous and long journey, European migrants were glad to finally set foot on the American continent, their new home.

The stories of these generalized experiences only tell part of the story of nineteenth-century migration. To illustrate the continued vibrancy of the Atlantic world, some quantitative material is necessary. However, nineteenth-century statistical compilations for migration are rare. The north German port cities of Hamburg and Bremen as well as Great Britain provide some insights into the movement of people in their annual trade compilations, which still only provide a fragmented record. Nevertheless, the three statistics clearly show that migrants continued to prefer states around the Atlantic when seeking a new home.

Bremen and Hamburg attracted migrants from the German states as well as other parts of Central and Eastern Europe. The vast majority who departed the Elbe or Weser ports went to the United States. In Bremen's case, as Table 2.1 shows, there was a small uptick of migrants to Australia in the late 1840s and early 1850s, but Australia remained unattractive to

---

[8] Ibid., 70–72.

[9] Ibid., 74–76; Dagmar Bellmann, *Von Höllengefährten zu schwimmenden Palästen die Passagierschifffahrt auf dem Atlantik (1840–1930)* (Frankfurt a.M., Germany: Campus Verlag, 2015).

Table 2.1 Migrates leaving from Bremen

	United States	Brazil	Cape Colony	Australia
1847	32,769	25	189	699
1848	29,365	–	–	582
1849	28,320	–	–	286
1850	25,552	20	8	150
1851	35,998	5	4	258
1855	31,378	21	109	–
1856	36,202	201	90	–
1857	48,123	329	935	–
1858	22,406	28	675	–
1859	21,669	278	–	–
1860	30,158	80	–	–
1864	38,942	2	–	–
1865	60,501	1	–	–
1866	89,962	–	–	–
1867	115,879	3	–	–
1868	107,920	–	–	–
1869	110,931	–	–	–

Sources *Tabellarische Uebersicht des Bremischen Handels im Jahre 1851*, 191; *Tabellarische Uebersicht des Bremischen Handels im Jahre 1860*, 228; *Jahrbuch für die Amtliche Statistik Bremischen Staats im Jahre 1870*, 196

Germans. Since many migrants traveled on ships that also carried cargo and since Bremen's trade was Atlantic-focused, Germans who desired to settle in Australia simply did not find shipping opportunities in Bremen and went instead to Hamburg or Great Britain. However, Bremen attracted a significant number of migrants who desired to find a new home in Brazil. As a consistently important trade partner, passage to the Portuguese American Empire was easy to obtain. Nevertheless, throughout the middle decades of the century, the United States was by far the most important destination for migrants, even combined the other regions only accounted for between 1 and 5% of migrants. The Atlantic focus of Bremen's trade meant that migrants from the Weser port city predominantly left for various countries in the Americas.

Bremen's traditional rival Hamburg remained in the shadow of the Weser port for much of the nineteenth century when it came to immigration. Nevertheless, Hamburg's migration movement followed a similar pattern to Bremen (Table 2.2). Only about 10% of Hamburg's migrants departed for non-US countries. The Hanseatic City on the

Table 2.2 Migrates leaving from Hamburg

	United States	Central America	Argentina	Brazil	Chile	Africa	Australia
1836	2870						
1837	2177			250			
1838	484			55		71	345
1839	1415			154			
1840	1407						
1841	1071	20		13		15	258
1842	495						120
1843	1756						
1844	1774						
1845	2388						
1846	3960			498			
1847	5439			758			
1848	4741						1069
1849	3800			37			1468
1850	5879			240	215		368
1851	8533	190		1950	245		530
1852	13,886	128		2047	571		1195
1853	14,027	49	23	546	326	20	1825
1854	21,001	81	76	1395	263	17	4880
1855	8708	42	66	1978	196	16	2996
1856	16,782	84	80	1529	703	29	1747
1857	20,949	158	81	1772	332	52	1233
1858	10,823	21	41	3431	160	2580	969
1859	8650	17	23	1757	151	163	1041
1860	12,205	27	64	897	167	533	436
1861	9370	17	45	1017	107	586	762
1862	14,300	20	52	1025	74	102	934
1863	15,721	14	47	847	199	33	2494
1864	17,050	14	28	447	83	32	641
1865	32,000	248	168	414	96		2832
1866	35,074	224	199	417	41	33	549
1867	33,996	17	96	1155	41	41	143
1868	37,274	6	18	3425	30	47	151
1869	37,261	7	71	3475	62	23	73
1870	24,874		8	1169	18	3	1259

Sources Imre Ferenczi, *International Migrations: Statistics Compiled with Introduction and Notes* (New York: National Bureau of Economic Research, 1929), 695

Elbe River was significantly better connected with railroads, canals, and the Elbe to the rest of the German states, Eastern, and Northeastern Europe.[10] Furthermore, the city's merchant class had established a diverse trade portfolio and could provide passage to almost any corner of the world. Despite Hamburg's trade being far less focused on the United States, the vast majority of migrants departed for the United States. By the 1850s, other countries gained in popularity as destinations for migration, but they were never as popular. In Hamburg, more migrants decided to leave for Australia, with over a thousand travelers on average per year in the 1850s and 1860s and at times as many as 4800. Nevertheless, Australia never gained the same allure as the Americas. Similarly, Hamburg sent a constant stream of migrants to Latin America. Just like in Bremen, Brazil attracted most of those going to South America, but Chile and Argentina appealed to a substantial number of migrants. Hamburg was a port with a diverse trade portfolio around the globe and its migration statistics confirm this, but the Atlantic region continued to attract most of the migrants.

Meanwhile, Great Britain was not only the most important export/import market and the world's largest shipper, but the country was also an important departure point for migrants. Tens of thousands crossed the Channel or North Sea to leave Europe from a British port. Migrants from Great Britain favored the British colonies, especially Canada and Australia. As a result, migration to both was significantly larger from Great Britain than from the two German ports. Nevertheless, the United States and Canada combined attracted at least twice as many migrants as Australia did. Unfortunately, it is unclear from the statistics provided by Great Britain what the distribution of "Others" is. It seems safe to assume that places like the Cape Colony, Brazil, and Argentina would feature relatively prominent since all three regions actively attracted settlers. From the migration statistics of the three countries, it is clear that migrants continued to think in Atlantic terms. Australia was too distant to attract as many migrants as the United States or Brazil (Table 2.3).

As migrants contemplated their destinations, the persistence of slavery especially in the southern parts of the United States played a role in their decision making, avoiding regions where slave labor competition

---

[10] Berquist, *Daily Life in Immigrant America*, 68.

Table 2.3 Migrates leaving from Great Britain

	Canada	United States	Australia	other
1847	109,680	142,154	4949	1487
1848	31,065	188,233	23,904	4887
1849	41,367	219,450	32,191	6490
1850	32,961	223,078	16,037	8773
1851	42,605	267,357	21,532	4472
1852	32,873	244,261	87,881	3749
1853	34,522	230,885	61,401	3129
1854	43,761	193,065	83,237	3366
1855	17,966	103,414	52,309	3118
1856	16,378	111,837	44,584	3755
1857	21,001	126,905	61,248	8721
1858	9704	59,716	39,295	5257
1859	6689	70,303	31,013	12,427
1860	9786	87,500	24,302	6881
1861	12,707	49,764	23,738	5561
1862	8328	48,726	38,828	1881
1863	9665	130,528	50,157	2514
1864	11,371	130,165	40,073	5472
1865	14,424	118,463	36,683	5321
1866	9988	131,840	23,682	4543
1867	12,160	126,051	14,023	4748
1868	12,332	108,490	12,332	5033
1869	20,921	146,737	14,457	4185
1870	27,168	153,466	16,526	5351
1871	14,954	150,788	11,695	5314
1872	24,382	161,782	15,248	9082
1873	29,045	166,730	25,137	7433
1874	20,728	113,774	52,581	10,189
1875	12,306	81,193	34,750	12,426
1876	9335	54,554	32,196	13,384

Sources *Statistical Abstract for the United Kingdom in Each of the last Fifteen Years* (1861), 71; *Statistical Abstract for the United Kingdom in Each of the last Fifteen Years* (1876), 131

undercut free labor prices. Thankfully, there was a vast literature providing potential migrants with information about the various destinations available. For example, the radical Schleswig-Holstein revolutionary Theodor Olshausen, who migrated to the United States in the aftermath of the failed uprising in the Dano-German borderland in 1848, arrived in St. Louis in 1851 and soon moved up the river to Davenport in Iowa where a substantial immigrant population from Schleswig-Holstein provided him with a home away from home. As Olshausen settled in the United States, he wrote three books on the geography, environment, and economy of the states of the Mississippi Valley. In *Das Mississippi-Thal*, Olshausen claimed that the region had great potential for Germans because every year many came to settle down. He praised the agricultural possibilities and admired the free labor attitude of the region, blasting the slave territories as backward.[11] Olshausen was not the only promoter of the Mississippi Valley. Many migrants wrote similar books and promoted settlement in the United States and other regions. E. A. Wiemann reported favorable on the prospects of colonization in Central America.[12] More focused, Johann Heinrich Siegfried Schultz visited and promoted the predominantly Belgium settlement at Santo Tomás de Castilla, Guatemala, attracting about one hundred Germans. Sadly, like many projects and colonization schemes, this one did not work out for the migrants and the settlement never prospered.[13] With all these options, migrants could at least rely on a vast literature to select their eventual destination whether eventually prosperous or not.

Newspapers, like the German *Allgemeine Auswanderungs-Zeitung* or *Die Auswanderer-Zeitung*, provided readers with detailed information about the conditions in various regions, land offers, ship schedules, and many other helpful items of advice. In its January 17, 1848 edition, the *Allgemeine Auswanderungs-Zeitung* brought to the reader's attention that around Port Natal in South Africa good agricultural land was available for settlers. Furthermore, the newspaper contained advertisements for land in Texas that migrants should take advantage of, which the paper covered in detail. Finally, the paper listed the ships leaving for desirable locations around the world, including in some cases advertisements for them. The newspaper finally included a report of the vessels that had

---

[11] Theodor Olshausen, *Das Mississippi Thal* (Kiel, Germany: Akademische Buchhandlung, 1854), 1–39; Theodor Olshausen, *Der Staat Iowa: Geographische und statistische beschrieben* (Kiel, Germany: Akademische Buchhandlung, 1855); Theodor Olshausen, *Der Staat Missouri* (Kiel, Germany: Akademische Buchhandlung, 1854).

[12] E. A. Weimann, *Mittel-Amerika als Gemeinsames Auswanderungs-Ziel: Ein Beitrag im Interesse der Centralisation Deutscher Auswanderung und Kolonisation* (Berlin: Gustav Hempel, 1850).

[13] Johann Heinrich Siegfried Schultz, *Ueber Colonisation mit Besonderer Rücksicht auf die Colonie zu Santo Thomas im Staate Guatemala* (Cologne, Germany: M. DuMont-Schauberg, 1843).

departed in 1847. In all, 227 ships had departed Bremen with 32,769 passengers for the United States. One had left for Port Natal with 189 passengers. Three ships with 25 passengers had gone to Brazil. An unusual high number of four ships with 699 passengers had departed for Australia. Migration favored the North Atlantic region, and the newspapers promoted opportunities within the Atlantic region.[14] With all of these public advertisements available, sometimes migrants trusted personal connections over newspaper reports.

The German migrants to Chile are an illustrative example, since the community came about largely as a nineteenth-century creation. After independence, Chile opened its doors for immigrants, hoping their industriousness would stimulate the economy. German migration was slow to pick up, but the existence of a robust merchant enclave in Valparaiso provided a basis for migration. Leading the way. Berlin-born Prussian merchant Bernhard Eunom Philippi worked on a merchant ship before doctors in Valparaiso recommended southern Chile as a better climate to deal with his health issues.[15] As a result of an agricultural survey, he discovered the vast potential of southern Chile for migration.

Asking migrants to venture on a three-month ocean journey to settle in Chile came as no easy task. Undeterred, Philippi desired a homogenous community of Germans for his agricultural experiment. In 1848, the government authorized Philippi to visit the German states to recruit potential immigrants for a colony in Valdivia and Chiloé, Región de Los Ríos. A pilot group of nine families decided to leave for Chile. About 300 migrants soon followed and arrived in Valdivia in 1851 where they discovered a problem. The land promised to them was not available and the large landowners refused to hand over or sell any property. The local authorities under Vicente Pérez Rosales, who was Chile-born, French-educated, and a California gold rush veteran, tried their best to obtain land for the German settlers. They eventually located some land for the colony. The project and promotion started to pay off with some 600 Germans migrating to Chile over the following five years.[16] The establishment of a German enclave with German culture and newspapers

---

[14] *Allgemeine Auswanderungs-Zeitung*, January 17, 1848.

[15] George F. W. Young, *The Germans in Chile: Immigration and Colonization, 1849–1914* (New York: Center for Migration Studies, 1974), 23, 30–33.

[16] Ibid., 47, 57, 85–88.

provided a sense of home and encouraged the small number of German migrants to settle in faraway Chile.

Not only German immigrants looked for settlement opportunities outside of the United States. Even among the Irish, migration to countries other than the United States was not uncommon and communal enclaves to maintain an Irish personality attracted migrants. In the 1850s, the Irish revolutionary Thomas Francis Meagher visited Central America where he explored the possibility for an Irish settlement. "I visit Central America.—Costa Rica especially," he wrote later, "for the purpose of ascertaining the true conditions of affairs there, and becoming familiar with a noble region."[17] Meagher restricted his activities to supporting migration, but did not leave the United States himself.

However, permanent settlement was not the only reason why people moved about during the nineteenth century. The period was in part a continuation of the old Atlantic world and many migrants sought a temporary refugee from revolution or prosecution. They desired a temporary exile, forced or self-imposed, to escape political turmoil.

An example of this revolutionary crisscrossing of the Atlantic is Juan García Del Río (1794–1856). García was born in Cartagena in what is now northern Colombia. In 1802, at the behest of his father, he went to study in Spain, where he came into contact with modern liberal ideals about constitutional government and natural rights. Since his father had embraced the idea of Cartagena's independence, García supported the cause as well. He worked temporarily for the revolutionary government of Cartagena as emissary in Europe, but upon the government's defeat was without employment. In 1818, he went to Chile and joined forces with the revolutionaries. He worked as a newspaper editor and entered politics. From 1822 to 1828, García represented Peru and other Latin American countries in Europe, with his primary residence in London. Upon the end of his mission, he determined to exploit economic opportunities in Mexico. When he arrived in the United States, the Mexican minister denied him the right to work in Mexico, because rumors called him an emissary of the Spanish government. He left the United States for New Granada in 1829 and returned to politics again. The disintegration of the federated New Granada forced García to pick sides once

---

[17] Michael Cavanagh, *Memoirs of General Thomas Francis Meagher: Comprising the Leading Events of His Career Chronologically Arranged* (Worcester, MA: Messenger Press, 1892), 347.

more; he ended up in Ecuadorian exile for almost ten years. After a short stint from 1842 to 1843 in Chile, García finally left for Mexico and commercial enterprise.[18] García's life illustrates migration patterns during the early nineteenth-century Atlantic world. He was not the typical nineteenth-century migrant, professional revolutionary, and business entrepreneur; however, just like Garcia, thousands used the ability to cross the Atlantic on a regular basis to locate opportunities and a new home.

Besides García, dozens of political and intellectual leaders from Latin America crisscrossed the Atlantic on a regular basis during the nineteenth century. Another example, Miguel García Granados y Zavala (1809–1878) was born in Spain, but García Granados's parents moved to Guatemala when he was two years old. Interested in a military career, he traveled by way of the United States to London in 1823. Upon the urging of his older brother, Granados studied engineering, but remained interested in military history. When their father died, the brothers returned to Guatemala in 1826. The conflicts in the region offered Granados an opportunity to make his military dream a reality. However, he failed and for over ten years had to accept exile in Mexico. He remained committed to change and helped transform the government in 1871.[19] Despite spending only a limited amount of time in Europe, Granados traversed the Atlantic world to seek out opportunities, just like his early modern predecessors would have done.

These two examples of Latin American migrants demonstrate the frequency of movement of people across the Atlantic. In addition to Latin America, there were those who sought a safe haven in London or Paris. Either city had long served as a place of refuge during revolutionary or reactionary periods for Europeans, but an ocean voyage did not stop Americans from seeking shelter in these two cities and countries. Among the most well-known refugees from Latin Americans was Juan Manuel de Rosas (1793–1877) who was instrumental in a number of conflicts in the Rio de la Plata region. After failing to address the federalist tendencies and liberal demands in Argentina, Rosas was ousted from power in 1852 and forced into exile in Great Britain. He remained in Southampton until his death in 1877. Rosas like many politicians and

---

[18] Pam Decho, Claire Diamond, and Rory Miller, *Latin Americans in London: A Select List of Prominent Latin Americans in London, c.1800–1996* (London, UK: Institute of Latin American Studies, 1998), 21–22.

[19] Ibid., 67–68.

intellectuals found in exile safety and a possibility to plan a return to politics, though in his case that never happened.

Importantly, as the examples above indicate, the flow of people never remained one directional, migrants crisscrossed the Atlantic. Many individuals departed Europe for the Americas and eventually returned to Europe. As well as the Latin Americans, another example of Atlantic movement comes from former rebel Confederates from the United States. They sought new opportunities outside the United States but returned once the opportunities did not meet their expectations or worse, never materialized at all. A substantial number of former Confederates determined that the best way to deal with defeat and the imposition of US nationalism on their homeland was to seek their fortunes elsewhere. Confederate migration was small as the moved to Mexico, Europe, British Honduras, and Venezuela, but some left their mark on their new homelands.[20] The Brazilian Confederate community, the Confederados, sought to reestablish a semblance of their former life. Those who landed in Brazil found a semblance of the home they wanted with the continuation of slavery. However, despite Brazil still having slavery and welcoming Confederate exiles, the new arrivals were not handed large plantations; they had to start as laborers, a position contrary to their personal views and attitudes. Being told off by rich and royal-protected black slaveholder was a major insult to these Confederate migrants with their white supremacy ideals.[21] Their search for a new home often became guided by the question, if there was a possibility to retain one's former planter status. As a result, the two

---

[20] For general works on Confederate migrants see Alfred J. Hanna and Kathryn A. Hanna, *Confederate Exiles in Venezuela* (Tuscaloosa, AL: Confederate Publishing Company, 1960); Christopher L. Jones, "Deserting Dixie: A History of Emigres, Exiles, and Dissenters from the American South, 1866–1925," Ph.D.diss, Brown University, 2009; Donald C. Simmons, Jr., *Confederate Settlements in British Honduras* (Jefferson, NC: McFarland, 2001).

[21] For works on the Confederate exiles in Brazil, see Cyrus B. Dawsey and James M. Dawsey, *The Confederados Old South Immigrants in Brazil* (Tuscaloosa: University of Alabama Press, 1995); William C. Griggs, *The Elusive Eden: Frank McMullan's Confederate Colony in Brazil* (Austin: University of Texas Press, 1987); Eugene C. Harter, *The Lost Colony of the Confederacy* (Jackson: University Press of Mississippi, 1985); Alicja Iwańska, *British American Loyalists in Canada and U.S. Southern Confederates in Brazil: Exiles from the United States* (Lewiston, NY: E. Mellen Press, 1993); Laura Jarnagin, *A Confluence of Transatlantic Networks: Elites, Capitalism, and Confederate Migration to Brazil* (Tuscaloosa: University of Alabama Press, 2008).

remaining slave societies in the Americas became a focus of attention, Brazil and Cuba, but only Brazil attracted a substantial number of permanent Confederate migrants.

By the late nineteenth century, the amount of people crisscrossing the borders and waters of the Atlantic world increased in frequency as individuals sought to advance their financial status before returning home. Modern large vessels allowed for easier and more frequent crossing of the once so imposing ocean. Mexican migrant workers in the southwestern part of the United States frequently engaged in cross-border migration for financial gain.[22] However, some migrant workers, for example from Austria and Hungary, voyaged much longer distances and relied on the improved, modern, and fast communication lines to call on their home government for protection in case of accident or injury. The 157,000 migrants from the Habsburg realm in Pennsylvania frequently needed help as injury and death were common in the dangerous mines. The Habsburg government desired to have its subjects overseas only for a short period to earn enough money to return home to enrich the general financial well-being of the Austro-Hungarian state. At the Jackson Lumber Company in Alabama, the Austrian consuls had to protect subjects against exploitation similar to slavery, urging them to avoid the southern parts of the country entirely.[23] Migrants remained protected from such exploits until they decided to naturalize in their new home.

Over time, migration flows and attitudes started to change. Where in 1904, the Hungarian government signed an agreement with Cunard to provide 30,000 annual passengers to the United States; within three years, the government changed direction and considered a repatriation program. Where the United States desperately tried to assume a melting pot identity in immigration matters, Hungary and other European states desired for their subjects to maintain national feelings, which could be used to bring them home eventually.[24] The Hungarian repatriations program was largely the exception in the nineteenth-century Atlantic world, but people flowed in many directions and did return home at times.

---

[22] John M. Hart, *Border Crossings: Mexican and Mexican-American Workers* (Wilmington, DE: Scholarly Resources, 1998).

[23] Nicole M. Phelps, *U.S.-Habsburg Relations from 1815 to the Paris Peace Conference: Sovereignty Transformed* (New York: Cambridge University Press, 2013), 158–161, 166, 171–172.

[24] Ibid., 185–186.

By the early twentieth century, when Austro-Hungarian workers temporarily or permanently relocated to the United States, the size of vessels that traversed the ocean had dramatically increased and the various shipping companies separated cargo from passenger travel; some built entire fleets solely devoted to passenger travel. Companies competed to build the largest, fastest, and most luxurious Atlantic liners. Some companies actively worked to improve the migrant experience. In 1886, HAPAG hired Albert Ballin to direct passenger services. He eventually assumed direction of the entire company in 1899. Within the next decade, HAPAG ordered with *Imperator* and *Vaterland* two ships in excess of 52,000 gross tons. More importantly, Ballin created an entire operation to direct migrants to HAPAG and house them in his immigrant halls in the Hamburg district of Veddel, along an Elbe tributary. Here, migrants were housed, feed, medically checked, their clothing decontaminated, and preparations made to insure their acceptance by US immigration officials.[25] The size of the ships had increased and the operations grown. New migrant streams came from Spain, Russia, Italy, and Austria-Hungary, in addition to the traditional regions like Germany, Ireland, and Great Britain.[26] However, even as different groups arrived in the Americas, the general patterns of movement had changed little since the early modern Atlantic world.

During the nineteenth century, people continued to crisscross the Atlantic in various and convoluted ways: Hungarian workers traveled to the Americas and back, Latin American revolutionary sought refuge in Europe, and migration promoters continued to encourage those interested in resettling to look to the Americas for a better future. The quantitative as well as qualitative material illustrates that migrants still favored the Atlantic region to the lesser-known and distant Australia. Migration and the movement of people continued in well-established patterns. Little changed, migrants in the bottom of ships faced serious, if shortened hardship as they journeyed across the Atlantic in smelly, confined spaces with stall water and potentially spoiled food. However, European

---

[25] Rebekka Geitner, "'Das größte Gasthaus der Welt?' Die Auswandererhallen der HAPAG auf der Veddel in den Jahren von 1901 bis 1934," in *Die hanseatisch-amerikanischen Beziehungen seit 1790*, eds. Rolf Hammel-Kiesow, Heiko Herold, and Claudia Schnurmann (Trier, Germany: Porta Alba Verlag, 2017), 311–313, 318–327.

[26] Walter T. K. Nugent, *Crossings: The Great Transatlantic Migrations, 1870–1914* (Bloomington: Indiana University Press, 1992), 12.

migrants were lucky since they made the trip voluntarily. In contrast, millions of Africans were forced to make the journey in desolate conditions that threatened their lives and forced into slavery once in the Americas. Migrants sought opportunities in a wide variety of locations, from emerging urban and industrial areas, to frontier towns, and tropical regions in the Caribbean. The Atlantic world had not ended as some historians claim and neither had migration patterns globalized, migration patterns remained Atlantic. The Atlantic world remained as vibrant, if not more so, than ever before. Thousands crisscrossed the ocean during the nineteenth century and dramatically altered the entire region, creating just like the early modern Atlantic, a unique and dramatically different Atlantic region from what it would have been without these interactions.

Bibliography

Bellmann, Dagmar. *Von Höllengefährten zu schwimmenden Palästen die Passagierschifffahrt auf dem Atlantik (1840–1930)*. Frankfurt a.M., Germany: Campus Verlag, 2015.

Berquist, James M. *Daily Life in Immigrant America, 1820–1870*. Westport, CT: Greenwood Press, 2008.

Bethell, Leslie. *The Abolition of the Brazilian Slave Trade Britain, Brazil and the Slave Trade Question*. Cambridge, UK: Cambridge University Press, 1970.

Cavanagh, Michael. *Memoirs of General Thomas Francis Meagher: Comprising the Leading Events of His Career Chronologically Arranged*. Worcester, MA: Messenger Press, 1892.

Dawsey, Cyrus B., and James Dawsey. *The Confederados: Old South Immigrants in Brazil*. Tuscaloosa: University of Alabama Press, 1995.

Decho, Pam, Claire Diamond, and Rory Miller. *Latin Americans in London: A Select List of Prominent Latin Americans in London, c.1800–1996*. London, UK: Institute of Latin American Studies, 1998.

Geitner, Rebekka. "'Das größte Gasthaus der Welt?' Die Auswandererhallen der HAPAG auf der Veddel in den Jahren von 1901 bis 1934." In *Die hanseatisch-amerikanischen Beziehungen seit 1790*. Edited by Rolf Hammel-Kiesow, Heiko Herold, and Claudia Schnurmann. Trier, Germany: Porta Alba Verlag, 2017.

Griggs, William Clark. *The Elusive Eden: Frank McMullan's Confederate Colony in Brazil*. Austin: University of Texas Press, 1987.

Hanna, Alfred J., and Kathryn A. Hanna. *Confederate Exiles in Venezuela*. Tuscaloosa, AL: Confederate Publishing Company, 1960.

Hart, John M. *Border Crossings: Mexican and Mexican-American Workers.* Wilmington, DE: Scholarly Resources, 1998.

Harter, Eugene C. *The Lost Colony of the Confederacy.* Jackson: University Press of Mississippi, 1985.

Iwańska, Alicja. *British American Loyalists in Canada and U.S. Southern Confederates in Brazil: Exiles from the United States.* Lewiston, NY: E. Mellen Press, 1993.

Jarnagin, Laura. *A Confluence of Transatlantic Networks: Elites, Capitalism, and Confederate Migration to Brazil.* Tuscaloosa: University of Alabama Press, 2008.

Jones, Christopher L. "Deserting Dixie: A History of Emigres, Exiles, and Dissenters from the American South, 1866–1925." Ph.D.diss, Brown University, 2009.

Nugent, Walter T. K. *Crossings: The Great Transatlantic Migrations, 1870–1914.* Bloomington: Indiana University Press, 1992.

Olshausen, Theodor. *Das Mississippi Thal.* Kiel, Germany: Akademische Buchhandlung, 1854.

Olshausen, Theodor. *Der Staat Missouri.* Kiel, Germany: Akademische Buchhandlung, 1854.

Olshausen, Theodor. *Der Staat Iowa: Geographische und statistische beschrieben.* Kiel, Germany: Akademische Buchhandlung, 1855.

Phelps, Nicole M. *U.S.-Habsburg Relations from 1815 to the Paris Peace Conference: Sovereignty Transformed.* New York: Cambridge University Press, 2013.

Rediker, Marcus. *The Amistad Rebellion: An Atlantic Odyssey of Slavery and Freedom.* New York: Penguin Books, 2013.

Schultz, Johann Heinrich Siegfried. *Ueber Colonisation mit Besonderer Rücksicht auf die Colonie zu Santo Thomas im Staate Guatemala.* Colonge, Germany: M. DuMont-Schauberg, 1843.

Simmons, Donald C., Jr. *Confederate Settlements in British Honduras.* Jefferson, NC: McFarland, 2001.

Weimann, E. A. *Mittel-Amerika als Gemeinsames Auswanderungs-Ziel: Ein Beitrag im Interesse der Centralisation Deutscher Auswanderung und Kolonisation.* Berlin: Gustav Hempel, 1850.

Young, George F. W. *The Germans in Chile: Immigration and Colonization, 1849–1914.* New York: Center for Migration Studies, 1974.

CHAPTER 3

Trade Relations

I strongly supported the formation of the "Ocean Steam Navigation Company" in 1846-7, which represented the beginning of transatlantic steamshipping and required the need for a larger harbor entrance, an optical telegraph was built between Bremen and its port city, which was replaced several years later by an electric telegraph, the Morse system, the first electric telegraph line on the continent. In 1847, I entered into negotiations with English entrepreneurs for the construction of a railway from Bremerhaven to Bremen. The Hanoverian Minister von Falk had promised me the concession. Our mayor, Smidt, who grasped the matter most vividly, promised me his support. A financial crisis after my return from England prevented construction in 1847, in 1848 political events in Germany held it back, so that the railway was not completed until 1862 at the expense of Hanover and Bremen.[1]

Since its opening, the Atlantic world had economically connected its adjacent continents, bringing unknown foods and goods to the various parts of this trade network. Trade created new economic opportunities, industry, and eventually prosperous port cities. With the independence of the Americas and these markets leaving the restrictive colonial trade system, a vast array of merchants desired to benefit. With profits multiplying and home economies demanding goods from other parts of the Atlantic world or requiring markets to sell finished products, merchants and

[1] Moritz Lindeman, *Der Norddeutsche Lloyd: Geschichte und Handbuch* (Bremen, Germany: Schünemann, 1892), 63.

political leaders faced demands for closer commercial ties. As the above statement by Bremen merchant Hermann Henrich Meier signaled, every port city around the Atlantic had to improve its communication lines and port facilities to remain relevant in the transforming Atlantic trade patterns. The nineteenth-century Atlantic world relied like its predecessor in the sixteenth, seventeenth, and eighteenth centuries on trade as a means to bring together the diverse people and regions surrounding the ocean. Merchants had brought slaves to the Americas, carried goods from one region to the other, and stimulated a dynamic interchange of commodities, ideas, and people. The nineteenth century increased trade ties and improved the connectivity within the Atlantic world. Vessels crossed the Atlantic in increasing numbers and at ever-faster speeds. By the mid-nineteenth century, many ports desired the opening of steamship lines to make trade faster and easier, bringing about the birth of such Atlantic institutions like Cunard and the Norddeutscher Lloyd. The Atlantic world remained a vibrant market economy where merchants traded commodities and port cities desired faster and more frequent connections to enhance the exchange of goods.

Steam became essential in enhancing the Atlantic economy. Steam engines not only powered machines but also means of transportation, a new age in ocean-going commerce started. Early steam vessels still relied on wind, unable to carry enough coal for an ocean crossing. Even more, captains found sailing more economical in the early stages of paddle wheel steamers. By the late 1830s, steamship companies emerged such as the British and American Steam Navigation Company and Great Western Steamship Company. They pioneered the use of steamships across the Atlantic Ocean. However, transporting goods and passengers across the ocean did not always end profitably.

At the same time, mail was still contractually carried on slower and unreliable sailing vessels. In 1836, the British government determined to use steamships to carry mail, which became known as mail packets. Placed in charge as Comptroller of Steam Machinery and Packet Service by the Lord Commissioners of the Admiralty was the famous Arctic explorer William Edward Parry. In 1839, the comptroller office issued the first tender asking for bids to carry mail by steamship across the Atlantic to Halifax and New York. With limited interest, the proposals were not to the Admiralties satisfaction.

Eventually, Parry located a group, which permanently transformed the Atlantic transportation landscape.[2]

A major breakthrough in transatlantic shipping came with the arrival, in Great Britain, of the Nova Scotian Samuel Cunard. Upon his landing in Liverpool, Cunard secured enough funding to purchase vessels and make a bid for the mail package tender from Liverpool to Halifax and Boston, a deviation from the original tender calling for New York as the terminus. To increase revenue and appease the Admiralty, Cunard promised to also provide service to Quebec, as long as, the St. Lawrence River remained ice-free and open to navigation. Cunard's company received payment based on the amount of mail carried per voyage, which averaged about £3295 per trip. The British and North American Royal Mail Steam Packet Company, the original name of Cunard, contracted in Liverpool for four paddle-wheel vessels, the *Britannia*, *Acadia*, *Caledonia*, and *Columbia*. Cunard's first ship left Liverpool on July 4, 1840, with an estimated arrival in Boston fourteen and a half days later. The ship arrived 4 hours ahead of schedule. Cunard's successful arrival created much cause for celebration, and he received almost 2000 dinner invitations for his one day stay.[3] Cunard had flung wide open the door to a new age of Atlantic commerce.

Cunard built a success story under his red funnel with two or three narrow black bands and a black top. However, he had initially to convince passengers and merchants about the reliability and safety of steam-powered ocean navigation. Marine engine-builder Robert Napier warned in 1840 that it was "of the utmost importance at first to gain the public confidence in steam vessels, for should the slightest accident happen so as to prevent the vessel making her passage by steam it would be magnified by the opposition & thus for a time mar the prospects of the company." In large part, Napier and Cunard avoided problems by focusing on what their ships did instead of what they ought to do; eventually,

---

[2] Daniel A. Butler, *The Age of Cunard: A Transatlantic History 1839–2003* (Annapolis, MD: Lighthouse Press Publication, 2004), 38; A. Fraser-Macdonald, *Our Ocean Railways* (London, UK: Chapman and Hall, 1893), 79, 81; Francis E. Hyde, *Cunard and the North Atlantic, 1840–1973: A History of Shipping and Financial Management* (London, UK: Macmillan, 1975), 4; Nick S. Robins, *The Coming of the Comet: The Rise and Fall of the Paddle Steamer* (Barnsley, UK: Seaforth Publishing, 2012), 5–6.

[3] Hyde, *Cunard and the North Atlantic*, 8; Fraser-Macdonald, *Our Ocean Railways*, 81–82.

promises raised expectations that companies had to meet. Furthermore, proficiencies were needed in the design and construction of the vessels to avoid flaws that could eventually spell disaster, but also in their day-to-day management on the ocean. Within a decade of operation, Napier's work and guidance gained Cunard the reputation of being a safe and reliable company.[4] Cunard's safety record insured his rise to the top in Atlantic shipping.

Within three years of commencing service, shipbuilding engineers realized that iron-hulled ships with screw propellers worked superior to wooden-haul paddle steamers. As a result, Cunard invested in new ships to keep up with technological advances, unwilling to surrender his position to competitors. On July 19, 1843, Cunard took delivery of the new iron-hulled *Great Britain*. Equipped with six watertight compartments, Cunard needed two years to outfit and decorate the ship for its 350 passengers. Making the journey to New York in only fifteen days, the *Great Britain* once more transformed the Atlantic world only three years after her sister ships' groundbreaking journey. The *Great Britain* unfortunately ran aground in incorrectly charted waters off Ireland and remained out of service for over a year, raising questions about iron as a construction material. Nevertheless, Cunard remained committed and iron soon took over as the new shipbuilding standard, before steel replaced the softer metal to allow even larger vessels.[5]

By the mid-1850s, Cunard had a fleet of sixteen ships operating lines to New York, Boston, and the Canadian provinces. When the Crimean War with Russia broke out, the British Admiralty realized that the Royal Navy lacked ships to transport troops. The Navy called on the patriotism of Cunard, who provided eleven of his ships for troop transportation to the Black Sea, leaving the company with the bare minimum of five vessels to conduct the contractual mail packet runs to the United States. When the Royal Navy requested even more ships, Cunard informed them that he would not be able to fulfill his obligation, bringing a quick about-face by the Royal Navy. Nevertheless, Boston temporarily lost service and never regained its status as an important transatlantic port for Cunard. The company's focus shifted to the more lucrative trade with New York.[6]

---

[4] Crosbie Smith and Anne Scott, "'Trust in Providence': Building Confidence into the Cunard Line of Steamers," *Technology and Culture* 48 (July 2007), 474, 482, 493.

[5] Butler, *The Age of Cunard*, 82–83.

[6] Ibid., 86–87.

Shipping businesses could not escape the international political realities of the nineteenth century, which took a toll on oceanic trade. However, Cunard laid the foundation for an ever more integrated nineteenth-century Atlantic world.

With the rise of steamship lines across Europe, everybody wanted a share of the postal contacts with the Americas. When the Hanseatic City of Bremen, a major German port on the Weser River along the North Sea coast, established direct diplomatic representation in the United States in 1853, they instructed their representative Rudolph M. Schleiden to seek a new postal treaty that subsidized a steamship line from Bremen to New York.[7] The new postal treaty laid the foundation for the success story of the Norddeutsche Lloyd. While in Bremen, rich merchants, politicians, and shipowners created a localized steamship business in the early 1850s, German and US financiers brought into existence the Ocean Steam Navigation Company, in New York, which provided a direct line between Bremen and New York. However, in 1857, the Ocean Steam Navigation Company discontinued the service. Meanwhile, Bremen merchants W. A. Fritze and C. Lemkuhl bought two steamships to run between Bremen and New York, but they never achieved much success. In 1856, Heinrich H. Meier approached possible investors like Eduard Crüsemann to establish a direct steamship line. Originally working between Bremen and Great Britain, by 1858, two ships traversed the Atlantic to New York. The schedule eventually included Baltimore and New Orleans. After a slow start, the Norddeutsche Lloyd developed into a powerful business that would come to dominate with the Hamburg-Amerikanische Packetfahrt-Actien-Gesellschaft (HAPAG), transatlantic shipping between Germany and the Americas.[8]

The desire for steamship lines became universal. Ports like Charleston, Richmond, and Savannah frequently inquired with foreign consuls

---

[7] December 29, 1850, pp. 191–192, book 13, January 3, 1853, p. 172, March 11, 1853, p. 201, June 22, 1853, pp. 275–278, June 30, 1853, pp. 285–286, book 15, Landesbibliothek Schleswig-Holstein, Kiel, Germany; Rudolph M. Schleiden, *Schleswig-Holsteins erste Erhebung, 1848–1849* (Wiesbaden, Germany: Verlag von J. F. Bergmann, 1891), 11.

[8] Ludwig Beutin, *Bremen und Amerika: Zur Geschichte der Weltwirtschaft und der Beziehungen Deutschlands zu den Vereinigten Staaten* (Bremen, Germany: C. Schünemann, 1953), 80–81.

whether any interest existed to open steamship lines and profit from the valuable trade in cash crops.[9] In addition, Brazil worked on the opening of a steamship line in the early 1860s connecting Rio de Janeiro with New York alongside an intermediary stop in Charleston, South Carolina.[10] The universal demand opened the door for shrewd businessmen to profit. Among them was the US entrepreneur Cornelius Vanderbilt.

Cornelius Vanderbilt laid the foundation for his transportation empire when he commanded the first run of his own steamship, the *Thistle*, from New York to New Brunswick on April 19, 1824. Initially, Vanderbilt's ships provided coastal steamboat journeys in the northeastern part of the United States. Eventually, he provided service through the Isthmus in Central America to California to profit from the mass of people traveling to the goldfields. His Accessory Transit Company offered a transit through Nicaragua along the San Juan River and Lake Nicaragua. Vanderbilt pursued his shipping business ruthlessly and drove competition, such as the Collins line, out of the market. By the 1860s, Vanderbilt switched to railroads as the more lucrative means of transportation.[11] Enterprising individuals like Cunard and Vanderbilt transformed the ways people and commodities traveled the Atlantic and brought the various communities closer together. They built on the established networks created in the colonial Atlantic world.

Only a small percentage of ships traversing the Atlantic for trade or passenger purposes were steamers. In 1840, the British government recorded 1370 ships built in the country, of which 74 were steamers. The number of steamships built over the next decade stagnated, but the number of newly constructed sailing vessels decreased dramatically, by 1850, only 621 sailing vessels left British shipyards. Nevertheless, by 1850, 426 steamships compared to 17,406 sailing vessels were registered in Great Britain. The sailing vessel still predominated at mid-century. By 1869, the situation looked dramatically

---

[9] Johannes Nicolaus Hudtwalcker to Carl Hermann Merck, January 31, 1861, CL VI no. 16p, Vol. 4b, Fasc 13c, 111–1 Senat, Staatsarchiv der Freien und Hansestadt Hamburg.

[10] James Watson Webb to William Henry Seward, October 8, 1863, M121, Despatches From U.S. Ministers to Brazil, 1809–1906, National Archives, Washington, DC.

[11] T. J. Stiles, *The First Tycoon: The Epic Life of Cornelius Vanderbilt* (New York: Vintage Books, 2010), 64, 218–220, 225, 259.

different. The number of sailing vessels had modestly increased to 24,187 and stood in contrast to 2972 steamers.[12] The emergence of steamers made passenger travel easier, but cargo remained predominantly on sailing vessels. But within a few short decades, steam and steel would vastly outperform wind as the main means of Atlantic transportation.

Despite the perception that global trade trends replaced Atlantic ones in the early nineteenth century, trade remained centered on the Atlantic world. The trade with China and Japan grew after each country opened, respectively, during the Opium War (1839–1842) and the visit of Commodore Matthew C. Perry in 1853–1854. Nevertheless, Australia, China, Japan, and India never gained the same importance that any one state in the Atlantic basin had. Merchants, shipowners, and traders looked to the Atlantic world to find raw materials and sell the industrial products of the European states.

Ships of the various Atlantic states crisscrossed the ocean. The end of the Navigation Acts, which had limited the colonial trade to ships from the colonial power, and the embrace of free trade, at least in regard to shipping, allowed shipowners from practically any country to carry commodities to any other country. Merchants were no longer restricted to carry goods from or to their native country; they engaged in the so-called carrying trade. A good example of how the carrying trade worked can be found by looking at the trade conducted by the German merchants and shipowners in the United States. In the fiscal year from July 1859 to June 1860, 341 German-flagged ships visited ports in the United States. Besides the flags of the Hanseatic Cities of Bremen, Hamburg, and Lübeck, ships from Hanover, Mecklenburg, Oldenburg, and Prussia were present. These ships were not solely engaged in trade between the United States and their homeports. They carried goods to Australia, Austria-Hungary, Belgium, Brazil, the British Isles, the British West Indies, Canada, Chile, China, Cuba, Dutch West Indies, Haiti, Hawaii Islands, Holland, Italy, Mexico, Peru, Puerto Rico, Russia, San Domingo, and Spain. At the same time, they arrived with cargos from Australia, Austria-Hungary, Belgium, Brazil, the British Isles, British East Indies, British West Indies, Chile, China, Cuba, Dutch East Indies,

---

[12] *Statistical Abstract for the United Kingdom in Each Year from 1840 to 1853* (London, UK: George Edward Eyre and William Spottiswoode, 1854), 20; *Statistical Abstract for the United Kingdom in Each of the Last Fifteen Years from 1862 to 1876* (London, UK: George Edward Eyre and William Spottiswoode, 1877), 94.

Dutch West Indies, France, Gibraltar, Hawaii Islands, Holland, Italy, Mexico, Puerto Rico, San Domingo, Spain, and Venezuela. Almost 50% of the German ships engaged in the carrying trade, while the rest came directly from or returned to the German states.[13] However, this list appears rather global in nature and would give the impression that German merchants traded equally with almost all parts of the globe. Their trade too was largely Atlantic.

Bremen, an early member of the once-powerful Hanseatic League, had a rich history of international trade and quickly rebuilt its trade empire in the aftermath of the Napoleonic wars. Especially, the opening of Bremerhaven at the mouth of the Weser River allowed larger ships to trade with Bremen and to avoid the lengthy trip down the river to the city itself.[14] Bremen, however, was a trade hub and transit port. Goods arrived in Bremen and after a short storage continue their voyage into the German states or other parts of Europe. Bremen was among the first European countries to trade with the United States and developed a strong trade connection with the North American republic. About 15% of Bremen's trade was solely devoted to the United States (Tables 3.1 and 3.2). Over a third of Bremen's trade was with the Americas, including Cuba, Brazil, and New Granada as important commodity providers. However, they were not as important as export markets. Similarly, Asia was of relatively small importance. While a significant amount of trade went to India, the India trade never reached the same value as the trade with Brazil, which was only one of many countries in the Americas. Clearly, Bremen's merchant continued to think in Atlantic terms.

Similarly, French merchants and shipowners focused on North America. The French had diversified their trade portfolio over time. Especially after the commercial treaty of 1860 with Great Britain, France strengthened its commercial ties with the political rival across the Channel. Within a few years, Great Britain was responsible for a quarter of the French trade (Tables 3.3 and 3.4). Asia played only a minor role for France's trade development. Japan, China, and the various European colonies in Asia barely accounted for 1% of the French trade. In contrast, the United States alone provided France with well over 10% of its

---

[13] *Report of the Secretary of the Treasury … Commerce and Navigation, 1859–1860* (Washington, DC: George W. Bowman, 1860), 534–545.

[14] Beutin, *Bremen und Amerika*, 27–29.

Table 3.1 Imports of Bremen by value

	(L d'or) 1851	(L d'or) 1855	(L d'or) 1860	(Thaler) 1865	(Thaler) 1870
Great Britain	2,050,842	3,462,303	8,752,682	15,562,445	12,097,249
France	593,161	232,072	635,404	874,214	537,110
Spain	32,738	450,678	164,497	240,091	135,935
Italy	85,145	100,158	97,343	113,994	93,690
Netherlands	587,444	350,780	451,958	470,471	871,412
Belgium	114,653	113,536	243,854	214,268	588,126
United States	5,911,527	8,661,334	15,761,513	10,847,602	29,958,327
British Canada	–	–	–	36,170	–
Cuba	1,766,279	2,654,492	2,291,385	3,494,597	1,158,976
Haiti	391,483	677,794	590,148	161,990	244,515
Jamaica	144,933	254,606	250,377	462,796	108,271
San Juan	622,294	851,567	724,947	869,332	511,297
Mexico	77,976	152,552	261,641	26,671	111,112
Venezuela	376,796	360,481	172,397	592,773	239,090
Brazil	1,900,508	2,429,004	2,528,645	2,552,908	3,132,707
Argentina	232,921	106,506	279,923	183,921	406,826
New Granada	57,316	451,603	2,407,033	3,209,441	3,056,164
Chile	3375	–	–	2740	–
Peru	44,605	39,012	9322	7989	35,535
China	78,390	92,423	121,544	175,333	315,718
India	–	1,191,549	1,274,536	2,162,050	1,428,829
Japan	–	–	–	300	4309
Australia	–	165	–	–	610
Dutch East Indies	160,922	458,126	309,004	390,683	584
All	37,546,116	53,254,978	71,504,302	77,294,373	92,303,438

Sources *Tabellarische Uebersicht des Bremischen Handels im Jahre 1851*, 22–23; *Tabellarische Uebersicht des Bremischen Handels im Jahre 1860*, 218–221; *Jahrbuch für die Amtliche Statistik Bremischen Staats im Jahre 1870*, 178–185

imports and offered a similar size market for French exports. In addition, the Spanish colonies of Cuba, Mexico, Argentina, Peru, and Chile emerged as essential trade partners of France. Brazil received about 3% of French exports and about 2% of the imports arriving in France came from Brazil, making Brazil the largest trade partner in South America. The patterns of French trade show similarities to Bremen's and further illustrate how these two continental European states remained focused on the Atlantic when it came to trade relations. States in Europe and the Americas were the essential trade partners and not Asian countries.

Table 3.2 Export of Bremen by value

	(L d'or) 1851	(L d'or) 1855	(L d'or) 1860	(Thaler) 1865	(Thaler) 1870
Great Britain	336,633	1,127,174	1,802,820	4,015,825	4,122,066
France	24,844	117,425	85,088	356,797	440,057
Spain	188	–	38,791	228,649	134,040
Italy	336	26,887	116,592	446,500	3791
Netherlands	534,369	583,955	959,029	865,702	1,472,146
Belgium	56,799	54,953	267,927	519,928	1,079,413
United States	8,510,969	12,697,334	13,099,918	13,002,370	17,518,124
British Canada	31,577	93,805	36,136	30,247	92,133
Cuba	240,622	310,271	477,813	664,910	618,401
Haiti	94,830	80,050	103,317	45,012	2174
Jamaica	54,014	35,594	35,234	127,450	120,606
San Juan	31,070	64,787	209,936	148,164	200,073
Mexico	204,929	181,749	91,892	17,245	60,865
Venezuela	175,714	348,050	126,407	246,393	119,741
Brazil	90,010	348,050	126,407	86,985	34,570
Argentina	11,484	70,956	255,194	263,767	254,941
New Granada	159,521	3204	54,979	142,831	34,589
Chile	20,603	1891	5472	9754	37,818
Peru	193,816	88,447	77,866	46,692	120,361
China	935	3713	6048	189,544	285,472
India	–	14,362	9681	105,582	65,971
Japan	–	–	–	32,097	73,992
Australia	12,719	15,919	6493	6592	9886
Dutch East Indies	37,849	34,567	116,306	8689	3892
All	32,868,947	48,924,319	70,068,298	70,879,843	90,947,474

Sources *Tabellarische Uebersicht des Bremischen Handels im Jahre 1851*, 30–31; *Tabellarische Uebersicht des Bremischen Handels im Jahre 1860*, 218–221; *Jahrbuch für die Amtliche Statistik Bremischen Staatsim Jahre 1870*, 178–185

A markedly different pattern emerges with British trade. The diversity of Great Britain's trade portfolio shows the country's merchant fleet traded with virtually every part of the world. As a result, Albion did not rely on any one country for commodities or as a market (Tables 3.5 and 3.6). Certain states like France, the German states, the United States, or India were more important than other countries but even then, the four largest trade partners combined only constituted about 40% of Britain's export trade. For Great Britain, Asia remained more significant as a result

Table 3.3 Export of France by value in million Francs

	1845	1850	1855	1860	1865
Great Britain	147.9	295.2	377.1	681.7	1294.9
Spain	90.4	106.3	120.9	138.4	217.6
Netherlands	24.9	36.3	31.2	30.5	37.8
Germany	105.9	54.8	74.1	194.6	235.5
Belgium	69.9	117.1	150.9	168.9	287.7
United States	143.1	272.6	341.5	321.6	133.4
British Canada	0.8	0.6	1.2	1.7	3.7
Cuba	14.5	11.1	19.1	30.9	28.7
Haiti	5.5	6.5	11.1	13.4	7.7
Mexico	12.7	22.8	26.1	19.4	70.7
Venezuela	3.0	4.7	7.5	3.8	6.3
Brazil	29.6	32.5	50.7	77.6	118.9
Argentina	5.2	13.8	17.1	45.9	51.9
New Granada	2.4	5.5	6.6	6.1	8.1
Chile	12.3	14.7	28.3	38.1	41.9
Peru	3.7	14.2	31.9	44.1	36.3
China	0.8	0.5	1.3	3.0	4.6
India	3.7	4.7	7.1	8.7	10.4
Japan	–	–	–	–	0.7
Dutch East Indies	1.2	1.7	1.5	1.2	1.4
All	1187.4	1531.0	2026.9	2949.4	4086.5

Sources *Tableau Général du Commerce de la France* (Paris, 1850), xxxviii–xxxix; *Tableau Général du Commerce de la France* (Paris, 1855), xxxiv–xxxv; *Tableau Général du Commerce de la France* (Paris, 1860), xxxvi–xxxvii; *Tableau Général du Commerce de la France* (Paris, 1866), xxxv–xli

of the deep imperial connections. Especially, Australia and British India provided markets for about 15% of British exports. However, both these colonies became part of the empire a long time ago and had therefore been integrated into the British trade network for well over a century. More recently opened Asian markets like China and Japan continued to fluctuate and failed to attain even remotely the same importance as the British colonies in Asia. Taking all this into consideration, even combined Asia only made up about a quarter of Britain's trade. The rest focused on the Atlantic world.

Throughout the middle decades of the nineteenth century, the United States ranked among the top five markets for Great Britain. At times, the country was the single largest market for Great Britain. While the other American countries could not even remotely live up to the importance of

Table 3.4 Import of France by value in million Francs

	1845	1850	1855	1860	1865
Great Britain	138.9	121.5	334.4	412.4	700.2
Spain	44.9	49.9	91.1	163.4	284.4
Netherlands	24.6	22.2	30.7	33.2	45.4
Germany	82.8	54.2	147.3	240.6	271.9
Belgium	134.2	157.9	261.5	215.6	423.5
United States	172.2	136.8	225.0	283.5	56.2
British Canada	0.1	–	–	0.8	3.9
Cuba	12.9	22.1	26.9	18.1	54.6
Haiti	7.8	7.1	11.1	14.3	31.1
Mexico	7.8	8.5	5.9	6.1	5.7
Venezuela	1.9	2.5	4.9	5.6	18.6
Brazil	14.7	17.7	34.1	34.3	96.1
Argentina	11.5	13.7	15.1	29.7	57.2
New Granada	1.0	1.5	0.5	2.3	1.4
Chile	4.3	3.9	4.7	7.1	13.0
Peru	2.0	5.0	2.9	6.9	21.0
China	3.3	2.0	3.6	3.3	44.7
India	40.5	44.6	53.3	59.4	88.5
Japan	–	–	–	–	8.3
Dutch East Indies	9.2	5.3	5.9	6.9	2.9
All	1240.1	1174.1	1951.7	2392.4	3527.4

Sources *Tableau Général du Commerce de la France* (Paris, 1850), xxxvi–xxxvii; *Tableau Général du Commerce de la France* (Paris, 1855), xxxii–xxxiii; *Tableau Général du Commerce de la France* (Paris, 1860), xxxiv–xxxv; *Tableau Général du Commerce de la France* (Paris, 1866), xxxv–xli

the United States, they did contribute to the still heavily Atlantic-centric trade portfolio of Great Britain. Among the Latin American countries, Brazil prevailed as by far the largest trade partner, followed by Argentina, Colombia, Peru, and Chile. Since Great Britain had its own Caribbean colonies, the country did not rely as much on Cuban and Haitian products as its European competitors. Nevertheless, Britain's trade was just as Atlantic-centric as the trade of the other European countries. Asia was not yet fully integrated into the trade networks, and a global economy was still in the making, at least for Europeans.

Located between the Atlantic and Pacific Oceans, the United States looked well-positioned to engage in global trade and bridge two ocean worlds. However, even the United States focused on the Atlantic world during most of the nineteenth century. The country was responsible for the opening of Japan with Commodore Perry's mission and benefitted

Table 3.5   Export of the United Kingdom by value in Pound

	1851	1855	1860	1865	1870
France	2,028,463	6,012,658	12,701,372	25,355,072	21,982,999
Spain	1,015,493	1,158,800	2,623,291	3,015,458	3,113,751
Italy	3,108,083	2,542,456	5,277,720	6,123,612	6,293,277
Netherlands	3,542,673	4,558,210	9,752,962	14,960,949	17,303,845
Germany	7,694,059	9,877,796	16,659,306	28,153,392	28,065,534
Belgium	984,501	1,707,693	3,964,670	6,896,157	8,949,154
United States	14,362,976	17,318,086	22,907,681	25,170,788	31,306,089
British Canada	3,740,880	2,802,368	3,986,810	5,720,498	7,584,427
Cuba	1,164,177	1,059,606	1,609,696	2,327,802	2,820,411
Haiti	239,146	160,128	417,072	348,419	401,220
Mexico	577,901	585,898	538,949	1,967,389	1,058,128
Venezuela	349,701	378,491	3,27,357	397,956	147,944
Brazil	3,518,684	3,312,728	4,571,308	5,771,024	5,543,803
Argentina	458,329	742,442	1,820,935	1,988,565	2,428,182
New Granada	319,889	588,935	854,500	2,419,347	2,201,367
Chile	1,181,837	1,330,385	1,737,929	1,626,315	2,767,048
Peru	1,208,253	1,285,160	1,428,172	1,205,876	1,853,706
China	1,528,869	888,679	2,915,542	3,688,414	6,363,391
India	7,022,296	9,949,154	17,683,669	18,833,190	20,093,749
Japan	–	–	2	1,654,028	1,777,293
Australia	2,636,347	3,530,497	9,935,368	12,445,838	9,110,021
Dutch East Indies	759,361	529,815	1,425,724	931,559	902,642
All	74,448,722	95,688,085	164,521,351	218,831,576	244,080,577

Sources *Annual Statement of the Trade and Navigation of the United Kingdom* (1855), 9–10; *Annual Statement of the Trade and Navigation of the United Kingdom* (1860), 6–7; *Annual Statement of the Trade and Navigation of the United Kingdom* (1865), 2–5; *Annual Statement of the Trade and Navigation of the United Kingdom* (1870), 2–5

from the British engagement in the Opium War, when US merchants continued to trade with China. China and India combined only received about 4% of the exports of the United States based on value (Tables 3.7 and 3.8). The United States, however, imported about 6% of the commodities reaching the country from both Asian countries. Other Asian countries added little to the equation. Even Japan developed slowly and not until the mid-1870s could the country pass China in export and become an important contributor to the imports of the United States.

48   N. EICHHORN

Table 3.6 Imports of the United Kingdom by value in Pound

	1851	1855	1860	1865	1870
France	8,083,112	6,737,560	17,774,037	31,625,231	37,607,514
Spain	1,070,982	2,555,358	3,992,386	4,769,277	6,067,018
Italy	2,321,042	2,069,029	2,748,525	2,486,997	3,843,605
Netherlands	3,749,560	3,809,889	8,256,690	12,413,404	14,315,717
Germany	5,414,795	8,483,386	14,541,562	12,611,852	15,404,218
Belgium	1,253,066	2,298,967	4,079,245	7,354,845	11,247,864
United States	23,616,455	26,969,947	44,727,202	21,624,210	49,804,835
British Canada	1,716,899	1,219,015	6,826,551	6,350,178	8,515,364
Cuba	1,929,121	1,973,020	3,288,116	5,063,839	5,362,339
Haiti	185,719	87,357	123,147	23,287	230,832
Mexico	374,740	677,726	490,221	3,216,924	299,813
Venezuela	79,359	62,682	24,940	221.331	81,915
Brazil	2,893,751	2,938,517	2,269,180	6,797,241	6,127,448
Argentina	1,006,420	737,857	1,101,428	1,014,329	1,486,425
New Granada	193,578	342,049	555,177	1,566,973	906,279
Chile	621,704	1,305,220	2,586,217	3,798,543	3,828,225
Peru	2,373,862	3,114,739	2,581,142	4,002,150	4,881,075
China	7,971,491	10,664,315	9,323,764	10,499,034	9,481,737
India	12,280,996	12,805,412	15,106,595	37,395,452	25,090,163
Japan	–	–	167,511	6,14,743	96,173
Australia	1,630,276	1,663,106	6,025,001	9,007,150	11,943,284
Dutch East Indies	139,036	160,709	333,816	226	259,846
All	110,484,997	117,402,366	210,530,873	271,072,285	303,257,493

Sources *Annual Statement of the Trade and Navigation of the United Kingdom* (1855), 5–6; *Annual Statement of the Trade and Navigation of the United Kingdom* (1860), 4–5; *Annual Statement of the Trade and Navigation of the United Kingdom* (1865), 2–5; *Annual Statement of the Trade and Navigation of the United Kingdom* (1870), 2–5

In contrast, trade with Great Britain retained a dominant position. In any given year, at least half of the exports of the United States went to and about 40% of the imports arrived from Great Britain. In addition, European countries like France, Spain, the Netherlands, Belgium, and the German states were of lesser but still significant importance. Especially, the German states and France grew dramatically in importance. Between the early 1860s and mid-1870s, French imports grew from 10 to 14%, but the same trend did not hold true with exports. The German states increased their share from 5 to 7%. Europe persisted as an immensely important market for the United States.

Table 3.7 Export of the United States by value in Dollar

	1849/1850	1855/1856	1860/1861	1865/1866	1870/1871	1874/1875
Great Britain	73,170,373	162,360,807	120,535,923	342,278,458	344,632,550	366,799,869
France	19,833,347	42,510,973	24,257,843	61,845,449	27,117,512	50,133,711
Spain	3,987,434	7,434,318	1,841,025	5,688,746	10,248,329	7,540,086
Netherlands	2,604,665	3,586,428	3,719,373	2,430,431	12,381,161	7,483,010
Germany	5,305,158	16,127,879	12,591,657	28,271,020	34,610,021	52,517,913
Belgium	2,543,760	6,500,623	2,754,011	6,900,732	11,610,950	12,387,590
British Canada	9,549,035	29,029,349	22,745,613	29,356,572	29,790,894	34,309,761
Cuba	4,990,297	7,809,263	12,892,077	15,772,160	14,200,496	15,586,658
Haiti	1,350,188	2,126,454	2,427,626	3,730,271	2,791,057	4,870,812
San Juan	909,653	1,142,724	1,381,064	2,574,744	3,400,291	2,377,757
Mexico	2,012,827	3,702,239	2,215,890	4,588,218	5,082,533	3,895,792
Venezuela	1,018,470	1,712,744	1,220,786	1,360,737	1,440,141	2,423,254
Brazil	3,197,114	5,094,904	5,023,217	5,785,504	5,945,397	7,634,865
Argentina	1,064,642	1,259,863	1,166,625	1,801,498	1,216,458	1,301,294
New Granada	1,256,219	1,611,392	1,586,992	3,791,941	4,182,567	4,272,950
Chile	1,422,721	2,867,743	2,626,652	1,161,384	1,548,411	2,062,190
Peru	275,725	1,244,223	394,940	1,215,835	3,479,773	2,443,657
China	1,605,217	2,558,237	6,917,427	10,149,824	3,920,216	1,465,934
India	659,459	767,629	629,901	582,828	273,513	473,049
Japan	–	4000	40,553	532,772	9,87,675	1,647,197
Australia	–	5,034,972	3,431,036	6,108,999	2,369,346	3,505,435
Dutch East Indies	443,485	210,156	254,069	161,053	203,785	1,034,159
All	151,898,720	326,964,908	249,344,913	565,426,394	562,518,651	643,094,767

Sources *Report of the Secretary of the Treasury, 1849–1850*, 306–307; *Report of the Secretary of the Treasury, 1855–1856*, 544–545; *Report of the Secretary of the Treasury, 1860–1861*, 602–603; *Report of the Secretary of the Treasury, 1865–1866*, 394–395; *Annual Report of the Chief of the Bureau of Statistics on the Commerce and Navigation of the United States, 1870–1871*, 190–191; *Annual Report of the Chief of the Bureau of Statistics on the Commerce and Navigation of the United States, 1874–1875*, 326–327

Table 3.8 Imports of the United States by value in Dollar

	1849/1850	1855/1856	1860/1861	1865/1866	1870/1871	1874/1875
Great Britain	75,159,424	122,266,082	139,206,367	202,440,242	220,880,367	146,597,827
France	27,538,025	49,016,062	34,245,549	22,930,289	28,103,025	63,342,631
Spain	2,082,395	2,232,466	3,259,361	2,675,009	4,188,445	4,534,873
Netherlands	1,686,967	2,426,479	2,811,334	2,778,314	2,047,962	2,353,658
Germany	8,815,343	14,619,687	15,341,989	26,257,936	25,093,635	40,893,386
Belgium	2,404,954	3,106,511	2,271,528	2,267,362	4,178,714	6,189,098
British Canada	5,644,462	21,310,421	19,062,936	54,704,959	35,501,746	32,763,870
Cuba	10,292,398	24,435,693	33,536,357	37,795,812	58,240,584	66,745,527
Haiti	1,544,771	1,924,259	1,716,173	1,161,719	1,055,675	2,207,173
San Juan	2,067,866	3,870,963	3,395,433	6,175,018	9,453,945	6,930,082
Mexico	2,135,366	3,568,681	3,689,213	4,155,603	17,511,163	11,634,983
Venezuela	1,920,247	4,202,692	2,999,949	2,476,449	2,975,629	5,690,224
Brazil	9,324,429	19,262,657	18,100,456	16,831,423	30,560,648	42,033,046
Argentina	2,653,877	2,322,161	3,200,836	6,832,266	7,040,575	5,834,709
New Granada	591,992	2,325,019	3,186,052	1,692,067	6,436,776	12,942,305
Chile	1,796,877	2,467,819	3,186,052	740,250	716,544	789,242
Peru	170,753	217,759	306,428	807,238	4,731,439	1,344,595
China	6,593,462	10,454,436	11,351,719	10,132,683	20,066,315	13,480,440
India	2,865,016	7,005,911	8,745,768	6,181,668	13,702,787	15,584,099
Japan	–	16,821	102,566	1,815,364	5,387,991	7,772,302
Australia	–	139,452	129,334	424,018	285,411	3,755,590
Dutch East Indies	444,404	1,399,289	1,045,791	776,255	3,043,131	6,775,399
All	178,138,318	314,639,942	335,650,153	437,640,354	541,493,708	553,906,153

Sources *Report of the Secretary of the Treasury, 1849–1850*, 306–307; *Report of the Secretary of the Treasury, 1855–1856*, 544–545; *Report of the Secretary of the Treasury, 1860–1861*, 602–603; *Report of the Secretary of the Treasury, 1865–1866*, 394–395; *Annual Report of the Chief of the Bureau of Statistics on the Commerce and Navigation of the United States, 1870–1871*, 68–69; *Annual Report of the Chief of the Bureau of Statistics on the Commerce and Navigation of the United States, 1874–1875*, 100–101

The same held true for Latin America and the Caribbean basin. By the mid-1870, the United States imported more commodities from Cuba than it did from France and more goods arrived from Brazil than from the German states. Nevertheless, Brazil and Cuba did not even take half of the export that went to France. Latin America was not a major export market, US consumer goods found few buyers, and cash crops had no takers in South America. The United States exported manufactured goods, competing with European producers. In addition, the United States exported especially high-priced cash crops and sought-after food crops. A similar pattern holds true for the commodities the United States received from Latin America and the Caribbean countries to satisfy its own consumer and industrial needs. Like the European states, merchants, traders, and shipowners in the United States focused their trade interactions on the Atlantic world during the nineteenth century. By the mid-1870s, Asia grew in importance, but had not reached Atlantic world levels. An Atlantic trade world persisted.

These trade statistics illustrate that during most of the nineteenth century, the Atlantic world remained a bustling center of trade. The trade patterns for Bremen, France, Great Britain, and the United States indicate that the Atlantic world continued to be the place where trade networks centered. The European powers still relied heavily on commodities from the Americas for their industry and on the Americas as markets for finished products. Asia was not, despite the desire to satisfy the huge China market and the opening of Japan, a huge market where European or US products were widely sought. The continued economic interconnectedness of the Atlantic region meant that merchants and political leaders desired to improve their position, calling for steamship lines, expanded port facilities, and other technological innovations. The growth in Atlantic trade brought about the emergence of lines like Cunard and the Norddeutscher Lloyd. European steam lines dominated Atlantic transportation as they connected various parts of the region in a speedy and safe fashion. These lines transformed the Atlantic world; where travel took months in the early days of the Atlantic world, by the end of the nineteenth century, ships could make the crossing in less than a week, furthering trade relations. The Atlantic world contained a vibrant trade network.

Bibliography

Beutin, Ludwig. *Bremen und Amerika: Zur Geschichte der Weltwirtschaft und der Beziehungen Deutschlands zu den Vereinigten Staaten.* Bremen, Germany: C. Schünemann, 1953.

Butler, Daniel A. *The Age of Cunard: A Transatlantic History 1839–2003.* Annapolis, MD: Lighthouse Press Publication, 2004.

Despatches from U.S. Ministers to Brazil, National Archives. Washington, DC.

Fraser-Macdonald, A. *Our Ocean Railways.* London, UK: Chapman and Hall, 1893.

Hyde, Francis E. *Cunard and the North Atlantic, 1840–1973: A History of Shipping and Financial Management.* London, UK: Macmillan, 1975.

Lindeman, Moritz. *Der Norddeutsche Lloyd: Geschichte und Handbuch.* Bremen, Germany: Schünemann, 1892.

Robins, Nick S. *The Coming of the Comet: The Rise and Fall of the Paddle Steamer.* Barnsley, UK: Seaforth Publishing, 2012.

Schleiden Papers. Landesbibliothek Schleswig-Holstein. Kiel, Germany.

Schleiden Papers. Staatsarchiv. Bremen, Germany.

Schleiden, Rudolph M. *Schleswig-Holsteins erste Erhebung, 1848–1849.* Wiesbaden, Germany: Verlag von J. F. Bergmann, 1891.

Smith, Crosbie, and Anne Scott. "'Trust in Providence': Building Confidence into the Cunard Line of Steamers." *Technology and Culture* 48 (July 2007): 471–496.

Stiles, T. J. *The First Tycoon: The Epic Life of Cornelius Vanderbilt.* New York: Vintage Books, 2010.

United Kingdom. *Statistical Abstract for the United Kingdom in Each Year from 1840 to 1853.* London, UK: George Edward Eyre and William Spottiswoode, 1854.

United States. *Report of the Secretary of the Treasury … Commerce and Navigation, 1859–1860.* Washington, DC: George W. Bowman, 1860.

CHAPTER 4

National Revolutions

By *people* we mean the ENTIRETY OF HUMAN BEINGS THAT MAKE UP THE NATION. However, a multitude of individuals does not yet constitute a *Nation*, unless it is directed by common principles, governed by the same laws, and united in a fraternal bond. *Nation* is a word that stands for *Unity: Unity of principles*, of *purpose*, and of *rights*.[1]

As the Atlantic world transitioned from the eighteenth into the nineteenth century, revolutionary upheavals touched virtually every part of the region. People formed new notions about what unified them, as suggested above by the Italian revolutionary Giuseppe Mazzini. They could look to language, history, or culture to find commonalities. When the French Revolution broke out in 1789, intellectual elites agreed that a nation was only a political state with geographic limitations whose people abided by the same laws and spoke the same language. The modern idea of nationalism remained in its infancy around 1800.[2] However, people started to search for identities that unified and defined them, beyond language and law. They were keen to acquire an identity especially those suffering from imperial oppression. Nevertheless, as Benedict Anderson

---

[1] Giuseppe Mazzini, "On the Superiority of Representative Government," 1832, in *A Cosmopolitanism of Nations*, 48.

[2] Jacques Godechot, "The New Concept of the Nation and Its Diffusion in Europe," in *Nationalism in the Age of the French Revolution*, ed. Otto Dann (London, UK: Bloomsbury Publishing, 1988), 13.

suggests, defining nationalism required much imagining and the even more difficult task of convincing the general population to embrace the newly developed identity.[3]

The earth-shattering reverberations of the French Revolution, the wars that followed, and the occupation of vast lands by French Revolutionary soldiers weakened the old state systems. As monarchs toppled from their thrones and states disappeared new loyalties emerged. Intellectual elites around the Euro-Atlantic, started to imagine identities in light of the local environment, shared linguistic-cultural characteristics, and historic backgrounds. Some of these imagined communities were designed to transform a series of separate entities into one nation-state, such as Italy or the United States. In other cases, the new imagined community ran counter to an imperial overlord, often the remnants of the older imperial Atlantic world, to create new small nation-states on the peripheral, such as the southern parts of the United States or Greece. During the first half of the nineteenth century, a wide variety of societies struggled to turn the vague outlines of their nationalism into full-fledged states. The independence struggles in Latin America and the Revolutions in 1830 and 1848 highlight these struggles to formulate coherent nation-states. This chapter will comparatively explore a series of national revolutionary struggles in Europe and the Americas, linking the language used by these nationalist movements to bring about independence or unity. Many of these challenges were possible because of the dissemination of ideas along the trade networks and the inspiration from conflicts in other parts of the Atlantic world.

When Antoine Furetière's posthumously published *Dictionnaire Universel* came out in 1690, he used a limited definition of nation, referring to people within a state of shared governance and language. A half century, hence, Voltaire continued to use nation in a Furetière-esque style, but also talked about "nation allemande (German nation)" and "la nation juive (Jewish nation)" whereas the existence of a German nation may be up for debate in the late eighteenth century, to classify the Jewish population of Europe as a nation was unusual considering how dispersed Jews were across Europe.[4] However, as a group of a shared faith,

---

[3] Benedict Anderson, *Imagined Communities: Reflections on the Origin and Spread of Nationalism* (London, UK: Verso, 1983).

[4] Jacques Godechot, "The New Concept of the Nation and Its Diffusion in Europe," in *Nationalism in the Age of the French Revolution*, ed. Otto Dann (London, UK: Bloomsbury Publishing, 1988), 13.

set of culture, and expatriate history, much united Jewish people to justify classifying them as a nation, which, however, in the second half of the century also served as basis for proto-fascist movements against them. As Benedict Anderson notes, the imagining of a community required not only a scholarly elite to craft historic or cultural ties into a coherent identity, but the mechanical innovations of the printing press and an educated people who could turn "print-languages" into "national consciousness."[5] The imagining of community cut across both ethnic as well as civic nationalism.

The French Revolution altered the entire conversation regarding nationalism and the meaning of nation. Resistance to the French military occupation and perceived outside oppression provided a powerful bond as people fought to regain their freedom. In 1815, the German historian and politician Friedrich Christoph Dahlmann gave a commemorative speech to mark the end of the Napoleonic Wars, but also to remind people not to throw away the accomplishments of the war years, especially the shared identity crafted in the wars of liberation. In his Waterloo speech, Dahlmann noted that a unified Europe had shed the despotism of French rule. He asked the German people to maintain the just created bond. The German people and nation existed and no law or decision by a cabinet could change that. Dahlmann closed with the powerful call, "Hail to the Germans, who have found rescue in the most dire moment, … Hail Blüchern and his warriors of the German fatherland."[6] The Napoleonic wars had awoken a national feeling that needed molding in the course of the century. However, a German nation-state was still far in the future and Dahlmann was hardly the first and only one to appeal to national consciousnesses.

Already, in 1807, German intellectual Johann Gottlieb Fichte suggested an ethnic-based nationalism. He claimed, "we, the immediate heirs of their soil, their language, and their way of thinking—for being Germans still, for being still borne along on the stream of original and independent life. It is they whom we must thank for everything that we have been as a nation since those days, and to them we shall be indebted for everything that we shall be in the future, unless things come to an

---

[5] Anderson, *Imagined Communities*, 37, 44–45.

[6] Friedrich Christoph Dahlmann, *Die Waterloo-Rede von Friedrich Christoph Dahlmann am 7. Juli 1815*, ed. Utz Schliesky (Kiel, Germany: Lorenz-von-Stein-Institut für Verwaltungswissenschaften an der Christian-Albrechts-Universität zu Kiel, 2015).

end with us now and the last drop of blood inherited from them has dried up in our veins." He imagined a connection between soil and people, a lasting linkage in ethnic nationalism.[7] While Fichte's idea of ethnic nationalism worked well in some parts of Europe, the vast majority of locations in the Atlantic world could not use the soil-based nationalism definition. The Americas in particular were populated by people with widely different backgrounds who required a different type of identity.

In contrast to Fichte, Giuseppe Mazzini attached a political meaning to nationalism; he desired a republican nation-state. His national identity divorced itself from soil, ethnicity, or race and instead was malleable to different people and locations. A political revolution was meaningless to Mazzini if not associated with a national revolution. He specifically believed in the inevitability of the creation of a liberal Italian nation-state. "Republican–because theoretically every nation is destined by the law of God and humanity, to form a free and equal community of brothers"; he wrote, "and the republican is the only form of government that insures this future. Because all true sovereignty resides essentially in the nation, the sole progressive and continuous interpreter of the supreme moral law."[8] Mazzini's nationalism was universal and a mix of civic and ethnic nationalism with a political system of government attached, a system applicable to many parts of the Atlantic world.

Where Fichte envisioned an ethnic-based national identity and Mazzini imagined a national community that mixed aspects of civic and ethnic nationalism, modern nationalism studies no longer support such a simplistic dichotomy of ethnic or civic nationalism. Michael Mann claims, "As states transformed first into national states, then into nation-states, classes became caged, unintentionally 'naturalized' and politicized."[9]

---

[7] Johann Gottlieb Fichte, *Addresses to the German Nation*, trans. R. F. Jones and G. H. Turnbull (Chicago, IL: University of Chicago Press, 1922), 136–138, 143–145; for a new study on the need to move beyond the dichotomy of ethnic and civic nationalism see: Timothy Baycroft and Mark Hewitson, eds., *What Is a Nation? Europe, 1789–1914* (Oxford, UK: Oxford University Press, 2006).

[8] Giuseppe Mazzini, "General Instructions for the Members of Young Italy," reprinted in *Selected Writings*, ed. Nagendranath Gangulee (London, UK: L. Drummond, 1945), 129–131.

[9] Lloyd S. Kramer, *Nationalism in Europe and America: Politics, Cultures, and Identities Since 1775* (Chapel Hill: University of North Carolina Press, 2011), 1; Michael Mann, *The Sources of Social Power: The Rise of Classes and Nation-States, 1760–1914* (Cambridge, UK: Cambridge University Press, 1986), 20. Interestingly, Mann does not include Poland, Latin

However, besides the underpinnings of class, nationalism frequently invokes irrational fears of enemies within and abroad. At the same time, nation-states maintained regional and local identities, superimposing a new national identity.[10] Furthermore, a dichotomy of civic and ethnic nation-state does not take into consideration many different forces, such as religion, language, economic development, political institutions, and war, contributing to a larger national identity.

However, what neither Mazzini nor Dahlmann out rightly said, but both implied, is that the creation of nations was a top-down affair, not involving the people who provided the backbone of the nation. Elites, especially intellectuals, professors, and students, were usually responsible for the formation of identities and then provided the rest of the state's population with a framework for their new identity. In the Americas, where identity had to embrace civic rather than ethnic definitions, elites drafted constitutions and developed pride in a shared history, language, heritage, and culture, which increasingly formed a basis for a statewide identity. As Benedict Anderson argues in *Imagined Communities*, "I propose the following definition of the nation: it is an imagined political community – and imagined as both inherently limited and sovereign."[11] The process of forming these communities was long and arduous. Even more, the formation process often brought different national identities into conflict.

On February 11, 1811, Cartagena, a city on the northern coast of the Viceroyalty of New Granada, declared its independence from the Spanish Empire. The effects of the French Revolution and occupation had destabilized Spain and its empire, raising questions about who legitimately ruled Spain. By February, relations in Cartagena had escalated when Spanish-born merchants and army officers called for the restoration

---

America, or the African continent in his analysis. While Irish independence desires briefly appear because of the impact of the American Revolution on British policy makers, Ireland otherwise is of little importance to Mann with its lack of industrialization.

[10] Michael Jeismann, "Nation, Identity, and Enmity: Towards a Theory of Political Identification," Jörn Leonhard, "Nation-States and War: European and Transatlantic Perspectives," Maiken Umbach, "Nation and Region: Regionalism in Modern European Nation-States," in *What Is a Nation? Europe, 1789–1914*, eds. Timothy Baycroft and Mark Hewitson (Oxford, UK: Oxford University Press, 2006), 27, 63–80, 231–254.

[11] Anderson, *Imagined Communities*, 6.

of Spanish rule. The local junta reasserted itself and prevented the usurpation of power. Nevertheless, the junta remained torn between moderate and radical political elements. By November, the latter had gained influence and decided to declare the province officially independent from Spain.[12] Cartagena's declaration of independence justified the decision to separate from the Spanish Empire by pointing to the three hundred year of "de vejaciones, de miserias, de sufrimientos de todo género."[13] The authors of the declaration resented the lack of equality within the empire and did not trust the monarchy or Cadiz Cortes, which governed in the name of the deposed king in opposition to the French occupiers. Pointing to Spanish hypocrisy, the writers claimed "fue un espectáculo verdaderamente singular e inconcebible ver que al paso que la España europea con una mano derribaba el trono del despotismo, y derramaba su sangre por defender su libertad, con la otra nuevas echase nuevas cadenas a la España Americana."[14] Like similar movements before and after, Cartagena's political elite voiced their desire to break the chains of oppression, end their enslavement. The Spanish government had lost its right to rule when it had violated the rights of the people. After establishing that all means to find reconciliation were exhausted, Cartagena's leaders distinguished themselves from "la nación Española." The declaration closed with "la Provincia de Cartagena de Indias es desde hoy de hecho y por derecho Estado libre, soberano e independiente; que se halla absuelta de toda sumisión, vasallaje, obediencia, y de todo otro vínculo de cualquier clase y naturaleza que fuese, que anteriormente la ligase con la corona y gobiernos de España, y que como tal Estado libre y absolutamente independiente." Henceforth, Cartagena was "naciones libres e independientes."[15] However, Cartagena's independence desires eventually had to give way.

---

[12] Brian R. Hamnett, *The End of Iberian Rule on the American Continent, 1770–1830* (Cambridge, UK: Cambridge University Press, 2017); Anthony McFarlane, *War and Independence in Spanish America* (New York: Routledge, 2013), 103–104.

[13] Translation: "humiliations, miseries, sufferings of all kinds."

[14] Translation: "it was a truly singular and inconceivable spectacle to see that while European Spain with one hand was demolishing the throne of despotism, and spilling its blood to defend their freedom, with the other cast new chains to American Spain."

[15] Acta de Independencia de Cartagena available at https://es.wikisource.org/wiki/Acta_de_Independencia_de_Cartagena.

In the course of the independence wars against Spain, Cartagena provided Simón Bolívar with an early outlet to call for a broad liberation struggle against Spain. A year after Cartagena's declaration of independence, Bolívar delivered his Cartagena Manifesto. As he appealed to the residents of New Granada to stand strong against Spanish rule and oppose oppression, he distinguished between his audience, Granadans, and their neighbors, Venezuelans. Even as Bolívar pointed to the lack of a republican political identity in Venezuela and New Granada, he observed that a federal-state structure was "the most suitable for guaranteeing human happiness in society."[16] Cartagena and Bolívar's attempts to bring independence failed in the 1810s, but El Libertador eventually returned. Independence desires lingered in places like Cartagena and a federal state, mimicking the United States, failed as localism prevailed.

New Granada and Cartagena did not stand alone in their challenge to balance independence desires and a federal-state system. The República Federal de Centroamérica, which emerged after independence from Spain and existed from 1821 until 1841, was a combination of the six Central American provinces of the Spanish Empire. Just like Bolívar's experimental Gran Colombia, this unified state lacked a national identity and eventually internal divisions and rivalries tore the experiment apart. Similarly, Mexico initially envisioned a federated system of government. However, the state soon faced separatist tendencies where identities collided, and political ambitions called for centralized government.[17]

The border province of Tejas, settled predominately by individuals from the United States, had an identity crisis within the Mexican state. By 1830, the Anglos vastly outnumbered the Hispanic Tejanos.

Translation: "the Province of Cartagena de Indies is from now on and by right a free, sovereign and independent state; that she is absolved of all submission, vassalage, obedience, and of any other bond of any kind and nature whatsoever, that previously linked her with the crown and governments of Spain, and that as such a free and absolutely independent State, it can do everything that free and independent nations can do."

[16] Simón Bolívar, *El Libertador: Writings of Simón Bolívar*, ed. David Bushnell (New York: Oxford University Press, 2010), 6.

[17] Marco C. Geserick, "Ephemeral Nations: Rise and Fall of Nations in Latin America During the Revolutionary Era, 1808–1842," Paper presented at Consortium on the Revolutionary Era, 1750–1850, Oxford, MS, February 20–22, 2014; Ralph L. Woodward, *Rafael Carrera and the Emergence of the Republic of Guatemala, 1821–1871* (Athens: University of Georgia Press, 2008), 115–117.

Complicating matters, in 1833, Antonio de Padua María Severino López de Santa Anna y Pérez de Lebrón rose to political power, having established himself as a successful military leader. He desired to address political instability with a centralization campaign. As a result, separatist rebellions broke out in various parts of Mexico, including the Yucatan and Tejas regions. Tejanos, both of Mexican and US origin, initially demanded the restoration of the original, federalist constitution of 1824 and political autonomy. When Mexico did not respond to the demands, Tejas declared its independence on March 2, 1836.[18] The declaration took inspiration from the United States, sans some of the more subtler word choices. Instead of "pursuit of happiness," the Tejas declaration called it for what it was, property. After a significant elaboration about the political reasons for the separation, including Mexico's violation of the rights of Tejanos. Tejas desired to escape the dungeons and mercenary armies of Mexico, which refused their petitions for remonstration. Despite, the substantial Mexican population in the province, the Anglo settlers distinguished themselves from their Mexican neighbors and claimed a separate identity, giving credence to their claim for independence. The declaration read, "A statement of a part of our grievances is therefore submitted to an impartial world, in justification of the hazardous but unavoidable step now taken, of severing our political connection with the Mexican people, and assuming an independent attitude among the nations of the earth."[19] As the Mexican government tried to reassert authority over the separatist province, young adventurers from New Orleans came to Texas' assistance. After the disasters at Goliad and the Alamo, the Texan armies defeated the Mexicans at San Jacinto on April 21, 1836. Despite Santa Anna trading his freedom for Texas' independence, the Mexican congress refused ratification. Texas became nominally independent and further fragmented another federal state with conflicting national identities.

Besides the Spanish speaking regions of Latin America, Portuguese Latin America faced a similar national instability that resulted in conflict and war. The Portuguese Empire in Brazil fragmented between widely diverse environmental and economic regions. The majority of the colony

---

[18] Daniel W. Howe, *What Hath God Wrought: The Transformation of America, 1815–1848* (New York: Oxford University Press, 2007), 661, 662, 665–669.

[19] Declaration of Independence of Texas, 1836, available at https://www.tsl.texas.gov/treasures/republic/declaration.html.

relied heavily on slave-produced cash crops; however, Rio Grande do Sul, on Brazil's southern border, relied on Gaucho-guarded cattle for income. Brazil did not take the region's economy into consideration when passing trade rules and regulations. On September 11, 1836, Rio Grande do Sul declared its independence from Brazil and started the Guerra dos Farrapos. Until 1845, the Republic Rio-Grandense held on, but eventually succumbed to the Brazilian army's reconquest.[20] Separatist independence desires based on a local identity faced serious difficulty as the Latin American examples illustrate.

Similar to Latin American anti-oppression arguments to bring about national independence and freedom from tyranny, the people in Greece suffered from within an oppressive empire where their overlords embraced with Islam a different religion. Furthermore, the elite could use the long history of Greece to craft a national identity. In 1797, Greek revolutionary Rigas Feraios/Rigas Velestinlis outlined the Greek demands. He claimed, "Ottoman despotism" having caused "the most unbearable tyranny." Indicting the sultan of the Ottoman Empire for being focused more on his personal pleasures than on the well-being of the empire, Feraios called on all people to throw "off the worthless yoke of despotism and embracing the cherished freedom of their glorious forebears." Finally, Feraios asserted that people had allowed themselves to be treated as slaves and needed to shed those chains of oppression. He concluded with thirty-five articles, which he called "The Rights of Man," many of which dealt with the specific situation in Greece. The French Revolution clearly influenced Greece.[21] Feraios showed the communality in language among Atlantic national revolutionary movements.

By 1820, the desire for independence had grown, especially among Greek exiles and elites. Alexandros Ypsilantis helped orchestrate an invasion from Russia that was to set in motion a rebellion in Greece. When Ypsilantis arrived in the Danubian Principalities, he outlined the demands of the Greek people. Like Feraios, Ypsilantis related the struggle

---

[20] Robert L. Scheina, *Latin America's Wars: The Age of the Caudillo, 1791–1899* (Washington, DC: Brassey's, 2003), 151–154.

[21] Rigas Velestinlis, "Revolutionary Proclamation 1797," *The Movement for Greek Independence, 1770–1821: A Collection of Documents*, ed. Richard Clogg (London, UK: Macmillan, 1976), 149–150; David Brewer, *The Greek War of Independence: The Struggle for Freedom from Ottoman Oppression and the Birth of the Modern Greek Nation* (Woodstock, NY: Overlook Press, 2001), 6–7, 14–16, 23–24.

for Greek independence to other revolutions, asking other subjects of the Ottoman Empire to join the rebellion. Assuming Europe would support Greek independence, the revolutionary called for the formation of "national phalanxes" and "patriotic legions" to shed the despotism of the Ottoman Empire. Knowing that the struggle would be long and difficult, he asked the people for financial support. Ypsilantis closed his proclamation in powerful nationalistic language. He asked, "Let us then once again, O brave and magnanimous Greeks, invite Liberty to the classical land of Greece! Let us do battle between Marathon and Thermopylae! Let us fight on the tombs of our fathers, who, so as to leave us free, fought and died there! ... To arms then, friends! The Motherland calls us!"[22] His appeal to a shared history of greatness was common among revolutionary movements as was his definition of nationalism.

Like their Latin American counterparts earlier in the decade, the Greek nationalists faced a difficult struggle. In the conservative age of the Congress of Vienna, conservative European political leaders desired to stamp out any revolutionary upheaval in its infancy. Therefore, Austrian troops subdued the upheaval in the Two Sicilies and French troops did likewise in Spain. Despite their initial reluctance to get involved in the domestic affairs of the Ottoman Empire, perspectives changed when Sultan Mahmud II enlisted the help of his vassal, Muhammad Ali Pasha al-Mas'ud ibn Agha of Egypt. Egyptian involvement changed the character of the conflict and opened the door for Great Britain, France, and Russia to intervene. Not until suffering defeat in the Russo-Ottoman War of 1828/1829 did the Ottoman Empire accept the independence of Greece, but the international community imposed upon them the Bavarian Otto Friedrich Ludwig von Wittelsbach the first Greek monarch.[23] Greek nationalism had succeeded, but remained dependent on outside involvement.

While Greece became the puppet of European diplomats, separatism successfully gripped another region of the continent. Having once

---

[22] Alexandros Ypsilanstis, "Fight for Faith and Motherland," February 24, 1821, *Movement for Greek Independence*, 201–203; Brewer, *The Greek War of Independence*, 32–35, 45–47, 49–61, 65–67, 70–71.

[23] Brewer, *The Greek War of Independence*, 135–144, 247–257, 349–351; Douglas Dakin, *The Greek Struggle for Independence, 1821–1833* (Berkeley: University of California Press, 1978), 132–138; Wolf Seidl, *Bayern in Griechenland: Die Geburt des griechischen Nationalstaats und die Regierung König Ottos* (Munich, Germany: Prestel Verlag, 1981).

stood as one of Europe's great maritime powers, the Netherlands had suffered decline in the eighteenth century. The industrialized southern provinces of the Netherlands perceived that the tax burden and lack of tariff protection placed an undue financial obligation on their region. Furthermore, the distinctive Dutch-speaking Protestant Flemish community and French-speaking Catholic Wallonia community raised issues of national and cultural separateness. Perceptions of national, religious, political, and economic suffering spread widely. On August 25, 1830, the opera in Brussels staged *The Deaf Girl of Porici*, a nationalist play about the 1648 uprising of Napoli against Spain. That evening, the people rose up against Dutch rule and its symbols.[24] The conflict quickly escalated as the southern provinces of the Netherlands determined to change their relationship with the Dutch monarchy. On October 4, 1830, the provisional government decreed that "Les provinces de la Belgique, violemment détachées de la Hollande, constitueront un *état independent*."[25] Despite the declaration of independence, it required international pressure for sovereignty to materialize. A conference in London in 1830 proposed the division of the Netherlands into the Netherlands and Belgium. The Dutch monarchy initially refused and mounted an unsuccessful ten-day war against Belgium. In July 1831, King Leopold I, a member of the House of Saxe-Coburg and Gotha, received the crown of Belgium to govern the constitutional monarchy. Within a decade over ten new states had appeared in the Atlantic world, building on the perception that their national interests and identity were no longer protected within the existing state framework.

Meanwhile in the northern borderland of the German states, in Schleswig-Holstein, German nationalism grew in the face of what many perceived as Danish oppression. The Danish king had ruled the duchies of Schleswig and Holstein in personal union and had long upheld the obligation of the 1460 Treaty of Ribe, which included the "Up Ewig Ungedeelt," or "Forever Undivided," clause maintaining the unity

[24] Clive H. Church, *Europe in 1830: Revolution and Political Change* (London: Allen and Unwin, 1983), 81, 84–85, 93; Robert Demoulin, *La Révolution de 1830* (Brussels, Belgium: Renaissance du Livre, 1950), 8–11, 14, 17, 127–131; J. S. Fishman, *Diplomacy and Revolution: The London Conference of 1830 and the Belgian Revolt* (Amsterdam, Netherlands: CHEV, 1988), 137–152.

[25] *Le Belge*, October 6, 1830. Translation: "The Provinces of Belgium, violently detached from Holland, will constitute an independent State."

of the two duchies. Uwe Jens Lornsen was an early voice calling for greater national autonomy. In his nationalist publications, Lornsen energized the youthful nationalist movement. In *Ueber das Verfassungswerk in Schleswigholstein*, Lornsen intentionally left out the hyphen that usually connected the names of the two duchies. He called for a united Schleswig-Holstein to stand up against the oppressive Danish king. The Danish monarch could not tolerate such a radical rabble rouser. After two years of incarceration, Lornsen departed for Brazil to improve his mental and physical health but did not find the desired results. He eventually returned to Europe in 1837.[26] Lornsen influenced a generation of German nationalists in the duchies.

Within a decade of Lornsen's writing, the radical "Neuholsteiner," a group of politicians who called for the complete separation of Holstein from Schleswig, emerged. Among the leading voices of the group was Theodor Olshausen, the editor of the *Correspondenz-Blatt*, which perpetuated Holstein-German nationalist propaganda. While Olshausen, as a German, highlighted German qualities, he frequently questioned Danish policy makers and the lack of a national identity in Schleswig, which comprised part Danish and part German population. Olshausen perceived of the Danish population of Schleswig as a backward people without culture.[27] Like so many nationalist movements that felt oppressed, the editors at the *Correspondenz-Blatt* called for autonomy in financial matters, including tax policies.[28] Even more, Olshausen demanded German as the official language of instruction and politics in Schleswig, acknowledging, however, that language supremacy could "turn home into a foreign environment." At the same time, he asserted that Denmark lagged behind intellectually, including in philosophy and theology.[29] The rise of German nationalism in Schleswig-Holstein increasingly alienated people away from their Danish rulers.

---

[26] Uwe Jens Lornsen, *Die Unions-Verfassung Dänemarks und Schleswigholsteins: Eine geschichtliche staatsrechtliche und politische Erörterung*, ed. Georg Beseler (Jena, Germany: Frommann, 1841); Silke von Bremen, "Von der inneren Gefangenschaft eines Freiheitskämpfers: Uwe Jens Lornsens seelische Not," *Nordfriesland* 169 (March 2010), 22–27.

[27] *Correspondenz-Blatt*, May 4, 1839, May 25, 1839.

[28] *Correspondenz-Blatt*, June 5, 1839.

[29] *Correspondenz-Blatt*, June 19, 1839, June 26, 1839.

In late January 1848, the death of King Christian VIII exasperated the conflict between the two nationalities. The new king Frederik VII promulgated a new constitution that integrated Schleswig into Denmark. On March 23, 1848, the duchies rose up.[30] In their explanatory declaration, the provisional government of Schleswig-Holstein noted that they acted legally in the name of their "unfree sovereign." Claiming legitimacy for their national cause and ruler, the proclamation condemned the Danish assault on sovereign German land, when the Danes tried to incorporate Schleswig into the Danish state.[31] Meanwhile, the Danish king's appeasing promise of freedom of press and electoral reform fell short when he referred to Schleswig as "our duchy."[32] The two nationalities had collided and for the next three years intermittent conflict destabilized the region. Eventually, the German nationalists surrendered when their German allies deserted them. In February 1851, the revolutionary government surrendered.[33] National identities that aimed at breaking states apart came as a double-edged sword and successes for separatist-minded independence movements were increasingly rare.

The United States stood out as a key example other people looked to as they formulated their separatist nationalism. Britain's-colonial subjects

[30] Rudolph M. Schleiden, *Erinnerungen eines Schleswig-Holsteiners* (Wiesbaden, Germany: Verlag von J. F. Bergmann, 1890), 277; Ulrich Lange, ed., *Geschichte Schleswig-Holsteins: Von den Anfängen bis zur Gegenwart* (Neumünster, Germany: Wachholz Verlag, 1996), 442.

[31] Provisional Government, *Proclamation*, March 24, 1848, *Aktenstücke zur neuesten Schleswig-Holsteinischen Geschichte*, ed. Rudolph M. Schleiden (Leipzig, Germany: Verlag von Wilhelm Engelmann, 1852), 2:1–2.

[32] Danish king to deputation from Holstein, March 24, 1848, Fasc. 6, Nachlass Schleiden, CAU.

[33] For studies of the Schleswig-Holstein uprising see Jens Ahlers, ed., *Aufbruch und Bürgerkrieg: Schleswig-Holstein, 1848–1851* (Kiel: Schleswig-Holsteinische Landesbibliothek, 2012); Claus Bjørn, ed., *1848: Det Mærkelige Ar* (Copenhagen, Denmark: Museum Tusculanums Forlag, 1998); Claus Bjørn, *1848: Borgerkrig og Revolution* (Copenhagen, Denmark: Gyldendal, 1998); William Carr, *Schleswig-Holstein, 1815–1848: A Study in National Conflict* (Manchester, UK: Manchester University Press, 1963); Steen Bo Frandsen, "Denmark, 1848: The Victory of Democracy and the Shattering of the Conglomerate State," in *Europe in 1848: Revolution and Reform*, eds. Dieter Dowe et al. (New York: Berghahn Books, 2001), 289–311; Alexander Scharff, *Schleswig-Holstein und die Auflösung des dänischen Gesamtstaates, 1830–1864/1867* (Schleswig, Germany: Gesellschaft für schleswig-holsteinische Geschichte, 1973, 1980); Nick Svendsen, *The First Schleswig-Holstein War 1848–1850* (Solihull, UK: Helion, 2007).

gradually felt the government in London overstepped its constitutional and legal bounds after the Seven Years' War (1754–1763). While the Declaration of Independence built on established English political theory and closely mimicked arguments made in 1688 (discussed in the next chapter), the document provided dozens of movements with inspiration as they wrestled with oppression and the need to establish an identity of their own.[34] As a primarily political revolution, the colonies did not come together as a unified state with a coherent national identity. Competing state and national identities remained at odds well past the mid-nineteenth century. Regionalism continued as a powerful force in the United States. New England contemplated leaving the United States over the disastrous policies leading into the War of 1812. Even more, the southern states increasingly felt like an oppressed minority within the country.

In the last years of the eighteenth century, as the United States had to navigate the complex environment of the French Revolutionary wars, the government put in place a series of laws undermining the civil liberties of the people, including freedom of speech. As a result, southerners worried about their place within the country, or, as John Taylor phrased it, "the southern states must lose their capital and commerce and … America is destined to war … and oppressive taxation." In opposition to the so-called Alien and Sedition Acts, Thomas Jefferson and James Madison prepared opposition memorials for Kentucky and Virginia respectively. Jefferson worried that these two acts could function as the precursor to assaults on freedom of religion or turn the presidency into a lifetime position. He claimed that states had the right to review federal laws for their constitutionality and if found unconstitutional to declare such laws "void and of no force." Despite Kentucky dismissing Jefferson's word choice of nullification, he went a step further in August 1799 when he suggested to Madison that the southern states should "sever ourselves from that union we so much value rather than give up the rights of self-government which we have reserved, and in which alone we see liberty."[35] The ideas and arguments of a southern separatist national identity were born.

[34] David Armitage, *The Declaration of Independence: A Global History* (Cambridge, MA: Harvard University, 2007).

[35] Gordon S. Wood, *Empire of Liberty a History of the Early Republic, 1789–1815* (New York: Oxford University Press, 2009), 267–271.

By 1828, tensions escalated as southern nationalists argued that their section needed to defend against growing northern oppression. That year, Congress passed a new tariff, southern anger triggered national opposition. Some viewed the tariff as a tax and price increase of 40%. The theory became known as "Forty Bales," because "the manufacturer actually invades your barns, and plunders you of 40 out of every 100 bales that you produce," explained a contemporary. In reality, the tariff came as a scapegoat for structural problems such as population increases, soil depletion, and overproduction dropping prices. When the Tariff of 1832 did not alter the situation, South Carolina's governor James Hamilton, Jr., called for a nullification convention to end the danger of a northern majority imposing its will. The convention declared both the Tariffs of 1828 and 1832 null and void. After February 1, 1833, the government could no longer collect the tariff in South Carolina. President Andrew Jackson fumed and prepared for conflict, but also asked Congress for additional tariff reductions. Realizing that Jackson was serious and South Carolina isolated, compromise seemed the only possible solution. South Carolina's Senator, and former Vice-President, John C. Calhoun cautioned, "secession, 'the most fatal of all steps,' should occur only 'in the last extremity.'" With Henry Clay, Calhoun worked out a compromise that prevented the secession of South Carolina and a military standoff. However, Robert B. Rhett expressed the feeling among separatists in the South, "Until this Government is made a limited Government ... there is no liberty—no security for the South."[36] Separatism in the United States was still in its infancy. However, only after mid-century did southerners try again to challenge the state authority and unsuccessfully bring about the independence of the nation.

By the 1870s, nationalism had succeeded in the creation of rudimentary nation-states with identities supported by a significant portion of the population. Where Voltaire, Fichte, Dahlmann, and Mazzini argued about the theoretical abstract of what a nation might entail, by the last quarter of the century, intellectuals had a vast body of evidence and examples to draw from when they decided to define a nation. In a speech at the Sorbonne in Paris, Ernest Renan asked in March 1882, "Qu'est-ce qu'une nation?" He started out saying that nations were

---

[36]William W. Freehling, *The Road to Disunion: Secessionists at Bay* (New York: Oxford University Press, 1990), 1:255–256, 276–278, 282, 285.

something new, that had not existed in ancient times. He questioned the national unities of Great Britain and Italy. "The union of England, Ireland, and Scotland was likewise a dynastic fact. Italy only tarried so long before becoming a nation," Renan argued, "because, among its numerous reigning houses, none, prior to the present century, constituted itself as the centre of [its] unity, Strangely enough, it was through the obscure island of Sardinia, a land that was scarcely Italian, that [the house of Savoy] assumed a royal title."[37] He agreed that nations and nation-states were largely a construct of the nineteenth century.

For Renan, who became also an early thinker of race theory and proto-fascism, race played a significant role in the formation of nations. He aligned closely with Fichte's ethnic base for nationalism. He propagated the idea of an ethnic nationalism, but worried about the purity of races. In contrast to contemporaries and modern scholars, Renan did not believe in language or religion as providing an adequate basis for nation-state formations. Powerfully, Renan established, "A nation is a soul, a spiritual principle. Two things, which in truth are but one, constitute this soul or spiritual principle. One lies in the past, one in the present. One is the possession in common of a rich legacy of memories; the other is present-day consent, the desire to live together, the will to perpetuate the value of the heritage that one has received in an undivided form." The process of nation-state formation was a difficult one as states searched for and constructed identities. By the time of his speech, these nation-states were a permanent fixture in the Atlantic world.

The French Revolution had awoken national desires among people as they resisted the occupation of their state by French forces or worse the disappearance of their state. European intellectual leaders used the opportunity of French oppression to craft the basis for national identities, starting struggles that would last into the middle of the nineteenth century as new nation-states formed. Meanwhile, Spanish-Americans faced a difficult struggle as conflicting local and regional identities clashed. There was the desire for regionalism; the independence of a city and its surrounding, as well as for the creation of larger states and even federated states. These conflicts were not easily settled and some independence desires, like the one in Cartagena, were subsumed in the independence wars

[37] Ernest Renan, "Qu'est-ce qu'une nation," March 11, 1882, translation in *Modern Political Doctrines*, ed. Alfred E. Zimmern (London, UK: Oxford University Press, 1939), 186–205.

and disappeared as new states made their appearance in Latin America. Many people took inspiration from the Declaration of Independence of the Thirteen Colonies as they struggled with their own perceptions of oppression and crafted their own statements. As a result, the language of declarations of independence across the Atlantic was remarkably similar. People were well aware of new ideas of nationalism and frequently, the political declarations of freedom went hand in hand with national ones. People not only established that they were a politically oppressed people, but also that they were a distinct group in contrast to their oppressors. Without the events in North America and France and the news of these events passed along the line of communications around the Atlantic world, there likely would not have been independence movements in Spanish America, Greece, or Belgium. The Atlantic world was a conduit for nation-state struggles to ferment and grow.

Bibliography

Ahlers, Jens, ed. *Aufbruch und Bürgerkrieg: Schleswig-Holstein, 1848–1851*. Kiel: Schleswig-Holsteinische Landesbibliothek, 2012.
Anderson, Benedict. *Imagined Communities: Reflections on the Origin and Spread of Nationalism*. London, UK: Verso, 1983.
Armitage, David. *The Declaration of Independence: A Global History*. Cambridge, MA: Harvard University Press, 2007.
Baycroft, Timothy, and Mark Hewitson, eds. *What Is a Nation? Europe, 1789–1914*. Oxford, UK: Oxford University Press, 2006.
Bjørn, Claus, ed. *1848: Det Mærkelige År*. Copenhagen, Denmark: Museum Tusculanums Forlag, 1998.
Bjørn, Claus. *1848: Borgerkrig og Revolution*. Copenhagen, Denmark: Gyldendal, 1998.
Bolívar, Simón. *El Libertador: Writings of Simón Bolívar*. Edited by David Bushnell. New York: Oxford University Press, 2010.
Brewer, David. *The Greek War of Independence: The Struggle for Freedom from Ottoman Oppression and the Birth of the Modern Greek Nation*. Woodstock, NY: Overlook Press, 2001.
Carr, William. *Schleswig-Holstein, 1815–1848: A Study in National Conflict*. Manchester, UK: Manchester University Press, 1963.
Church, Clive H. *Europe in 1830: Revolution and Political Change*. London: Allen and Unwin, 1983.
Clogg, Richard, ed. *The Movement for Greek Independence, 1770–1821: A Collection of Documents*. London, UK: Macmillan, 1976.

Dahlmann, Friedrich Christoph. *Die Waterloo-Rede von Friedrich Christoph Dahlmann am 7. Juli 1815*. Edited by Utz Schliesky. Kiel, Germany: Lorenz-von-Stein-Institut für Verwaltungswissenschaften an der Christian-Albrechts-Universität zu Kiel, 2015.

Dakin, Douglas. *The Greek Struggle for Independence, 1821–1833*. Berkeley: University of California Press, 1978.

Dann, Otto, ed. *Nationalism in the Age of the French Revolution*. London, UK: Bloomsbury Publishing, 1988.

Demoulin, Robert. *La Révolution de 1830*. Brussels, Belgium: Renaissance du Livre, 1950.

Fichte, Johann Gottlieb. *Addresses to the German Nation*. Translated by R. F. Jones and G. H. Turnbull. Chicago, IL: University of Chicago Press, 1922.

Fishman, J. S. *Diplomacy and Revolution: The London Conference of 1830 and the Belgian Revolt*. Amsterdam, Netherlands: CHEV, 1988.

Freehling, William W. *The Road to Disunion*. 2 vols. New York: Oxford University Press, 1990, 2007.

Hamnett, Brian R. *The End of Iberian Rule on the American Continent, 1770–1830*. Cambridge, UK: Cambridge University Press, 2017.

Howe, Daniel W. *What Hath God Wrought: The Transformation of America, 1815–1848*. New York: Oxford University Press, 2007.

Kramer, Lloyd S. *Nationalism in Europe and America: Politics, Cultures, and Identities Since 1775*. Chapel Hill: University of North Carolina Press, 2011.

Lange, Ulrich, ed. *Geschichte Schleswig-Holsteins: Von den Anfängen bis zur Gegenwart*. Neumünster, Germany: Wachholz Verlag, 1996.

Lornsen, Uwe Jens. *Die Unions-Verfassung Dänemarks und Schleswigholsteins: Eine geschichtliche staatsrechtliche und politische Erörterung*. Edited by Georg Beseler. Jena: Frommann, 1841.

Mann, Michael. *The Sources of Social Power: The Rise of Classes and Nation-States, 1760–1914*. Cambridge, UK: Cambridge University Press, 1986.

Mazzini, Giuseppe. *Selected Writings*. Edited by Nagendranath Gangulee. London, UK: L. Drummond, 1945.

Mazzini, Giuseppe. *A Cosmopolitanism of Nations: Giuseppe Mazzini's Writings on Democracy, Nation Building, and International Relations*. Translated and edited by Stefano Recchia and Nadia Urbinati. Princeton, NJ: Princeton University Press, 2009.

McFarlane, Anthony. *War and Independence in Spanish America*. New York: Routledge, 2013.

Scharff, Alexander. *Schleswig-Holstein und die Auflösung des dänischen Gesamtstaates, 1830–1864/1867*. Schleswig, Germany: Gesellschaft für schleswig-holsteinische Geschichte, 1973, 1980.

Scheina, Robert L. *Latin America's Wars: The Age of the Caudillo, 1791–1899.* Washington, DC: Brassey's, 2003.
Schleiden, Rudolph M., ed. *Aktenstücke zur neuesten Schleswig-Holsteinischen Geschichte.* Leipzig, Germany: Verlag von Wilhelm Engelmann, 1852.
Schleiden, Rudolph M. *Erinnerungen eines Schleswig-Holsteiners.* Wiesbaden, Germany: Verlag von J. F. Bergmann, 1890.
Seidl, Wolf. *Bayern in Griechenland: Die Geburt des griechischen Nationalstaats und die Regierung König Ottos.* Munich, Germany: Prestel Verlag, 1981.
Svendsen, Nick. *The First Schleswig-Holstein War 1848–1850.* Solihull, UK: Helion, 2007.
von Bremen, Silke. "Von der inneren Gefangenschaft eines Freiheitskämpfers: Uwe Jens Lornsens seelische Not." *Nordfriesland* 169 (March 2010): 22–27.
Wood, Gordon S. *Empire of Liberty a History of the Early Republic, 1789–1815.* New York: Oxford University Press, 2009.
Woodward, Ralph L. *Rafael Carrera and the Emergence of the Republic of Guatemala, 1821–1871.* Athens: University of Georgia Press, 2008.
Zimmern, Alfred E., ed. *Modern Political Doctrines.* London, UK: Oxford University Press, 1939.

CHAPTER 5

Constitutional Revolutions

Le régime légal est … interrompu, celui de la force est commencé. Dans la situation où nous sommes placés, l'obéissance cesse d'être un devoir. … Aujourd'hui donc, des ministres criminels ont violé la légalité. Nous sommes dispensés d'obéir. Nous essaierons de publier nos feuilles sans demander l'autorisation qui nous est imposée.[1]

The Age of Revolutions (1776–1825) not only witnessed the birth of independence desires among nationalities but also the demand for political reform, casting a long political shadow into the middle of the nineteenth century. States grappled with political inequalities and demands for constitutional governments. As early as 1688, when England suffered through the Glorious Revolution, revolutionary challenges appeared Atlantic in nature. The events in 1688 and more importantly, the Revolution of the Thirteen Colonies provided a new language against oppressive rulers and highlighted the demands for constitutional government. Those demands reappeared in the French Revolution, the revolutions in Spanish America, and continued into the 1830s and 1840s.

---

[1] Maurice La Châtre, *Histoire des Papes: Rois, Reines, Empereurs a travers les Siècles* (Paris: Docks de la Librairie, 1870), 3:135.
Translation: "The legal regime is … interrupted, that of the force is begun. In the situation where we are placed, obedience ceases to be a duty. … Today, then, criminal ministers have violated the law. We are excused from obeying. We will try to publish our sheets without asking for the authorization that is imposed on us."

As kings abandoned constitutional and legal requirements toward their subjects, people did not feel bound to obey royal commands, like the complaint by the French press to King Louis-Philippe above indicates. As monarchs ignored the rights of their subjects, revolutions tried to reign in kings with constitutional governments and governing charters.

The traditional end of the Age of Revolutions with the victory of Spanish American independence is problematic as the previous chapter already indicated, the work to form nation-states did not conclude or slow down in 1825. Similarly, constitutional government had become a common rallying cry for political reformers, who sought legal rights and obligations enshrined in codes obeyed by everybody regardless of birth or status. However, this did not mean the abandoning of monarchy or the embrace of democracy, a system of elections opens to a wide body of people. Well into the middle of the nineteenth century, revolutionaries continued to employ the language used by revolutionaries in the Thirteen Colonies and the French Revolution. The Age of Political Revolution lasted until at least 1848, when for one last time reformers tried to bring about political change in the process of revolution based on the enlightened principles of government first employed in 1688. This was an Atlantic Age of Political Revolution as politicians around the Atlantic basin sought a similar set of constitutional limitations of their rulers and learned from each other's successes and failures.

One of the first instances of an Atlantic revolutionary exchange of ideas came as early as 1688. Facing the usurpation of power by James II, Willem of Oranje invaded England to claim the throne in the name of his wife. After James II's escape from Britain, Parliament declared the throne vacant and laid out the arguments against James to justify the change in dynastic leadership. Parliamentary leaders pointed to "evil councilors, judges, and ministers" for the actions of the king, to give legitimacy to their action and leave monarchical institutions blameless. At the same time, Parliament asserted its authority by noting that "the pretended power of suspending of laws by regal authority without consent of Parliament is illegal." Even more, they asserted the right of people to petition government, opposition to standing armies, taxing people without Parliamentary consent, free elections for Members of Parliament, jury trials, and the regular meeting of Parliament. Parliament effectively provided a blueprint for future revolutions to seek redress against oppressive rulers and a bill of rights that governed rulers and ruled.[2] The Declaration of Rights of 1688 became the basis for future revolutions, especially in the English Colonies and France, which in turn became symbols in the future.

The Glorious Revolution was not restricted to the European mother country. Since King James had "invaded the privileges and seized on the charters of most of those towns that have a right to be represented by their burgesses in Parliament" and become an outspoken proponent of Catholicism, the North American colonies faced a decision which king to support.[3] The often-times rebellious colonists, just like their English counterparts, quickly bought into the anti-Catholic Popish plots to overthrow the English system of government. Furthermore, settlers in the colonies believed "in the sovereignty of the king," "that local people, and the institutions of local governance, should have broad latitude," and the rulers "obligation to keep people safe, to defeat whatever enemies threatened from within or without."[4] The memory of 1688 lasted within Greater Britain and language used in 1688 eventually helped bring about the revolution and independence of the Thirteen Colonies.

When after the Seven Years' War Great Britain asserted itself in the affairs of the colonies by collecting taxes and finally enforcing trade laws, the colonists looked back at the legacies of 1688 for the proper language to use against political oppression. Even as the colonists adjusted the grievances to their particular situation, similar items appeared, such as the imposition of taxes, jury trials, the maintenance of a military in peacetime, the right to petition, and the removal of charters and rights undermining the freedom of the people. However, the Declaration of Independence took on a more universal character and laid a new claim to the right of people to rebel against oppressive rulers. After all, the drafter, Thomas Jefferson, started with the assertion that "whenever any

---

[2] The Declaration of Rights, February 19, 1689, reprinted in *England's Glorious Revolution, 1688–1689: A Brief History with Documents*, ed. Steven C. A. Pincus (Boston, New York: Bedford/St. Martin's, 2005), 69–71.

[3] The Declaration, October 1688, reprinted in *England's Glorious Revolution, 1688–1689: A Brief History with Documents*, ed. Steven C. A. Pincus (Boston, New York: Bedford/St. Martin's, 2005), 40.

[4] Owen Stanwood, *The Empire Reformed: English America in the Age of the Glorious Revolution* (Philadelphia: University of Pennsylvania Press, 2011), 4.

Form of Government becomes destructive of these ends, it is the Right of the People to alter or to abolish it, and to institute new Government." The new United States had dramatically changed the language of revolution against oppressive rulers by placing an obligation on people to rebel.[5] Nevertheless, there remained questions about the direction and meaning of the revolution.

Though the Declaration of Independence leaned on Parliament's Declaration of Rights, the colonists remained uncertain where the true problem lay. Some pointed to Parliament having usurped power from the king and preventing him from ruling for and in protection of his subjects. Others questioned if Parliament was an important institution to prevent the overreach of the monarchy. As historian Eric Nelson has shown, "a great many colonists … had rebelled against the British Parliament in the name of the Crown, desperate to transform and revivify 'that Government under which we had lived so long and happily formerly.'" In the end, the United States adopted a monarchical constitution without the monarch. In the course of the rebellion, the drafting of the new Constitution, and politics of the Early Republic, political leaders in the United States recycled the arguments of their English predecessors.[6] As a result, the revolution in the Thirteen Colonies was a limited political revolution that only had a limited impact on the Atlantic world.

The United States' political evolution between the Revolution and the assumption of office by George Washington under the new constitution put many political theories into practice and allowed enlightened thinkers to enhance their ideas about good government with practical experiences. Theories had long existed about the inviolability of property and the importance of civil society to avoid the chaos of a state of nature, by way of a social contract. Even more philosophers debated the best approach for responsible government. In light of the frequent usurpation of power by monarchs, Charles-Louis de Secondat, Baron de La Brède et de Montesquieu suggested that a separation of power was needed for governments to avoid despotism. He believed that the

---

[5] "The Declaration of Independence," July 4, 1776, https://www.archives.gov/founding-docs/declaration-transcript.

[6] Lance Banning, *The Jeffersonian Persuasion: Evolution of a Party Ideology* (Ithaca, NY: Cornell University Press, 1978); Eric Nelson, *The Royalist Revolution: Monarchy and the American Founding* (Cambridge, MA: Harvard University Press, 2014), 230.

administrative powers of executive, legislative, and judicial branches of government should be separate but dependent upon each other. Thus, the three branches would check each other, preventing one from becoming too powerful, balancing each other out. Using virtue or honor respectively, monarchy or republic could provide stable and freedom-embracing governments. In contrast, Jean-Jacques Rousseau firmly believed in the smaller scale of republican government, assuming France too large for an effective and stable republican government. In an ideal world, Rousseau preferred direct democracy, where all the people could vote on decisions. These and other political philosophies clashed in the French Revolution.

The French Revolution started moderate enough with demands to restrict the king's powers and challenge the outdated estate system of representation. In January 1789, Emmanuel Joseph Sieyès questioned the social organization of France when he asked why the Third Estates should bear all the burden of the overstretched French tax system without reaping any of the benefits. He wondered how the state could continue to tolerate the parasitic nature of the First and Second Estate and not grant the Third Estate a fair representation in government.[7] As the Estates General reconstituted as a Constitutional Assembly, the new leaders made sure to secure basic rights for the French people. The Declaration of the Rights of Man and Citizens of 1789 provided that all men were equal. Inspired by enlightened thought, the declaration said, "The source of all sovereignty resides essentially in the nation; no body, no individual can exercise authority that does not proceed from it in plain terms."[8] However, the moderate personality of the French Revolution quickly disintegrated with the attempted escape of the king, murder of the king by radical elements, foreign attacks on the revolution, domestic civil war, and the massive slave rebellion in Saint-Domingue. Nevertheless, the French Revolution influenced events well beyond Europe.

While the French Revolution sent shock waves across Europe and reverberated in the French Colonial Empire, Spain tried to guard against the incendiary information of the revolution. The authorities in Caracas

---

[7] Emmanuel Joseph Sieyès, "What Is the Third Estate?" in *The French Revolution: A Document Collection*, eds. Laura Mason and Tracey Rizzo (Boston: Houghton Mifflin, 1999), 51–54.

[8] "Declaration of the Rights of Man and Citizens," in *The French Revolution*, 102–103.

and other colonies arrested French residents and anyone who showed sympathy to the French Revolutionary cause. In the colonies, a growing concern came about the impact and possible repetition of the slave rebellion in Saint-Domingue. With its diverse caste system, many people in the Spanish colonies sympathized with the slave and free black population in the French Caribbean. Even more, refugees from the French colony arrived in various colonies around the Caribbean basin, causing anxieties about a destabilization. There grew a concern that just like in the United States, the white elite of the colonies would create a republican system of government designed to benefit them and leave people of color in a state of slavery or oppression. Spanish Americans had already tasted the danger of non-white resistance during the Tupac Amaru rebellion, which relied on an Inca identity to challenge the Bourdon reforms to the empire.[9] The process to gain political independence from Spain lasted an additional ten years after the French Revolutionary and Napoleonic Wars concluded.

Conversely, the French Revolution impacted the rest of the Atlantic world. In 1798, with French assistance, Ireland attempted unsuccessfully to gain its independence. Forced to accept the dissolution of the Irish Parliament in the Act of Union of 1800/1801, a growing Irish national movement demanded political independence, autonomy, or at least a fair treatment in Parliament. In 1828, the Catholic Daniel O'Connell challenged the political status quo when he ran in the County Clare by-election. Revealingly, his Catholicism prevented O'Connell from taking the Oath of Supremacy required by the Test and Corporation Acts. His election victory forced the government of Arthur Wellesley, the Duke of Wellington and Home Secretary Sir Robert Peel to repeal the Test and Corporation Acts. Parliament divided on the subject. Some sympathized with the views expressed by John Smith of Midhurst who reminded his fellow members that "The Dissenters of the present day were as intelligent, as loyal, as prosperous, and as industrious, a class of people as any within his majesty's dominions. It was now three or four and twenty years ago since the people had enrolled themselves as volunteers for

---

[9] Charles F. Walker, *The Tupac Amaru Rebellion* (Cambridge, MA: Harvard University Press, 2014); Michael Zeuske, "The French Revolution in Spanish America," in *The Routledge Companion to the French Revolution in World History*, eds. Alan I. Forrest and Matthias Middell (Abingdon, UK: Routledge, 2015), 78–84.

the defence of their common country."[10] However, the Irish Tory and Protestant Robert Jocelyn, Earl of Roden hoped "that some measure would immediately be adopted for suppressing that abominable nuisance, the Catholic Association. …, there could be only one as to the evil effects produced by the inflammatory speeches of the demagogues now meeting in Dublin. The suppression of the Association was not only of importance to the safety of the loyal Protestants of Ireland, but to the peace and happiness of the Catholic peasantry."[11] Despite the warnings of the Earl of Roden, the more pragmatic political voices won, wishing to prevent something like the French Revolution. Parliament abolished the Test and Corporation Acts, which allowed O'Connell to take his seat. A limited political revolution had started aimed at revising the English constitutional system.

The limited reform measure to remove religion as a barrier to office holding and the growing turmoil on the continent as a result of the Revolutions of 1830 left Britain's elite concerned about the country's stability. Fearful that the disenfranchised workers and middling sort could rise up against the oligarchic political system, the British government decided to take action.[12] However, democratic reform was not on the agenda. On March 1, 1831, Lord John Russell rose in the House of Commons and proposed a reform bill. The bill shifted voting power from rural area to the new urban centers as well as reduce property qualification.[13] The debate whether to include a large number of subjects in the body politic started without the violence associated with political revolution on the continent.

In Great Britain, democracy tended to invoke the image of mob rule as practiced in the opinions of many in the United States and the

---

[10] John Smith, February 26, 1838, Repeal of the Test and Corporation Acts, Hansard, vol. 18, 696.
[11] Robert Jocelyn, Earl of Roden, March 7, 1828, Catholic Association, Hansard, vol. 18, 1054–1055.
[12] Edward Pearce, *Reform!: The Fight for the 1832 Reform Act* (London: Jonathan Cape, 2003), 185–186, 208–209.
[13] Ibid., Chapters 6, 9–11. For additional works on the Great Reform Act of 1832 see Gilbert A. Cahill, *The Great Reform Bill of 1832: Liberal or Conservative?* (Lexington, MA: Heath, 1969); Eric J. Evans, *The Great Reform Act of 1832* (London: Methuen, 1983); Elie Halévy, *The Triumph of Reform* (London: Ernest Benn, 1961); John A. Phillips and Charles Wetherell, "The Great Reform Bill of 1832 and the Rise of Partisanship," *Journal of Modern History* 63 (December 1991), 621–646.

excesses of the French Revolution. Nevertheless, when Parliament debated the First Reform Act, the issue of democracy arose. Members of Parliament wondered whether to enlarge the electoral franchise and the implications of such a decision. Everybody employed powerful arguments for and against franchise reform. On February 28, 1832, Sir George Murray, representing Perthshire in Scotland, rose in the House of Commons and summarized: "democracy was the source of liberty, but that was no reason why that source should be swelled till it burst; for if it were swollen, it would overflow and destroy its barriers. The great danger of the Bill was, the power it would give to democracy." He continued that democracy caused the end of ancient republics like Athens and Rome and should not bring down Great Britain.[14] Democracy, perceived still as dangerous, prone to mob rule, few states were ready to move beyond the limits of constitutional monarchy.

Even as Great Britain temporarily satisfied the demand for political reform, the Irish people continued to demand great autonomy. Divided between the moderate Catholic forces under Daniel O'Connell and the radical independence-minded non-sectarian Young Ireland movement, there was major disagreement about the use of violence and how history condoned its uses. In the speech that drove a permanent wedge between the two factions, Thomas Francis Meagher on July 28, 1846, made a powerful comparison that forced the Irish to retain military power as a means of last resort. He asserted, "Abhor the sword–stigmatise the sword? No, my lord, for, at its blow, a giant nation started from the waters of the Atlantic, and by its redeeming magic, and in the quivering of its crimson light, the crippled colony sprang into the attitude of a proud republic–prosperous, limitless, and invincible! Abhor the sword–stigmatise the sword? No, my lord, for it swept the Dutch marauders out of the fine old towns of Belgium–scourged them back to their own phlegmatic swamps–and knocked their flag and sceptre, their laws and bayonets, into the sluggish waters of the Scheldt."[15] Meagher used the American and Belgium revolutions to justify the importance of retaining violence as a last resort but also the need for an Irish revolution.

With the economic and human disaster of the potato famine, the time seemed right for a revolution. When the British government botched the

[14] George Murray, February 28, 1832, Parliamentary Reform Bill, Hansard, vol. 10, 935.

[15] Michael Cavanagh, *Memoirs of General Thomas Francis Meagher* (Worcester, MA: Messenger Press, 1892), 65–66.

relief efforts to alleviate the hardship of the famine, resistance to British rule increased. Furthermore, the suspension of the Writ of Habeas Corpus on July 22, 1848, allowed the authorities to crack down on the radicals of the Young Ireland movement. Young Ireland's leadership determined to embrace revolution to bring about Irish independence. In the following seven days, the movement called on the people in the counties of Wexford, Kilkenny, and Tipperary to rise up against their British lords. By July 28, the uprising had started. The rebels were ill-prepared for the challenges ahead. There was only one encounter between rebels and authorities.[16] The uprising had failed, and political freedom continued to elude the Irish.

While the British state faced the Irish national revolution in 1848, the political revolution started by O'Connell twenty years earlier was not yet complete. Within a few years of the Reform Act, a new organization had started to petition parliament for additional reforms. The so-called Chartists demanded that all residents of Great Britain over the age of twenty-one be allowed the right to vote. To create not only fair elections but allow every vote to count equally, the Chartists demanded that the House of Commons reapportion to create districts equal in population.[17] The petitions in 1839 and after failed as Parliament refused to consider any reforms that looked like democracy. In 1848, inspired by the events in Paris and elsewhere, the Chartist one last time unsuccessfully attempted to bring about political change. With the failure of the newest Chartist petition, the political revolutionary era in Great Britain closed and the focus turned to reform within the parliamentary system, eventually accomplished by conservative political forces.

However, the center for political revolution remained France. Having set a global precedent with the French Revolution of 1789 and the ouster of King Louis XVI, France had laid an irrevocable foundation for constitutional government. No king could govern without a

---

[16] Laurence Fenton, *The Young Ireland Rebellion and Limerick* (Blackrock, Ireland: Mercier Press, 2010); Denis Gwynn, *Young Ireland and 1848* (Cork, Ireland: Cork University Press, 1949); Christine Kinealy, *Repeal and Revolution: 1848 in Ireland* (Manchester, UK: Manchester University Press, 2009); Robert Sloan, *William Smith O'Brien and the Young Ireland Rebellion of 1848* (Dublin, Ireland: Four Courts Press, 2000).

[17] People's Charter of 1839 available at https://www.marxists.org/history/england/chartists/peoples-charter.htm.

constitution or parliamentary system henceforth and France illustrated that fact with two more revolutions before mid-century. Upon the conclusion of the Napoleonic Wars, the Bourbon dynasty returned to power, but neither Louis XVIII nor Charles X had absolute powers. By the late 1820s, France suffered under an economic crisis and people realized that Charles X did not intend to accept the constitution or parliamentary framework. Furthermore, he seemed resolved to restore the CatholicChurch to its former position of prominence and compensate royalist who had lost property during the first French Revolution.[18] However, as dissatisfaction with the monarchy elevated so to did fears of democracy and the unruly masses,[19] therefore, a second French republic was out of the question.

On July 25, 1830, the king issued the July Ordinance or Ordinance of Saint-Cloud, which suspended "the liberty of the periodical press" and established harsh penalties if a paper tried to avoid the law. Furthermore, the ordinance dissolved the Chamber of Deputies and called for new elections. Finally, to attain a Chamber of Deputies favorable to the king, the electoral franchise was limited by raising the property qualification. Protest immediately followed in what became the *Trois Glorieuses*. The Parisian population followed a well-established precedent when they claimed that "The Government has violated legality, we are absolved from obedience." A Paris journalist claimed, "The government has to-day lost the character which commands obedience. We are resisting it in that which concerns us; it is for France to decide how far its own resistance must extend." On July 30, 1830, Marie Joseph Louis

[18] J. Lucas-Dubreton, *The Restoration and the July Monarchy* (New York: G. P. Putman's Sons, 1929), 2–3, 16–17, 115–116, 145–155.

[19] For additional works on the French revolution of 1830 see Henry Contamine, "La Révolution de 1830 a Métz," *Revenue d'Histoire Moderne* 6 (July 1931), 115–123; R. Durand, "La Révolution de 1830 en Côte-d'Or," *Revenue d'Histoire Moderne* 6 (July 1931), 161–175; Shirley Gruner, "The Revolution of July 1830 and the Expression 'Bourgeoisie'," *Historical Journal* 11 (1968), 462–471; John M. Merriman, *1830 in France* (New York: New Viewpoints, 1975); Pamela M. Pilbeam, *The 1830 Revolution in France* (Basingstoke: Macmillan, 1991); Pamela M. Pilbeam, "The 'Three Glorious Days': The Revolution of 1830 in Provincial France," *Historical Journal* 26 (December 1983), 831–844; David H. Pinkney, "The Crowd in the French Revolution of 1830," *American Historical Review* 70 (October 1964), 1–17; Roger Price, "Legitimist Opposition to the Revolution of 1830 in the French Provinces," *Historical Journal* 17 (December 1974), 755–778; William Sewell, *Work and Revolution in France: The Language of Labor from the Old Regime to 1848* (Cambridge, UK: Cambridge University Press, 1980).

Adolphe Thiers announced: "Charles X can no longer return to Paris: he has caused the blood of the people to flow. The Republic would expose us to frightful divisions: it would embroil us with Europe. The Duke of Orleans is a prince devoted to the cause of the Revolution. ... It is from the French people that he will hold the crown." The leadership of France passed into the hands of the so-called citizen King Louis-Philippe of the Orleans dynasty.[20] France embraced a limited political revolution in 1830, but its accomplishments did not last.

On July 31, the Chamber of Deputies announced to the French people, "France is free. The absolute power was raising its flag; the heroic population of Paris overthrew it." Liberty was preserved by the quick action of the people. Like Thiers, the deputies informed the French that the "Duke of Orleans is devoted to the national and constitutional cause; he has always defended its interests and professed its principles." Similar to 1688, the American Revolution, or the Rights of Men and Citizens, the new government promised the French people that their rights would be protected, included the National Guard, juries for press offenses, and the replacement of deputies call on for public office.[21] With the new king, constitutional and legal rights returned to France. However, Louis-Philippe never felt secure in his position and desired to enhance his legitimacy. By the 1840s, he faced a similar crisis to the one that toppled Charles X.

In February 1848, Louis-Philippe confronted domestic dissent. His first minister François Pierre Guillaume Guizot's policies against constitutionalism and economic hardship gave liberals reasons for opposition. In early February, Guizot prohibited two banquets, which served the political opposition as a platform to express dissent. After prohibiting a second banquet, students, workers, and political reformers flooded the streets of Paris. As barricades went up, Guizot decided to resign on February 23, 1848. Louis-Philippe followed suit and left France for Great Britain. France declared a republic. "A retrograde

---

[20] July Ordinance, July 25, 1830, Protest of the Paris Journalists, July 26, 1830, Thiers' Orleanist Manifesto, July 30, 1830, *The Constitutions and Other Select Documents Illustrative of the History of France, 1789–1901*, ed. Frank M. Anderson (Minneapolis, MN: H. W. Wilson, 1967), 496–502; Lucas-Dubreton, *The Restoration and the July Monarchy*, 159–171.

[21] Proclamation of the Deputies, July 31, 1830, *Constitutions and Other Select Documents*, 502–503.

and oligarchical government has just been overthrown by the heroism of the people of Paris," the official proclamation cheered. Referencing 1830, the proclamation noted that in both cases the monarchy killed its own people. Therefore, the Parisian revolutionaries asked the rest of France to fall in line and support the new republic, "The unity of the nation, constituted henceforth of all the classes of citizens who compose it; the government of the nation by itself." Finally, the proclamation invoked the old principles of the French Revolution, "Liberty, equality, and fraternity."[22] Barely half a century in the past, France and Europe worried if this new republican experiment might end as disastrously as the first.

Aware that the last French republic devastated Europe and tumbled the continent into a quarter century of violence and warfare, the leaders of the Second French Republic desired to illustrate they had learned from the past. On March 7, 1848, Alphonse Marie Louis de Prat de Lamartine appeased the people of Europe about French intention. Lamartine called it a "victory of the people, their heroism, moderation, and tranquility." "France is a republic," Lamartine cheered. Most importantly, Lamartine calmed, "The French republic, however, desiring to enter into the family of the already instituted governments as a regular Power and not as a phenomenon that disturbs European order." This was not to be a repetition of the French Revolution of 1789. To dispel the perception, the French politician argued, "in 1792, liberty was a novelty, equality a scandal, and the republic a problem." Things had changed. France did not intend to use war to spread republican principles.[23]

On April 23, the people of France pass their verdict on the Parisian revolution, when the country held a democratic election to determine the composition of the constitutional assembly. French voters returned a conservative majority. Worse still, in June, the provisional government ran out of financial resources and shuttered the workshop program for the unemployed. Faced with a possible social revolution, the government

---

[22] Proclamation of the Overthrow of the July Monarchy, February 24, 1848, *Constitutions and Other Select Documents*, 515–516; Lucas-Dubreton, *Restoration and the July Monarchy*, 350–367.

[23] Alphonse Lamartine, "Manifest to Europe," in *Orations from Homer to William McKinley*, ed. Mayo Williamson Hazeltine (New York: P. F. Collier, 1902), 12:4922–4929.

used the army to put down the worker protests.[24] By November, the French Revolution ran its course when the people overwhelmingly elected the conservative royalist Louis Napoleon, nephew of the late Emperor Napoleon, as their first president.[25] By 1852, Napoleon turned the Second Republic into the Second Empire.

The demise of the Second Republic was synonymous with the failure of many political experiments around the Atlantic world. Contemporaries frequently blamed the unpreparedness of the French people, their lack of proper education to protect the republic and their continued subscription to conservative Catholic leaders. Only with an educated electorate that vigilantly guarded the principles of the political system could a republic win. In 1848, few had developed those skills. Conservative powerholders could derail political reforms with their influence over the mass of people, especially if they could use the pulpit to their benefit, which applied both in France and Ireland. As elsewhere, French reformers clashed with their conservative counterparts, progressive thinkers clashed with Catholics, and middle-class fears of the working classes all undermined the success of political experiments.[26]

From France, the revolutionary upheavals spread across the Atlantic world. In the Italian and German states, national ambitions called for unification and the creation of coherent nation-states, but there was also a strong desire for political, constitutional reform. People demanded the limitation of state and royal powers with the creation of constitutional government. They wanted representative bodies to hold leaders accountable. Furthermore, what revolutionaries in 1688 had demanded

---

[24] For works on the French revolution of 1848 see Frederick A. De Luna, *The French Republic Under Cavaignac, 1848* (Princeton, NJ: Princeton University Press, 1969); Roger Price, *1848 in France* (Ithaca, NY: Cornell University Press, 1975); Roger Price, *The French Second Republic: A Social History* (Ithaca, NY: Cornell University Press, 1972).

[25] For biographies on the President/Emperor Napoleon III see David Baguley, *Napoleon III and His Regime: An Extravaganza* (Baton Rouge: Louisiana State University Press, 2000); Albert Guérard, *Napoleon III: A Great Life in Brief* (New York: Alfred A. Knopf, 1955); James F. McMillan, *Napoleon III* (London, UK: Longman, 1991); F. A. Simpson, *The Rise of Louis Napoleon* (London, UK: Frank Cass and Co. 1968).

[26] Contemporary criticism of the republican experiment is illustrated by Maurice Agulhon, *The Republican Experiment, 1848–1852*, trans. Janet Lloyd (New York: Cambridge University Press, 1983); John M. Merriman, *The Agony of the Republic: The Repression of the Left in Revolutionary France, 1848–1851* (New Haven: Yale University Press, 1978).

reappeared in Central European proclamations regarding rights. In 1847, the residents of Offenburg demanded freedom of press and freedom of thought. To ensure the stability and future of the constitutional government, reformers understood the need to have the military loyal to the constitution and no longer the state or king. Like in France, there was the demand for a National Guard, an armed people to protect the interested of the constitution. Finally, reformers called for abrogation of all legal privileges and the creation of jury trials.[27] Despite these lofty goals, political revolution stalled in the German lands, but others continued the fight.

By March 15, 1848, the Habsburg rulers in Vienna faced Hungarian demands for an end of press censorship, liberal political reforms, and economic and tax changes. Realizing that they had to agree to some of these demands or face Hungarian independence, the Austrians placated their Hungarians subjects for the moment to maintain moderates in power.[28] However, as the revolution faced conservative repressions and internal divisions, stemming the tide against political changes proved difficult. On April 19, 1849, Hungary declared its independence. Inspired by their predecessors in North America, the Hungarian "Declaration Relative to the Separation of Hungary from Austria" charged that "The House of Austria has publicaly [sic] used every effort to deprive the country of its legitimate independence and constitution, designing to reduce it to a level with the other provinces long since deprived of all freedom, and to unite all in a common link of slavery."[29] The Hungarian definition of their relationship with Austria in terms of oppression and slavery was a common threat among revolutionaries at the time and reused older language from 1688.[30] By August 1849, Hungary stood

[27] Die Forderungen des Volkes in Baden, September 12, 1847, available on https://de.wikisource.org/wiki/Die_Forderung_des_Volkes.

[28] For studies on the Hungarian uprising of 1848 see István Deák, *The Lawful Revolution: Louis Kossuth and the Hungarians, 1848–1849* (New York: Columbia University Press, 1979); Laszlo Deme, *The Radical Left in the Hungarian Revolution of 1848* (Boulder: East European Quarterly, 1976).

[29] Henry W. DePuy, *Kossuth and His Generals: With a Brief History of Hungary* (Buffalo, NY: Phinney, 1852), 203–204.

[30] For studies on the Austrian uprising of 1848 see Edward Crankshaw, *The Fall of the House of Habsburg* (New York: Penguin Book, 1983); Friedrich Engel-Janosi and Helmut Rumpler, *Probleme der Franzisko-Josephinischen Zeit 1848–1916* (Munich, Germany: R. Oldenbourg Verlag, 1967); R. John Rath, *The Viennese Revolution of 1848* (Austin: University of Texas Press, 1957).

isolated and the Hungarian army surrendered to the Austro-Russian invasion force. The Hungarian revolution was one of the most brutal and bloody of the 1848 uprisings. Mixing national and political demands, the Hungarian independence declaration was influenced by its political predecessors and mirrored their demands and style.

Along the vast trade routes of the Atlantic, news of these revolutionary events in France travels to the Americas. Even the country that has set off the revolutionary age was not immune to political challenges. The United States had set the standard for political revolutions, limited in scope and eventually conservative in outcome. The United States did not embrace outright democracy and remained slow to extend the political franchise to less well-off individuals who lacked the necessary amount of property. By the late 1820s, the United States headed toward a political revolution. In 1824, the sitting president James Monroe did not endorse a member of his cabinet for president. As a result, the country faced a four-candidate presidential election race: the New Englander John Quincy Adams, William H. Crawford from the South, and two Westerners in Andrew Jackson and Henry Clay. Since no candidate received the necessary majority in the Electoral College, the House of Representatives crowned John Q. Adams president. Supporters of the defeated Andrew Jackson saw in the appointment of the Speaker of the House, Henry Clay, as Secretary of State so close after their favored candidate had lost, a "corrupt bargain."[31] A political revolution swept the United States.

As a result of defeat, Jackson's supporters launch a campaign to ensure their candidate's success in the next election. New electioneering tactics emerged, which included camp meetings, stump speeches, barbecues, and other festivities. George Caleb Bingham illustrated the new style of electioneering in a painting in 1852, *The County Election*. In the artwork neither Democrats nor Whigs challenge the voters of the other party. However, in the center of the line, one person seems to be carrying a passed-out voter. Once voters have done their civic duty, the drinks are ready. Until the last minute, political campaigners try to influence voters and their decisions. The most charismatic and appealing politician

---

[31] Daniel W. Howe, *What Hath God Wrought: The Transformation of America, 1815–1848* (New York: Oxford University Press, 2007), 203–211; Sean Wilentz, *The Rise of American Democracy: Jefferson to Lincoln* (New York: W. W. Norton, 2005), 240–257.

received popular support.[32] Nevertheless, even in the United States, politicians distrusted the people. Especially, in the eastern parts of the country, many feared that with a Westerner becoming president, the country would be placed on a downhill trajectory and destroy the moral foundation of the country. Religion served as one means to combat those dangerous trends and could school the un- or undereducated electorate in the West. In addition, Martin Van Buren's spoils system created political loyalty with the party awarding patronage jobs in government.[33] The political groundswell brought changes to the electoral system with more elections placed directly in the hands of the voters, such as the selection of electors for the president. The embrace of democracy left many wondering if the United States had fallen under the spell of mobocracy as it passed through this political revolution. At the same time, the rest of the Americas continued to suffer from the political instability created by the independence movements.

Among Latin American countries, Brazil most closely, in time and style, emulated the European revolutions of 1848. By the 1840s, Brazil faced the abysses of a political revolution as concerns about the regency grew. Even with the coronation of Dom Pedro II in 1841, political opposition continued within the framework of a conservative-liberal dichotomy. The lack of political opportunity and the encrusted nature of the system brought about a third-party challenge in Pernambuco province in the 1840s: the Partido Nacional de Pernambuco, often called Praieira. The new party aimed to overcome inequality and elite power. Since conservatives were bent on maintaining control by any means, members of the Praieira rose up in revolt in late 1848. The so-called Praieira Revolt was short-lived as Brazilian national forces

---

[32] Lois W. Banner, "Religious Benevolence as Social Control: A Critique of an Interpretation," *Journal of American History* 60 (June 1973), 23–41; Clifford S. Griffin, "Religious Benevolence as Social Control, 1815–1860," *Mississippi Valley Historical Review* 44 (December 1957), 423–444.

[33] Charles Sellers, *The Market Revolution: Jacksonian America, 1815–1846* (New York: Oxford University Press, 1991), 353, 364. Not all Jackson scholars would agree with Seller's argument but all see a new move toward democracy but also the limits of democracy, see Lee Benson, *The Concept of Jacksonian Democracy: New York as a Test Case* (Princeton, NJ: Princeton University Press, 1961); Howe, *What Hath God Wrought*; Edward Pessen, *Jacksonian America: Society, Personality, and Politics* (Urbana: University of Illinois Press, 1985); Robert V. Remini, *The Election of Andrew Jackson* (New York: J. B. Lippincott, 1963).

quickly subdued the rebels.[34] In the aftermath, Dom Pedro realized that he would need to turn himself into the country's first citizen or face a similar fate to Louis-Philippe. Political upheaval spread and did not end always as favorably to the holders of power.

Like Brazil, other parts of Latin America witnessed attempts to bring the reign of the caudillo to a close. In the Rio de la Plata region, the Manuel Oribe-Fructuoso Rivera skirmish in Uruguay ended in 1851 with the temporary defeat of Oribe's Blancos, which undermined the Rosas dictatorship in Buenos Aires. Already during the last stages of the civil war, Rosas faced challenges from competing caudillo Justo José de Urquiza y García. In 1851, Urquiza defeated Rosas, forcing the former dictator into exile. Rosas left for Great Britain, where he joined other revolutionary or counterrevolutionary exiles of 1848 such as Fürst von Metternich, Louis-Philippe, and Lajos Kossuth.[35] Argentina continued to suffer under political instability, since nationalism and a liberal constitutional system of government were still absent.

Meanwhile in Chile, the late 1840s witnessed growing political turmoil over financial disagreements and personal political ambitions. In early 1850, the Chilean congress approved a new tax law, which pitched the liberal-minded Bruno de Larraín y Aguirre against the conservative Manuel Francisco Antonio Julián Montt Torres. Larraín worried that Chile faced the possibility of a constitutional crisis as congress tried to challenge the independence of the presidency. Montt already foreshadowed that tyranny loomed, if taxes were suspended, which would create a cause for legitimate revolution. He noted that, "Revolution! Civil war! Why – when the Constitution leaves us the freedom to obtain the reforms we desire through peaceful means?" While conflict was temporarily prevented, the assault against the Chilean government structures increased, especially with the creation of the *Sociedad de la Igualdad* (Society for Equality) in 1850. The founder, Santiago Acros, resided in Paris until 1848, when he returned to Chile, likely after seeing some of

---

[34] Nancy P. Naro, "Brazil's 1848: The Praieira Revolt," Ph.D.diss, University of Chicago, 1981; Nancy P. Naro, "Brazil's 1848: The Praieira Revolt in Pernambuco, Brazil," in *The European Revolutions of 1848 and the Americas*, ed. Guy Thomson (London, UK: Institute of Latin American Studies, 2002), 100–124.

[35] John Lynch, *Argentine Caudillo: Juan Manuel de Rosas* (Wilmington, DE: Scholarly Resources, 2001), 121–162; David Rock, "The European Revolutions in the Rio de la Plata," in *The European Revolutions of 1848*, 125–141.

the upheavals of the French Revolution that year. He was later joined by Francisco Bilbao, who remained in Paris until February 1850. The organization worried that independence could be lost to new tyrants.[36] The groundwork for political revolution was in place as conservatives solidified their grasp on power and progressives contemplated rebellion.

In September 1851, the election of the conservative Montt caused a rebellion. Liberals assumed that the election had been rigged. Even more, they worried that his victory would spell "the absolute and perpetual loss of liberty and the Republic." Even before the election, the government faced challenges. On April 20, Easter Sunday, the liberal general Pedro Urriola Balbontín staged a coup d'état with the Valdivia Regiment at Cerro Santa Lucía. Urriola died in the fight that day along with 200 others under his command. Once Montt's election was confirmed, liberals rebelled in both the northern and southern parts of the country. The government sent a large army of over 3300 soldiers against the rebels and within a month subdued the political opponents. *El Copiapino* commented that "it was necessary for us to suffer an eruption, so as to be able to await more bounteous and lasting peace and quiet."[37] For the moment Chile was at peace and the liberal political challenge ended in defeat, just like they had done in Europe.

To the north, in New Granada, which was the most republican among the Latin American countries, the presidential election of 1849 brought the liberal José Hilario López Valdés to power. Valdés and the liberals implemented reforms such as an end of Jesuit education and broadening the electoral franchise. In 1851, conservatives rebelled against these reforms, but liberal forces subdued the uprising. However, much like in France where universal manhood suffrage brought the election of a conservative-monarchical president, so too did the 1856 election bring a conservative victory in New Granada.[38] Across the Atlantic World, a

---

[36] Simon Collier, *Chile: The Making of a Republic, 1830–1865: Politics and Ideas* (New York: Cambridge University Press, 2003), 76, 82–85.

[37] Collier, *Chile*, 94, 97, 100–102; Kurt Weyland, "The Diffusion of Revolution: '1848' in Europe and Latin America," *International Organization* 63 (Summer 2009), 391–423.

[38] Eduardo Posada-Carbó, "New Granada and the European Revolutions of 1848," in *The European Revolutions of 1848*, 217–240; Nancy P. Applebaum, *Muddied Waters: Race, Region, and Local History in Columbia, 1846–1948* (Durham, NC: Duke University Press, 2003); James E. Sanders, *Contentious Republicans: Popular Politics, Race, and Class in Nineteenth-Century Columbia* (Durham, NC: Duke University Press, 2004).

comparative struggle over political and constitutional reforms meshed with a nation-state formation process.

When revolutionaries in 1848 demanded constitutional government from their monarchical overlords, they fell back on time tested arguments dating back as far as the Glorious Revolution of 1688. In the Anglo-American Atlantic world, political leaders questioned royal oppression with the implementation of constitutional rules limiting the power of monarchs. They made a lasting claim that oppressed people had an obligation to rebel. Despite these two limited political revolutions, the watershed moment for the nineteenth-century Atlantic world came in 1789 with the French Revolution. Overthrowing the oppressive French monarchy, the encrusted and unequal social structures, and inculcating a universal code of rights dramatically altered the perception of people regarding their relationship to government and the monarchy. Spanish American revolutionaries looked to the events in France to free themselves from Spanish oppression. By 1830, some states still languished seeking constitutional governments, but few were prepared to embrace universal suffrage, democracy. The Age of Political Revolution desired to prevent oppression from above, royal oppression, and below, from the people, to insure a stable government. As a result, France and Great Britain made limited constitutional changes to enlarge the political franchise, but they shied away from more dramatic reforms. Even the United States was concerned about the outgrowth of democracy, as seen in the election of Andrew Jackson. In 1848, reformers tried one last time to bring about constitutional changes in the face of resilient monarchs. Meanwhile, Latin America struggled with constitutional instability and the continuation of the Age of the Caudillo. However, even here, the demands of constitutional government and political rights were heard frequently after independence. The Age of Political Revolution was running its course by the 1850s, revolutionary leaders had sought inspiration from each other, and revolutionary ideas had crisscrossed the Atlantic in every direction. Revolutionaries looked back at the events in 1688 for inspiration and arguments. The Atlantic world dramatically transformed as political leaders exchanged and adopted revolutionary constitutional ideas.

Bibliography

Agulhon, Maurice. *The Republican Experiment, 1848–1852*. Translated by Janet Lloyd. New York: Cambridge University Press, 1983.

Anderson, Frank M., ed. *The Constitutions and Other Select Documents Illustrative of the History of France, 1789–1901*. Minneapolis, MN: H. W. Wilson, 1967.

Applebaum, Nancy P. *Muddied Waters: Race, Region, and Local History in Columbia, 1846–1948*. Durham, NC: Duke University Press, 2003.

Baguley, David. *Napoleon III and His Regime: An Extravaganza*. Baton Rouge: Louisiana State University Press, 2000.

Banner, Lois W. "Religious Benevolence as Social Control: A Critique of an Interpretation." *Journal of American History* 60 (June 1973): 23–41.

Banning, Lance. *The Jeffersonian Persuasion: Evolution of a Party Ideology*. Ithaca, NY: Cornell University Press, 1978.

Benson, Lee. *The Concept of Jacksonian Democracy: New York as a Test Case*. Princeton, NJ: Princeton University Press, 1961.

Cahill, Gilbert A. *The Great Reform Bill of 1832: Liberal or Conservative?* Lexington, MA: Heath, 1969.

Cavanagh, Michael. *Memoirs of General Thomas Francis Meagher*. Worcester, MA: Messenger Press, 1892.

Châtre, Maurice La. *Histoire des Papes: Rois, Reines, Empereurs a travers les Siècles*. Paris: Docks de la Librairie, 1870.

Church, Clive H. *Europe in 1830: Revolution and Political Change*. London: Allen and Unwin, 1983.

Collier, Simon. *Chile: The Making of a Republic, 1830–1865: Politics and Ideas*. New York: Cambridge University Press, 2003.

Contamine, Henry. "La Révolution de 1830 a Métz." *Revenue d'Histoire Moderne* 6 (July 1931): 115–123.

Crankshaw, Edward. *The Fall of the House of Habsburg*. New York: Penguin Book, 1983.

De Luna, Frederick A. *The French Republic Under Cavaignac, 1848*. Princeton, NJ: Princeton University Press, 1969.

Deák, István. *The Lawful Revolution: Louis Kossuth and the Hungarians, 1848–1849*. New York: Columbia University Press, 1979.

Deme, Laszlo. *The Radical Left in the Hungarian Revolution of 1848*. Boulder: East European Quarterly, 1976.

Demoulin, Robert. *La Révolution de 1830*. Brussels, Belgium: Renaissance du Livre, 1950.

DePuy, Henry W. *Kossuth and His Generals: With a Brief History of Hungary*. Buffalo, NY: Phinney, 1852.

Desan, Suzanne, Lynn Hunt, and William Max Nelson, eds. *The French Revolution in Global Perspective*. Ithaca: Cornell University Press, 2013.

Dowe, Dieter, et.al. *Europe in 1848: Revolution and Reform.* New York: Berghahn Books, 2001.
Durand, R. "La Révolution de 1830 en Côte-d'Or." *Revenue d'Histoire Moderne* 6 (July 1931): 161–175.
Engel-Janosi, Friedrich, and Helmut Rumpler. *Probleme der Franzisko-Josephinischen Zeit 1848–1916.* Munich, Germany: R. Oldenbourg Verlag, 1967.
Evans, Eric J. *The Great Reform Act of 1832.* London: Methuen, 1983.
Fenton, Laurence. *The Young Ireland Rebellion and Limerick.* Blackrock, Ireland: Mercier Press, 2010.
Griffin, Clifford S. "Religious Benevolence as Social Control, 1815–1860." *Mississippi Valley Historical Review* 44 (December 1957): 423–444.
Gruner, Shirley. "The Revolution of July 1830 and the Expression 'Bourgeoisie'." *Historical Journal* 11 (1968): 462–471.
Guérard, Albert. *Napoleon III: A Great Life in Brief.* New York: Alfred A. Knopf, 1955.
Gwynn, Denis. *Young Ireland and 1848.* Cork, Ireland: Cork University Press, 1949.
Halévy, Elie. *The Triumph of Reform.* London: Ernest Benn, 1961.
Hazeltine, Mayo Williamson, ed. *Orations from Homer to William McKinley.* New York: P. F. Collier, 1902.
Howe, Daniel W. *What Hath God Wrought: The Transformation of America, 1815–1848.* New York: Oxford University Press, 2007.
Jones, Peter. *The 1848 Revolutions.* London, UK: Longman, 1991.
Kinealy, Christine. *Repeal and Revolution: 1848 in Ireland.* Manchester, UK: Manchester University Press, 2009.
Lucas-Dubreton, J. *The Restoration and the July Monarchy.* Translation by E. F. Buckley. New York: G. P. Putman's Sons, 1929.
Lynch, John. *Argentine Caudillo: Juan Manuel de Rosas.* Wilmington, DE: Scholarly Resources, 2001.
Mason, Laura, and Tracey Rizzo, eds. *The French Revolution: A Document Collection.* Boston: Houghton Mifflin, 1999.
McMillan, James F. *Napoleon III.* London, UK: Longman, 1991.
Merriman, John M. *1830 in France.* New York: New Viewpoints, 1975.
Merriman, John M. *The Agony of the Republic: The Repression of the Left in Revolutionary France, 1848–1851.* New Haven: Yale University Press, 1978.
Naro, Nancy P. "Brazil's 1848: The Praieira Revolt." Ph.D.diss, University of Chicago, 1981.
Nelson, Eric. *The Royalist Revolution: Monarchy and the American Founding.* Cambridge, MA: Harvard University Press, 2014.
Pearce, Edward. *Reform!: The Fight for the 1832 Reform Act.* London: Jonathan Cape, 2003.

Pessen, Edward. *Jacksonian America: Society, Personality, and Politics.* Urbana: University of Illinois Press, 1985.

Phillips, John A., and Charles Wetherell. "The Great Reform Bill of 1832 and the Rise of Partisanship." *Journal of Modern History* 63 (December 1991): 621–646.

Pilbeam, Pamela M. "The 'Three Glorious Days': The Revolution of 1830 in Provincial France." *Historical Journal* 26 (December 1983): 831–844.

Pilbeam, Pamela M. *The 1830 Revolution in France.* Basingstoke: Macmillan, 1991.

Pincus, Steven C. A., ed. *England's Glorious Revolution, 1688–1689: A Brief History with Documents.* Boston, New York: Bedford/St. Martin's, 2005.

Pinkney, David H. "The Crowd in the French Revolution of 1830." *American Historical Review* 70 (October 1964): 1–17.

Price, Roger. *The French Second Republic: A Social History.* Ithaca, NY: Cornell University Press, 1972.

Price, Roger. "Legitimist Opposition to the Revolution of 1830 in the French Provinces." *Historical Journal* 17 (December 1974): 755–778.

Price, Roger. *1848 in France.* Ithaca, NY: Cornell University Press, 1975.

Rath, R. John. *The Viennese Revolution of 1848.* Austin: University of Texas Press, 1957.

Remini, Robert V. *The Election of Andrew Jackson.* New York: J. B. Lippincott, 1963.

Sanders, James E. *Contentious Republicans: Popular Politics, Race, and Class in Nineteenth-Century Columbia.* Durham, NC: Duke University Press, 2004.

Sellers, Charles. *The Market Revolution: Jacksonian America, 1815–1846.* New York: Oxford University Press, 1991.

Sewell, William. *Work and Revolution in France: The Language of Labor from the Old Regime to 1848.* Cambridge, UK: Cambridge University Press, 1980.

Simpson, F. A. *The Rise of Louis Napoleon.* London, UK: Frank Cass and Co. 1968.

Sloan, Robert. *William Smith O'Brien and the Young Ireland Rebellion of 1848.* Dublin, Ireland: Four Courts Press, 2000.

Stanwood, Owen. *The Empire Reformed: English America in the Age of the Glorious Revolution.* Philadelphia: University of Pennsylvania Press, 2011.

Thomson, Guy, ed. *The European Revolutions of 1848 and the Americas.* London, UK: Institute of Latin American Studies, 2002.

Walker, Charles F. *The Tupac Amaru Rebellion.* Cambridge, MA: Harvard University Press, 2014.

Weyland, Kurt. "The Diffusion of Revolution: '1848' in Europe and Latin America." *International Organization* 63 (Summer 2009): 391–423.

Wilentz, Sean. *The Rise of American Democracy: Jefferson to Lincoln.* New York: W. W. Norton, 2005.

CHAPTER 6

Garibaldi's Revolutionary Atlantic

The first half of the nineteenth-century Atlantic world was a period characterized by the exchange of goods, people, and ideas both national and constitutional. The wide variety of trade routes spanning the Atlantic region allowed for people to reach faraway places, escape prosecution, and for new ideas in newspapers, pamphlets, and books to reach receptive audiences in distant places. The Revolutionary Atlantic stood as a crossroads and nobody better illustrates this interchange of ideas and people, of revolutionary crosscurrents around the Atlantic world, than the Italian revolutionary Giuseppe Garibaldi.

Like no other, Garibaldi left his imprint on the nineteenth-century Atlantic world. He participated in the revolutions of 1830 on both sides of the Atlantic and remained an active participant in 1848 and into the 1860s national struggles. Born in the border town of Nice on July 4, 1807, Garibaldi grew up in the Kingdom of Piedmont-Sardinia. Coming from a seafaring family, the young Garibaldi aspired to a maritime career and went to sea at the relatively late age of fifteen. During the frequent quarantines in Mediterranean ports, Garibaldi read nationalist tracts, including works by Giuseppe Mazzini. Mazzini's *La Giovine Italia* (Young Italy) became a symbol for revolutionaries in the Atlantic region. In the organization's manifesto, Mazzini noted, "revolutions are the work of principles rather than of bayonets." He called for "every effort at emancipation" to accomplish "unity, liberty, and independence." Fear should never force people to accept compromises; instead, they should work to overthrow tyranny. Italy would not accept "assistance and the

© The Author(s) 2019
N. Eichhorn, *Atlantic History in the Nineteenth Century*,
https://doi.org/10.1007/978-3-030-27640-9_6

pity" of Europe to bring about Italian national unity.[1] Based on the founding principles, La Giovine Italia determined to start an uprising in Piedmont-Sardinia in 1833. Garibaldi got caught up in the revolutionary upheavals as he tried to recruit member of the navy for the *carbonari*. The authorities put Garibaldi on trial in absentia, sentencing him to death. Disguised as a peasant, Garibaldi left Genoa on January 5, 1834, and in Marseilles, hired on with a merchant vessel on its way to Brazil. He was just one of many exiles during this period. Garibaldi left revolution torn Europe to face South American revolutions.

In Brazil, Garibaldi encountered a state suffering from the legacies of colonial rule and an identity crisis. With the Portuguese court located in Brazil since the French invasion of 1807, the Portuguese people demanded the return of the court to Lisbon. As a result, Dom João VI (1816–1826) faced a crisis. When the king decided to return to Portugal, his son Pedro refused and declared the independence of Brazil on September 7, 1822, assuming the title of Emperor Dom Pedro I. However, by the late 1820s, dynastic problems in Portugal, economic hardship, and constitutional demands for reform placed the six-year-old Dom Pedro II on the throne of Brazil on April 7, 1831.[2] The regency caused many disagreements, internal divisions, and destabilized Brazilian politics. Garibaldi arrived into this crisis in Rio de Janeiro, where he was supposed to recruit an Italian legion among the Italian immigrants and fashion a revolutionary navy for the Italian independence fight. Initially, Garibaldi employed the vessels in the coastal trade of Brazil, but soon found better use for the vessels.

Brazil's southern province of Rio Grande do Sul had embraced separatism, feeling oppressed and unfairly treated within the Brazilian Empire. Garibaldi joined the freedom cause as a privateer. As a Farrapos "buccaneer," Garibaldi with the twelve sailors on the *Mazzini* preyed

---

[1] Giuseppe Mazzini, *A Cosmopolitanism of Nations: Giuseppe Mazzini's Writings on Democracy, Nation Building, and International Relations*, trans. and eds. Stefano Recchia and Nadia Urbinati (Princeton, NJ: Princeton University Press, 2009), 33–38.

[2] Roderick J. Barman, *Brazil: The Forging of a Nation, 1798–1852* (Stanford, CA: Stanford University Press, 1988), 43–44, 142–146, 148–149, 158–159; *Citizen Emperor: Pedro II and the Making of Brazil, 1825–1891* (Stanford, CA: Stanford University Press, 1999), 26–29; Neill Macaulay, *Dom Pedro: The Struggle for Liberty in Brazil and Portugal, 1798–1834* (Durham, NC: Duke University Press, 1986), 226–227, 241–252, 283–301; Jeffrey D. Needell, *The Party of Order: The Conservatives, the State, and Slavery in the Brazilian Monarchy, 1831–1871* (Stanford, CA: Stanford University Press, 2006).

on Brazilian vessels. However, his privateering career was short-lived. He evaded the authorities in a Uruguayan port, but faced temporarily imprisonment after capture in Argentina soon after. In his much later published memoirs, he wrote disdainfully about the naval engagement he fought: "The Italians—all but one—fought stoutly; the foreigners and freed blacks—of whom there were five—hid themselves in the hold."[3] Garibaldi had turned from a European into a Brazilian revolutionary, an Atlantic career.

Regardless of losing the *Mazzini*, the government of Rio Grande do Sul gave Garibaldi command of the small secessionist navy, but he also fought a number of battles on solid ground. When Rio Grande do Sul's war effort turned south, Garibaldi went into exile once more. Looking for peace, he wrote: "I had now passed six years of my life in hardship and privation, severed from all the associations of my youth, and from my parents, of whose fate ... I was absolutely ignorant. This naturally made me desirous of getting back some place where I might be able to hear from home."[4] Unfortunately, his new exile in Uruguay came about as no less volatile.

The Banda Oriental was a late addition to the Spanish Empire. Garibaldi termed the state's problem this way: "The Republic of Uruguay was, like the greater number of the South American republics, in that state of civil war which, long-continued and almost chronic as it is, forms the greatest hindrance to the progress of which that splendid country ... is susceptible."[5] The conflict centered on the Colorado leader Fructuoso Rivera's attempt to overthrow the Blanco government of Manuel Oribe, which was allied with Rosas government in Buenos Aires. Garibaldi called Rosas "the tyrant of that Republic" and wrote, "But to the nation, the real people, Ourives was not the opponent of Ribera, but the paid leaders of a foreign army, the instrument of a tyrant whose weapons were invasion, slavery, and death. And the people rushed to the

---

[3] Giuseppe Garibaldi, *Garibaldi: An Autobiography*, ed. Alexandre Dumas, trans. William Robson (London, UK: Routledge, Warne, and Routledge, 1861), 1:24, 26–29, 43–47, 38; Alfonso Scirocco, *Garibaldi: Citizen of the World*, trans. Allan Cameron (Princeton, NJ: Princeton University Press), Chapters 4 and 5.

[4] Garibaldi, *Garibaldi*, 1:53–76, 80–84, 108–121, 133–134.

[5] Ibid., 1:138.

defense, fully conscious of their sacred rights."[6] Many foreigners rushed to the defense of Uruguay.

The Uruguayan civil war quickly escalated and Garibaldi, who recruited an Italian legion among the Italian residence of Montevideo, helped to defend the city against Oribe's forces. Garibaldi wrote happily, "The Italians assembled to the number of about five hundred, few enough compared with the total of our compatriots settled in the country, yet more than I had ever hoped for, considering our daily habits and the nature of our education." In addition, Garibaldi relied on his naval experience, commanding the corvette *Constitucion* to relief the besieged troops in the city. Eventually, international support from Brazil, Great Britain, and France contributed to the victory of the Rivera faction. Ironically, the financial burden of French involvement in the Rio de la Plata states contributed to the downfall of the French government in 1848.[7] By the time the conflict in the region ended, Garibaldi had returned to Europe.

In the first month of 1848, the Italian national and constitutional desires had brought major challenges to the rulers on the peninsula. Calls came from Mazzini for a unified, republican nation-state, the people in Sicily desired a separate nation-state that restored some of the ancient privileges to the island's elite, and finally there was the universal desire to remove Habsburg rule. Furthermore, since 1846, when Pope Pius IX embraced liberal ideas of government, he seemed likely to become a leadership figure in the unification of Italy. From Uruguay, Garibaldi congratulated the pope and encouraged him to continue his reform plans. Garibaldi wrote: "If these hands, used to fighting, would be acceptable to his Holiness, we most thankfully dedicate them to the service of him who deserves so well of the Church and of our fatherland. Joyful indeed shall we and our companions in whose name we speak be, if we may be allowed to shed our blood in defence of Pio Nono's work of redemption."[8] By the late 1840s, Garibaldi was ready to return to Italy and assist the unification process.

---

[6] Garibaldi, *Garibaldi*, 1:137, 165; John Lynch, *Argentine Caudillo: Juan Manuel de Rosas* (1981. Wilmington, DE: Scholarly Resources, 2001).

[7] Garibaldi, *Garibaldi*, 1: 137, 169–170; Scirocco, *Garibaldi*, Chapter 8.

[8] Giuseppe Garibaldi to Pope Pius XI, October 12, 1847; Garibaldi, *Garibaldi*, 3:68; Simonetta Soldani, "Approaching Europe in the Name of the Nation: The Italian Revolution, 1846/1849," in *Europe in 1848: Revolution and Reform*, eds. Dieter Dowe et al. (New York: Berghahn Books, 2001), 63–66, 68.

Garibaldi wished for a unified Italy, explaining his decision to return home: "At that time—the beginning of 1848, I think—we heard the news of the recent pontifical reform, while it had already for some time been evident, from all the correspondence which reached La Plata, that Italian intolerance of foreign dominion had reached its height. The idea of returning to our own country and giving strength for her redemption had long made our hearts beat high."[9] The new prospects brought Garibaldi and "a handful of our bravest" back to Europe. He returned with sixty-three of his followers from Uruguay, but he worried about the implications of aligning with a revolutionary cause. In almost religious language, Garibaldi described the feelings he had on the voyage: "We were marching towards the fulfillment of the longing, the passion of our whole life; we were hastening to dedicate the weapons gloriously wielded in the service of the oppressed of other countries to our own beloved land. That thought more than compensated for the dangers, hardships, suffering of a whole life of tribulation. Our hearts throbbed high with lofty hopes and enthusiasm." Once in Italy, Garibaldi offered his services to Carlo Alberto of Piedmont-Sardinia, who had assumed the mantle of unification and the ouster of Austria, in order to "save Italy and fight against her enemies, whatever might be the political leaning of our leaders in the war of emancipation." The king rebuffed Garibaldi, worrying about the prospect of a Mazzinian republic. Even decades later, Garibaldi angrily wrote: "I would have served Italy under that king's order with the same fervour as if the country had been a republic, and would have persuaded the young men who trusted me to follow on the same path of self-denial." As a result, the Italian Revolutionary offered his services to the revolutionary government of Lombardy, which gladly accepted. As the armies of Carlo Alberto performed dismally at the Battle of Custoza (July 24–25, 1848), Garibaldi fought valiantly, but could not change the fate of Italy.[10] After the Custoza ceasefire, Garibaldi searched for new opportunities.

When in November 1848, Mazzini declared a radical republic in the Papal States and ousted the pope, Garibaldi accepted command of one of the republican armies. The pope did not accept his exile and called for

---

[9] Garibaldi, *Garibaldi*, 1:257; Peter Jones, *The 1848 Revolutions* (London, UK: Longman, 1991), 89–91.

[10] Garibaldi, *Garibaldi*, 1:257–259, 266–267; Scirocco, *Garibaldi*, 142–146; Alan Sked, *The Survival of the Habsburg Empire: Radetzky, the Imperial Army and the Class War, 1848* (London, UK: Longman, 1979).

assistance from the Austrians, French, and Bourbons in the Two Sicilies. Their armies soon converged on the Roman Republic. Garibaldi commented on the situation: "That dagger-stroke [referring to the assassination of Minister of Justice Pellegrino Rossi] announced to all advocated of compromise with foreign powers that the people knew them, and would not return to the slavery to which they sought, by falsehood and treachery, to entice them back." The radical republicans faced numerically superior armies. Garibaldi temporarily held the soldiers' reactions at bay, like when he fought with Rivera in Uruguay. The South American lessons and experiences could not overcome a vastly superior enemy. On July 3, the revolutionaries evacuated Rome. The radical Roman experiment ended.[11] Offered passage to the United States by the US minister to the Papal States, Lewis Cass, Garibaldi kindly refused, wanting to remain with his men and continue the fight in Venice. Garibaldi fled to the independent duchy of San Marino, where he disbanded his soldiers.[12] Garibaldi's return had not ended with the desired result; however, his Atlantic journey was not yet over.

Garibaldi continued to support the Italian unification process as a nationalist, fighting in Sicily against the Bourbon dynasty, trying twice to bring Rome under Italian control, and finally against the Austrians in 1866. His international reputation made him a sought-after leader. The United States offered him a command as the rebellion of the southern states commence and newly Republican France accepted his assistance against the German invasion of 1870. Nobody better represented the revolutionary first half of the Atlantic nineteenth century then Garibaldi. While he did not care about the systems of government he fought for, aligning with republican, monarchical, and even caudillo regimes, he fought first and foremost for the people's right to reside in nation-states whether that was in Rio Grande do Sul, Uruguay, or Italy. The expatriate migrant communities allowed Garibaldi to recruit Italians in South Americas and the trade networks allowed for the speedy dissemination of ideas and news, making him aware of the events in Italy far across the Atlantic. Finally, Garibaldi found an abundance of opportunities to lend his sword as states and people experimented with political, social, and national changes throughout the region. He was a truly Atlantic revolutionary.

[11] Garibaldi, *Garibaldi*, 1:299, 2:1, 19, 20; Jones, *1848 Revolutions*, 97; Soldani, "Approaching Europe in the Name of the Nation," 77, 80.

[12] Garibaldi, *Garibaldi*, 2:20, 26–29.

Bibliography

Barman, Roderick J. *Brazil: The Forging of a Nation, 1798–1852*. Stanford, CA: Stanford University Press, 1988.

Barman, Roderick J. *Citizen Emperor: Pedro II and the Making of Brazil, 1825–1891*. Stanford, CA: Stanford University Press, 1999.

Dowe, Dieter, et.al. *Europe in 1848: Revolution and Reform*. New York: Berghahn Books, 2001.

Garibaldi, Giuseppe. *Garibaldi: An Autobiography*. 3 vols. Edited by Alexandre Dumas. Translated by William Robson. London, UK: Routledge, Warne, and Routledge, 1861.

Jones, Peter. *The 1848 Revolutions*. London, UK: Longman, 1991.

Lynch, John. *Argentine Caudillo: Juan Manuel de Rosas*. Wilmington, DE: Scholarly Resources, 2001.

Macaulay, Neill. *Dom Pedro: The Struggle for Liberty in Brazil and Portugal, 1798–1834*. Durham, NC: Duke University Press, 1986.

Mazzini, Giuseppe. *A Cosmopolitanism of Nations: Giuseppe Mazzini's Writings on Democracy, Nation Building, and International Relations*. Translated and edited by Stefano Recchia and Nadia Urbinati. Princeton, NJ: Princeton University Press, 2009.

Needell, Jeffrey D. *The Party of Order: The Conservatives, the State, and Slavery in the Brazilian Monarchy, 1831–1871*. Stanford, CA: Stanford University Press, 2006.

Scirocco, Alfonso. *Garibaldi: Citizen of the World*. Translated by Allan Cameron. Princeton, NJ: Princeton University Press, 2007.

Sked, Alan. *The Survival of the Habsburg Empire: Radetzky, the Imperial Army and the Class War, 1848*. London, UK: Longman, 1979.

CHAPTER 7

Slave Trade and the Return to Africa

> As soon as we had fairly got under way, and about bidding adieu to the African coast forever, the captain and many of the officers made choice of such of the young women as they chose to sleep with them in their Hammocks, whom they liberated from chains and introduced into their several apartments. After the officers had provided themselves with mistresses of color, they made arrangements for the keeping and feeding the slaves. We were fastened in rows, as before observed, so that we could set upon our ramps or lie upon our backs, as was most convenient, and as our exercises were not much, we, it was concluded, could do with little food; our allowance was put at two scanty meals per day, which consisted of about six ounces of boiled rice and Indian corn each meal, with the addition of about one gill of fresh water.[1]

Slavery was an integral part of the Atlantic world and the involuntary movement of people within Africa and from the continent to other parts of the Atlantic world was part of the slave trade experience since well before the Atlantic world even came into existence. The trade in human beings dislocated millions from Africa creating new cultures in the African community in the Americas. Despite increasingly vocal abolitionist movements and their calls to outlaw the inhuman trade, the forceful removal of African people to the New World continued well past mid-century. During the 360 years that the slave trade operated

[1] Boyrereau Brinch and Benjamin F. Prentiss, *The Blind African Slave, or Memoirs of Boyrereau Brinch* (St. Albans, VT: Harry Whitney, 1810), 87.

within the Atlantic world, 9,913,677 Africans arrived in the Americas. However, in the last seventy years (19%) of the Atlantic slave trade, 3,303,396 Africans arrived in the Americans, primarily in Brazil and the colonies of Spanish America. They represented 33% of the total slaves who arrived in the Americas.[2] During the first half of the nineteenth century, when Great Britain slowly exerted its considerable maritime influence to close down the inhuman trafficking, the slave trade was at the prime of its operation and its most lucrative. The actual suppression of the trade was difficult to enforce as traders in Africa and the Atlantic world generally remained unwilling to surrender and abandon this profitable business. As a result, philanthropists tried to alter Africa and undermine the reasons for the trade by bringing modern farming technology to the interior; their efforts had little success. Even as millions of Africans suffered through the Middle Passage to the Americas and into the clutches of slavery, there were a few thousands who decided to escape the racism of the Americas, especially in the United States, and return to their ancestral homeland. The idea of colonization of freedpeople, an early iteration of the abolition movement in the United States, continued and persisted until the end of the century. For Africans, the Atlantic remained a crossroads as they were forced into slavery or as they tried to escape racism in the Americas and return to their roots. The movement of Africans across the ocean contributed to transformations on both sides of the Atlantic.

The Middle Passage was a devastating experience. One of the most powerful accounts of the slave experience came from Olaudah Equiano. Kidnapped from his village in Africa with his sister, they got separated in the course of their transport to the coast. He was initially passed from one slave trader and owner to another; he even briefly reunited with his sister. After six or seven months of travel and work, he reached the Atlantic coast. The unkept and unintelligible way of the European traders and seafarers scared Equiano, fearing what future awaited him. After his African captors sold him on board one of the slavers, Equiano said that he was "overpowered with horror and anguish, I fell motionless on the deck and fainted." He worried that the mariners would eat him, but the African slavers tried to alleviate that concern. Equiano felt "abandoned to despair" and "deprived of all chance of returning to my

---

[2] Data on Sums of Disembarkation from the Slave Voyages.

native country, or even the least glimpse of hope gaining the shore."[3] His anguish had only started.

After a brief time on deck of the slave ship, they forced Equiano below deck. He commented later that he "received such a salutation in my nostrils as I had never experienced in my life; so that with the loathsomeness of the stench." When Equiano refused to eat, two crewmembers flogged him. Any thoughts of escape were killed by the netting the crew had put in place, which slaves would have to scale before jumping overboard. Despite slowly easing his mind into the new situation, he continued to worry that the brutish white seaman might kill him, claiming that he had never seen "so savage a manner; for I have never seen among any people such instances of brutal cruelty." Flogging was a common occurrence on the vessel and Equiano even witnessed one of the seamen whipped to death and tossed overboard.[4]

Even more than the flogging, the below deck spaces drew frequent comments from Equiano. He noted on a number of occasions the "stench of the hold" wondering how dangerous the "absolutely pestilential" smell could be. Adding to the discomfort was the absolute lack of air circulation creating an overbearing hot environment in the tropical climates of Africa, not to mention the limited spaces that left "scarcely room to turn ... almost suffocated us." Equiano explained that such an environment could cause sickness to arise and spread quickly among the slaves. He later wrote that "The shrieks of the women, and the groans of the dying, rendered the whole a scene of horror almost inconceivable." As a result, some of the slaves contemplated suicide to avoid the misery of the journey and what awaited them. When three slaves jumped overboard to their death, the crew confined the most active slaves underdeck to prevent others from following suit. Even Equiano, who was lucky that the situation took such a toll on his body that he was permitted on deck for extended periods of time, was sent below. The crew rescued one of the slaves and "flogged him unmercifully, for thus attempting to prefer death to slavery."[5] Equiano's experience and printed account served anti-slave trade political figures to push for the outlawing of the inhuman

---

[3] Olaudah Equiano, *The Interesting Narrative of Olaudah Equiano: Or Gustavus Vassa, the African* (London: Printed for, and sold by the author, 1794), 32–33, 41, 46–47.

[4] Ibid., 47–49.

[5] Ibid., 51–53.

trade, especially the horrific details related in the account help to undermine the slave trade.

Despite numerous calls since the 1770 by religious and humanist groups and the enlightened language of the new political age, the slave trade continued to thrive in the Age of Revolutions. The maritime conflicts associated with the French Revolution and Napoleonic Wars offered a chance to undermine the Atlantic trade in human beings. In 1807, the British government finally determined to act on the prolonged lobbying from humanitarian elements and deal with the growing French threat on the high seas. Parliament passed a law stating unequivocally, "That from and after the First Day of *May* One thousand eight hundred and seven, the *African* Slave Trade, and all manner of dealing and trading in the Purchase, Sale, Barter, or Transfer of Slaves, or of Persons intended to be sold, transferred, used, or dealt with as Slaves, practiced or carried on, in, at, to or from any Part of the Coast or Countries of *Africa*, shall be, and the same is hereby utterly abolished, prohibited, and declared to be unlawful."[6] Henceforth, the British Royal Navy policed the implementation of the law, and in the course of the Napoleonic Wars, used wartime measures to detain slavers from other countries. Coincidentally, the United States outlawed the international trade in human beings that same year. After 300 years, the horrors of the Middle Passages seemed to slowly come to a close, but ending the slave trade was no easy task.

Within a decade, the British desired to broadly prohibit the Atlantic slave trade. The conclusion of the Napoleonic Wars offered an opportunity to enlist other European countries and in the postwar treaties include anti-slave trade stipulations. Furthermore, the independence of the Spanish colonies in the Americas required separate treaties with all of them to suppress the trade. By the mid-1840s, the British devoted dozens of vessels to the anti-slave trade patrols along the African coast. When the Royal Navy captured a slave ship, they usually released the slaves in Sierra Leone, not their original homelands. Most concerning, the United States jealously guarded its neutral rights against searches preventing the treaties from being effective. Even the Treaty of Ghent, ending the War of 1812, did not settle the question about search and seizure. As a result, the United States maintained its own inadequate fleet

---

[6] "An Act for the Abolition of the Slave Trade," in *Select Statutes, Cases and Documents to Illustrate English Constitutional History, 1660–1832: With a Supplement from 1832–1894*, by Charles G. Robertson (London, UK: Methuen, 1904), 167.

of warships off the West African coast to hunt down slavers flying the US flag. Despite British pressure, Brazil and Spanish-Cuba continued to import slaves until 1850 and 1862, respectively. Spanish-Cuba accepted the end of the trans-Atlantic slave trade because the protection of the US flag had disappeared. By 1867, naval forces had captured over 570 slave ships and liberated 150,000 slaves.[7] A rather small figure considering the 3,303,396 slaves brought to the Americas in the nineteenth century; treaty enforcement worked significantly better than naval enforcement against violators.

In 1862, Great Britain and the United States, as leading maritime powers in the Atlantic world, finally agreed to a new slave trade treaty. Freed by the secession of the southern states, opposition to a fiercer enforcement of the anti-slave trade treaty disappeared in the United States. Secretary of State William H. Seward and the British representative in Washington, Richard Bickerton Pemell, Lord Lyons, agreed to a new anti-slave trade treaty. In the treaty, the United States surrender prohibition against searches of neutral vessels regarding the slave trade. The treaty read, "The two high contracting parties mutually consent that those ships of their respective navies which shall be provided with special instructions for that purpose, … may visit such merchant vessels of the two nations as may, upon reasonable grounds, be suspected of being engaged in the African slave trade, or of having been fitted out for that purpose." The treaty did limit the right to conduct searches to war vessels and only ships suspected to engage in the slave trade, but it was a major step forward.[8] Two of the most powerful navies finally stood together in opposition to the trade, final legal loopholes were gone, and the demise of the trade set in motion.

---

[7] Laird W. Bergad, *Comparative Histories of Slavery in Brazil, Cuba, and the United States* (New York: Cambridge University Press, 2007), 258; Donald L. Canney, *Africa Squadron: The U.S. Navy and the Slave Trade, 1842–1861* (Washington, DC: Potomac Books, 2006); Peter Grindal, *Opposing the Slavers: The Royal Navy's Campaign Against the Atlantic Slave Trade* (London, UK: I. B. Tauris, 2016); Christopher Lloyd, *The Navy and the Slave Trade: The Suppression of the African Slave Trade in the Nineteenth Century* (London, UK: Longmans, Green, 1949).

[8] Charles I. Bevans, ed., *Treaties and Other International Agreements of the United States of America, 1776–1949* (Washington, DC: U.S. Government Printing Office, 1969), 12:137; Philip E. Myers, *Caution and Cooperation: The American Civil War in British–American Relations* (Kent, OH: Kent State University Press, 2008), 211–212.

Despite long-standing international agreements against the trade, some politicians in the Americans, especially the southern region of the United States and in Peru openly talked about the reopening of the slave trade in the 1850s. After relocating to Knoxville, Tennessee, the Irish revolutionary John Mitchel called in his *Southern Citizen* for the repeal on the prohibition on the international slave trade. Already in New York, he had suggested that because most people in Africa were "ignorant and brutal negroes," they should be brought to the United States to improve their situation. He firmly believed that "the cause of negro slavery is the cause of true philanthropy, so far as that race is concerned."[9] Mitchel supported not only slavery but the Atlantic slave trade as well.

Northern abolitionists questioned Mitchel's position. *The New York Tribune* suggested that Mitchel should remain silent on the issue. "But the Africans are black, and the Irishmen are white, when they are not very dirty … color has not therefore saved the Irish people from the most terrible oppression, as, we think, J. M. will admit," the paper posited. There were many other comparisons between the Irish and Africans, such as their "shiftless and degraded" state. The paper suggested an important question to Mitchel, "when an Irish patriot, as Mitchel professes to have been, argues that the black man is not fit for freedom because he is not free, it is perfectly proper for us to ask this Irishman why the rule is not applicable to the condition of his own countrymen?"[10] Mitchel remained undeterred in his support for the slave trade.

Mitchel was not alone in the southern states to suggest the reopening of the Atlantic slave trade was necessary. Unsurprisingly a son of South Carolina, Leonidas W. Spratt led the way. In 1853, he made the suggestion to import Africans to fulfill the labor needs of the southern states and insure that the lowest rank of white southern society did not have to engage in the menial labor that had created a working class in the northern parts of the country. The argument by Spratt and Mitchel found willing listeners. In 1857, South Carolina's legislature failed to approve the reopening of the slave trade. Similarly, Georgia and Louisiana almost approved the reopening of the slave trade.

---

[9] "The South," *Hinds County Gazette* [Raymond, MS], October 14, 1857; Aidan Hegarty, *John Mitchel: A Cause Too Many* (Belfast, UK: Camlane Press, 2005), 94; James Quinn, *John Mitchel* (Dublin, Ireland: University College Dublin Press, 2008), 57–58, 64.

[10] "The Renegade John Mitchel," *The Liberator* [Boston, MA], September 18, 1857.

With legislative inaction, enterprising hotspurs determined to take matters into their own hands. Historian William Freehling reports, "On August 21, 1858, the U.S.S. *Dolphin* captured the slaver *Echo* off Cuba." Another vessel, the Wanderer was apprehended a few months later. Despite government efforts to charge the crews, judges in Charleston and Savannah refused.[11] Even so the Atlantic slave trade was supposedly dead, many profiteers persisted desiring the reopening for financial gain, despite the trade's inhumanity.

In contrast to the United States, where slaveholders and traders openly debated the reopening of the Atlantic slave trade in defiance of international treaty, Peru actually acted in part on these notions. Even so Peruvian politicians did not promote the reopening of the Atlantic slave trade, they passed a law in July 1845 that allowed for the "importation of slaves from other American republics." Critics pointed to a recent incident with Ecuador to suggest that Great Britain would not oppose the international slave trade within the Americas. The policy to bring slaves into the country was the government's quick and easy solution to Peru's dilemma; landowners badly needed workers to restore agricultural prosperity. However, the small number of slaves brought into Peru from New Granada was a trickle and not the hoped-for mass of new workers. Furthermore, several slaves arrived from the Cauca Valley, where recent slave unrest raised doubts about the slave loyalty. Only the prohibition against the exportation of slaves by New Granada ended Peru's slave trade experiment.[12] Despite the decline and international outrage against the international slave trade, there was a retrograde movement that desired to reimplement if not the Atlantic, then at least the intra-American slave trade to supply workers to the various agricultural pursuits in the New World.

Since the enforcement of the anti-slave trade treaties was difficult in light of continued evasion and even calls for the reopening of the trade, some abolitionists, with their missionary instinct, suggested fighting the slave trade at its source in Africa. They hoped that by providing a better economic base, they would eliminate reasons for selling and trading human beings. Missionaries and humanitarians converged on Africa to

---

[11] William W. Freehling, *Road to Disunion* (New York: Oxford University Press, 2007), 2:168, 170–171.

[12] Peter Blanchard, *Slavery and Abolition in Early Republican Peru* (Wilmington, DE: Scholarly Resources, 1992), 53–57.

enlighten the people and provide education and agricultural advancements. As a result, a group of private individuals with government support determined to ascend the Niger River in 1841 to establish a model farm deep in the interior and negotiate anti-slave trade treaties with local rulers along the way. Tropical diseases, climate issues, and insufficient resources in money and manpower prevented the expedition form permanently changing African attitudes. Its model farm quickly succumbing to the harsh realities of the interior's tribal rivalries and traditionalisms. More successful were the missionaries whom the expedition had met along the way in Sierra Leone and Liberia. Many missionaries who went to Africa truly embodied the Atlantic migrant spirit. In Sierra Leone, the Niger expedition met with John Carr. Carr, born in Trinidad, received a law degree from University College in London, before coming to Africa to uplift the continent's population.[13] In the end, treaties, naval enforcement, and international pressure ended the transatlantic slave trade; however, millions suffered before the trade finally ended.

Despite efforts to end the slave trade after 1808, the number of people transported to the Americas remained staggering and their suffering horrifying. Even after the United States outlawed the trade in 1808 and the number of imported slaves declines from a last-ditch purchase boom from 1806 to 1810 of 34,841 slaves, the importation did not stop. According to the Trans-Atlantic Slave Trade—Database of the Slave Voyages project, between 1856 and 1860, 1541 slaves arrived in Mainland North America. In total, after the prohibition of the trade, 3680 slaves arrived in the region. The numbers however pale in comparison with the continued trade with Brazil and the Spanish Caribbean colonies of Cuba and Puerto Rico. Working in the labor-intensive, harsh, and deadly conditions of the sugar production region, Spanish planters received thousands of new slaves every year. The first half of the 1810s was a difficult one for Spain, still suffering from the French occupation, with slave imports dramatically decreased. The trade remained cyclical for the next decades. Going as high as 122,807 slaves imported in the five years between 1816 and 1820 and as low as 35,106 in the last few years of the trade. However, the trade was not slowing down. Just as slavery remained a profitable institution until its

---

[13] Howard Temperley, *White Dreams, Black Africa: The Antislavery Expedition to the Niger, 1841–1842* (New Haven: Yale University Press, 1991), 76–79.

very end, so too remained the slave trade a profitable undertaking, even after the international community outlawed the involuntary movement of human beings.

The situation in Brazil was no different. Instead of the growing international desire to end the atrocious trade bringing about a rethinking in the Portuguese colony and eventually independent empire, Brazilian planters continued to import a growing number of slaves. Starting with 112,886 in the first five years of the nineteenth century, the number increased to 293,289 from 1826 to 1830. Things changed that decade. Great Britain and the Brazilian monarchy negotiated an anti-slave trade treaty in 1826, which Emperor Dom Pedro announced to take effect in May 1830. However, by 1833, the trade grew once again, much to the concern of the British representative in Rio de Janeiro.[14] As a result, the five years following the implementation of the slave trade treaty saw a decline in the arrival of enslaved people to 25,982. The trade rapidly increased again with 200,045 slaves arriving in Brazil from 1836 to 1840. For the next decade, the trade remained high, but British pressure forced Brazil to relinquish the importation of human beings by the early 1850s. During that decade, only 7900 slaves arrived in the country.

Unfortunately, the record for the African side of the trade leaves much to be desired. In most years during the nineteenth century, the origin of half of the slaves departing Africa is only categorized as "Other Africa" in the Trans-Atlantic Slave Trade—Database. At the start of the century, from 1801 to 1805, 434,689 slaves embarked on the devastating Middle Passage. About 17% of the slaves came from undisclosed location in Africa, the largest share of 38% or 165,139 slaves arrived from West-Central Africa and St. Helena. In addition, Senegambia contributed 19,644 slaves, Sierra Leone 11,312, the Windward Coast 7195, the Gold Coast 32,968, the Bight of Benin 39,180, and the Bight of Biafra 61,614. By the time Brazil had reinstituted the slave trade, little had changed. From 1836 to 1840, 381,157 slaves left Africa for the Americas. In this five-year stretch, only 21% or 79,211 slaves came from undisclosed locations. Like four decades earlier, 42% of the enslaves people or 161,600 came from West-Central Africa and St. Helena. In addition, only 2478 slaves came from the Senegambia region, 1685 slaves

---

[14] Leslie Bethell, *The Abolition of the Brazilian Slave Trade: Britain, Brazil and the Slave Trade Question, 1807–1869* (Cambridge, UK: Cambridge University Press, 1970), 62–63, 67, 75.

boarded their vessels on the Windward Coast, and only 702 on the Gold Coast. Meanwhile, 23,119 slaves embarked in the Bight of Benin region and a further 23,669 in the Bight of Biafra region. Interestingly enough, 13,580 slaves left the Sierra Leone region, which was where British slave patrols deposited freedpeople. Until the very end of the slave trade, the regions of West-Central Africa and St. Helena provided slaves to the Americas. The numbers hardly convey the suffering experiences by Africans in the course of the Middle Passages, but they illustrate how devastating, significant, and lucrative this trade remained well into the nineteenth century, tying Africa and the Americas together.

Importantly, the flow of Africans in the Atlantic world was not only one from east to west; there was a remarkable flow also from west to east, back to Africa, especially from the United States. Few Africans, freed from slavery, moved back to the continent of their ancestors. Nevertheless, for a long time, emancipation and a return to Africa went hand in hand in Anglo-American society, since many white politicians perceived Africans incapable of republicanism. In the United States, the dual desire for emancipation and deportation fundamentally tied together the emergence of the American Colonization Society. In 1816, the organization, whose full title was the Society for the Colonization of Free People of Color of America, came into existence under the guiding hands of Robert Finley of New Jersey. Eventually leading politicians, like Henry Clay and James Madison, supported the idea. The perception that colonization was essential grew from the steady and natural increase of the slave population in the United States. Manumissions freed some slaves; then there was a growing free black population. Many misconceptions, created in the aftermath of Saint-Domingue, played into the fear by white people of what slaves would do once freed.[15]

The first attempt to transition freedmen back to Africa came under the guidance of Paul Cuffee, a Quaker shipowner with Ashanti-Wampanoag parents. He returned a group of 38 freedmen to Sierra Leone. However, his goals were entirely selfish: gain personal wealth. The trip laid the foundation for the emergence of an organization to

---

[15] Eric Burin, *Slavery and the Peculiar Solution: A History of the American Colonization Society* (Gainesville: University Press of Florida, 2005), 1, 13–19; Allan Sarema, *The American Colonization Society: An Avenue to Freedom?* (Lanham, MD: University Press of America, 2006), 18, 24–26, 71.

promote the movement of people back to Africa. On December 21, 1816, the American Colonization Society established itself in Washington and lobbied Congress for money to acquire a piece of land in Africa where freedpeople could settle. A number of southern politicians, especially in the border states, understood the negative impact of slavery, but also that free people of color and white society would never integrate well. However, asking Congress to financially support the purchase of land in Africa and assist in obtaining ships to transport freedmen was a difficult task. Many southern congressmen saw the use of federal money for this enterprise as an encroachment on their section's power and negative judgment of their section's economic and social structures. A federal financial allocation helped to precipitate the Nullification Crisis in 1832.[16]

Regardless of antagonisms toward colonization both among individuals of African-decent in the United States and slave-owning southerners, colonization schemes continued. As a result, early leaders of colonization, like Robert Stockton and Jehudi Ashmun, acquired additional land from tribal people in the Liberia coastal regions. However, just like any indigenous people in the Atlantic region, the local chiefs eyed the newcomers with suspicion, forcing a number of bloody engagements to prevent the theft of their land. Furthermore, the colony suffered from a lack of adequate food supplies and a reluctance on the part of the ACS to provide the necessary supplies, fearing a dependence on shipments from the United States. The establishment of the first settlement and subsequent arrivals found the colony resembling a graveyard rather than a thriving enterprise. About 42% of the arrivals died of disease, war, or accidents.[17] A return migration to Africa was a dangerous undertaking and the ancestral continent not the hoped-for paradise.

Only about 2500 Afro-Americas migrated from the United States to Liberia, among them was John Brown Russwurm. Born on October 1, 1799, Russwurm was the offspring of a white merchant from the United States, sometimes also describes as English, and a black mother, likely a

---

[16] Freehling, *Road to Disunion*, 1:272–274; Beverly C. Tomek, *Colonization and Its Discontents Emancipation, Emigration, and Antislavery in Antebellum Pennsylvania* (New York: New York University Press, 2011), 142–143.

[17] James Ciment, *Another America: The Story of Liberia and the Former Slaves Who Ruled It* (New York: Hill and Wang, 2013), 31–36, 39–42, 46–47, 58.

slave woman. Russwurm spent the first nine years of his life in Jamaica, at which time his father decided that his son needed a respectable education. In contrast to Caribbean norms, Russwurm enrolled in a school in Montreal, Canada. Shortly after sending his son to Canada, his father relocated to Portland, Maine. An ironic decision considering the year he moved was also the year Great Britain and the United States went to war. From 1824 to 1826, Russwurm studied at Bowdoin College in Maine, becoming the college's first black graduate. With Samuel Cornish, also an offspring of an interracial couple, Russwurm published the *Freedom's Journal* in New York from 1827 to 1829. The journal gave voice to the black community in the United States, refusing to allow others to speak for and misrepresent their cause. However, readers soon grew outraged when Russwurm offered space and eventually agreed with supporters of colonization.[18] The abolition movement in the United States was deeply divided on colonization as the proper way to free African people.

By March 1829, Russwurm determined to leave the financially struggling *Freedom's Journal* and migrate to Africa. Leaving from Baltimore, Russwurm arrived in Monrovia, the capital of Liberia on November 12, 1829. He viewed his transition from the Americas to Africa as a step toward the civilizing of the continent. In Liberia, Russwurm worked not only for the American Colonization Society, but also as the editor of the *Liberia Herald* and superintendent of schools. Historians claim that the *Liberia Herald* was "West Africa's, and probably the continent's, first black newspaper." Promoting the migration of free blacks to West Africa, the *Liberia Herald* was supposedly in great demand on both sides of the Atlantic. In 1836, Russwurm gained even more prominence within the colonization community when the Maryland State Colonization Society appointed him governor of New Maryland. Russwurm retained the governorship until his death in 1851. During his fifteen years as governor, historians claim the colony suffered little internal and external strife.[19] Russwurm connected the Americas with Africa. Nevertheless, the idea of colonizing African slaves upon gaining their freedom in the Americas back to Africa never became a prominent undertaking and only a small number of individuals took up the call.

---

[18] Winston James, *The Struggles of John Brown Russwurm: The Life and Writings of a Pan-Africanist Pioneer, 1799–1851* (New York: New York University Press, 2010), 5–7, 13, 44.

[19] Ibid., 49, 59–61, 64.

Despite the failure of colonization in its first decades, the notion of removing African people from the Americas remained an intellectual movement among some abolitionists in the United States. In his Preliminary Emancipation Proclamation, President Abraham Lincoln noted "the effort to colonize persons of African descent, with their consent, upon this continent, or elsewhere, with the previously obtained consent of the Governments existing there, will be continued."[20] Lincoln had embraced colonization in his early political career, which he carried into the Civil War era. In large part, the debate revitalized in 1862 as the United States inched closer to emancipation as a war policy. Civilian and military decision makers had to determine what to deal with the freed population as the war dragged on and slaves made their way to US lines. In April 1862, Lincoln met with representatives from Liberia, which some newspapers misconstrued as an investigation into colonization, a rumor Lincoln vehemently denied. Nevertheless, he did consider and initially support colonization projects in the Caribbean and Central America, much to the resentment of local leaders in the regions.[21] Even with emancipation, the removal, voluntarily or compulsorily, of Africans from the United States lingered into the end of the century.

By the later nineteenth century, Booker T. Washington claimed, "Somebody else conceived the idea of colonizing the coloured people, of getting territory where nobody lives, putting the coloured people there, and letting them be a nation all by themselves." Washington objected to the proposal. He pointed to the irony that white people desired Africans in the United States to return to Africa, but he argued, "If you were to build ten walls around Africa to-day you could not keep the white people out." Despite claiming respect for those advocating an escape from southern discrimination in the United States, Washington cautioned that European racism, exploitation, and land/resource hunger would make African people migrating back to the continent just as likely to suffer from discrimination or worse. He pointed to Cecile Rhodes and Henry M. Stanley as examples of that exploitation. After chronicling the various

---

[20] Preliminary Emancipation Proclamation, September 22, 1862 Document available at www.archives.gov.

[21] Eric Foner, *The Fiery Trial: Abraham Lincoln and American Slavery* (New York: W. W. Norton, 2010), 221–224. Also see Phillip W. Magness and Sebastian N. Page, *Colonization After Emancipation Lincoln and the Movement for Black Resettlement* (Columbia: University of Missouri Press, 2011).

European colonial enterprises in Africa and the lack of empty, unclaimed territory remaining, Washington advised that a return to Africa was not going to bring a change in status and called on his fellow blacks to tackle the struggle for equality at home.[22]

Regardless of Washington's warnings, a small group of individuals decided to depart the United States. Ironically, as thousands wanted to enter the promised land of freedom and economic opportunity, others realized the country's oppressive nature and determined to escape. Liberia attracted many in the United States who desired to return to Africa being a country run by people of African-decent and the local government offered free land to settlers. In addition, Liberia could allow an escape from the lynchings Africans faced in the United States and the serious economic downturn of cotton prices. As historian Kenneth C. Barnes notes, "Liberia represented a chance for a better life for the South's black farmers." About a third of all the black migrants from the US South to Liberia between 1879 and 1899 were from Arkansas. However, only about 600 Arkansans made the journey to Africa. The movement to return people to Africa was formalized with the Liberian Exodus Joint Stock Steamship Company, which by 1878 raised $6000 and purchased a vessel in Boston, the *Azor*, to take people back to Africa. The maiden voyage of the *Azor* carried 206 individuals back to Africa; however, the cost of the project exceeded the financial resources of its backers, preventing a second trip. Even with these failures, the notion of returning to Africa did not die and even by 1913, projects were underway for the resettlement of Africans from the United States to Africa.[23] The return migration was miniscule in comparison with the millions forced to the Americas. Nevertheless, the Atlantic was a two-way street and to escape economic crisis and oppression some Africans looked to the opportunity their ancestors' home continent provided.

Despite his misgivings about colonization in Africa both by European powers and individuals of Africans decent in the United States, Booker T. Washington was not shy about bringing his agricultural expertise to bear on behalf of the imperial powers in Africa, creating an intellectual reverse migration. Washington gained an international reputation

---

[22] Booker T. Washington, *The Future of the American Negro* (Boston, MA: Small, Maynard and Company, 1899), 158–164.

[23] Kenneth C. Barnes, *Journey of Hope: The Back-to-Africa Movement in Arkansas in the Late 1800s* (Chapel Hill: University of North Carolina Press, 2004), 2, 11, 179.

with his skill-based teaching at Tuskegee Institute. Upon request by the German Imperial government, individuals from the Tuskegee Institute traveled to the German colony of Togo to bring their knowledge about cotton growing and associated labor practices to Togo in order to help develop a sound economy. It was certainly an odd combination that Washington's Tuskegee Institute engaged in. Having suffered from slavery, oppression, economic exploitation, segregation, and racial violence, they joined forces with a state that had only in the late 1840s abolished serfdom and whose record with non-German ethnic groups was not dissimilar to how white southerners treated the black population in the United States. Despite its own racism, the German political leadership realized they could learn much from the southern states to increase the agricultural output of its West African colony.[24]

When Washington spoke in 1895 at the Atlanta International Cotton State Exposition in the audience was the German agricultural attaché, Baron Beno von Herman auf Wain who used the opportunity to report to Berlin about the cotton economy in the southern states of the United States. Besides realizing that blacks in the United States possessed important knowledge about the cultivation of cotton, he also noted that the German colonial people would work for significantly lower wages, making German colonial cotton more profitable. Herman approached Washington during a speaking engagement of the latter in Boston in the summer of 1900 and requested "two negro-cottonplanters and one negro-mechanic" who could teach the population of Togo about cotton planting. James Nathan Calloway, Allen Lynn Burks, Shepherd Lincoln Harris, and John Winfrey Robinson agreed to go to Togo and assist the German government. As the leader of the group, Calloway had extensive experience with training people and planting cotton. Furthermore, as a graduate of Fisk University, he was well connected with the black leadership in the United States.[25] This was certainly not a mass migration of people, but like in so many other moments of the Atlantic world, essential knowledge about agricultural production traversed the Atlantic with people. While all three parts of the Atlantic framework were involved,

---

[24] Andrew Zimmerman, *Alabama in Africa: Booker T. Washington, the German Empire, and the Globalization of the New South* (Princeton, NJ: Princeton University Press, 2010), 1–4.

[25] Ibid., 4–6.

the players were different, and it was an unusual reverse migration of people and knowledge.

Once in Lomé, the capital of the Togo colony, the four men set to work on their project to cultivate cotton. Two separate experimental cotton estates were put into operation. In 1902, another five Tuskegee students traveled to Togo to join the operations; however, two died when their landing craft capsized in the rough surf. In addition, tropical disease and exhaustion took their toll on the arrivals from Alabama. By 1904, all the Tuskegee educators had either died or returned home. Nevertheless, this small group left a significant legacy on Togo's landscape. Their cotton project paid off well. The educational institutions established by the Tuskegee faculty remained in existence until the colony changed hands to the French in 1914 and remain in operation today. The cotton variations created by the Tuskegee group for Africa had an impact beyond the German colony.[26] Members of Tuskegee in Africa followed a long-established trajectory of African migration back and forth across the Atlantic.

Africans suffered unspeakable humiliation as a result of the slave trade. The story of Equiano brought awareness to the inhumanity slaves faced on board the ships carrying them to the Americas. Regardless of the growing challenges to the slave trade by the late eighteenth and early nineteenth century, the outlawing of the trade hardly stopped the lucrative business in human beings. One-third of the slaves, who arrives in the New World, arrived during the nineteenth century, as pressure mounted to prevent their sailing. Therefore, not only the slave experience, but also the slave trade remained an integral part of the African participation in the Atlantic world. The suffering continued, even with the small yet continuous movement of Africans back to their continent of origin. This return migration was an early approach to abolition, to remove the freed population back to Africa. While the American Colonization Society's experiment in Liberia was of mixed results and many abolitionists opposed the idea of a repatriation of freedmen, the notion of leaving the Americas for Africa, to escape racial oppression never went away. Even by the end of the nineteenth century, some Africans contemplated voluntary migration to Africa, some like the Tuskegee faculty even saw it in an uplifting of the African people spirit. Africans had been instrumental in

---

[26] Ibid., 6–8.

making the Atlantic world and they continued to do so in the nineteenth century. The interconnectedness of the nineteenth-century Atlantic dramatically altered African experiences, be that in the continuation of the slave trade, in the possibility to return to Africa, or to assist colonial efforts in Africa with agricultural knowledge. Africa and Africans still lived in a world dramatically different as a result of their connection with the Atlantic trade and political networks.

Bibliography

Barnes, Kenneth C. *Journey of Hope: The Back-to-Africa Movement in Arkansas in the Late 1800s*. Chapel Hill: University of North Carolina Press, 2004.
Bergad, Laird W. *Comparative Histories of Slavery in Brazil, Cuba, and the United States*. New York: Cambridge University Press, 2007.
Bethell, Leslie. *The Abolition of the Brazilian Slave Trade: Britain, Brazil and the Slave Trade Question, 1807–1869*. Cambridge, UK: Cambridge University Press, 1970.
Bevans, Charles I., ed. *Treaties and Other International Agreements of the United States of America, 1776–1949*. Washington, DC: U.S. Government Printing Office, 1969.
Blanchard, Peter. *Slavery and Abolition in Early Republican Peru*. Wilmington, DE: Scholarly Resources, 1992.
Brinch, Boyrereau, and Benjamin F. Prentiss. *The Blind African Slave, or Memoirs of Boyrereau Brinch*. St. Albans, VT: Harry Whitney, 1810.
Burin, Eric. *Slavery and the Peculiar Solution: A History of the American Colonization Society*. Gainesville: University Press of Florida, 2005.
Canney, Donald L. *Africa Squadron: The U.S. Navy and the Slave Trade, 1842–1861*. Washington, DC: Potomac Books, 2006.
Ciment, James. *Another America: The Story of Liberia and the Former Slaves Who Ruled It*. New York: Hill and Wang, 2013.
Equiano, Olaudah. *The Interesting Narrative of Olaudah Equiano: Or Gustavus Vassa, the African*. London: Printed for, and sold by the author, 1794.
Foner, Eric. *The Fiery Trial: Abraham Lincoln and American Slavery*. New York: W. W. Norton, 2012.
Freehling, William W. *The Road to Disunion*. 2 vols. New York: Oxford University Press, 1990, 2007.
Grindal, Peter. *Opposing the Slavers: The Royal Navy's Campaign Against the Atlantic Slave Trade*. London, UK: I. B. Tauris, 2016.
Hegarty, Aidan. *John Mitchel: A Cause Too Many*. Belfast, UK: Camlane Press, 2005.

James, Winston. *The Struggles of John Brown Russwurm: The Life and Writings of a Pan-Africanist Pioneer, 1799–1851*. New York: New York University Press, 2010.

Lloyd, Christopher. *The Navy and the Slave Trade: The Suppression of the African Slave Trade in the Nineteenth Century*. London, UK: Longmans, Green, 1949.

Magness, Phillip W., and Sebastian N. Page. *Colonization After Emancipation Lincoln and the Movement for Black Resettlement*. Columbia: University of Missouri Press, 2011.

Myers, Philip E. *Caution and Cooperation: The American Civil War in British–American Relations*. Kent, OH: Kent State University Press, 2008.

Quinn, James. *John Mitchel*. Dublin, Ireland: University College Dublin Press, 2008.

Robertson, Charles G., ed. *Select Statutes, Cases and Documents to Illustrate English Constitutional History, 1660–1832: With a Supplement from 1832–1894*. London, UK: Methuen, 1904.

Temperley, Howard. *White Dreams, Black Africa: The Antislavery Expedition to the Niger, 1841–1842*. New Haven: Yale University Press, 1991.

Tomek, Beverly C. *Colonization and Its Discontents Emancipation, Emigration, and Antislavery in Antebellum Pennsylvania*. New York: New York University Press, 2011.

Washington, Booker T. *The Future of the American Negro*. Boston, MA: Small, Maynard and Company, 1899.

Yarema, Allan. *The American Colonization Society: An Avenue to Freedom?* Lanham, MD: University Press of America, 2006.

Zimmerman, Andrew. *Alabama in Africa: Booker T. Washington, the German Empire, and the Globalization of the New South*. Princeton, NJ: Princeton University Press, 2010.

CHAPTER 8

Emancipation

> We can and should discuss whether abolition should be simultaneous or gradual. We advocate simultaneous abolition and with indemnification paid immediately because we believe that it is best to end the old system and begin another, unburdened and aided by the ten million pesos that will enter the country.—José Julián Acosta y Calbo[1]

The nineteenth century was a period of great change for people of African descent within the Atlantic World. In the Americas and Africa, they struggled to shed the bonds of slavery and gain their freedom. Human bondage created the Atlantic world, its plantations with their cash crop agricultural system dramatically transformed every part of the region. According to historian Thomas Benjamin, the end of slavery undermined the cohesive nature of the Atlantic world. However, the transition from slavery to freedom was not an easy one, often wrought with conflict and suffering. People of African descent were active participants in obtaining their own freedom, often fighting on the frontlines of those conflict. However, emancipation of human property frequently was a top-down affair determined by distant governments with little interest in assisting freedpeople or in making sure freedpeople had an economic and political future. As the quote above by José Julián Acosta

---

[1] José Julián Acosta y Calbo, quoted in Christopher Schmidt-Nowara, *Empire and Antislavery: Spain, Cuba, and Puerto Rico, 1833–1874* (Pittsburgh, PA: University of Pittsburgh Press, 1999), 136.

© The Author(s) 2019
N. Eichhorn, *Atlantic History in the Nineteenth Century*,
https://doi.org/10.1007/978-3-030-27640-9_8

y Calbo, a Spanish supporter of emancipation, illustrates, there were two traditions of Atlantic emancipation during the nineteenth century: gradual and immediate. The century started with the embrace of gradual emancipation in the newly independent North American colonies. The events in French Saint-Domingue derailed the hope for a peaceful and slow transition when a massive slave rebellion raised the specter of violence and racial conflict as part of emancipation. Where the Saint-Domingue slave rebellion hindered emancipation debates for the first half of the nineteenth century, Great Britain altered the conversation with its gradual and compensated emancipation process, which greatly benefitted the planter aristocracy but left freedmen in a state of dependence. The precedent set by emancipation in the British Empire provided many Latin American countries with a new framework, how to shed one of the final vestiges of colonial rule, as the examples of Peru will illustrate below. Next, the United States altered the conversation one last time with the uncompensated and immediate emancipation of slaves in the course of the southern rebellion. With compensation off the table, the Spanish Empire in Cuba and Brazil eventually adopted the precedent set by the United States but avoided civil conflict to accomplish the freedom of people of African descent. At the same time, the end of slavery in the America was not accompanied by a similar push for abolition in Africa, where slavery continued, tolerated by European imperial powers. Abolition persisted as part of an Atlantic reform conversation.

Abolition permanently transformed the Atlantic world. Already during the colonial period slaves sought their freedom in the alien environment of the Americas by establishing maroon camps, which were a mainstay of slavery in the Americas. Primarily in the Caribbean, slaves escaped the harsh system of the plantations or mines and moved to the frontier areas of European colonization. In the Caribbean, maroons settled in the impassable interiors or isolated stretched of the coast. Whereas on the mainland, they went into hiding in the swampy and impassable areas on the coast or the colonial hinterland. Nevertheless, survival as self-liberated people was difficult since colonial authorities desired to stamp out the maroons's threat to slavery. In addition, the camps had to grow food for their survival, making them vulnerable.[2] Maroons were the first

---

[2] Sylviane A. Diouf, *Slavery's Exiles: The Story of the American Maroons* (New York University Press, 2014); Alvin O. Thompson, *Flight to Freedom: African Runaways and Maroons in the Americas* (Kingston, Jamaica: University of West Indies Press, 2006).

to seek their freedom within the colonial slave culture; nevertheless, it took the cataclysm of revolution to challenge the slave system on an Atlantic scale.

The enlightened insistence on the equality of man and inherent freedoms enjoyed by everybody questioned slavery's existence by the end of the eighteenth century. Despite religion having long served as a justification for slavery, by the second half of the eighteenth century, religious groups challenged the slave system. As early as the 1770s, groups in the BritishEmpire called for an end of human bondage and the trade in human beings. Particularly, Quakers worked to end the worst form of human bondage and human trafficking. However, even Quakers had come to abolition by a circuitous route, since many owned slaves themselves and felt the guilt of owning another human being. As early as 1688, Quakers protested the institution of slavery in Pennsylvania, but they remained a fringe movement until the next century. By the middle of the eighteenth century, London Quakers spoke out against the international slave trade and their Pennsylvania counterparts voiced their opposition to slaveholding itself.[3] Quakers were a cornerstone of the Atlantic abolition movement with communities in Europe and the Americas calling for an end of slavery.

Early abolition was by design a slow process, or a gradual abolition. In 1777, Vermont in the United States passed the country's first abolition law. Building on the enlightened ideals of liberty and equality, the state established "That all men are born equally free and independent, and have certain natural, inherent, and unalienable rights." Since slavery seemed counter to this spirit, the state leaders asserted that nobody "ought to be holden by law to serve any person as a servant, slave, or apprentice." The law declared individuals brought to the state in such manner free after they reached twenty-one for men and eighteen for women.[4] This gradual approach to emancipation was slow and, in some cases, like New Jersey, allowed slavery to survive for half a century. Many slaves were unwilling to wait that long when the promise of freedom finally emerged, leading to slave rebellion.

---

[3] Brycchan Carey and Geoffrey Plank, "Introduction," in *Quakers and Abolition*, eds. Brycchan Carey and Geoffrey Gilbert Plank (Urbana, IL: University of Illinois Press, 2014), 1–4; Seymour Drescher, *Abolition: A History of Slavery and Antislavery* (Cambridge, UK: Cambridge University Press, 2009), 128, 209–218.

[4] *The African Observer* [Philadelphia, PA], November 1827, 177.

The first transformative events for the abolition of slavery came when the French revolution in Saint-Domingue escalated into a slave rebellion. As news of the events in France arrived in Saint-Domingue, the white population and free people of color fought among each other for additional rights. The slave population initially remained excluded from this conversation, but as false rumors of emancipation being withheld by the planter elite circulated among the slave population, unrest took hold. On August 21, 1791, events escalated when slaves under the leadership of Dutty Boukman rebelled in the Northern Province of the colony. As the revolt for freedom from enslavement spread across the island and France got embroiled in international conflict with its European enemies, Saint-Domingue was an easy target. Faced with civil unrest and foreign invasion, one of the revolutionary commissioners to the colony decided to enlist the assistance of the rebelling population. Léger Félicité Sonthonax established that "All Negroes and people of mixed blood currently enslaved are declared free and will enjoy all rights pertaining to French citizenship. They will, however, be subject to a regimen described in the following articles." Even after Sonthonax promised freedom to the enslaved population, he required plantation slaves to remain on their master's estate. If a plantation slave desired to leave for another position before the annual contract expired, he/she needed the permission of the local magistrate. Besides freedom, there were some small advances such as the outlawing of whipping and payment for agricultural labor.[5] Sonthonax and French Saint-Domingue transformed the process of emancipation with slave rebellion bringing about emancipation.

Saint-Domingue cast an even larger shadow over the Atlantic world. As the people of Saint-Domingue and its tropical climate wreaked havoc on the foreign occupation forces, events in France took a turn toward conservativism. With Napoleon Bonaparte, Saint-Domingue faced the nightmare of slavery's reestablishment. Aware of the desolate economic situation created by emancipation and social upheavals, Charles Victoire Emmanuel Leclerc, the new commander in Saint-Domingue, suggested to Napoleon, "Attempting to smash quickly this idol of liberty, in whose name so much blood has been shed, might mean starting all over again." He advised Napoleon against the reestablishment of slavery at the time to avoid unnecessary bloodshed. By May 1802, Napoleon, nevertheless,

---

[5] David Patrick Geggus, ed., *The Haitian Revolution: A Documentary History* (Indianapolis, IN: Hackett Publishing, 2014), 107–109.

decided to reestablish slavery in the colonies, erasing ten years of freedom for the formerly enslaved population.[6] The abolition of slavery in Saint-Domingue set a hazardous precedent. Emancipation became associated with violence, race war, and socio-economic destruction.

Pro-Slavery advocates used the events in Saint-Domingue to their benefits. They could point to the violence and slave rebellion as specters of what would happen when people talked too freely about abolition. The influential writer Bryan Edwards in *Historical Survey of the French Colony of St. Domingo* listed the crimes or "horrors" as he called it suffered by the white population, including a "general massacre," the violation of white women, and other atrocities. Edwards, like many others, pointed to the causative relations between the publication of print material about abolition and slave rebellions. For pro-slavery advocates, the lessons of the events in Saint-Domingue were clear, talking about emancipation caused slave rebellion, violence, and murder of white people, followed by a decline in the economy.[7] In the paranoid mind of slaveholders, events in the second quarter of the nineteenth century confirmed that causation.

The abolition debates transformed once more in 1831 when William Lloyd Garrison published the first edition of *The Liberator*. In contrast to the colonization scheme embraced in the United States by groups like the American Colonization Society, Garrison promoted a new approach to emancipation, immediatism. Garrison was born on December 12, 1805, into a merchant family and grew up in Massachusetts. He gained early experiences as co-editor of the *Genius of Universal Emancipation* in Baltimore, Maryland. He was an outspoken critic of slavery and the domestic slave trade.[8] On January 1, 1831, the first issue of Garrison's new paper appeared in Boston. *The Liberator* called for an immediate end of slavery and no colonization of freedmen in Africa. In his first column, Garrison wrote that "Assenting to the 'self-evident truth' maintained in the American Declaration of Independence, 'that all men are created equal, and endowed by their Creator with certain inalienable

[6] Ibid., 172.

[7] Edward B. Rugemer, *The Problem of Emancipation: The Caribbean Roots of the American Civil War* (Baton Rouge: Louisiana State University Press, 2008), 50–52.

[8] William L. Garrison, "Comments on John B. Russwurm Going to Liberia," *The Liberator* [Boston, MA], May 7, 1831; Henry Mayer, *All on Fire: William Lloyd Garrison and the Abolition of Slavery* (New York: St. Martin's Press, 1998), 51–54, 84–91.

rights – among which are life, liberty and the pursuit of happiness,' I shall strenuously contend for the immediate enfranchisement of our slave population." Garrison refused to stop until the slave population in the United States was free. He promised to be "as harsh as truth, and as uncompromising as justice." Garrison created a new language and founded the New-England Anti-Slavery Society in January 1832, which became the cornerstone of the American Anti-Slavery Society. Garrison's radical views eventually included support for women's right as well as political rights for African Americans, which created a rupture in the abolition movement. The break manifested forcefully during the World Anti-Slavery Convention in Londonwhen Garrison unsuccessfully supported the attendance of women. Moderate reformers, including the Tappan brothers, distanced themselves from Garrison and formed the American and Foreign Anti-Slavery Society.[9]

The anti-slavery movement relied on African Americans to illustrate the dehumanizing effects of slavery. Most notably, Frederick Douglass provided a unique voice to the movement. Douglass spent his first twenty years as a slave in Maryland until he escaped in September 1838 on the Philadelphia, Wilmington and Baltimore Railroad. He made his way to New York City, where he married, and then continued to Massachusetts. He took a keen interested in the anti-slavery movement. After some coaching, he became a powerful orator relying on his first-hand experiences with slavery. In 1845, Douglass published his account, an instant bestseller. His newfound fame made him a target for slave catchers. As a result, Douglass went on his first tour of Ireland and Great Britain, where for two years he gave a series of speeches and met with such anti-slave trade voices like Thomas Clarkson. Douglass, just like the abolition movement itself, was an Atlantic abolitionist. He did not visit continental Europe because the anti-slavery movement was primarily an Anglo-US development. Others, like Georgia's Ellen and William Craft, followed his example to avoid slave catchers.[10]

[9] William L. Garrison, "To the Public," *The Liberator* [Boston, MA], January 1, 1831; Mayer, *All on Fire*, 231–239, 281–285, 288–293.

[10] For works on the transatlantic odysseys of former slaves see Frederick Douglass, *My Bondage and My Freedom* (Auburn, NY: Miller, Orton, 1857); Tom Chaffin, *Giant's Causeway: Frederick Douglass's Irish Odyssey and the Making of an American Visionary* (Charlottesville: University of Virginia Press, 2014); Ellen Craft and William Craft, *Running a Thousand Miles for Freedom: Or, the Escape of William and Ellen Craft from Slavery*, ed. Richard J. M. Blackett (Baton Rouge: Louisiana State University Press, 1999, 1860).

Criticisms of slavery did not sit well with slaveholders in the United States, who increasingly feared a repetition of the slave uprising in Saint-Domingue. Henry Nott of South Carolina College worried "Europe is against us, & the North is against us … Incendiary publication" could encourage revolt and "open rebellion and secret poison." Similarly, Arthur P. Hayne of South Carolina wrote that only "if the Non-Slave-Holding States … will come forward patriotically, generously, and fairly and unite with the South to prevent Insurrection and to organize a moral power in favour of the South—*then and only then will the south be safe.*" The perception expressed by Nott and Hayne was widespread in the southern states after 1831. On August 21, 1831, Nat Turner, a slave, led a slave uprising in Southampton County in southeastern Virginia. Armed with knives, hatchets, and axes, about 70 slaves invaded plantation homes and killed some sixty white residents. As soon as news of the uprising spread, the white south went into a hysterical defense of the institution. Turner and his companions were hunted down. Mob violence ruled as southerners held the image of the rebellion of Saint-Domingue in their minds. Resisting emancipation, southern slaveholders found much evidence in the Caribbean basin to justify the continuation of slavery.[11]

Regardless of the defensiveness of US planters, slave rebellions usually reminded authorities about the need to change policies. On December 25, 1831, slaves in the British colony of Jamaica rose up, in what became an eight-day rebellion of about one-fifth of the slaves on the island. The leader of the revolt was Samuel Sharpe, a Baptist minister and missionary to the slave population. Missionaries and abolitionists worked closely together, raising new fears among the planters. As a result, missionaries among the slaves talked about abolition and freedom. The Baptist War was in part an uprising by the slaves to demand better working conditions in the face of a shrinking supply of labor and general economic hardship on the island. Troops under the command of Sir Willoughby

---

[11] Nott to Hammond, March 8, 1836, Hammond Paper, Hayne to Jackson, March 8, 1836, Jackson Papers, quoted in William W. Freehling, *Road to Disunion* (New York: Oxford University Press, 1990), 1:293; David F. Allmendinger, *Nat Turner and the Rising in Southampton County* (Baltimore, MD: Johns Hopkins University Press, 2014), 136–214; Herbert Aptheker, *Nat Turner's Slave Rebellion* (New York: American Institute for Marxist Studies, 1966), 51–58; Patrick H. Breen, *The Land Shall Be Deluged in Blood: A New History of the Nat Turner Revolt* (New York: Oxford University Press, 2015).

Cotton quickly defeated the slaves and the ruling planters engaged in brutal retaliations with the death toll exceeded 500 slaves. In the colony, missionaries and slaves came under closer supervision to prevent a similar incident from reoccurring as planters adopted a defensive posture. Meanwhile, in the mother country, the authorities reacted differently.[12]

Having lead the way with the closure of the slave trade, freedom-loving Great Britain could no longer reconcile slavery with its socio-political identity. Three days after the death of William Wilberforce, the architect of the anti-slave trade law, on August 1, 1833, Parliament passed a law abolishing slavery. Only slaves under six gained their freedom immediately. All others became apprentices and continued to work for their old masters until 1840, when they finally gained their freedom. The wait was to allow slaves time to adjust and slowly transition from slavery to freedom. Slaves received their freedom and masters received part of the £20 million compensation allocated for property lost. With resistance to the delay in emancipation, full emancipation occurred on August 1, 1838. Slavery ended in the British Empire. Great Britain set a new example, illustrating that emancipation could be peaceful and not ruin the plantation economy.[13] Many other countries over the next twenty years followed the example of compensated emancipation.

In Latin America, slavery had been on the decline since the wars of independence but continued to exist. During the wars, both sides offered freedom to any slave who joined their cause. The promise was mostly honored, but not every slave gained freedom. Chile, Mexico, and the Central American states abolished the institution shortly after independence; the majority of the new states retained a small slave population and resisted the idea of complete and immediate abolition. Free womb laws, a slow gradual approach to emancipation, where slaves born

---

[12] Mary Reckord, "The Jamaican Slave Rebellion of 1831," *Past and Present* 40 (July 1968), 108–125; Mary Turner, *Slaves and Missionaries: The Disintegration of Jamaican Slave Society, 1787–1834* (Kingston, Jamaica: Press University of the West Indies, 1998), 148–178.

[13] Claudius K. Fergus, *Revolutionary Emancipation: Slavery and Abolitionism in the British West Indies* (Baton Rouge: Louisiana State University Press, 2013), 181–198. Furthermore, modern scholarship on emancipation takes a nuances look at the variety of factors that contributed to the end of slavery. However, there remains the ground breaking work of Eric Williams, *Capitalism and Slavery* (Chapel Hill: University of North Carolina Press, 1944) which makes the argument that purely economic factors caused the rethinking of slavery as a labor system.

after a certain date were freed upon reaching a specified age, put slavery on a path toward extinction across the Americas, but such an approach could take a long time. In New Jersey, which adopted gradual emancipation in 1804, the last slaves gained their freedom in 1865 as a result of the Thirteenth Amendment to the US Constitution. However, slavery could have lasted until 1892, when Jinny, a former slave died.[14] Free womb laws could take almost a century to eradicate slavery. Those Latin American countries that retained slavery after independence faced a growing challenge by the middle of the century to finally act against the inhuman institution of bondage.

Slaves were not treated any better in Peru or Colombia than they were in the United States or on the sugar islands, but there were many legal loopholes slaves could use to their benefit. While the United States debated the territorial expansion of slavery in the aftermath of the war with Mexico, Latin American countries too debated the future of slavery. Latin American abolition debates were never as heated and violent as in North America. In part, this was due to the relative absence of anti-slavery societies, which if they even existed were smaller than in the northern regions.[15] Furthermore, abolition often occurred, much like later in the United States, in the context of a civil war. Peru is an illustrative example.

Peru had a relatively small slave population. Nevertheless, many slaveholders considered slavery essential to the country's economy, fearing economic problems if slavery ended. In contrast to the North American slave societies, the Peruvian legal system offered many opportunities for slaves to sue and obtain their freedom. Sickness or mistreatment were often used by slaves to sue to have their value reduced, thus making it easier for them to buy their freedom. Much like in the Caribbean, where Chinese and Indian workers became an essential labor force even before the end of slavery, so too did Chinese coolies, as well as Germans, and Irish immigrants replace slaves in Peru. However, neither Irish nor German immigrants accepted treatment equal to indentured servitude or

---

[14] George R. Andrews, *Afro-Latin America, 1800–2000* (New York: Oxford University Press, 2004), 55–67; James J. Gigantino, *The Ragged Road to Abolition: Slavery and Freedom in New Jersey, 1775–1865* (Philadelphia: University of Pennsylvania Press, 2014), 240–251.

[15] Andrews, *Afro-Latin America*, Chapters 2–3; Peter Blanchard, *Slavery and Abolition in Early Republican Peru* (Wilmington, DE: Scholarly Resources, 1992), Chapter 4.

slavery. Slave owners continued to view slavery as a viable labor practice. They, therefore, looked for ways to replenish their labor supply, such as the reopening of the slave trade.[16] Considering the resilience of slavery in Latin America in the 1850s, the demise in Peru was eventually anticlimactic.

Much like in the United States, political rebellion brought slavery to its knees benefitting from the political instability and economic problems that plagued Peru. In late 1853, dissatisfied with the election victory of José Rufino Echenique Benavente, Domingo Elías revolted against the elected president. The initial rebellion suffered immediate setbacks. As a result, Elías contacted Ramón Castilla y Marquesado in the southern province of Arequipa. The two dissatisfied and ambitious politicians joined forces to bring about political change. Their cooperation provided the momentum needed for success. In an attempt to add strength to his side, Echenique promised freedom to any slave who joined his army. Castilla countered with a proclamation freeing all slaves.[17] Much like Lincoln's Emancipation Proclamation seven years hence, only victory in the war would bring freedom to the slaves.

Peru's emancipation edict followed largely the British example of compensation and assumed a high moral tone of humanity. Castilla's proclamation of December 3, 1854, established in the first sentence, "That it is due to justice to restore to man his freedom."[18] His political challenge was not just about gaining power but intended to "recognise and guarantee the rights of humanity, oppressed, denied, and scorned by the tribute of the Indian, and Slavery of the negro." The intent behind the proclamation looked humanitarian, not like the military order Abraham Lincoln eventually issued. Castilla blamed Echenique for holding back on emancipation and liberty because he "desired not to excite distrust respecting the indemnification due to the masters." Echenique was selfish in his demands and only interested in gaining additional soldiers for his cause; Castilla had a higher moral standard.

---

[16] Blanchard, *Slavery and Abolition*, Chapter 6.

[17] Ibid., Chapter 9; Mark Thurner, *From Two Republics to One Divided: Contradictions of Postcolonial Nationmaking in Andean Peru* (Durham, NC: Duke University Press, 1997), 44–47.

[18] "Emancipation Declared in Peru," *Anti-slavery Reporter* [London, UK], July 2, 1855, 154.

Powerfully, the Castilla government decreed "The men and women held until the present time in Peru as slaves, or serving freedmen, whether in that condition by sale or birth, and in whichever mode held in servitude, perpetual or temporary—all, without distinction of age, are from this day wholly and for ever free." This was not a gradual approach like in the British colonies or halfhearted one like in the United States. Castilla radically demolished the remains of slave society in Peru with the stroke of his pen. Even more, Castilla promised that the Peruvian government would take care of the "old and infirm." The only exemption was for "those slaves or servants shall be debarred from freedom who take up arms to sustain the tyranny of Don Jose Rufino Echineque, who made war against the liberties of the people." To put the slave owners at ease, Castilla promised fair compensation for the property lost. As in every post-emancipation society, slaves gained little besides their freedom. Castilla's government, like the British government, compensated slave owners for their lost property. Peru's competing political faction had ended slavery because of political needs during a time of war and therefore failed to provide any benefits to the freed population.

Similarly, emancipation in the United States was a war measure to win a political conflict, but neither did Lincoln embrace the same moral language that Castilla used nor did the country compensate masters for lost property. During the early 1850s, slavery was a hotly debated issue in the United States. The organization of the remainder of the Louisiana Purchase and opening of the territory to popular sovereignty, where the settlers determined the future of slavery in the territory spelled the end of the Whig party as well as undermined the political future of the Know-Nothing/American party thus paving the way for the sectional Republican party.[19] The territorial slavery question not only brought

---

[19] For work see Frederick J. Blue, *No Taint of Compromise: Crusaders in Antislavery Politics* (Baton Rouge: Louisiana State University Press, 2005); Eric Foner, *Free Soil Free Labor Free Men: The Ideology of the Republican Party Before the Civil War* (New York: Oxford University Press, 1970); Freehling, *The Road to Disunion*; William E. Gienapp, *The Origins of the Republican Party, 1852–1856* (New York: Oxford University Press, 1987); Michael F. Holt, *The Political Crisis of the 1850s* (New York: Wiley, 1978); David M. Potter, *The Impending Crisis, 1848–1861* (New York: Harper Perennial, 1976); Roger L. Ransom, *Conflict and Compromise: The Political Economy of Slavery, Emancipation, and the American Civil War* (New York: Cambridge University Press, 1989); Elizabeth R. Varon, *Disunion! The Coming of the American Civil War, 1789–1859* (Chapel Hill: University of North Carolina Press, 2008).

about a political realignment, but also foreshadowed the coming of civil war in the United States with violent clashes in the Kansas Territory between pro- and anti-slavery settlers. The authorities in Washington were not prepared to deal with the situation.[20] Despite the relative absence of slaves from Kansas Territory, southerners perceived Kansas's addition as a slave state essential for the future prosperity of their section.

The slavery-related disagreements between the two sections manifested during the election of 1860. Southern states at the Democratic National Convention in Charleston, South Carolina, demanded some form of national protection for slavery. Unable to agree, the Democratic party ran campaigns in the southern half with a southern candidate and in the northern half with a northern candidate. The split of the only remaining national party allowed for the election victory of Abraham Lincoln and new the Republican party. Fearful, that the sectional party president would destroy slavery, South Carolina, followed by ten other slave states, seceded from the Union. The Vice-President of the new Confederate States of America explained that the secession of the southern states was to defend slavery. In his "Corner Stone Speech," Alexander Stephens asserted "Our new government is founded upon exactly the opposite idea; its foundations are laid, its corner-stone rests, upon the great truth that the negro is not equal to the white man; that slavery subordination to the superior race is his natural and normal condition."[21] Therefore, all grievances and demands among the southern states were part of the defense of slavery.

President Lincoln was cautious not to embrace emancipation as a war goal as long as the loyalty of the slave-holding border states, like Kentucky, Missouri, and Maryland, remained in question. As the war dragged on, Confederate forces used the labor of slaves in the war effort, forcing the Union to strategically rethink their policies and embrace emancipation as a moral justification and military tool. Following the stalemate at the Battle of Antietam/Sharpsburg on September 17,

---

[20] For works related to Kansas and the West in Civil War causation, see Nicole Etcheson, *Bleeding Kansas: Contested Liberty in the Civil War Era* (Lawrence: University Press of Kansas, 2004); Michael A. Morrison, *Slavery and the American West: The Eclipse of Manifest Destiny and the Coming of the Civil War* (Chapel Hill: University of North Carolina Press, 1999).

[21] Henry Cleveland, *Alexander H. Stephens in Public and Private: With Letters and Speeches, Before, During, and Since the War* (Philadelphia, PA: National Publishing Company, 1886), 717–729.

1862, Lincoln issued the Preliminary Emancipation Proclamation on September 22, 1862. From the outset, Lincoln made perfectly clear that his goal was about "practically restoring the constitutional relation between the United States, and each of the states, and the people thereof, in which states that relation is, or may be suspended, or disturbed." The president still toyed with colonization and compensation for slave owners, embracing both the peculiar history of the US abolitionist movement and the way abolition had been done thus far. Nevertheless, Lincoln announced in unequivocal words "That on the first day of January ... one thousand eight hundred and sixty-three, all persons held as slaves within any state, or designated part of a state, the people whereof shall then be in rebellion against the United States shall be then, thenceforward, and forever free." Compared with Castilla's emancipation, Lincoln's was halfhearted and gave the seceded states three months to return to the Union and thus retain their slaves.[22] Despite Lincoln issuing the Emancipation Proclamation on January 1, 1863, setting free slaves in the rebelling territories, Congress had to pass and states had to ratify the Thirteenth Amendment to finally end slavery in the United States.[23]

Emancipation in the United States placed the two remaining slave societies in Brazil and the Spanish Empire on notice, but over twenty years passed before either acted. Brazil had only in 1850 abolished the slave trade and Cuba followed sixteen years later when the British–US anti-slave trade treaty eliminated remaining loopholes that had made the trade possible. As early as the 1820s, anti-slave trade advocates emerged in Cuba suggesting the "whitening" of society by encouraging European migration. Meanwhile, Spain abolished slavery on the Spanish Peninsula in 1837.[24] Finally, in the 1860s, an abolitionist movement emerged in

---

[22] Abraham Lincoln, "Preliminary Draft of Final Emancipation Proclamation," in *The Collected Works of Abraham Lincoln*, ed. Roy P. Basler (New Brunswick, NJ: Rutgers University Press, 1953), 6:23–26, 28–31; Eric Foner, *The Fiery Trial: Abraham Lincoln and American Slavery* (New York: W. W. Norton, 2012), 206–290; Edna G. Medford, *Lincoln and Emancipation* (Carbondale: Southern Illinois University Press, 2015), 61–74.

[23] Patrick R. Cleburne, "Negro Enlistment Proposal," in *The War of the Rebellion: A Compilation of Official Records* (Washington, DC: Government Printing Office), Series I, vol. 52, Part 2, 586–592.

[24] Laird W. Bergad, *Comparative Histories of Slavery in Brazil, Cuba, and the United States* (New York: Cambridge University Press, 2007), 275–276.

Spain and its colonies. Furthermore, especially in Cuba, there was growing resentment of Spanish colonial rule. The anger culminated in 1868 in the Guerra de los Diez Años. Carlos Manuel de Céspedes del Castillo led the uprising against the Spanish in Cuba. In the Declaration of Yara, on December 27, 1868, Céspedes condemned slavery but accepted the existence of the institution. Nevertheless, he decreed all slaves free who wished to enlist in the army but prevented from doing so by their masters. The war ended with Cuba gaining greater autonomy under the Pact of Zanjón but slavery remained in existence for the moment.[25] Both sides in the conflict had considered the joined future of slavery and the island, requiring action by the Spanish government once the war was over.

Already during the *Guerra de los Diez Años*, the Spanish government determined to address the slavery issue to counter the emancipation decree issued by the rebel faction. In 1870, the Moret Law, named after Segismundo Moret y Pendergast, took effect and provided freedom to all slave children born after September 1868. However, this gradual approach to emancipation was no longer acceptable. The Pact of Zanjón, which ended the Guerra de los Diez Años, was followed by an emancipation decree by the Spanish government in 1880, which transformed slavery into a patronato, a type of apprenticeship common in post-emancipation society. Slavery ended in name but the masters' prerogatives remained. The law allowed slaves to purchase their freedom. By 1886, the number of patronato declined to 25,381 from a slave population of 199,094 in 1877.[26] That year the Spanish Empire determined to finally end slavery, including the patronato.

In Brazil, the process was drawn out significantly longer, combining both internal and external conflicts. The war between Brazil, part of the Triple Alliance, and Paraguay in the 1860s brought about a rethinking regarding slavery. Paraguay emancipated its slave population in the course of the war and Brazilian forces resorted to conscripting slaves when volunteers dried up. By the 1860s, Emperor Dom Pedro desired to free Brazil from slavery. He followed through by freeing the slaves owned by the state and ordered an end to whippings of slaves as a punishment in 1864. Three years later, a proposed law called for the end

---

[25] Bergad, *Comparative Histories of Slavery*, 282; Schmidt-Nowara, *Empire and Antislavery*, 127, 134, 162.

[26] Schmidt-Nowara, *Empire and Antislavery*, 137–138, 162.

of slavery by the end of the century. However, the law never passed.[27] Nevertheless, Brazil was slowly moving toward emancipation.

Like so many other slave societies, Brazil adopted a gradual approach to emancipation, slowly freeing the slave population. In 1871, José Paranhos, Viscount of Rio Branco, pushed through the Brazilian parliament the Rio Branco Law, a free womb law. All slave children born after September 28, 1871, gained their freedom upon reaching 28. The law provided for a slow and gradual demise of slavery and could have lasted another 60 or more years. In the first fifteen years of the law's existence, only 20,000 slaves gained their freedom. However, the domestic, political pressure for emancipation increased dramatically. Especially political leaders from the Northern Province embraced abolition since the slave population and cash crop agricultural focus shifted southward toward the coffee belt. By 1884, an abolition movement emerged in Rio de Janeiro and slave-free regions appeared where slave could run away too. Faced with growing opposition, abolition gained political support. On May 13, 1888, the Lei Áurea took effect in Brazil and permanently abolished slavery in the country.[28] The Lei Áurea was part of a broad political reform agenda in Brazil that a year later also ended the monarchy.

However, slavery was far from over in the Atlantic world when Brazil, as the last state in the Americas, abolished slavery. By the early nineteenth century, a new power arose in the African interior, the Sokoto Caliphate. Estimates claim that the caliphate had about 4 million slaves, more than any of the slave societies in the Americas. The slave population constituted about half of the caliphate's populace. Slaves labored on plantations around the empire producing food crops as well as indigo and cotton but not in the cash crop fashion as slaves in the Americas. Slavery in West Africa expanded in the course of the nineteenth century, but not because of an advancing agricultural frontier or a search for fresh cash crop land, but in large part because the Sokoto empire expanded its territorial and religious reach across the region. Just like in Europe's colonization of the Atlantic world, Sokoto justified the enslavement of defeated enemies in religious terms.[29] Sokoto had by mid-century developed a powerful slave base state.

---

[27] Bergab, *Comparative Histories of Slavery*, 284.

[28] Ibid., 285–287.

[29] Enrico Dal Lago, *American Slavery, Atlantic Slavery, and Beyond: The U.S. "Peculiar Institution" in International Perspective* (Boulder, CO: Paradigm Publishers, 2012), 65–66, 81.

At the same time, Sokoto's control of slaves was just as tenuous as that of planters in other parts of the Atlantic world. Religious revivals in the United States sparked immediate abolitionism; in the caliphate, slaves too embraced millennial movements to challenge the institution of slavery and their master's power. In 1900, slavery was still alive in the Sokoto Caliphate. By the first decade of the new century, Britain, France, and Germany carved the Sokoto Caliphate into parts of their emerging empires. Colonial rules prohibited the trade in slaves and enslavement of people but left those already enslaved in a legal gray area. In some colonies, slavery continued into the 1930s.[30] The champions of abolition were often reluctant to emancipate by the end of the century as new notions of white supremacy and white men's burdens justified imperial designs.

Where Great Britain lead the way within the Atlantic world on the issue of abolishing the slave trade and the emancipation of slavery, by the 1860s, British imperial policies required changes to this humanitarian attitude. When the British determined to establish a colonial presence in Lagos, they were about to integrate a region that relied heavily on slavery and the slave trade. Initially, British officials avoided the subject to maintain the new colony's economic stability. Since slavery was officially dead in the BritishEmpire, the Law Officers opinioned that annexation abolished slavery in Lagos. Nevertheless, British officials did not publicize the end of slavery and allowed slavery to naturally die out.[31] Despite the abolition of slavery in the Americas, slavery remained alive in Africa and thus part of the Atlantic world well into the twentieth century.

The involuntary movement of African people to the Americas and their suffering on plantations, in mines, or in urban environments characterized the Atlantic world. The spirit of reform to bring an end to the slave trade and slavery itself increased during the late eighteenth and early nineteenth century. The process of abolition transformed in the course of the century. Starting with the violence of the slave rebellion in Saint-Domingue, the institution of slavery faced a growing threat as slaves desired an immediate end to their enslavement, which undermined the pervious notion of a gradual abolition. However, the

---

[30] Ibid., 89–90, 179.
[31] Kristin Mann, *Slavery and the Birth of an African City: Lagos, 1760–1900* (Bloomington: Indiana University Press, 2010), 5.

violence associated with the events in Saint-Domingue worried many and allowed slaveholders to make powerful arguments against abolition. As the specter of abolition and slave rebellion loomed, the British dramatically altered the conversation, transforming the abolition story in the Atlantic world. The gradual and compensated abolition of slavery, which granted freedom to slaves, but not economic or political power, became a standard throughout the Americans. Having already assumed a moral high ground over the abolition of the slave trade, emancipation further increased the British role model function. Henceforth, abolition followed the British model as the example of Peru indicated, with slaveholders receiving compensation. However, gradualism was on the decline as the resilience of slave holders increased to maintain their property and the lucrative business, they engaged in. The rebellion in the United States signaled a new style in the abolition of slavery when President Lincoln ended slavery as a war measure in the territories in rebellion. Without compensation and immediately, the end of slavery was dramatic, rapid, and unprecedented. The end of slavery in the United States put Brazil and the Spanish Empire on notice, neither went through a civil war to emancipate the enslaved, but there was no compensation either. The irony in all this was that the moral power which led the way on abolition, Great Britain happily tolerated slavery in its new African colonies by the time Brazil and Cuba ended slavery in the Americas. The long struggle for emancipation during the nineteenth century culminated with all people of African descent in the Americas free. However, Africans in Africa face a much longer road ahead to gain that anticipated freedom. Abolition was an Atlantic debate and transformed the very nature of the Atlantic world away from enslavement and plantation agriculture.

BIBLIOGRAPHY

Allmendinger, David F. *Nat Turner and the Rising in Southampton County.* Baltimore, MD: Johns Hopkins University Press, 2014.

Andrews, George R. *Afro-Latin America, 1800–2000.* New York: Oxford University Press, 2004.

Aptheker, Herbert. *Nat Turner's Slave Rebellion.* New York: American Institute for Marxist Studies, 1966.

Basler, Roy P., ed. *The Collected Works of Abraham Lincoln.* New Brunswick, NJ: Rutgers University Press, 1953.

Bergad, Laird W. *Comparative Histories of Slavery in Brazil, Cuba, and the United States.* New York: Cambridge University Press, 2007.
Blanchard, Peter. *Slavery and Abolition in Early Republican Peru.* Wilmington, DE: Scholarly Resources, 1992.
Blue, Frederick J. *No Taint of Compromise: Crusaders in Antislavery Politics.* Baton Rouge: Louisiana State University Press, 2005.
Breen, Patrick H. *The Land Shall Be Deluged in Blood: A New History of the Nat Turner Revolt.* New York: Oxford University Press, 2015.
Carey, Brycchan, and Geoffrey Gilbert Plank, eds. *Quakers and Abolition.* Urbana, IL: University of Illinois Press, 2014.
Chaffin, Tom. *Giant's Causeway: Frederick Douglass's Irish Odyssey and the Making of an American Visionary.* Charlottesville: University of Virginia Press, 2014.
Cleveland, Henry. *Alexander H. Stephens in Public and Private: With Letters and Speeches, Before, During, and Since the War.* Philadelphia, PA: National Publishing Company, 1886.
Craft, Ellen, and William Craft. *Running a Thousand Miles for Freedom: Or, the Escape of William and Ellen Craft from Slavery.* Edited by Richard J. M. Blackett. Baton Rouge: Louisiana State University Press, 1999.
Dal Lago, Enrico. *American Slavery, Atlantic Slavery, and Beyond: The U.S. "Peculiar Institution" in International Perspective.* Boulder, CO: Paradigm Publishers, 2012.
Diouf, Sylviane A. *Slavery's Exiles: The Story of the American Maroons.* New York: New York University Press, 2014.
Douglass, Frederick. *My Bondage and My Freedom.* Auburn, NY: Miller, Orton, 1857.
Drescher, Seymour. *Abolition: A History of Slavery and Antislavery.* Cambridge, UK: Cambridge University Press, 2009.
Etcheson, Nicole. *Bleeding Kansas: Contested Liberty in the Civil War Era.* Lawrence: University Press of Kansas, 2004.
Fergus, Claudius K. *Revolutionary Emancipation: Slavery and Abolitionism in the British West Indies.* Baton Rouge: Louisiana State University Press, 2013.
Foner, Eric. *Free Soil Free Labor Free Men: The Ideology of the Republican Party Before the Civil War.* New York: Oxford University Press, 1970.
Foner, Eric. *The Fiery Trial: Abraham Lincoln and American Slavery.* New York: W. W. Norton, 2012.
Freehling, William W. *The Road to Disunion.* 2 vols. New York: Oxford University Press, 1990, 2007.
Geggus, David Patrick, ed. *The Haitian Revolution: A Documentary History.* Indianapolis, IN: Hackett Publishing, 2014.
Gienapp, William E. *The Origins of the Republican Party, 1852–1856.* New York: Oxford University Press, 1987.

Gigantino, James J. *The Ragged Road to Abolition: Slavery and Freedom in New Jersey, 1775–1865*. Philadelphia: University of Pennsylvania Press, 2014.
Holt, Michael F. *The Political Crisis of the 1850s*. New York: Wiley, 1978.
Mann, Kristin. *Slavery and the Birth of an African City: Lagos, 1760–1900*. Bloomington: Indiana University Press, 2010.
Mayer, Henry. *All on Fire: William Lloyd Garrison and the Abolition of Slavery*. New York: St. Martin's Press, 1998.
Medford, Edna G. *Lincoln and Emancipation*. Carbondale: Southern Illinois University Press, 2015.
Morrison, Michael A. *Slavery and the American West: The Eclipse of Manifest Destiny and the Coming of the Civil War*. Chapel Hill: University of North Carolina Press, 1999.
Potter, David M. *The Impending Crisis, 1848–1861*. New York: Harper Perennial, 1976.
Ransom, Roger L. *Conflict and Compromise: The Political Economy of Slavery, Emancipation, and the American Civil War*. New York: Cambridge University Press, 1989.
Reckord, Mary. "The Jamaican Slave Rebellion of 1831." *Past and Present* 40 (July 1968): 108–125.
Rugemer, Edward B. *The Problem of Emancipation: The Caribbean Roots of the American Civil War*. Baton Rouge: Louisiana State University Press, 2008.
Schmidt-Nowara, Christopher. *Empire and Antislavery: Spain, Cuba, and Puerto Rico, 1833–1874*. Pittsburgh, PA: University of Pittsburgh Press, 1999.
Thompson, Alvin O. *Flight to Freedom: African Runaways and Maroons in the Americas*. Kingston, Jamaica: University of West Indies Press, 2006.
Thurner, Mark. *From Two Republics to One Divided: Contradictions of Postcolonial Nationmaking in Andean Peru*. Durham, NC: Duke University Press, 1997.
Turner, Mary. *Slaves and Missionaries: The Disintegration of Jamaican Slave Society, 1787–1834*. Kingston, Jamaica: Press University of the West Indies, 1998.
Varon, Elizabeth R. *Disunion! The Coming of the American Civil War, 1789–1859*. Chapel Hill: University of North Carolina Press, 2008.
Williams, Eric. *Capitalism and Slavery*. Chapel Hill: University of North Carolina Press, 1944.

CHAPTER 9

Conquest of Frontiers

> What the Mediterranean Sea was to the Greeks, breaking the bond of custom, offering new experiences, calling out new institutions and activities, that, and more, the ever-retreating frontier has been to the United States directly, and to the nations of Europe more remotely. And now, four centuries from the discovery of America, at the end of a hundred years of life under the Constitution, the frontier has gone, and with its going has closed the first period of American history.[1]

The Atlantic world from its inception was about pushing back the frontiers to the unknown. Initially European explorers made their way down the African coast, across the Atlantic, and eventually into the interior of the Americas. Exploration was a key aspect of the advancing frontiers. Shortly after the explorers came the settlers. European settlers around the Atlantic advanced frontiers in a permanent and devastating fashion, coming into conflict with the indigenous peoples of the Americas and Africa. Even by the nineteenth century, blank spots and uncartographed regions remained that allowed explores to gain fame and recognition. Even worse for indigenous peoples, a growing stream of settlers flowed into the interiors, where settlers and indigenous people came into conflict. As settlers claimed indigenous land, they often fell for the propaganda that suggested the unlimited fertility of the frontier regions.

---

[1] Frederick J. Turner, *The Frontier in American History* (New York: Henry Holt, 1921), 39.

© The Author(s) 2019
N. Eichhorn, *Atlantic History in the Nineteenth Century*,
https://doi.org/10.1007/978-3-030-27640-9_9

However, as frontier promoters in Brazil and the United States suggest, there were voices of caution against the forces of nature. By the end of the century, as the words of historian Frederick Jackson Turner in Chicago highlight, the frontier in the United States had disappeared. In contrast, the frontier remained alive in South America and Africa. During the nineteenth century, across the Atlantic world, states struggled with the continued process of exploring the interiors of the continents around the Atlantic, as the examples of the Lewis and Clark expedition, the Peruvian Amazonian Cartography mission, and the search for Timbuktu illustrate. In addition, the perceived empty lands needed settling in the mind of many to put the land to proper use. Yet, even as some promoters called for settlement, others cautioned against settling arid regions without the proper resources for agriculture. Frontier settlers occupied the interiors often after taking arduous trips into the interiors, like the Mormons and Boer. As settlers flooded into the interiors, conflict with the indigenous populations occurred as the examples of the Plains people in North America, the Zulu of South Africa, and the indigenous people in Argentina and Chile will illustrate. Just like in the Early Modern period, the frontiers of the nineteenth-century Atlantic world were a region of conflict, a clash of the perceived civilized and barbaric, and the struggles continued to remake and define the states around the Atlantic.

Frontier history or Western History is a popular topic in the United States and the frontier deeply ingrained in US popular culture. However, comparative frontier histories are rare. Latin American historians have difficulty reconciling the idea of a frontier as outlined by Frederick Jackson Turner and the realities in Latin America. If applying the US census definition of two persons per square miles, then large parts of Latin America and Africa remain frontiers even today. In addition, Latin American historians, more interested in the social and cultural history of their ethnically diverse countries, have not paid close attention to the inward movement of people. Meanwhile, US historians developed an entire subfield of Western History to study the people inhabiting the western regions of the country. Western History has changed dramatically since Turner laid the foundation with his essentially white narrative of conquest.[2] Few studies exist comparing the Mexican, Canadian, and

---

[2] For leading studies on the West in the United States, see Particia N. Limerick, *The Legacy of Conquest: The Unbroken Past of the American West* (New York: W. W. Norton, 2006); Robert M. Utley, The *Indian Frontier of the American West, 1846–1890*

US experiences. There are some comparative works that bring together the frontier experiences in South Africa and the western plains, especially with regard to the struggle between the US government and the Lakota on the one hand and the British/Boer and the Zulu on the other.[3] Latin American remains an unwritten page in frontier studies.[4] This chapter will suggest some possible frontier comparisons across the nineteenth-century Atlantic world.

By the end of the 1500s, the Americas and Africa had attracted European interests. Since Cristoforo Colombo, hundreds explored the two continents in search of material wealth, a waterway to Asia, or sheer adventurism. The Italian Giovanni Cabot worked for the English to find a route around the Americas to Asia. Fellow Italian, Giovanni da Verrazzano served the French in search of a similar route. Meanwhile, Iberian explorers Vasco Núñez de Balboa and Fernão de Magalhães discovered routes to the Pacific Ocean and helped to establish the size of the American obstacle. For a long time, Europeans continued to hope for an all-water route to Asia, leading to many dead in the search for a Northwest Passage and a series of cross-continental explorations. Other Spanish and Portuguese seafarers and conquistadors explored the interior of the Americas and Africa. They laid the foundation for their nineteenth-century counterparts.[5]

Across the Americas, even by 1800, the interior remained unknown and maps showed many blanks. Political instability often delayed exploration and cartography missions. Among the most well-known explorations of the early years of the nineteenth century was the Meriwether Lewis and William Clark expedition. Authorized by the Thomas

---

(Albuquerque: University of New Mexico Press, 1984); Richard White, *"It's Your Misfortune and None of My Own": A New History of the American West* (Norman: University of Oklahoma Press, 1991).

[3] James O. Gump, *The Dust Rose Like Smoke: The Subjugation of the Zulu and the Sioux* (Lincoln: University of Nebraska Press, 1994); Bruce Vandervort, *Indian Wars of Mexico, Canada and the United States, 1812–1900* (New York: Routledge, 2006).

[4] Alistair Hennessy, *The Frontier in Latin American History* (Albuquerque: University of New Mexico Press, 1978), 3, 9–27; David Maybury-Lewis, Theodore Macdonald, and Biorn Maybury-Lewis, eds., *Manifest Destinies and Indigenous Peoples* (Cambridge, MA: Harvard University David Rockefeller Center for Latin American Studies, 2009).

[5] Felipe Fernández-Armesto, *Pathfinders: A Global History of Exploration* (New York: W. W. Norton, 2006), 236–238.

Jefferson administration to explore the Louisiana Purchase territory and Colombia River basin, Jefferson outlined in his instructions, "The object of your mission is to explore the Missouri river, & such principal stream of it, as, by it's course & communication with the waters of the Pacific Ocean, may offer the most direct & practicable water communication across this continent, for the purposes of commerce." Jefferson's hope was that the expedition would find either an all-water route connecting Missouri and Columbia or at least an easy portage between the two river systems. However, when the expedition finally reached the great divide, disappointment set in. Meriwether Lewis wrote in his diary on July 27, 1905, about his concern of not knowing how much distance lay between them and the nearest navigable branch of the Columbia River.[6] The expedition put to rest all assumptions that there was a water connection between the Atlantic and Pacific; however, Lewis and Clark's work left still many unexplored areas in North America.

In the aftermath of the expedition, fur traders explored and exploited the western interior of North America. Since Lewis and Clark had laid a powerful claim to the Oregon territory, trappers and eventually settlers made their way to the Pacific Northwest. However, when Oregon attracted settlers, the need for a safe and reliable transcontinental transit route emerged. In 1842, John C. Frémont and Kit Carson embarked from St. Louis up the Missouri River to South Pass and in a follow-up expedition, mapped the route from South Pass to the Pacific Ocean. Frémont had opened the Oregon Trail for thousands of settlers. Frémont was aware of the long line of explorers he had just joined. He wrote upon reaching the Great Salt Lake, "As we looked eagerly over the lake in the first emotions of excited pleasure, I am doubtful if the followers of Balboa felt more enthusiasm when, from the heights of the Andes, they saw for the first time the great Western Ocean."[7] Frémont was not alone in opening the interior for settlers.

When the United States considered a transcontinental railroad to the west coast since wagon trails and even relay riders could not provide the necessary all-weather communication needed by such a large country,

---

[6] Thomas Jefferson to Meriwether Lewis, June 20, 1803, Meriwether Lewis, July 27, 1805, in *The Journals of Lewis and Clark*, ed. Bernard De Voto (Boston, MA: Houghton, Mifflin, 1953), 168–169, 481–487.

[7] John C. Frémont, *Narratives of Exploration and Adventure*, ed. Allan Nevins (New York: Longmans Green, 1956), 243.

the government employed the US Army Corps of Topographical Engineers to map out the best route. Between 1853 and 1855, the engineers traveled the West: Issac Stevens explored the region between the 47th and 49th parallel to see if a route between St. Paul, Minnesota and the Puget Sound area was possible; John W. Gunnison was responsible for the central sector between the 37th and 38th parallel from St. Louis to the San Francisco area; and Amiel W. Whipple explored the 35th parallel route to Los Angeles. However, even by the 1860s unknown regions remained, such as the deep and rugged valleys of the Colorado River. The one-armed war veteran John Wesley Powell took small wooden boats down the rough waters of the river to eliminate the last great unknown of the United States.[8] While the interior of North America fascinated explorers, a similar lack of knowledge existed from a European perspective in Africa and drove explorations.

Despite European exploration and colonization starting in Africa, by the early nineteenth century, there was still a limited knowledge in Europe about the African interior since most trade centered along the coastline and its immediate vicinity. Very much like the limited knowledge about great rivers in North America, there was a vague understanding about the major rivers in Africa, such as the Nile or Congo and their sources deep in the African interior. Similarly, European lacked comprehension about the extent of the Sahara and the people populating the reaches of that desert. There were many myths and legends surrounding the West African kingdoms and their wealth, especially the fabled Timbuktu. In 1824, the Société de Géographie in Paris offered 10,000 francs to the first European to visit and, most importantly, return alive from Timbuktu. Edinburgh-born Alexander Gordon Laing desired to claim the prize. He worked for a number of years in Barbados and served as an officer in the York Light Infantry Regiment. In 1822, he joined the Royal African Colonial Corps and worked along the West African coast, where he fought in the Ashanti War of 1823–1824. In July 1825, Laing set out to find the source of the Niger and Timbuktu. He reached the city in August of the following year, but was likely murdered

---

[8] Even so dated, a good start on the subject is William H. Goetzmann, *Army Exploration in the American West, 1803–1863* (New Haven: Yale University Press, 1959); a newer account exists in Frank N. Schubert, *The Nation Builders: A Sesquicentennial History of the Corps of Topographical Engineers, 1838–1863* (Fort Belvoir, VA: Office of History, U.S. Army Corps of Engineers, 1988).

the following month, before he could lay claim to fame and monetary wealth.[9] Following in Laing's footstep was the French-born René Caillié. Born in 1799, Caillié had spent time along the African coast becoming familiar with the customs and traditions of the African people. From April 20 to May 4, 1828, Caillié visited Timbuktu, staying only a short time to avoid detection. He returned to North Africa along the caravan routes by August.[10] Laing and Caillié continued the time-honored tradition of European explorers in Africa.

However, just like in North America, the rivers of the interior remained a mystery, especially the source of the Nile and the lakes in central Africa puzzled European geographers and attracted imperial fantasies. Among the most prominent individuals in this search were David Livingstone and Henry Morton Stanley. Born in Scotland in 1813, David Livingstone joined the London Missionary Society. After finishing his religious education he received a mission appointment in southern Africa. After his mission station closed, Livingstone explored the African interior. He was the first European to see Victoria Falls and to cross the African continent between Luanda in Angola and Quelimane on the Zambezi River. He later accompanied the Zambezi Expedition from 1858 to 1864 and unsuccessfully challenged the theory that the Nile started in the Lake Tanganyika and Victoria region.[11] In contrast, Welch-born John Rowlands, Sir Henry Morton Stanley, faced a lifelong uphill battle due to his illegitimate birth. In 1859, he departed England for New Orleans, where he met merchant Henry Hope Stanley, who eventually adopted Rowland into his family. After the southern rebellion, Stanley embraced a journalistic-adventurer career. In 1869, the *New York Herald*'s James Gordon Bennett, Jr. supported Stanley's desire to visit Africa and locate Robert Livingstone, which he successfully accomplished. In 1874, financed by the *New York Herald* and *Daily Telegraph*, Stanley explored the Congo River, laying the foundation for the Belgium

---

[9] Frank T. Kryza, *The Race for Timbuktu: In Search of Africa's City of Gold* (New York: HarperCollins, 2006), 47, 50–57, 209, 229–238.

[10] Ibid., 256–257.

[11] Andrew C. Ross, *David Livingstone: Mission and Empire* (London, UK: Hambledon, 2002), 16–18, 79–108, 125–150; Tim Jeal, *Livingstone* (New Haven: Yale University Press, 2013), 34–35, 89–159.

Free State of Congo.[12] Livingstone and Stanley shaped European understandings about the African interior and river systems. River systems and their sources not only attracted North American and African explorers, the massive Amazon River system also drew adventurers, explorers, and cartographers to South America.

In Latin America, exploration and naturalism initially combined to advance human knowledge. At the end of the eighteenth century, the well-known Prussian Friedrich Wilhelm Heinrich Alexander von Humboldt visited Central America and the northern parts of South America, reporting on the geography, environment, and flora in the region. In the 1830s, following in Humboldt's footsteps, Charles Darwin visited South America as part of a British expedition, leading to his groundbreaking discoveries in zoology.[13] However, the Amazon's many tributaries continued to mystify Latin American statesmen. After the war with Peru and Chile on one side and Spain on the other, Peru was stuck with a group of former Confederate naval officers. Instead of returning home, John R. Tucker, David P. McCorkle, and Walter R. Butt went on a cartographic expedition into Peru's Amazonian rainforest. Tucker headed the Hydrographic Commission of the Amazon, which was established on May 25, 1867. They were transnational and Atlantic in personal with a wide range of individuals from different countries participating. Arturo Wertheman, or in his native German, Arthur Werthemann, joined the three Confederates to map the Amazon River's tributaries in Peru. Born in Mulhouse, France in 1842, Werthemann joined Ferdinand Lesseps's Suez Canal project in Egypt in 1862. He may have come to the United States in 1864 in the steerage of the *Grahams Polly* and appeared in Chile in 1865 to work on the Valparaiso

---

[12] Tim Jeal, *Stanley: The Impossible Life of Africa's Greatest Explorer* (London, UK: Faber and Faber, 2007), 31–34, 46–48, 69–70, 91–100.

[13] For works on Humboldt and Darwin's work in the Atlantic world, see Myron Echenberg, *Humboldt's Mexico: In the Footsteps of the Illustrious German Scientific Traveller* (Montreal: McGill-Queen's University Press 2017); Jeannette E. Jones and Patrick B. Sharp, *Darwin in Atlantic Cultures: Evolutionary Visions of Race, Gender, and Sexuality* (New York: Routledge, 2010); Vera M. Kutzinski, *Alexander von Humboldt's Transatlantic Personae* (New York: Routledge, 2012); Aaron Sachs, *The Humboldt Current: Nineteenth-Century Exploration and the Roots of American Environmentalism* (New York: Viking, 2006); Laura D. Walls, *The Passage to Cosmos: Alexander von Humboldt and the Shaping of America* (Chicago, IL: University of Chicago Press 2009).

to Santiago railroad.[14] Werthemann, the three Confederates, and the rest of the expedition worked on a purpose-US-built steam vessel. The Hydrographic Commission produced some of the most accurate and reliable maps of the region. At the same time, the group witnessed some of the conflicts between native inhabitants and white invaders. In 1876, Tucker departed Peru over payment issues with the Peruvian government. Werthemann stayed behind and continued mapping before eventually turning to mining as a more lucrative income source.[15] The group shows one example of the transnational personality of these explorations and cartography missions during the nineteenth century. Few individuals had such a transnational and Atlantic character as Werthemann, Stanley, or Laing, leaving legacies on three continents. Nevertheless, they show how vibrant and interconnected the frontiers in the Atlantic world were in the nineteenth century. Once these explorers opened the interiors, settlers followed them.

As settlers looked to the interiors for opportunities to farm, they encountered promotional materials, as well as warnings about the region they were heading into. In Brazil, the Amazonian frontier promised great wealth. Aureliano Cândido Tavares Bastos promoted the opening of the Amazon to free commerce to exploit the vast riches of the region. Besides the massive forests, the region could produce cotton, cocoa, chestnuts, rubber, and sugar. He called for a strong, farsighted, and innovative policy. Political leaders should try to attract European settlers to the region to put the natural resource to use. Without adequate and visionary political leadership, Brazil would never benefit from the Amazon and even more, any plan to make the region prosper required the integration and education of the indigenous population. Despite the number of slaves in the region, Tavares Bastos assumed slavery would soon disappear. Despite much promise, Tavares Bastos noted that the climate along the Amazon was extremely unhealthy with people reporting fevers. However, high water temperatures and lush vegetation along the

---

[14] Annemarie Seiler-Baldinger, "Basels Beitrag zur Kenntnis Lateinamerikas, 1493–1930," *Société Suisse des Américanistes / Schweizerische Amerikanisten-Gesellschaft Bulletin* 66–67 (2002–2003), 171; David P. Werlich, *Admiral of the Amazon: John Randolph Tucker, His Confederate Colleagues, and Peru* (Charlottesville: University Press of Virginia, 1990), 88, 143–145.

[15] Seiler-Baldinger, "Basels Beitrag zur Kenntnis Lateinamerikas," 171; Werlich, *Admiral of the Amazon*, 144.

banks of the rivers did paint a romantic image. There was much promise in the Amazon region.[16] Conversely, what the Amazon had in abundance; the western plains of the United States lacked: water.

The former US Army major turned geologist and explorer of the Colorado River, John Wesley Powell explained in his "Report on the Lands of the Arid Region of the United States," the need for an engineered solution to the aridity in the western parts of the country. Powell noted that "This Arid Region begins about midway in the Great Plains and extends across the Rocky Mountains to the Pacific Ocean." The lack of rainfall on the eastern side of the western mountain ranges created significant problems for farmers. He explained that if there was under 20 inches of rainfall per year, farmers needed to find ways to irrigate their crops. Because of this uncertainty, Powell suggested the use of irrigation, which would liberate the farmer from his dependence on rainfall and allow for an uninterrupted cultivation of crops. He desired to control the water flow to ensure that the rich sediment remained on the fields and not get washed away downstream. He suggested that "The diversion of a large stream from its channel into a system of canals demands a large outlay of labor and material. To repay this all the water so taken out must be used, and large tracts of land thus become dependent upon a single canal. It is manifest that a farmer depending upon his own labor cannot undertake this task." Therefore, the government had to assist with irrigation projects.[17] Brazil and the United States faced significantly different issues with their frontier regions as settlers encountered either an impenetrable rainforest or an arid region.

Regardless of the warnings and in spite of the threat posed by indigenous people, settlers actively moved the settlement frontier inward during the nineteenth century. In both Africa and the Americas, settlers continued to use the perceived unused, open, and free land in the interior to escape oppressive governments and discrimination, especially national and religious oppression. After the creation of the Church of Latter-Day Saints in New York, the Mormons moved around the Midwest, facing superstition and violence from their religious neighbors. The worst moment of this religious prosecution was the assassination of

---

[16] Aureliano Cândido Tavares Bastos, *O Valle do Amazonas* (Sao Paulo, Brazil: Companhia Editora Nacional, 1937), 196, 200, 211–212.

[17] John W. Powell, *Report on the Land of the Arid Region of the United States* (Washington, DC: Government Printing Office, 1879), vii, 1–2, 10.

founder Joseph Smith, Jr. on June 27, 1844.[18] The Mormons decided to move west to find religious freedom in unsettled land, which was hardly a new concept in the Atlantic world.

On April 5, 1847, a vanguard company of 148 settlers embarked across the plains. After six weeks, the company reached Fort Laramie where other settlers and members of the Mormon Battalion joined them. From here, they followed the Oregon Trail. Knowing the problems associated with crossing the Platte River, the Mormons used their portable boats and left behind a small group to help others by setting up a ferry. Near the Green River, the company ran into Sam Brannan, who had taken a different group of Mormon settlers to San Francisco. He urged Bingham Young to settle in California, but the Mormon leader remained set on his plans for the Great Basin. Once across South Pass, the company quickly reached their destination, the Salt Lake Valley. Eventually over 70,000 Mormons made the trek across the Plains to reach Salt Lake City, a religious safe haven. However, the Mormon paradise was not a peaceful one as they engaged with the US military in a battle-less war for control of the Utah territory in 1857.[19] The Mormons had a relatively peaceful trip to their new home on the banks of the Great Salt Lake; the Boers in the Cape Colony were not so lucky.

Like the Mormons, the Boers came into conflict with the British authorities in the Cape Colony. The Boers were a combination of Dutch, French Huguenot, and German farmers, who settled in the Cape Colony when the area was still Dutch controlled. The Boers, due to the relatively small size of their community, considered themselves part of one large family. Among the many issues, the Boers had with the British authorities were the abolition of slavery, the British attempt to Anglicize the Boer population, and the perceived indifference of the British authorities with frontier problems, especially the many attacks by the Xhosa people. Most of the voortrekkers were trekboers (semi-nomadic pastoralists) or gresnboere (frontier farmers). Despite some Boers holding slaves, the new states eventually banned slavery, but maintained a strict racial segregation. Furthermore, there were population pressures and land shortages

---

[18] Richard E. Bennett, *We'll Find the Place: The Mormon Exodus, 1846–1848* (Norman: University of Oklahoma Press, 1997), 2–3, 11–12, 21, 24.

[19] Bennett, *We'll Find the Place*, 83–88, 172–174, 182–184, 189–196, 218–220; David L. Bigler and Will Bagley, *The Mormon Rebellion: America's First Civil War, 1857–1858* (Norman: University of Oklahoma, 2011).

that pushed the Boers into the frontier regions. Regardless of the exact reasons, in the 1830s, thousands of voortrekers left the Cape Colony and moved inland.[20]

As the voortrekkers moved inland, they quickly came into conflict with the native Zulu population. On February 6, 1838, trek leader Piet Retief was killed by a Zulu chief, which started a continuous conflict between the two groups. Two months later, the Boers retaliated with a punitive raid, but a vastly superior Zulu army defeated them. In part, the strong individualism of the Boers undermined their ability to operate as an effective army. The conflict between Boers and Zulu escalated. The eventual result of the trek was the creation of Natal, Transvaal, and the Orange Free States, which remained in conflict with the Zulu, who like most indigenous people were confined to Bantustans, reservation like homelands.[21] Both the Boer and Mormons continued the tradition of religious dissenters, like the Puritans, who escaped religious prosecution by moving into a frontier region within the Atlantic world. At the same times, especially the Boers, illustrate the growing, violent tensions between settlers and indigenous people that states eventually had to intercede.

By the 1840s, settlers in the United States advanced the settlement frontier into the trans-Mississippi region encountering the Comanche in Texas and in the western parts of Iowa and Minnesota, settlers faced the Dakota and Pawnee. Furthermore, the pioneers on their way to Oregon or California encountered Cheyenne, Shoshone, and other tribes. As the land-robbing settlers came into conflict with the indigenous people, the US Army had to frequently come to the settlers' assistance, providing protection.[22] So far only two conflicts have attracted comparative scholarship: the Lakota War and the Zulu War.

The Lakota were an expansionist tribal group in the northern Plains of the United States. Settlers had forced the Lakota to move westward from

---

[20] Norman Etherington, *The Great Treks: The Transformation of Southern Africa, 1815–1854* (Harlow, UK: Pearson, 2001), 45–49, 57–60, 183–191, 203–207, 212–221, 243–262.

[21] Ibid., 262–266, 279–282.

[22] For some recent studies on the issue, see Robert M. Utley and Wilcomb E. Washburn, *Indian Wars* (Boston, MA: Houghton Mifflin, 2002); Elliott West, *The Contested Plains: Indians, Goldseekers, and the Rush to Colorado* (Lawrence: University Press of Kansas, 1998).

Minnesota, displacing other tribes in the upper Plains. Between 1854 and 1856, the US Army fought the Lakota following the Grattan Massacre, which started when Lieutenant John L. Grattan visited the camp of Conquering Bear to arrest a cattle thief. When a soldier killed Conquering Bear, the Lakota slayed all 31 soldiers. For the next twenty years, the plains suffered intermediate warfare. Tensions flared up again in 1862 and 1864. In 1866, the tenuous peace collapsed when a coalition of tribes under Red Cloud annihilated a relief column under William J. Fetterman outside of Fort Phil Kearny. In the aftermath of the conflict, the Lakota accepted a reservation in the western part of Dakota Territory.[23] However, peace did not last as settlers continued to encroach on Lakota land.

The economic panic of 1873 and the discovery of valuable minerals in the Black Hills created a stream of settlers onto the Lakota reservation. The government demanded more land concessions. As a result, Crazy Horse and Sitting Bull called on their people to resist the incursion and theft of their land. The hostile native population eventually reached around 7000. Therefore, General Philip Sheridan dispatched George Crook from the south, John Gibbon from the west, and Alfred Terry from the east to deal with the threat. After the inconclusive engagements at the Powder River and the Rosebud, a cavalry detachment from Terry's column located the native village along the Little Big Horn on June 25, 1876. The members of the 7th Cavalry under the flamboyant George Armstrong Custer charged the camp in divided columns, not knowing the disposition or strength of the enemy. The result was that Custer and 270 of his men were wiped out. The success did not win the war and the Lakota had to accept that stopping the steady advance of white settlement was impossible. By April 1877, the war was over and many of the victorious indigenous people had escaped into Canada.[24] However, other native tribes, the Nez Perce, Apache, and Modoc, continued to resist the theft of their land.[25] At the same time that Custer overconfidently

---

[23] Utley and Washburn, *Indian Wars*, 184–186, 203–205, 211–214.

[24] For studies of the Lakota War, see Jerome A. Greene, ed., *Lakota and Cheyenne: Indian Views of the Great Sioux War, 1876–1877* (Norman: University of Oklahoma Press, 2000); Charles M. Robinson, *A Good Year to Die: The Story of the Great Sioux War* (Norman: University of Oklahoma Press, 1996).

[25] Keith A. Murray, *The Modocs and Their War* (Norman: University of Oklahoma Press, 1959); Dan L. Thrapp, *The Conquest of Apacheria* (Norman: University of Oklahoma Press, 1979); Elliott West, *The Last Indian War: The Nez Perce Story* (Oxford: Oxford University Press, 2009).

rode into Sitting Bull's camp, British arrogance caused a similar result in South Africa.[26]

In southern Africa, the Zulu were a similarly expansionist people who continued to use traditional animal hide shield and short spear, but also increasingly firearms. The incursion of Boer settlers created tensions along the settlement frontier. In 1873, Cetshwayo became the new king of the Zulu. His opposite was Sir Henry Bartle Edward Frere, the ambitious first colonial governor of the federated Cape Colony and Transvaal. British and Zulu disagreed on the boundary between their respective territories. Gunning for war, Frere issued an ultimatum to the Zulu on December 11, 1878, demanding, among other things, the acceptance of missionaries and the toleration of a British agent with the Zulu. When Cetshwayo rejected the terms, British troops marched into Zululand on January 11, 1879. The Anglo-Zulu War pitched two powerful enemies against each other. Leading the British invasion force of 15,000 soldiers was Frederick Augustus Thesiger, Baron Chelmsford who faced some 35,000 Zulu warriors. Chelmsford encamped his part of the army near Isandlwana on January 22 but failed to place his troops in a defensive position. Despite the advantage of artillery and the powerful Martini-Henry rifle, the British failed to stop the steadily advancing and numerically superior Zulu army. At the end of the day, the British line broke and 1300 lay dead, including their commanders Anthony Durnford and Henry Pulleine. After the humbling defeat, the British gained the upper hand at Rorke's Drift and the Battle of Ulundi. The Zulu kingdom divided and Cetshwayo was imprisoned on Robben Island.[27] In both the United States and South Africa, native warriors gained signature victories in the 1870s, but their victories were hollow ones. Like all indigenous people during this era, they fought losing wars.

As a significant imperial power, Great Britain faced indigenous opposition in various parts of the Atlantic world. Along the West African coast, the British and Ashanti people engaged in a vicious struggle for territorial control over the Gold Coast, modern Ghana. In the first Anglo-Ashanti War from 1823 to 1831, the Ashanti tried unsuccessfully to

---

[26] For comparative studies, see Gump, *The Dust Rose Like Smoke*; Howard Lamar and Leonard Thompson, eds., *The Frontier in History: North America and Southern Africa Compared* (New Haven, CT: Yale University Press, 1981).

[27] Gump, *The Dust Rose Like Smoke*, 4–7, 13–26, 86–91, 106–109.

lay claim to the coastal regions. For thirty years, the Pra River became the border between the Ashanti and the BritishEmpire. In 1863/1864, the two sides skirmished but lack of British troops and sickness among the Ashanti ended the struggle prematurely. When in 1871 the Ashanti invaded the former Dutch Gold Coast region, which the British had only recently incorporated into their empire, the British reacted in force. Under Garnet Joseph Wolseley, thousands of British, West Indian, and African soldiers marched into Ashanti territory and occupied the Ashanti capital. In the aftermath of their defeat, the Ashanti accepted a harsh peace, which reduced their territory dramatically. The British fought two more wars to complete the conquest of the Ashanti.[28] The wars were swift and short, compared to the long drawn out ones in the Americas. Even Latin America faced conflicts as indigenous people resisted the encroachment on their land.

Argentina benefitted from the creation of a national identity, which developed during the Guerra del Paraguay and strong trade links within the Atlantic world. Argentinian politicians called for the pacification of the fertile Pampas of Patagonia and their integration into the national economy. As early as the 1830s, Juan Manuel de Rosas tried to pacify the region. However, even thirty years later, native people continued to raid the cattle-farming regions of the pampas, stealing cattle and killing settlers. In addition, there were concerns that the Chilean government might use the instability on the pampas to expand eastward. As a result, Alejo Julio Argentino Roca, first as commanding officer, then as secretary of war, and finally as president, directed the so-called Conquista del Desierto. Initially, the Argentinian government pushed the native people deeper into the pampas and to prevent their return, dug a 232-mile trench to separate the barbarian native and civilized white farming people. The usually fluid American frontier turned into a European style borderline. However, the trench did not stop raiding. In 1877, Roca changed policy. He argued that "Our self-respect as a virile people obliges us to put down as soon as possible, by reason or by force, this handful of savages who destroy our wealth and prevent us from definitely occupying, in the name of law, progress and our own security, the richest and most fertile lands of the Republic." Roca unleashed his army, equipped with superior breech-loading British rifles. The final campaign,

---

[28] Robert B. Edgerton, *The Fall of the Asante Empire: The Hundred-Year War for Africa's Gold Coast* (New York: Free Press, 1995), 71–102.

nevertheless, took seven years. In the process, the government removed over 15,000 natives in what is sometimes described as a genocide.[29] Like the US and British governments, Argentina's political and military leaders pursued a ruthless campaign against indigenous people to pacify the frontier region and allow settlers to exploit the region's economic opportunities.

Meanwhile in Chile, the Mapuche people in the Araucanía region resisted the settlement of the frontier region. Wheat farming and sheep herding increased in Chile after independence and farmers put more land under the plow. The Araucanía was the only place where such a farming expansion could take place, but at the expense of the Mapuche, who called the final stage of the conflict *La Ultima Matanza* (the Last Massacre). In 1861, the Chilean army established a military outpost at the confluence of the Mulchén and Búreo River. Nevertheless, the Chilean government was reluctant to let renegade settlers force it into a war with the Mapuche, especially while a conflict with Spain was ongoing. In the late 1860s, the Mapuche struck back against Chilean incursions, killing soldiers and taking livestock. However, the natives' bolas, spears, and slings had little chance against the modern repeater rifles of the Chileans. The conflict continued for a decade. By the 1880s, the Chileans had subdued most Mapuche resistance, inflicting significant casualties and claiming additional land for white settlement. Chile's frontier was largely pacified.[30]

When European explorers ventured into the Atlantic world in the 1500s, they established frontier zones between their settlements and the indigenous people, these areas of contact and frequently conflict advanced steadily inward in the course of the next 400 years.

---

[29] César Bustos-Videla, "The 1879 Conquest of the Argentine 'Desert' and Its Religious Aspects," *The Americas* 21 (July 1964), 36–57; Alfred Hasbrouck, "The Conquest of the Desert," *Hispanic American Historical Review* 15 (May 1935), 195–228; Richard O. Perry, "Warfare on the Pampas in the 1870s," *Military Affairs* 36 (April 1972), 52–58; Richard O. Perry, "Argentina and Chile: The Struggle for Patagonia 1843–1881," *The Americas* 36 (January 1980), 347–363; Kenneth M. Roth, *Annihilating Difference: The Anthropology of Genocide* (Berkeley: University of California Press, 2002), 45.

[30] Rosamel Millaman, "The Mapuche and 'El Compañero Allende': A Legacy of Social Justice Historical Contradictions, and Cultural Debates," in *The Routledge History of Latin American Culture*, ed. Carlos M. Salomon (New York: Routledge, 2018), 205–206; Chris Moss, *Patagonia: A Cultural History* (New York: Oxford University Press, 2008), 155–156.

The nineteenth century was no different. There were still many unknown regions that attracted explores in search of fame and adventure. The interiors of the vast continents around the Atlantic remained obscure; explorers and cartographers ventured into the unknown to finally bring the last remaining pieces of land to people's attention. Promoters of frontier settlement emphasized the unique climatic, environmental, and geographic features as well as vast resources available in the interiors to draw settlers. However, as John Wesley Powell indicates, there were also cautious voices warning against the environmental dangers looming in the frontier zones, where resources could be plenty or scarce. As settlers flooded into the interiors, they often followed established Atlantic patterns: seeking economic opportunities or escaping oppression and pursuing freedom, at times religious. The Boer and the Mormons illustrate this migration for religious freedom. In the end, the frontiers were zones of conflict, like they had been during the early colonial empires. The open lands of the interior, from the North American plains to the South American pampas and South Africa's Drakensberg Mountains, witnessed massive struggles in the course of the nineteenth century as indigenous people tried to stem the unstoppable tied of settler encroachment. Just like their predecessors, indigenous people suffered significant carnage. Nineteenth-century Atlantic frontiers remained zones of contentious encounters and conflict.

Bibliography

Bennett, Richard E. *We'll Find the Place: The Mormon Exodus, 1846–1848*. Norman: University of Oklahoma Press, 1997.

Bigler, David L., and Will Bagley. *The Mormon Rebellion: America's First Civil War, 1857–1858*. Norman: University of Oklahoma, 2011.

Bustos-Videla, César. "The 1879 Conquest of the Argentine 'Desert' and Its Religious Aspects." *The Americas* 21 (July 1964): 36–57.

Echenberg, Myron. *Humboldt's Mexico: In the Footsteps of the Illustrious German Scientific Traveller*. Montreal: McGill-Queen's University Press, 2017.

Edgerton, Robert B. *The Fall of the Asante Empire: The Hundred-Year War for Africa's Gold Coast*. New York: Free Press, 1995.

Etherington, Norman. *The Great Treks: The Transformation of Southern Africa, 1815–1854*. Harlow, UK: Pearson, 2001.

Fernández-Armesto, Felipe. *Pathfinders: A Global History of Exploration*. New York: W. W. Norton, 2007.

Frémont, John C. *Narratives of Exploration and Adventure.* Edited by Allan Nevins. New York: Longmans Green, 1956.

Goetzmann, William H. *Army Exploration in the American West, 1803–1863.* New Haven: Yale University Press, 1959.

Greene, Jerome A., ed. *Lakota and Cheyenne: Indian Views of the Great Sioux War, 1876–1877.* Norman: University of Oklahoma Press, 2000.

Gump, James O. *The Dust Rose Like Smoke: The Subjugation of the Zulu and the Sioux.* Lincoln: University of Nebraska Press, 1994.

Hasbrouck, Alfred. "The Conquest of the Desert." *Hispanic American Historical Review* 15 (May 1935): 195–228.

Hennessy, Alistair. *The Frontier in Latin American History.* Albuquerque: University of New Mexico Press, 1978.

Jeal, Tim. *Livingstone.* New Haven: Yale University Press, 2013.

Jeal, Tim. *Stanley: The Impossible Life of Africa's Greatest Explorer.* London, UK: Faber and Faber, 2007.

Jones, Jeannette E., and Patrick B. Sharp. *Darwin in Atlantic Cultures: Evolutionary Visions of Race, Gender, and Sexuality.* New York: Routledge, 2010.

Kryza, Frank T. *The Race for Timbuktu: In Search of Africa's City of Gold.* New York: HarperCollins, 2006.

Kutzinski, Vera M. *Alexander von Humboldt's Transatlantic Personae.* New York: Routledge, 2012.

Lamar, Howard, and Leonard Thompson, eds. *The Frontier in History: North America and Southern Africa Compared.* New Haven, CT: Yale University Press, 1981.

Lewis, Meriwether, and William Clark. *The Journals of Lewis and Clark.* Edited by Bernard De Voto. Boston, MA: Houghton, Mifflin, 1953.

Limerick, Particia N. *The Legacy of Conquest: The Unbroken Past of the American West.* New York: W. W. Norton, 2006.

Maybury-Lewis, David, Theodore Macdonald, and Biorn Maybury-Lewis, eds. *Manifest Destinies and Indigenous Peoples.* Cambridge, MA: Harvard University David Rockefeller Center for Latin American Studies, 2009.

Moss, Chris. *Patagonia: A Cultural History.* New York: Oxford University Press, 2008.

Murray, Keith A. *The Modocs and Their War.* Norman: University of Oklahoma Press, 1959.

Perry, Richard O. "Argentina and Chile: The Struggle for Patagonia 1843–1881." *The Americas* 36 (January 1980): 347–363.

Perry, Richard O. "Warfare on the Pampas in the 1870s." *Military Affairs* 36 (April 1972): 52–58.

Powell, John W. *Report on the Land of the Arid Region of the United States.* Washington, DC: Government Printing Office, 1879.

Robinson, Charles M. *A Good Year to Die: The Story of the Great Sioux War.* Norman: University of Oklahoma Press, 1996.

Ross, Andrew C. *David Livingstone: Mission and Empire.* London, UK: Hambledon, 2002.

Roth, Kenneth M. *Annihilating Difference: The Anthropology of Genocide.* Berkeley: University of California Press, 2002.

Sachs, Aaron. *The Humboldt Current: Nineteenth-Century Exploration and the Roots of American Environmentalism.* New York: Viking, 2006.

Salomon, Carlos M., ed. *The Routledge History of Latin American Culture.* New York: Routledge, 2018.

Schubert, Frank N. *The Nation Builders: A Sesquicentennial History of the Corps of Topographical Engineers, 1838–1863.* Fort Belvoir, VA: Office of History, U.S. Army Corps of Engineers, 1988.

Seiler-Baldinger, Annemarie. "Basels Beitrag zur Kenntnis Lateinamerikas, 1493–1930." *Société Suisse des Américanistes / Schweizerische Amerikanisten-Gesellschaft Bulletin* 66–67 (2002–2003): 161–175.

Tavares Bastos, Aureliano Cândido. *O Valle do Amazonas.* Sao Paulo, Brazil: Companhia Editora Nacional, 1937.

Thrapp, Dan L. *The Conquest of Apacheria.* Norman: University of Oklahoma Press, 1979.

Turner, Frederick J. *The Frontier in American History.* New York: Henry Holt, 1921.

Utley, Robert M. The *Indian Frontier of the American West, 1846–1890.* Albuquerque: University of New Mexico Press, 1984.

Utley, Robert M., and Wilcomb E. Washburn. *Indian Wars.* Boston, MA: Houghton Mifflin, 2002.

Vandervort, Bruce. *Indian Wars of Mexico, Canada and the United States, 1812–1900.* New York: Routledge, 2006.

Walls, Laura D. *The Passage to Cosmos: Alexander von Humboldt and the Shaping of America.* Chicago, IL: University of Chicago Press, 2009.

Werlich, David P. *Admiral of the Amazon: John Randolph Tucker, His Confederate Colleagues, and Peru.* Charlottesville: University Press of Virginia, 1990.

West, Elliott. *The Contested Plains: Indians, Goldseekers, and the Rush to Colorado.* Lawrence: University Press of Kansas, 1998.

West, Elliott. *The Last Indian War: The Nez Perce Story.* Oxford: Oxford University Press, 2009.

White, Richard. *"It's Your Misfortune and None of My Own": A New History of the American West.* Norman: University of Oklahoma Press, 1991.

CHAPTER 10

Imperial Projects and Expansion

Of admiring American institutions, and desiring their extension over this continent? Suspicion of cordially hating the stupid and barbarous despotism of Spain over the people of Cuba?... May those who inherit it be ever worthy to bear it, by opposition to all political despotism, and by stern, unyielding resistance to tyranny, whether boldly attempted to be enforced by the bayonet, or slyly and stealthily by the perversion of judicial powers.[1]

From its inception, empire characterized the Atlantic world. Spain, Portugal, France, and England competed to carve out ever-changing territorial sphere for economic exploitation, settlement, and the production of lucrative crops. Even so, the French Revolution temporarily put an end to empire building and dismantled much of the French and Spanish empires in the Atlantic world, the second half of nineteenth-century witnessed a renewed interest in imperial projects, both in the Americas and Africa. The Atlantic empires partially collapsed in the Age of Revolutions starting with the British colonies in North America and ending with the independence of most of the Spanish colonies. However, none of the European empires collapsed completely since Great Britain still occupied Canada and a series of Caribbean islands, Spain still held Cuba and Puerto Rico, and the vast majority of Caribbean islands remained European controlled. The Caribbean basin once more became

---

[1] John A. Quitman, August 15, 1854, in *Life and Correspondence of John A. Quitman*, by John Francis Hamtramck Clairborne (New York: Harper, 1860), 2:306.

a hotbed for imperial conflict after 1825. The Dominican Republic became victim of Haitian and Spanish imperial designs and almost fell prey to the United States. The imperial ambitions to expand placed the United States at odds with its southern neighbors, leading to the replacement of the Spanish Empire by the United States and the assumption of a hegemonic role by the Anglo-North American country by the end of the century. The shift of power from one empire to another illustrates the dramatic transformation of the nineteenth-century Atlantic world. As the European power surrendered the Americas to the United States, they set out to carve up the African continent. The Atlantic world remained dominated by empires, both formal and informal, as the focus shifted from the Americas to Africa and powers fought each other as well as the indigenous people to expand their territorial and economic hold over millions of people. The modern Age of Empire was part of the nineteenth-century Atlantic world experience.

On November 30, 1821, the Capitanía General de Santo Domingo gained its independence from Spain as the República del Haití Español . The new state was internally divided and ripe with political mistrust. Immediately, questions about the political future of the island emerged, including whether to join forces with one of the other republics in the region. Especially, the Afro-Caribbean population desired attachment to Haiti, which made every effort to convince the Spanish-speaking neighbors to join the two countries together. As a result, support for an annexation by Haiti appeared in the large cities. Attachment to Haiti promised political stability. In February 1822, Haitian president Jean-Pierre Boyer sent 12,000 soldiers to occupy Haití Español. Boyer claimed, "que no había entrado en ella como conquistador sino por la voluntad de sus habitants (I have not come into this city as a conqueror but by the will of its inhabitants)."[2] Hispaniola's French and Spanish halves unified under Haitian leadership.

Despite their promises, the Haitians acted like conquerors and forced heavy taxes on the occupied land to help pay for Haiti's looming enormous indemnity payment to France. In addition, the Haitian army of occupation was poorly supplied and commandeered food, at times at

---

[2] Anne Eller, *We Dream Together: Dominican Independence, Haiti, and the Fight for Caribbean Freedom* (Durham, NC: Duke University Press, 2016), 3–6; Franklin J. Franco Pichardo, *Historia del Pueblo Dominicano* (Santo Domingo, Dominican Republic: Ediciones Taller, 2009), 175–178.

10 IMPERIAL PROJECTS AND EXPANSION 161

gunpoint. Land redistribution and the enforcement of labor regulations on cash crop plantations soon followed. Furthermore, Haitian law prohibited the ownership of land by white residents and as a result, many elite white families lost their property and left the island. The Haitians, who connected slavery and Catholicism, ordered all religious leaders off the island. The occupation government made serious mistakes, alienating many and opening the door for resistance movements. By 1838, Juan Pablo Duarte Díez, Matías Ramón Mella Castillo, and Francisco del Rosario Sánchez created the nationalist *La Trinitaria*, which called for independence. They closely cooperated with a group of Haitians, who desired to overthrow Boyer. Unfortunately, their revolutionary plans became known and they were imprisoned. Nevertheless, on February 27, 1844, led by *La Trinitaria*, the Spanish-half of the island declared its independence as the República Dominicana.[3] However, independence was not secure as neighbors and imperial powers threatened the country's existence.

Over the next fifteen years, Buenaventura Báez Méndez and Pedro Santana y Familias governed the new republic. Faced with the constant threat of invasion from neighboring Haiti, legacies of misgovernment, and a desolate financial situation, Pedro Santana inquired with Spain whether the former colonial mother country was interested in reoccupying the former colony. Spain, which had just gained a significant victory against Morocco, jumped on the opportunity, especially with the United States unable to enforce the Monroe Doctrine. On March 18, 1861, Spain annexed the state and Pedro Santana became the colonies first governor-general. However, Spanish rule did not bring the hoped-for stability and prosperity. Spain quickly embraced a governing style similar to that of Haiti three decades before. The new rules alienated the people. Civilians had to hand overdraft animals to the Spanish military. Spanish officials dismissed the religious leaders on the island and replaced them with Spaniards. Higher tariffs and the integration into the Spanish colonial trade system undercut the merchant class and limited the economy. The dissatisfaction of the local residents became clear when on August 16, 1863, nationalist leaders, like José Antonio Salcedo Ramírez, launched a raid on Santo Domingo. The rebellion quickly escalated, but

---

[3] Eller, *We Dream Together*, 21–29.

the hoped-for assistance from the United States never materialized.[4] For the third time in half a century, the Dominican Republic sought its independence from colonial rule.

Despite high hopes of a restoration of great power status at the start of the decade, Spain soon faced an imperial overstretch. The Spanish realized, like so many other countries during this period, that fighting a guerilla war was no easy task. The Spanish Empire gained some recent military experiences with the successful war against Morocco, the support provided to the debt collection in Mexico, and military assistance for the French invasion of Indochina. Spain overestimated its military abilities. In the course of the two years of conflict, Spain suffered over 10,000 casualties, mainly from tropical diseases, and expanded 33 million pesos on an unwinnable war. With the popularity of the occupation decreasing, Leopoldo O'Donnell y Jorís vacated the prime minister-ship and opened the door for a Spanish withdrawal. With the Spanish Cortes refusing additional funding for the occupation, on March 3, 1865, the Spanish declared the annexation over, and Spanish forces withdrew from the island by mid-July. The República Dominicana gained its independence for a third time, but questions arose whether freedom would last.[5]

On January 10, 1870, US President Ulysses S. Grant dropped another bombshell for the suffering young republic, his Secretary of State Hamilton Fish submitted to the US Senate a treaty annexing Dominicana, with a promise of future statehood. The treaty was the result of private negotiations with President Ramón Buenaventura Báez Méndez. Grant noted in his address to Congress, accompanying the treaty, "I did not dream of instituting any steps for the acquisition of insular possessions [however] I believed ... that we should not permit any independent government within the limits of North America to pass from a condition of independence to one of ownership or protection under a European power." Once more, the independence of the island country was in question. Thankfully, Grant faced serious disapproval of his foreign policy in the Senate, which opposed empire building as

---

[4] Wayne H. Bowen, *Spain and the American Civil War* (Columbia: University of Missouri Press, 2011), 84–107; James W. Cortada, "A Case of International Rivalry in Latin America: Spain's Occupation of Santo Domingo, 1853–1865," *Revista De Historia De América* 82 (July 1976), 60–61, 73–75; Eller, *We Dream Together*, 21–58.

[5] Bowen, *Spain and the American Civil War*, 84–107; Cortada, "A Case of International Rivalry in Latin America," 79–82.

long as the country continued to reel over racial questions at home.[6] For once, República Dominicana retained its independence, but the United States had opened a political conversation about empire building.

Empire building or rebuilding in the Caribbean specifically and the Americas more generally was no easy task as the Spanish discovered. Spain's withdrawal from Hispaniola was only one disaster in its growing series of imperial failures. Inspired by the successes in Indochina, Morocco, Mexico, and Hispaniola, Spain wondered if the country could regain some of its lost empire in South America. In 1862, Spain dispatched a "scientific expedition" under Admiral Luis Hernández Pinzón to the west coast of the Americas. On August 4, 1863, the desired opportunity arose when for unknown reasons, a mob of Peruvians at the Talambó hacienda attacked two Spaniards, killing one. Pinzón used the occasion to demand an apology and reparations from Peru. When neither was offered since the incident was a domestic police matter, Pinzón unearthed old outstanding debt dating back to the wars of independence. Diplomatic negotiations soon broke down and the Spanish flotilla seized the Chincha Islands on April 14, 1864. The islands were rich in guano, an essential export commodity for the financially unstable Peruvian republic. Chile quickly entered into a formal alliance with Peru after Spain and Chile clashed over Chile's refusal to provide coal to the Spanish fleet. As a result, the Spanish fleet had no base where to refit its ships or take on supplies.[7] However, the two South American republics lacked a navy with a trained officer corps to challenge the Spanish. As a result, Peru asked its minister in the United States to recruit an experienced mariner, whom he found in John R. Tucker, a former Confederate naval officer who had experience with ironclads, submarines, and stationary torpedoes.[8] In Peru, Tucker found a recently modernized navy with a series of ironclad battleships from Great Britain, like the Laird-build

---

[6] Ulysses S. Grant, "Special Message," April 5, 1871; Dennis Hidalgo, "Charles Sumner and the Annexation of the Dominican Republic," *Itinerario* 21 (July 1997), 51–65.

[7] Robert L. Scheina, *Latin American's Wars: The Age of the Caudillo, 1791–1899* (Washington, DC: Brassey's, 2006), 333–334; David P. Werlich, *Admiral of the Amazon: John Randolph Tucker, His Confederate Colleagues, and Peru* (Charlottesville: University Press of Virginia, 1990), 79–86.

[8] Werlich, *Admiral of the Amazon*, 82, 87–88.

Huáscar, but the end of the war and domestic opposition precluded him from taking command.[9] Spain soon realized its impossible situation.

A change of government in Spain and the replacement of Pinzón by Vice-Admiral Juan Manuel Pareja had no impact on the conflict. The peace treaty signed by Pareja and General Manuel Ignacio de Vivanco, Peru's negotiator, in January 1865 crumbled under public pressure in Peru. Meanwhile, Pareja escalated relations with Chile. On September 17, 1865, he demanded that his ships visiting Valparaiso be given the regular twenty-one-gun salute. Since the visit and demand coincided with the Chilean Independence Day celebrations and would have embarrassed the government, Chile refused. As a result, and of other disagreements over Chilean neutrality, Pareja declared war on September 24. He proclaimed a paper blockade of the Chilean ports.[10] Despite the military distraction in Chile, the main war effort focused on Peru. However, victory was ever more distant for Spain. Therefore, the Spanish withdrew their navy from the South American coast. Spain had failed, its empire in decline, the great powers delegated Spain to third power status, which opened the door for more ambitious empire builders in the Americas to benefit from Spain's fall.

Where Spain tried to rebuild an empire lost at the start of the nineteenth century, the French similarly tried to recreate their lost empire. The French were no strangers to the idea of conquest and imperial expansion. Having lost most of their colonies during the Seven Years' War and the French Revolutionary/Napoleonic War era, some French leaders longed for an opportunity to regain lost glory. Charles X initiated the process of turning Algeria into a colony. The French invasion benefitted from the damage done to Algiers' defenses, insignificantly by the United States and the pounding by the Anglo-Dutch fleet.[11] In Algeria, Pierre Deval, the French consul, encounter problems when he tried to settle a wheat purchase agreement from the French Revolutionary period. On April 29, 1827, the ruler of Algiers and Deval had a contentious meeting during which the dey hit Deval with his fly whisk.

---

[9] Scheina, *Latin American's Wars*, 335; Werlich, *Admiral of the Amazon*, 82.

[10] Scheina, *Latin American's Wars*, 334–335.

[11] Robert Aldrich, *Greater France: A History of French Overseas Expansion* (Basingstoke, UK: Macmillan Press, 1996), 10–23; Frederick C. Leiner, *The End of Barbary Terror: America's 1815 War Against the Pirates of North Africa* (New York: Oxford University Press, 2007), 151–176.

Charles X used the so-called Fan Affair to undermine the Algerian government with a blockade. In 1829, after once more failing to negotiate a settlement, Charles X determined to take forceful action. A naval force under Admiral Guy-Victor Duperré assisted the 34,000 soldiers commanded by Louis Auguste Victor de Ghaisne, Comte de Bourmont in their landing in Sidi Ferruch on June 14, 1830. After three weeks of fighting, the French army occupied Algiers, ending over 300 years of nominal Ottoman rule. Algeria was the first nineteenth-century French colony.[12] Louis-Philippe inherited the Algerian colonial project, which was popular with the French people. France created a civil administration, which promoted the cultivation of cotton, commercial agriculture, and factories to turn the colony into a profitable enterprise. On June 22, 1834, France officially turned Algeria into a colony with a military governor and occupation force.[13] The dream of recreating the French Empire had taken its first step. Importantly, the French started the slow process of carving up the African continent among the imperial powers.

By the 1850s, after he had cemented his power in France, Napoleon cast a global eye with regard to rebuilding the French Empire. However, the main focus remained the Atlantic world. After joining the European debt collection expedition against civil war torn and cash-strapped Mexico, in the summer of 1863, Napoleon orchestrated with his conservative Mexican allies a takeover of Mexico. However, by 1866, with growing local resistance, financial strains on the French military, imperial overstretch, and European conflicts, Napoleon withdrew from the imperial projects in the Americas. Henceforth, French attention shifted to Africa. Already in the 1860s, France negotiated trade and territorial concession with the local leaders along parts of the West African coast, which in the next twenty years served as a basis for the territorial expansion of the French Empire into the African interior.[14] In effect, where Spain had been successful in North Africa and failed in the Americas, the French suffered a very similar fate during the mid-nineteenth century. Both foreshadowed that with independence in the Americas, imperial attention

---

[12] Aldrich, *Greater France*, 25–26; James McDougall, *A History of Algeria* (Cambridge, UK: Cambridge University Press, 2017), 50–58.

[13] Aldrich, *Greater France*, 26–27; Douglas Porch, *The French Foreign Legion: A Complete History of the Legendary Fighting Force* (New York: HarperCollins, 1991), 64–66.

[14] Aldrich, *Greater France*, 35–50.

shifted back to Africa, where the Atlantic world had started four hundred years ago.

Nevertheless, imperialism remained alive in the Caribbean and the new state continued to fear designs against their territorial integrity. The most persistent power, desiring to expand into the region, was the United States. By the 1850s, with the western expansion of slavery blocked, southerners debated expansion into the Caribbean basin. Since the incorporation of European colonies or independent states likely involved a hefty price tag or war, the US government shied away from expansion in a southerly direction. Instead, private individuals took up the cause by recruiting private armies and illegally attacking these sovereign states. The so-called filibusters brought fear and destruction in their wake. Many of these armies were recruited in the United States, but opportunity-seeking foreigners joined these transnational armies, which were often a combination of Atlantic residents. Whereas some politicians looked favorable toward these expeditions, others perceived them as illegal and wondered about the use of violence to force institutions of government on another people.[15]

Among the most prominent filibusters was Narciso López. Born on November 2, 1797, in Caracas, López grew up in a wealthy Basque merchant family. During the independence war, he participated on the Spanish side and after independence, left Venezuela for Spain. In Spain, he fought the Primera Guerra Carlista, before returning to Cuba. Working in the Cuban administration during the 1840s illustrated to López how much Spain oppressed the Cuban people. Within a decade, he unsuccessfully tried twice to free Cuba from Spain. On his second journey, the Spanish authorities captured López and most of his army, executing them after a swift trial. More importantly, López's army represented the diversity of the Atlantic world during this period. Among those captured by the Spanish authorities and convicted to hard labor in quicksilver mines were 41 men from the northern parts of the United States, 58 from the southern states, 20 Cubans, 15 Germans, 10 Irish,

---

[15] For works on expansionism contributing to the causation of the rebellion in the United States see Matthew Karp, *This Vast Southern Empire: Slaveholders at the Helm of American Foreign Policy* (Cambridge, MA: Harvard University Press, 2016); Robert E. May, *The Southern Dream of a Caribbean Empire, 1854–1861* (Baton Rouge: Louisiana State University Press, 1973).

9 Hungarians, 4 English, and a few others.[16] Of the nine Hungarians, six were soldiers with desperately needed military experiences. They had participated in the Hungarian revolution of 1848. Joseph Csermelyi, Augustus Kováts, Emeric Radnich, and Louis A. Schlesinger were part of the August 1851 filibuster. John Prágav surrendered after suffering an injury on August 13, 1851, but he committed suicide to avoid garroting. According to Schlesinger, the Hungarians joined an army of liberation to bring freedom to the oppressed Cubans.[17] They willingly overlook the racial slavery aspect of the filibusters in favor of the liberation of oppressed people from monarchical rule. Despite the facade of bringing territorial independence, filibusters were part of an imperial expansion of the United States into the Caribbean.

While Spain dealt with López, other parts of the Caribbean suffered from the pestilence of William Walker. At the time of the Lopez filibuster, Walker invaded Sonora and Baja California. He escaped capture by the Mexican authorities and prepared for new adventures in Central America, especially Nicaragua. Walker's activities destabilized Central America and created resentment among the people, which resulted in his eventual fateful meeting with a firing squad. However, Walker too took a diverse group of individuals with him on his filibuster expeditions, among them was Charles Frederick Henningsen. His birthplace is unknown but he had the unfortunate tendency of picking the losing side such as Don Carlos in the 1830s in Spain, the Russians in the early 1840s in Circassia, and finally Walker in Central America. Among Walker's troops were also the Cuban Domingo de Goicouria Cabrera, the Prussian Bruno von Natzmer, and a number of US citizens, along too was López-veteran Schlesinger. In March 1856, Walker orchestrated an invasion of Guanacaste. The four attacking companies were under the command of Schlesinger, and one company each was composed entirely

---

[16] Tom Chaffin, *Fatal Glory: Narciso Lopez and the First Clandestine U.S. War Against Cuba* (Charlottesville: University Press of Virginia, 1996); Anderson C. Quisenberry, *Lopez's Expeditions to Cuba, 1850 and 1851* (Louisville, KY: J. P. Morton, 1906), 126–131.

[17] Louis A. Schlesinger, "Personal Narrative of Louis Schlesinger of Adventures in Cuba and Ceuta," *United States Magazine and Democratic Review* (September 1852), 210; Eugene Pivány, *Hungarians in the American Civil War* (Cleveland, OH: Dongo, 1913), 9; István Kornél Vida, *Hungarian Émigrés in the American Civil War: A History and Biographical Dictionary* (Jefferson, NC: McFarland, 2012), 117, 162, 181.

of German and French residents.[18] The filibusters were colorful, transnational armies and they operated in the best tradition of the old diverse Atlantic world.

A good indication of how much people in the Caribbean basin feared filibusters came with the so-called Watermelon Riot of 1856 in Panama City. During the 1850s, Panama was still a province of New Granada. Like all Latin American regions, Panama's social instability increased with the construction of the Panama Railroad. The railroad, besides the trans-Isthmus boat-coach operation of the Accessory Transit Company in Nicaragua, served as one of the main transit routes through Central America to California. Therefore, many US citizens passed through Panama, creating fears of a possible US colonization of the region. On April 15, after an incident between a watermelon vendor and a US traveler, Panama City's stored up anger against these outsiders exploded. The mob attacked the symbols of exploitation. However, the fear of a filibuster coming to attack Panama City aided in the relatively speedy suppression of the revolt. The arrival of the authorities put an end to the riot. Race, nationalism, and dissatisfaction played their part in the riot.[19] Increasingly, the United States was no longer the northern sister republic but an imperial bully intending to colonize the people of Latin America.

After a brief delay because of the southern rebellion, some political leaders in the United States started to voice a desire to join the imperial competition for colonies. Therefore, a small group of imperialists called for an expansion of the battleship navy and the opening of new markets with a forceful foreign policy as the necessary precursors to empire. The primary objective of US Empire was an old expansionist target: Cuba. During the Guerra de los Diez Años, in the 1870s, the United States had largely abstained from becoming involved as the country struggled with the aftereffects of the southern rebellion. By the 1890s, when

---

[18] Charles H. Brown, *Agents of Manifest Destiny: The Lives and Times of the Filibusters* (Chapel Hill: University of North Carolina Press, 1980); Laurence Greene, *The Filibuster: The Career of William Walker* (Indianapolis, IN: Bobbs-Merrill Company, 1937); Robert E. May, *John A. Quitman: Old South Crusader* (Baton Rouge: Louisiana State University Press, 1985), 335–337; Robert E. May, *Manifest Destiny's Underworld: Filibustering in Antebellum America* (Chapel Hill: University of North Carolina Press, 2002), 97–101; William O. Scroggs, *Filibusters and Financiers: The Story of William Walker and His Associates* (New York: Macmillan, 1916), 7, 162, 183.

[19] Mercedes C. Daley, "The Watermelon Riot: Cultural Encounters in Panama City, April 15, 1856," *Hispanic American Historical Review* 70 (February 1990), 85–108.

Cubans once more tried to gain their independence, the United States was not going to remain a bystander. In 1895, the *Cuban Libre* once more violently challenged Spain in the eastern parts of Cuba, which the Spanish authorities tried to squash with an unprecedented level of brutality. A massive outcry followed the devastating and deadly reconcentration policy. International opposition forced the Spanish government to abandon the policy in 1897.[20] US interest in the Cuban conflict peaked in 1898 after the explosion of the USS *Maine* in Havana harbor. Between February 15, 1898, when the explosion took place and the declaration of war on April 25, policy makers in the United States whipped up public anger and pushed the country in the direction of war. The Cuban Junta in New York provided an effective propaganda machine to that end. The United States relied on Cuban assistance to conduct a war the country's military was ill-prepared for. The US Army lacked proper maps and tropical equipment, relying on the Cubans to clear the beaches and areas around the landing sites of Spanish forces. With the defeat of the Spanish in Cuba, the United States quickly dispatched troops to Puerto Rico to claim the island before the peace negotiations in Paris could commence.[21] The War of 1898 concluded Spain's imperial reign in the Atlantic world. Spain surrendered its final two territories in the Americas, ending 400 years of occupation. Despite earlier promises to allow Cuba its independence, the Teller Amendment of 1901 limited Cuban sovereignty to domestic affairs and gave the United States far-reaching powers in Cuban domestic and foreign affairs. Meanwhile, Puerto Rico was claimed as an outright colony. Having established its own empire, the United States guarded its imperial interest in the

---

[20] For works on the "New Diplomacy" see Robert L. Beisner, *From the Old Diplomacy to the New: 1850–1900* (Wheeling, IL: Harlan Davidson, 1986). For works on the Cuban Independence Struggle of 1895 see John L. Tone, *War and Genocide in Cuba, 1895–1898* (Chapel Hill: University of North Carolina Press, 2008).

[21] For works on the US engagement in the Cuban Independence War see George W. Auxier, "The Propaganda Activities of the Cuban Junta in Precipitating the Spanish–American War, 1895–1898," *The Hispanic American Historical Review* 19 (August 1939), 286–305; John Offner, *An Unwanted War: The Diplomacy of the United States and Spain Over Cuba, 1895–1898* (Chapel Hill: The University of North Carolina Press, 1992); Louis A. Pérez, Jr., *The War of 1898: The Unites States and Cuba in History and Historiography* (Chapel Hill: University of North Carolina, 1998).

Americas as imperial struggles for territory and influence heated up in the early twentieth century.[22]

By the late nineteenth century, the United States invigorated the Monroe Doctrine against imperial projects but also assumed a hegemonic status for the Americas. The new imperialism only added to the desire to maintain the Americas as the exclusive sphere of US influence. The United States worried when Great Britain and Germany determined to collect outstanding debt from Venezuela by blockading the country, raising fears of imperial schemes. The United States insisted on arbitration and in 1903, the Permanent Court of Arbitration at The Hague investigated the matter and sided with the two European powers. When a similar situation appeared in the Dominican Republic, the United States unilaterally preempted any European involvement and forced the payment of debts.[23] The Atlantic region by the late nineteenth century and early twentieth century was once more a region of imperial conflict. Furthermore, the remaining colonial possessions in the Americas desired increasingly more say in their domestic affairs.

As imperialism expanded outward, empires also faced internal revisions, especially the British Empire with its settler colonies was prone to political challenges. In the course of the nineteenth century, Ireland and Canada were continuous headaches to the power brokers at Westminster and Whitehall. After the events of 1848, Irish leaders renewed their struggle for independence by emphasizing a national identity conceived in exclusively Catholic terms. Some Irish nationalists hoped that by causing a war between Great Britain and the United States, they could gain their independence. Their agitation did not bring Irish freedom

---

[22] For works on the US occupation of Cuba see Carmen D. Deere, "Here Come the Yankees! The Rise and Decline of United States Colonies in Cuba, 1898–1930," *Hispanic American Historical Review* 78 (November 1998), 729–765; Lester D. Langley, *The Banana Wars: United States Intervention in the Caribbean, 1898–1934* (Lexington: University Press of Kentucky, 1983); Juan C. Santamarina, "The Cuba Company and the Expansion of American Business in Cuba, 1898–1915," *Business History Review* 74 (Spring 2000), 41–83; Marial Iglesias Utset, *A Cultural History of Cuba During the U.S. Occupation, 1898–1902*, trans. Russ Davidson (Chapel Hill: University of North Carolina Press, 2011).

[23] Langley, *The Banana Wars*, 13–26; Seward W. Livermore, "Theodore Roosevelt, the American Navy, and the Venezuelan Crisis of 1902–1903," *American Historical Review* 51 (April 1946), 452–471; Jay Sexton, *The Monroe Doctrine: Empire and Nation in Nineteenth-Century America* (New York: Hill and Wang, 2010), 199–240.

but unintentionally helped to create the Canadian Union. In 1858, James Stephens established the Irish Republican Brotherhood (usually called Fenians in the United States).[24] The attempt to stage an uprising in 1865 failed as the British authorities vigilantly checked all arrivals, temporarily suspended the Writ of Habeas Corpus, arrested suspected Fenians, and closed down *The Irish People*, a Fenian newspaper. In 1867, Stephens' successor Thomas Kelly tried to stage an uprising, but the uncoordinated rebellion quickly fell apart.[25] Irish independence was not making any headway, forcing a shift to guerilla warfare. On September 11, 1867, Manchester police arrested Kelly. A week later, Fenians sprang him from a prison transport and killed one of the guards. The British government had difficulty tracking down the conspirators and witnesses willing to testify. In November, another prison break plot at Clerkenwell Prison in London similarly failed when the explosion leveled a number of houses near the prison, killing twelve innocent bystanders. The British needed to make a decision: Should they stand by their liberal principles or should they adopt a police state that spied on its subjects? The Fenians caused a national identity crisis in Great Britain, but the British authorities determined to let the Irish separatist issue run its course and maintain the empire without major changes.[26] The government hastened the Fenian's demise by making concessions to Irish nationalism, such as the disestablishment of the Anglican Church of Ireland. The British Empire in Ireland seemed secure for the moment.

Meanwhile, the Fenian's leadership in the United States, guided by John O'Mahony and Michael Doheny, proposed to use the recent misunderstandings between the United States and Great Britain to provoke

---

[24] For works on the Fenians see James H. Adams, "The Negotiated Hibernian: Discourse on the Fenian in England and America," *American Nineteenth Century History* 11 (March 2010), 47–77; Leon O. Broin, *Revolutionary Underground: The Story of the Irish Republican Brotherhood, 1858–1924* (Totowa, NJ: Rowman and Littlefield, 1976); R. V. Comerford, *The Fenians in Context: Irish Politics and Society, 1848–82* (Dublin, Ireland, Wolfhound Press, 1985); Brian Jenkins, *Fenians and Anglo-American Relations During Reconstruction* (Ithaca, NY: Cornell University Press, 1969); Brian Jenkins, *The Fenian Problem: Insurgency and Terrorism in a Liberal State, 1858–1874* (Montreal, Canada: McGill-Queen's University Press, 2008); Desmond Ryan, *The Fenian Chief: A Biography of James Stephens* (Coral Gables, FL: University of Miami Press, 1967); Mabel G. Walker, *The Fenian Movement* (Colorado Springs, CO: Ralph Myers Publisher, 1969).

[25] Jenkins, *The Fenian Problem*, 39–40, 46–48, 60, 75, 85.

[26] Ibid., 105–108, 119–133, 149–163, 166–172.

a war and foster Irish independence. However, neither the British nor the United States desired an Atlantic war. Nevertheless, an 800-strong Fenian army crossed from Buffalo, New York into Canada under the leadership of John O'Neill on May 31, 1866, but with their supply lines cut by US authorities, they forced surrender. US and Canadian authorities coordinated to prevent other hostile border crossings. In 1871, the Fenians assumed they might be able to exploit the Red River Rebellion in western Canada, but US authorities immediately arrested Fenian lawbreakers.[27] The relations between Great Britain and the United States did not allow for a group of Irish separatists to cause a larger conflict. However, the Fenians activities illustrated Canada's vulnerability and created new impulses to alter the relationship between Canada and the mother country.

In the 1860s, Canada was a collection of different and independent colonies, which included Nova Scotia, Newfoundland, New Brunswick, Prince Edward Island, Quebec (Lower Canada), and Ontario (Upper Canada). The idea of a union between the various colonies was nothing new. The Act of Union of 1840 combined Upper and Lower Canada under one governor-general. Furthermore, all colonies had provincial self-government by the 1860s. The pressure for a union of the Canadian provinces increased when the United States refused to renew the Marcy-Elgin Reciprocity Treaty during the rebellion of the southern states.[28] The existing political structure in Canada was unable to provide a government strong enough to deal with the threat posed by the United States, deal with the expanding Canadian population, and create the infrastructure necessary for a prospering economy. On September 1, 1864, the premiers of New Brunswick, Nova Scotia, and Prince Edward Island met in Charlottetown to discuss the possibility of a union of the maritime colonies. John A. Macdonald, premier of the Province

---

[27] Jenkins, *The Fenian Problem*, 33, 58; Walker, *The Fenian Movement*, Chapters 10, 18, 180–182. For work on the Anglo-American post war relations see Charles S. Campbell, *From Revolution to Rapprochement: The United States and Great Britain, 1783–1900* (New York: Wiley, 1974); Phillip E. Myers, *Dissolving Tensions: Rapprochement and Resolution in British–American–Canadian Relations in the Treaty of Washington Era, 1865–1914* (Kent, OH: Kent State University Press, 2015).

[28] Myers, *Caution and Cooperation*, Chapter 12; Peter B. Waite, *The Life and Times of Confederation, 1864–1867: Politics, Newspapers, and the Union of British North America* (Toronto, ON: Robin Brass Studio, 2001), 123; also see Ged Martin, ed., *The Causes of Canadian Confederation* (Fredericton, Canada: Acadiensis Press, 1990).

of Canada, requested to participate. The four premiers kept Governor-General Charles Stanley Monck and the Colonial Office in London informed about their intentions. Macdonald's province especially suffered under a legislative paralysis since every government required a majority in East and West Canada, creating slow-working coalition governments. Macdonald and George-Étienne Cartier suggested a union of the colonies.[29] Where Great Britain opposed any change in the constitutional relationship or government of Ireland, Whitehall looked favorable at the Canadian efforts to establish self-government.

The leaders agreed to maintain close ties with Great Britain and representation in a bicameral system. Building on the Charlottetown conference the delegates met again a month later in Quebec to officially discuss the idea of a Canadian Union. On October 10, 1864, the meeting started and by October 27, the provinces came to an agreement, sending it to London for final approval. In January 1867, the drafting of the British North America Act started and after heated debate, Parliament agreed to the Dominion of Canada. With royal assent, the Dominion came into existence on July 1, 1867. Shortly after the law took effect, Manitoba, British Columbia, the Northwest Territories, and Prince Edward Island joined the Dominion of Canada as well.[30] The unification of Canada brought stability to Britain North America and represented a unique imperial devolution of power in an age of strengthening imperial projects and expansion.

The imperial age from 1875 to 1914 is sometimes seen as a global struggle. However, the attention of the European powers was primarily on Africa. With Europe suffering from the Long Depression (1873–1896), the powers searched for outlets to sell their overproduction. Even more Africa offered a vast array of useful and needed natural resources for European industry. As national rivalries grew, the European powers sought to increase their strengths through colonizing additional areas in other parts of the world. The stage was set for the Scramble for Africa, carving the continent up into colonies and potentially escalating imperial rivalries into global conflicts. In 1884, Otto von Bismarck hosted the Berlin Conference to address the Scramble for Africa. While the conference embraced humanitarian principles such as opposition to

---

[29] Waite, *The Life and Times of Confederation, 1864–1867*, Chapters 6, 9–10.
[30] Ibid., Chapters 7, 8, and 17.

the slave trade, the main goal was to figure out mechanisms to avoid conflict. Despite the lofty goals of the conference, the imperial powers came on a number of occasions, such as the Fashoda Incident and the Moroccan Crisis, close to fighting over patches of desert or jungle raising the specter of global war.[31] Like in the early days of the Atlantic world, Africa once more was the focus of European imperial projects for resources and trade.

The new imperialists in Africa did not act in any way different from their Spanish or Portuguese predecessors. The internationally most well-publicized incident was the atrocity committed by King Leopold's mercenaries in the Congo to force the indigenous population to collect rubber. When villages missed their quotas, the mercenaries cut off hands in punishment. Estimates claim that between one and fifteen million people died and millions more were mutilated. However, the Congo was just one of many atrocities. The German imperial government slaughtered the Herero people in their Southwest African colony by pushing these cattle pastoralists into the desert and preventing them access to their wells. Over 100,000 Herero and Nama died.[32] Where the slave trade had devastated Africa in the early Atlantic world, the imperial age left a permanent and devastating mark on the African continent.

Despite a brief decline at the start of the nineteenth century, empire remained a devastating experience for people around the Atlantic world. Imperial conflicts continued to define the Atlantic region. Especially, the Caribbean witnessed serious conflicts between independence desires and imperial expansion designs. The Dominican Republic immediately after

[31] For introductory works on the Scramble of Africa see Muriel E. Chamberlain, *The Scramble for Africa* (Harlow, UK: Longman, 2010); Thomas Pakenham, *The Scramble for Africa, 1876–1912* (New York: Random House, 1992); Henri L. Wesseling, *Divide and Rule: The Partition of Africa, 1880–1914* (Westport, CT: Praeger, 1996).

[32] For works on European genocide in Africa see Martin Ewans, *European Atrocity, African Catastrophe: Leopold II, the Congo Free State and Its Aftermath* (London, UK: Routledge, 2002); Adam Hochschild, *King Leopold's Ghost: A Story of Greed, Terror, and Heroism in Colonial Africa* (Boston, MA: Houghton Mifflin, 1999); David Olusoga and Casper W. Erichsen, *The Kaiser's Holocaust: Germany's Forgotten Genocide and the Colonial Roots of Nazism* (London: Faber and Faber, 2010); Jeremy Surkin, *Germany's Genocide of the Herero: Kaiser Wilhelm II, His General, His Settlers, His Soldiers* (Cape Town: UCT Press, 2010); Jürgen Zimmerer and Joachim Zeller, *Völkermord in Deutsch-Südwestafrika: Der Kolonialkrieg (1904–1908) in Namibia und seine Folgen* (Berlin, Germany: Links Verlag, 2003).

independence suffered the occupation of the country by Haitian forces and shortly after the recolonization by Spain. Only domestic dissent in the United States prevented the Dominican Republic falling prey to a third imperial conquest. Nevertheless, imperial schemes by especially the United States on the Caribbean basin continued and culminated with the ousting of Spain from Cuba and Puerto Rico and the replacement of the last vestiges of the Spanish Empire by the United States. The United States replaced Spain as the hegemon of the Americas by the early twentieth century. Following the surrender of the Americas to the United States, European attention shifted to Africa, where imperial powers left a devastating and permanent mark, just like when they had initially colonized and removed millions of Africans into slavery. The Atlantic world remained dominated and devastated by empires. The imperial actors may have changed over the past century, but by 1914, the Atlantic world was still a region ripe with imperial rivalries and conflicts.

Bibliography

Adams, James H. "The Negotiated Hibernian: Discourse on the Fenian in England and America." *American Nineteenth Century History* 11 (March 2010): 47–77.

Aldrich, Robert. *Greater France: A History of French Overseas Expansion.* Basingstoke, UK: Macmillan Press, 1996.

Auxier, George W. "The Propaganda Activities of the Cuban Junta in Precipitating the Spanish–American War, 1895–1898." *The Hispanic American Historical Review* 19 (August 1939): 286–305.

Beisner, Robert L. *From the Old Diplomacy to the New: 1850–1900.* Wheeling, IL: Harlan Davidson, 1986.

Bowen, Wayne H. *Spain and the American Civil War.* Columbia: University of Missouri Press, 2011.

Broin, Leon O. *Revolutionary Underground: The Story of the Irish Republican Brotherhood, 1858–1924.* Totowa, NJ: Rowman and Littlefield, 1976.

Brown, Charles H. *Agents of Manifest Destiny: The Lives and Times of the Filibusters.* Chapel Hill: University of North Carolina Press, 1980.

Campbell, Charles S. *From Revolution to Rapprochement: The United States and Great Britain, 1783–1900.* New York: Wiley, 1974.

Chaffin, Tom. *Fatal Glory: Narciso Lopez and the First Clandestine U.S. War Against Cuba.* Charlottesville: University Press of Virginia, 1996.

Chamberlain, Muriel E. *The Scramble for Africa.* Harlow, UK: Longman, 2010.

Clairborne, John Francis Hamtramck. *Life and Correspondence of John A. Quitman.* New York: Harper, 1860.

Clemente, Josep C. *Las Guerras Carlistas*. Barcelona, Spain: Ediciones Península, 1982.
Comerford, R. V. *The Fenians in Context: Irish Politics and Society, 1848–82*. Dublin, Ireland: Wolfhound Press, 1985.
Cortada, James W. "A Case of International Rivalry in Latin America: Spain's Occupation of Santo Domingo, 1853–1865." *Revista De Historia De América* 82 (July 1976): 53–82.
Daley, Mercedes C. "The Watermelon Riot: Cultural Encounters in Panama City, April 15, 1856." *Hispanic American Historical Review* 70 (February 1990): 85–108.
Deere, Carmen D. "Here Come the Yankees! The Rise and Decline of United States Colonies in Cuba, 1898–1930." *Hispanic American Historical Review* 78 (November 1998): 729–765.
Dosal, Paul J. *Cuba Libre: A Brief History of Cuba*. Wheeling, IL: Harlan Davidson, 2006.
Eller, Anne. *We Dream Together: Dominican Independence, Haiti, and the Fight for Caribbean Freedom*. Durham, NC: Duke University Press, 2016.
Ewans, Martin. *European Atrocity, African Catastrophe: Leopold II, the Congo Free State and Its Aftermath*. London, UK: Routledge, 2002.
Ferrer, Ada. *Insurgent Cuba: Race, Nation, and Revolution, 1868–1898*. Chapel Hill: University of North Carolina Press, 1999.
Franco Pichardo, Franklin J. *Historia del Pueblo Dominicano*. Santo Domingo, Dominican Republic: Ediciones Taller, 2009.
Greene, Laurence. *The Filibuster: The Career of William Walker*. Indianapolis, IN: Bobbs-Merrill Company, 1937.
Hidalgo, Dennis. "Charles Sumner and the Annexation of the Dominican Republic." *Itinerario* 21 (July 1997): 51–65.
Hochschild, Adam. *King Leopold's Ghost: A Story of Greed, Terror, and Heroism in Colonial Africa*. Boston, MA: Houghton Mifflin, 1999.
Jenkins, Brian. *Fenians and Anglo-American Relations During Reconstruction*. Ithaca, NY: Cornell University Press, 1969.
Jenkins, Brian. *The Fenian Problem: Insurgency and Terrorism in a Liberal State, 1858–1874*. Montreal, Canada: McGill-Queen's University Press, 2008.
Karp, Matthew. *This Vast Southern Empire: Slaveholders at the Helm of American Foreign Policy*. Cambridge, MA: Harvard University Press, 2016.
LaFeber, Walter. *The New Empire: An Interpretation of American Expansion: 1860–1898*. Ithaca, NY: Cornell University Press, 1963.
Langley, Lester D. *The Banana Wars: United States Intervention in the Caribbean, 1898–1934*. Lexington: University Press of Kentucky, 1983.
Leiner, Frederick C. *The End of Barbary Terror: America's 1815 War Against the Pirates of North Africa*. New York: Oxford University Press, 2007.

Levine, Robert S. *Dislocating Race and Nation: Episodes in Nineteenth-Century American Literary Nationalism.* Chapel Hill: University of North Carolina Press, 2008.

Livermore, Seward W. "Theodore Roosevelt, the American Navy, and the Venezuelan Crisis of 1902–1903." *American Historical Review* 51 (April 1946): 452–471.

Martin, Ged, ed. *The Causes of Canadian Confederation.* Fredericton, NB: Acadiensis Press, 1990.

May, Robert E. *John A. Quitman: Old South Crusader.* Baton Rouge: Louisiana State University Press, 1985.

May, Robert E. *Manifest Destiny's Underworld: Filibustering in Antebellum America.* Chapel Hill: University of North Carolina Press, 2002.

May, Robert E. *The Southern Dream of a Caribbean Empire, 1854–1861.* Baton Rouge: Louisiana State University Press, 1973.

McDougall, James. *A History of Algeria.* Cambridge, UK: Cambridge University Press, 2017.

Myers, Philip E. *Caution and Cooperation: The American Civil War in British–American Relations.* Kent, OH: Kent State University Press, 2008.

Offner, John. *An Unwanted War: The Diplomacy of the United States and Spain Over Cuba, 1895–1898.* Chapel Hill: The University of North Carolina Press, 1992.

Olusoga, David, and Casper W. Erichsen. *The Kaiser's Holocaust: Germany's Forgotten Genocide and the Colonial Roots of Nazism.* London: Faber and Faber, 2010.

Pakenham, Thomas. *The Scramble for Africa, 1876–1912.* New York: Random House, 1992.

Pérez, Louis A., Jr. *Cuba: Between Reform and Revolution.* New York: Oxford University Press, 2006.

Pérez, Louis A., Jr. *The War of 1898: The Unites States and Cuba in History and Historiography.* Chapel Hill: University of North Carolina, 1998.

Pivány, Eugene. *Hungarians in the American Civil War.* Cleveland, OH: Dongo, 1913.

Porch, Douglas. *The French Foreign Legion: A Complete History of the Legendary Fighting Force.* New York: HarperCollins, 1991.

Quisenberry, Anderson C. *Lopez's Expeditions to Cuba, 1850 and 1851.* Louisville, KY: J. P. Morton, 1906.

Ryan, Desmond. *The Fenian Chief: A Biography of James Stephens.* Coral Gables, FL: University of Miami Press, 1967.

Santamarina, Juan C. "The Cuba Company and the Expansion of American Business in Cuba, 1898–1915." *Business History Review* 74 (Spring 2000): 41–83.

Scheina, Robert L. *Latin American's Wars: The Age of the Caudillo, 1791–1899*. Washington, DC: Brassey's, 2006.

Schlesinger, Louis A. "Personal Narrative of Louis Schlesinger of Adventures in Cuba and Ceuta." *United States Magazine and Democratic Review* 31 (September 1852): 210.

Scroggs, William O. *Filibusters and Financiers: The Story of William Walker and His Associates*. New York: Macmillan, 1916.

Sexton, Jay. *The Monroe Doctrine: Empire and Nation in Nineteenth-Century America*. New York: Hill and Wang, 2010.

Surkin, Jeremy. *Germany's Genocide of the Herero: Kaiser Wilhelm II, His General, His Settlers, His Soldiers*. Cape Town: UCT Press, 2010.

Tone, John L. *War and Genocide in Cuba, 1895–1898*. Chapel Hill: University of North Carolina Press, 2008.

Utset, Marial Iglesias. *A Cultural History of Cuba During the U.S. Occupation, 1898–1902*. Translated by Russ Davidson. Chapel Hill: University of North Carolina Press, 2011.

Vida, István Kornél. *Hungarian Émigrés in the American Civil War: A History and Biographical Dictionary*. Jefferson, NC: McFarland, 2012.

Waite, Peter B. *The Life and Times of Confederation, 1864–1867: Politics, Newspapers, and the Union of British North America*. Toronto, ON: Robin Brass Studio, 2001.

Walker, Mabel G. *The Fenian Movement*. Colorado Springs, CO: Ralph Myers Publisher, 1969.

Werlich, David P. *Admiral of the Amazon: John Randolph Tucker, His Confederate Colleagues, and Peru*. Charlottesville: University Press of Virginia, 1990.

Wesseling, Henri L. *Divide and Rule: The Partition of Africa, 1880–1914*. Westport, CT: Praeger, 1996.

Zimmerer, Jürgen, and Joachim Zeller. *Völkermord in Deutsch-Südwestafrika: Der Kolonialkrieg (1904–1908) in Namibia und seine Folgen*. Berlin, Germany: Links Verlag, 2003.

CHAPTER 11

Henry Sylvester Williams's Black Atlantic

For many Africans, the nineteenth century was a transformative period. Depending on their location, they gained their freedom either as early as the 1790s or as late as the 1880s; however, freedom did not always mean political, economic, or social freedom. When slavery ended in the British Empire in 1838, plantation owners received compensation for their lost property, but slaves received no compensation for the lifetime of toil and suffering. The color of one's skin still limited professions, political careers, and economic well-being. With the Age of Empire increasing the European powers' contact with African people, racism remained a problem. Nevertheless, just like their European counterparts, Africans developed a variety of identities that prevented a unified opposition of Africans and African Americans against oppressive imperial policies. While their statues may have slightly improved, they remained on a whole an oppressed people. Thankfully, some like Henry Sylvester Williams, who would crisscross the Atlantic several times in his lifetime, stood up to fight against racism and for the rights of Africans.

Williams was born on March 24, 1867, in Barbados, but he grew up in Trinidad where his parents made sure he received a primary education. As an Afro-Caribbean on these small islands, Williams future career options were limited, and he determined to try to become a teacher. As a result, Williams realized how inadequate the education system in these British colonies remained and how much it placed Afro-Caribbeans at a disadvantage. Therefore, he decided to pursue a different career path and escape the confines of Trinidad. In 1891, he departed for the United

States, which by that time hardly had a reputation for racial equality where individuals of African descent faced lynch mobs and terrorism aimed at maintaining white racial supremacy. He did not stay long, leaving for Nova Scotia and Dalhousie University. Despite Nova Scotia's large black loyalist population dating back to the revolutionary era, Williams was only the university's second black student. He stayed briefly before leaving for London in September 1896 to enroll in college there. At age 30, Williams had for the first time crossed the Atlantic, but this would not be his last Atlantic crossing.[1]

As the center of banking, trade, and imperial politics, London offered a young, ambitious person a host of opportunities to advance their career, unless they racially did not fit into the white English expectations. However, being at the power center of the expanding British Empire also placed Williams in direct contact with the problems of that empire, including the abuses of power by imperialists and racial attitudes held by white Britons. Undeterred by the attitudes of his new surroundings or the high price tag, Williams decided to pursue a law degree. After passing his exams in June 1897, the Gray's Inn admitted Williams six months later. Besides admission fees, Williams also faced the cost of having to attend seventy-two dinners, paying for food and fine clothing. He joined an exclusive club of Oxford and Cambridge graduates creating a serious disadvantage and leading to him failing several of his exams. He eventually passed in 1902 and became one of the few black barristers in London. Nevertheless, racism made it difficult for him to prosper and side projects frequently distracted him from his law practice.[2]

Based on British racism, imperial oppression, and inequality, Williams determined to create the African Association to give Africans an independent voice, fight the "creation of the 'new form of slavery'" in Africa, and improve access to education. Importantly, the association promoted the interests of Africans in Africa and the West Indies. Despite an initially lukewarm reception among political, religious, and social leaders in London, the group quickly engage politics and reached out with lecture tours to illustrate the oppression still suffered by Africans, including the perception of a "re-enactment of slavery in South Africa." Just like abolition societies seventy years earlier, the African Association had an Atlantic

---

[1] Marika Sherwood, *Origins of Pan-Africanism: Henry Sylvester Williams, Africa and the African Diaspora* (New York: Routledge, 2011), 5–6, 12, 19–24.

[2] Ibid., 26–29, 31–32, 134–135.

reach and membership.[3] The pinnacle of the organization's short-lived existence was the Pan-African Conference of 1900.

Taking place in the shadow of the divisive Boer War (1899–1902) and the final Ashanti War (1900–1902), the conference planners invited leaders from Britain, the Americas, and Africa, a truly Atlantic world gathering. According to Williams and organization president H. Mason Joseph, the goal of the conference was to combat "wide-spread ignorance which is prevalent in England about the treatment of Native Races ... [and] to take steps to influence public opinion on existing proceedings and conditions affecting the welfare of Natives in the various parts of the Empire, viz. South Africa, West Africa and the British West Indies." They particularly concerned themselves with the false assumption that emancipation brought significant progress to African people, noting that Africans remained a "depressed race." In addition, the list of talking points for the conference was long, including the prohibition of liquor sales in Africa, improvement of education, and the end of slavery.[4] With these high hopes and far-reaching demands, the conference got underway.

On July 23, 1900, the Pan-African Conference started with C. W. French, chronicling the failures of the British government to provide an equal footing for Afro-Caribbeans in the colonies. French asked that "Black and white men should be allowed to compete for political and social rights without distinction." Others spoke in a similar manner. The harshest criticism of the British post-emancipation Caribbean came from J. E. Quinlan who pointed out that emancipation left freedmen penniless and homeless. Freedmen should receive land or be allowed to return to Africa if the government was unwilling to assist them in the Caribbean colonies. Even worse, recent tropical storms left the already destitute population further impoverished and financial support went solely to white residents. Having lambasted the British government, Quinlan closed with a different suffering region, "In South Africa the aim of the English capitalist seemed to be enslave the black people." Not only did Afro-Britons see an Atlantic struggle to gain equality for their peers, but this was also a conflict infused with the new language of working-class reformism.[5] The conference brought to light the continued

---

[3] Ibid., 38–39, 48–49.
[4] Ibid., 68, 77.
[5] Ibid., 81–85.

suffering of African people within the British Empire, but without regional support the organizers in London stood little change to bring about change.

In February 1901, Williams returned to his native Caribbean to enlist supporters for the Pan-African Conference and African Association. His welcome was unexpectedly cold. At a Jamaica meeting, the audience wondered why they should support an organization so devoted to the cause of South Africa when few of them had ties to that region. In almost Booker T. Washington like language (supported accommodation politics in the United States), *The Gleaner* suggested that the races should slowly overcome their difference, calling for "mutual sympathy and forbearance." While historians Marika Sherwood claims, there was interested in the African Association and its goal in the Caribbean, local chapters did not last. Williams could do little to change these attitudes despite claiming, "The African race in the West Indies needed and still needs a vigorous arousing to a full sense of what they owe themselves."[6] In other words, Williams and the Afro-Caribbean people believed in two different national identities, with Williams embracing a broad, trans-atlantic identity encompassing all African people regardless of their origin in Africa.

Undeterred Williams returned to London, where the African Association had disintegrated. Finding his work as a barrister limited by racism, Williams decided to try his luck in South Africa, where racial hostility was even worse. Using his contacts in South Africa to his benefit, Williams got admitted to the Cape Town Bar on October 29, 1903. Even as he earned an income as a barrister, Williams stayed active in the community. Going back to his roots, he continued to promote education as the "salvation of the coloured community." He stayed only eleven months, likely realizing he could not make enough income in South Africa. Nevertheless, his connections eventually allowed him to serve as agent of African people with the London bureaucracy.[7]

Still dissatisfied with his barrister career, Williams decided to enter politics. He joined the Liberal Party, Fabian Society, Freemasons, and the League of Universal Brotherhood in preparation of his running for office. In 1905, he ran for councillor of Marylebone Borough,

---

[6] Ibid., 106–107, 115.
[7] Ibid., 144–146, 155.

where he resided, and won as a Progressive and Labour party candidate. He was not the only African running for office that winter. He served his community diligently for two years, attending almost all council sessions and committee meetings. At the same time, Williams devoted himself to help African people seek recourse with the Colonial Office, focusing initially on South Africa. In 1907, he supported the Sotho Chiefs who demanded land from the British authorities for the assistance the tribe had rendered during the Boer Wars (1880–1881 and 1899–1902). Unfortunately, the Colonial Office stonewalled and pointed to the government in South Africa to adjudicate the situation. In the end, the Colonial Office claimed that no land was available for the tribesmen and that they should return home. Considering the many setbacks with the Colonial Office, Williams accepted an invitation by the President of Liberia, Arthur Barclay, and the National Bar Association to participate in the country's centennial celebrations in January 1908. Williams used the opportunity of his speech to reiterate the oppression suffered by African people under British rule.[8] After two years of council politics and stonewalling of African demands by the Colonial Office, Williams decided to leave Europe behind and return with his family to Trinidad.

On August 29, 1908, seven years since his last visit, Williams returned home for the last time. Only two days later, Williams was a member of the Trinidad Bar, ready to sustain his family with his barrister income. He quickly had cases to deal with; "his portfolio of civil and criminal cases, which involved travel between the various courts in the capital and the rural towns" kept him busy. Never one to focus simply on one career, Williams remained publicly involved, likely hoping to eventually recreate the defunct African Association. On March 26, 1911, Williams died of chronic nephritis, a slow, gradual, and at the time fatal kidney inflammation.[9]

Williams' death left a void in the Pan-African struggle for equality. For ten years, Williams was on the forefront of the struggle to bring unity to the African people on the two sides of the Atlantic Ocean and to use their combined strength to force the British government to make concessions. Nothing speaks more to the transformation of the nineteenth-century Atlantic world, then a Trinidadian working in London

---

[8] Ibid., 163–168, 174–175, 186, 196–202, 204.
[9] Ibid., 217, 223–226.

to united African Americans and Africans facing the oppression of white supremacy and imperial expansion. He failed to overcome the regional identities Afro-Caribbeans and Africans had developed in the course of the century. Nevertheless, Williams fought against the reappearance of slavery in South Africa and the legacies of slavery in the Caribbean, where Africans remained second class subjects. Williams represents the struggles and transformations of the late nineteenth-century and early twentieth-century Atlantic world. He was not a Garibaldi-like revolutionary who picked up weapon to fight for a constitutional nation-state, he fought with the pen and in the courtroom, but both desire an end of oppression and national unity for their people.

Bibliography

Sherwood, Marika. *Origins of Pan-Africanism: Henry Sylvester Williams, Africa and the African Diaspora*. New York: Routledge, 2011.

CHAPTER 12

Conservative Revolutions

> Se trata de poner en peligro nuestra nacionalidad, y yo que por mis principios y juramentos soy llamado á sostener la integridad nacional, la soberanía y la independencia, tengo que trabajar activamente, multiplicando mis esfuerzos para corresponder al depósito sagrado que la Nación, en el ejercicio de sus facultades, me ha confiado; sin embargo, me propongo, aunque ligeramente, contestar los puntos más importantes de su citada carta.[1]

The middle decades of the nineteenth century were a period of turmoil. Around the Atlantic world, states suffered from revolution, civil war, nationalist struggles, and frontier conflicts. What started at the end of the Napoleonic Wars, when educated elites called for the unification of nation-states and political reformers called for constitutional governments, little progress had been made in the first half of the century, especially during the revolutions of 1830 and 1848. After mid-century, things changed as conservative political leaders embraced the popular desire for nation-states with constitutional government. As political factions struggled to imprint their political vision on these emerging states, violent conflicts often followed. In Italy and Germany, conservative

---

[1] "It is about endangering our nationality, and I, because of my principles and oaths, I am called to sustain national integrity, sovereignty and independence, I have to work actively, multiplying my efforts to correspond to the sacred deposit that the Nation, in the exercise of his faculties, he has entrusted me; however, I propose, albeit slightly, to answer the most important points of your letter." Benito Juarez to Archduke Maximiliano, May 28, 1864, available at http://www.jornada.com.mx/2006/05/28/sem-carta.html.

political forces took the scepter of reform to form constitutional nation-states with limited public involvement. In Mexico, foreign invasion challenged the elected leadership of Benito Juarez, who with the words quoted above refused to hand over Mexico and relinquish his position of power to a foreign-imposed monarch. Meanwhile the United States and Argentina–Brazil–Paraguay suffered horrendous casualties as the states underwent rebellion or international conflict, eventually emerging with new political structures to strengthen their national identities. However, conservative political forces drove these reforms around the Atlantic world after they realized how their own political future rested on them embracing modern political identities. By the 1870s, conservatives created the nation-states their opponents had tried to bring into existence for the past half-century. As states struggled with reforms, this chapter will utilize the personal experiences of Felix Salm-Salm and Alexander Asbóth to illustrate how limited constitutional reforms and nation-states were the result of decades of fighting.

The 1860s started with a major success for unification nationalism. The Italian states finally achieved partial unification. However, the imposition of a northern Italian identity on the entire country created dissatisfaction and resistance. Across the ocean in the United States, diverging identities split the country along sectional lines and caused a fierce rebellion by the planter aristocracy of the southern states. Even with the surrender of the Confederate armies, the conflict did not stop. The United States, torn apart over territory added as a result of the war with Mexico, inadvertently jumpstarted a debate about Mexican identity. The Mexican government learned its lessons from the disastrous war. Mexico disintegrated into ten years of civil war, including a foreign invasion, as the country developed a national identity and cemented constitutional government. At the same time, the German states struggled with unification and some tried to resist a Prussian imposed nationalism. The Atlantic world was a contested region with many mercenaries, professional soldiers, and ideologues who helped to craft vibrant Atlantic world networks of exchange as these national-constitutional struggles unfolded.

After the failures of 1848, the Italian people continued to desire the ousting of the Austrians, their puppet rulers, and to create an Italian nation-state. After the revolutionary events of 1848, Italian unification remained dormant and the political and diplomatic constellation in Europe needed to change before an Italian state could again challenge the Austrians in northern Italy. In addition, Carlo Alberto abdicated the throne of Piedmont-Sardinia in favor of his son Vittorio Emanuele. A new political constellation emerged to bring about Italian unification.

As the next region of crisis in the nationalist struggles of Europe, northern Italy attracted several adventure-minded soldiers of fortune and political reformers. Born on Christmas Day 1828, Felix Constantin Alexander Johann Nepomuk zu Salm-Salm received a Prussian military education and fought with the Prussian army during the First Schleswig-Holstein War. Faced with mounting gambling debt, Salm-Salm escaped to the Austrian army where he participated in the campaigns to prevent the unification of Italy.[2] He fought under the viceroy of Lombardy-Venetia, Ferdinand Maximilian. The Austrian archduke had only recently married Marie Charlotte Amélie Augustine Victoire Clémentine Léopoldine of Belgium in July 1857 and was favorably disposed toward the Italian national cause. His rule is frequently described as liberal.[3] This was not the last time these two would fight side by side. As the struggle for Italian unification unfolded, Austria made a series of political and diplomatic errors. During the Crimean War (1853–1856), the Russians felt betrayed by Austria's favorable embrace of the western allies. France and Great Britain too felt betrayed by Austria's lack of support in their war against the Russians.[4] The stage was set for a major political realignment on the Italian peninsula.

Adding to the new leadership, in 1852, Vittorio Emanuele appointed Camillo Paolo Filippo Giulio Benso, Conte di Cavour Prime Minister. Cavour had a shrewd understanding of politics and diplomacy and was prepared to use all tools at his disposal to accomplish Italian unification under the leadership of Piedmont-Sardinia. He worked deliberately and carefully to challenge the Austrian Empire, searching for allies. Napoleon III was essential to Cavour's plans. In January 1858, Orso Teobaldo Felice Orsini attempted to kill the French Emperor, encouraging

---

[2] David Coffey, *Soldier Princess: The Life and Legend of Agnes Salm-Salm in North America, 1861–1867* (College Station: Texas A&M University Press, 2002), 14.

[3] Joan Haslip, *The Crown of Mexico: Maximilian and His Empress Carlota* (New York: Holt, Rinehart and Winston, 1971), 75–85, 94–96, 107–117.

[4] For studies on the impact of the Crimean War on Austrian diplomacy and Europe see J. B. Conacher, *Britain and the Crimea, 1855–1856: Problems of War and Peace* (New York: St. Martin's Press, 1987); Werner E. Mosse, *The Rise and Fall of the Crimean System, 1855–71: The Story of a Peace Settlement* (London, UK: MacMillan, 1963); Paul W. Schroeder, *Austria, Great Britain, and the Crimean War: The Destruction of the European Concert* (Ithaca, NY: Cornell University Press, 1972).

Napoleon to look more closely into the Italian national question. Cavour accepted an alliance with the unpredictable and adventurous-minded emperor.[5] Not everyone agreed with Cavour that the alliance with the French was necessary. Giuseppe Garibaldi later wrote: "It is true that his ally inspired me with no confidence, but what was I to do?" He was ready to make "war on the inveterate enemy of Italy," meaning Austria. He continued:

> The idea of making war on Austria by means of Piedmont was not new to me; nor was that of subordinating every political conviction to the one great aim of making, by whatever means, an Italian nation. This programme was the same as that adopted on our departure from Montevideo, and when Manin's and Pallavicini's noble resolution of uniting our country into one Italy under Victor Emmanuel was communicated to me at Caprera, it found me still with the same political creed.

However, Garibaldi wanted to take the field, having given up a high command in Uruguay to serve his country. He was not prepared to send volunteers, attached to him and by him, into battle under incompetent leaders.[6] The unification of Italy pitched the nationalist Garibaldi against the conservative-nationalist Cavour and the liberal-nationalist Mazzini.

Having coaxed the Austrians into an act of aggression with the mobilization of Piedmont-Sardinian's army, the allies declared war. After the victory at the Battle of Villafranca, Napoleon struck a deal with the Austrians which brought about the incorporation of Lombardy into Piedmont-Sardinia. Taking a page out of Napoleon's playbook, Cavour called for plebiscites incorporating the other northern Italian principalities. However, the incorporation of Lombardy came at a high price;

---

[5] Dennis Mack Smith, *Victor Emanuel, Cavour, and the Risorgimento* (London, UK: Oxford University Press, 1971), 28, 47–53, 92–93; Massimo Salvadori, *Cavour and the Unification of Italy* (Princeton, NJ: D. Van Norstrand Company, 1961). For important studies on the Risorgimento see Derek Beales, *The Risorgimento and the Unification of Italy* (London, UK: George Allen and Unwin, 1971); Charles F. Delzell, ed., *The Unification of Italy, 1859–1861: Cavour, Mazzini, or Garibaldi?* (Malabar, FL: Robert E. Krieger Publishing Company, 1976); Harry Hearder, *Italy in the Age of the Risorgimento, 1790–1870* (London, UK: Longman, 1983).

[6] Garibaldi, *Garibaldi*, 2:69–71, 124–126.

Napoleon received Nice and Savoy, Garibaldi's birthland.[7] In the end, the war with Austria accomplished the unification of northern Italy. Attention quickly shifted to the Bourbon-governed Two Sicilies to complete the unification of the peninsula. A violent incorporation of the Two Sicilies could have European ramifications; therefore, a plan was devised to allow Garibaldi to liberate the Sicilian people from the Bourbon dynasty. On May 5, 1860, Garibaldi left for Sicily, which soon came under his control. In the face of Garibaldi's popular forces, the Bourbon dynasty folded and on September 7, 1860, the victorious Garibaldi entered Naples.[8] He briefly thought about invading the Papal States and fighting his way into Rome, but for the moment, Rome as the capital of a unified Italy remained a dream.

Garibaldi was not alone thinking about the future; Cavour too considered his options and they did not involve Garibaldi. In Naples, Garibaldi encountered Cavour's scheming, which intended to prevent the revolutionary nationalist from becoming too powerful and Mazzini from declaring a republic. Garibaldi angrily wrote to Cavour's supporters: "They wanted to overthrow a monarchy only to put another in its place, without the power or the will to improve the condition of the unfortunate people." Despite Cavour's misgivings, King Vittorio Emanuele favored Garibaldi's undertaking, but the king could not escape the political consideration of what might happen if Garibaldi invaded Rome and fought the French army stationed there. As a result, Cavour and Vittorio Emanuele dispatched an army to stop Garibaldi. Since the only land route to the Two Sicilies was across the Papal States, this offered an opportunity to incorporate parts of the Papal States into the new Italy. The armies of Piedmont-Sardinia and Garibaldi met without battle. Garibaldi commented, "The Italian army of the north, sent by Farini

---

[7] Hearder, *Italy in the Age of the Risorgimento*, 223–230; Smith, *Victor Emanuel, Cavour, and the Risorgimento*, 5–7, 158–163.

[8] Garibaldi, *Garibaldi*, 2:149–151, 2:215. For works on the invasion of Sicily see Lynn M. Case, *Franco-Italian Relations 1860–1865: The Roman Question and the Convention of September* (New York: AMS Press, 1932); Christopher Hibbert, *Garibaldi and His Enemies: The Clash of Arms and Personalities in the Making of Italy* (Boston, MA: Little, Brown and Company, 1965); Dennis Mack Smith, *Cavour and Garibaldi, 1860: A Study in Political Conflict* (Cambridge, UK: Cambridge University Press, 1954); Dennis Mack Smith, "Cavour's Attitude to Garibaldi's Expedition to Sicily," *Cambridge Historical Journal* 9 (1949): 359–370; Samuel M. Osgood, *Napoleon III and the Second Empire* (Lexington, MA: D. C. Heath and Company, 1973).

and company to combat the 'revolution personified' in us, found us brothers; and to this army fell the task of completing the annihilation of Bourbonism in the Two Sicilies. ... They resolved to enjoy the fruits of conquest while banishing the conquerors."[9] For the Italian leadership, Garibaldi was as much a mercenary as he was a nationalist figurehead. On March 17, 1861, Vittorio Emanuele became king of the new Italy. However, Italian unification was not yet complete. Rome and Venetia remained in foreign hands until 1871 and 1866, respectively.[10] Garibaldi continued to accompany Italian unification.

While Garibaldi's Atlantic journey ended and he remained in Europe to continue the fight for Italy, Garibaldi's legacy and reputation drew the interested of the sectionally divided United States. At the start of the rebellion, a US representative in Austria suggested that Garibaldi should join the United States. Austria took offense and expelled the consul. Nevertheless, high-level negotiations ensued, involving two US ministers. The talks quickly broke down when the Italian insisted on command of all Union armies and a clear statement that the war was to end slavery.[11] The Abraham Lincoln administration could not grant a foreigner such extensive powers with the influential nativist element in the Republican party and abolition as a war goal could have dramatically complicated the war at such an early stage. Regardless, both sides in the United States continued to use his image. However, there was no shortage of foreigners willing to cross the Atlantic and pick up arms for the United States. Having once more accumulated significant debt, Felix Salm-Salm determined to escape his debtors by leaving Austrian service for the United States. He initially served on the staff of Louis Blenker, the commander of a division made up of German-speaking soldiers. In October 1862, he received command of the 8th New York Volunteer Regiment.[12] While Garibaldi was ready to help the United States based on his principles, Salm-Salm was doing it for the money and adventure.

---

[9] Garibaldi, *Garibaldi*, 2:216–220, 2:241; Scirocco, *Garibaldi*, Chapter 17–19; George M. Trevelyan, *Garibaldi and the Thousand* (London, UK: Phoenix Press, 2001).

[10] Garibaldi, *Garibaldi*, 2:254–282; Hearder, *Italy in the Age of the Risorgimento*, Chapter 10; Smith, *Victor Emanuel, Cavour, and the Risorgimento*, Chapter 13–15.

[11] Seward to Motley, October 9, 1862, Despatches from U.S. Ministers to Austria; Marsh to Seward, September 14, 1861, Despatches from U.S. Ministers to the Italian States.

[12] David Coffey, *Soldier Princess: The Life and Legend of Agnes Salm-Salm in North America, 1861–1867* (College Station: Texas A&M University Press, 2002), 14.

12 CONSERVATIVE REVOLUTIONS 191

In the end, regardless of their motivations, the soldiers in the United States reformulate the meaning of the US Constitution.

By the 1860s, two competing identities emerged in the United States. In the southern section, the elite created an identity centered on slavery. Southerners believed that the country was a confederation of independent states, that voluntarily joined together and who could voluntarily leave if they so desired. The state they envisioned was similar to the fragmented state of the German lands or Italian Peninsula. In their states' rights assumption, the southern states built on ideas voiced by Thomas Jefferson and James Madison in the late eighteenth century as well as the Nullification doctrine of John C. Calhoun. In its declaration of secession on December 20, 1860, South Carolina argued that the frequent violation of the rights of the states by the federal government justified the separation from the Union. The declaration read that "the State of South Carolina having resumed her separate and equal place among nations." Building on the Declaration of Independence of 1776, South Carolinians argued that the Union was between "free and independent states." The South Carolinians then quoted specific examples of how some of the states deliberately avoided constitutional obligations and oppressed the southern states. Most importantly, the northern states refused to return runaway slaves despite their constitutional obligation. With increasingly frequent violations and threats, South Carolina felt no longer safe within the Union. With the recent presidential election, the state feared "The Guaranties of the Constitution will then no longer exist; the equal rights of the States will be lost. The slaveholding States will no longer have the power of self-government, or self-protection, and the Federal Government will have become their enemy."[13] Other states followed the example of South Carolina as they laid out a new national identity of a fragmented and weak national union built around the principles of aristocratic slaveholding.

Meanwhile, President Abraham Lincoln outlined a different national identity in his inaugural address. Lincoln noted that the Constitution created "a more perfect Union." However, with secession, the perfect Union was in question. He argued "the Union is less perfect than before the Constitution, having lost the vital element of perpetuity." Therefore, Lincoln noted that secession was illegal. He asked the southern states,

---

[13] *Declaration of the Immediate Causes which Induce and Justify the Secession* (Charleston, SC: Evans and Cogswell, 1860).

which by the time of his inaugural formed the Confederate States of America, to evaluate what they were doing, "Before entering upon so grave a matter as the destruction of our national fabric, with all its benefits, its memories, and its hopes, would it not be wise to ascertain precisely why we do it?" In a letter to Horace Greeley in 1862, Lincoln asserted further that his primary goal was to restore and protect the United States. He desired the country to return to its old status. He did not agree with the idea that slavery had to end in order for the United States to survive. In his desire to protect the perpetual Union and restore the bond between the states, Lincoln wrote, "If I could save the Union without freeing any slave I would do it, and if I could save it by freeing all the slaves I would do it; and if I could save it by freeing some and leaving others alone I would also do that."[14] For Lincoln, the Union was of primary importance and an unbreakable contract between the people and the country.

With the two sides having created such divergent identities, the United States moved toward a collision, as southerners believed their section under attack. The conflict over the constitution in Kansas ended with a partial southern victory when the territory, after much violence, unsuccessfully applied with a pro-slavery constitution. However, the anger infused political climate of the 1850s with the Dred Scott decision, the caning of Massachusetts Senator Charles Sumner, and the attempted slave uprising at Harpers Ferry undermined the stability of the political parties in the country. With the Whig party disintegrating, the Republican party with its "free soil, free labor, free men" identity became a strong force in the North, contesting the Democratic party, which faced the accusation of blindly following their conservative, even reactionary, southern party members and being the party of the imaginary slave power conspiracy. Southerners with their pro-slavery and states' rights nationalism undermined their own position by insisting on a constitutional amendment protecting slavery at the Democratic National Convention in Charleston, South Carolina.[15] The United States disintegrated into war.

---

[14] First Inaugural Address, Lincoln to Greeley, August 22, 1862, Basler, *Collected Works of Abraham Lincoln*, 4:249–261, 5:388–389.

[15] For works on the escalating sectional tensions see William J. Cooper, Jr., *The South and the Politics of Slavery, 1828–1856* (Baton Rouge: Louisiana State University Press, 1978); Foner, *Free Soil Free Labor Free Men*; Freehling, *The Road to Disunion*; Michael F. Holt, *The Rise and Fall of the American Whig Party: Jacksonian Politics and the Onset of the Civil War* (New York: Oxford University Press, 1999); Potter, *The Impending Crisis*; Varon, *Disunion!*

The southern rebellion caused one of the bloodiest conflicts of the period. Despite the vast majority of individuals fighting in the conflict being born in the United States, this was a transnational war. Many people who migrated to the United States fought in the war, such as the Hungarian revolutionary and refugee Alexander Asbóth; others fought for the glory, money, and experience like Felix Salm-Salm. Among the European revolutionaries, a substantial number supported the new Republican party and infused their language into the conflict. Men like Carl Schurz, Gustav Philipp Körner, or Franz Sigel who fought in Europe for constitutional government against monarchy. In the United States, they saw the oppression of slaves and the lack of republican principles in the southern states as reason to oppose the slaveholder aristocracy. In a speech in March 1859, Carl Schurz outlined the perception of many, "In one word, that it is *not a federal, but a national government*; and second, that therefore the general government is the exclusive judge of its own powers." Schurz claimed an inseparable nature for the federal union. He eloquently mixed his European political views with historical evidence from the United States. Unfortunately, some contemporaries wondered how European separatists from Hungary or Ireland could fight with the Union. In 1864, Confederate troops captured the former Hungarian revolutionary Emeric Szabad, upon inquiry, Szabad claimed, "I came to America to fight for the Union, the destruction of which would cause joy to none but tyrants and despots." For this Hungarian, political oppression emanating from the South was the reason for the war and why the Union was in the right.[16]

In contrast, the Irish were a peculiar group and some sympathized with the arguments advanced by the southern states. The Irish revolutionary John Mitchel, who temporarily resided in Knoxville, Tennessee, favored slavery and the reopening of the international slave trade.

---

[16] Vida, *Hungarian Émigrés in the American Civil War*, 54, 59–60; Carl Schurz, "State Rights: Reply to Criticism, Kenosha, Wisconsin, on March 31, 1859," *Milwaukee Daily Sentinel*, April 4, 1859. For works on the so-called Forty-Eighters see Charlotte L. Brancaforte, ed., *The German Forty-Eighters in the United States* (New York: Peter Lang, 1989); Bruce Levine, *The Spirit of 1848: German Immigrants, Labor Conflict, and the Coming of the Civil War* (Urbana: University of Illinois Press, 1992); Carl Wittke, *Refugees of Revolution: The German Forty-Eighters in America* (Philadelphia: University of Pennsylvania Press, 1952); Adolph E. Zucker, ed., *The Forty-Eighters: Political Refugees of the German Revolution of 1848* (New York: Columbia University Press, 1950).

"He would be a bad Irishman," Mitchel claimed, "who voted for principles which jeopardized the present freedom of a nation of white men, for the vague hope of elevating blacks to a level which it is at least problematic whether God and Nature intended them." Even more, Mitchel wished for "a good plantation, well-stocked with healthy negroes, in Alabama."[17] While his compatriot, Patrick R. Cleburne did not care for slavery or the plantation system, he voiced his perception that freeing and arming slaves could help the South win its independence. He wrote:

> If this state continues much longer we must be subjugated.... It means the crushing of Southern manhood.... It is said slavery is all we are fighting for, and if we give it up we give up all. Even if this were true, which we deny, slavery is not all our enemies are fighting for. It is merely the pretense to establish sectional superiority and a more centralized form of government, and to deprive us of our rights and liberties.[18]

However, Cleburne's comments were unacceptable to the Confederate government. In contrast to the Irish residents of the South, Thomas Meagher had no problem with slavery but disagreed with the approach taken by southerners to rectify their grievances. He claimed:

> Duty and patriotism alike prompt me to it. The Republic, that gave us an asylum and an honorable career,—that is the mainstay of human freedom, the world over—is threatened with disruption.... Above all is it the duty of us Irish citizens, who aspire to establish a similar form of government in our native land. It is not only our duty to America, but also to Ireland. We could not hope to succeed in our effort to make Ireland a Republic without the moral and material aid of the liberty-loving citizens of these United States.[19]

Depending on their political interpretation, the protection of the Union and Irish independence were intimately connected for those fighting with the US Army, whereas for the Irish in the South, the war was not about slavery but freedom from northern oppression.

[17] Hegarty, *John Mitchel*, 88–89; Quinn, *John Mitchel*, 56–58.
[18] Patrick Cleburne, "Negro Enlistment Proposal," January 2, 1864, *The War of the Rebellion: A Compilation of the Official Records of the Union and Confederate Armies* (Washington, DC: GPO, 1880–1901), Series 1, vol. 52, Part 2, 586–592.
[19] Cavanagh, *Memoirs of Gen. Thomas Francis Meagher*, 369.

Meanwhile, Hungarians overwhelmingly fought for the Union. For some of them, fighting was a profession and they simply sought out wars to find employment. Nevertheless, there were some ideological reasons to support one side or the other. Once the war started, Alexander Asbóth, an officer and close confident of Lajos Kossuth in 1848, published a call to arm for the Hungarian community in the United States. Asbóth asked his fellow countrymen to join the Union army. Hoping for a future uprising in Hungary, he wrote: "we see with deep sorrow the glorious Republic of the United States, our adopted Country, upon the verge of dissolution, the realization of which would be a triumph for all despots and the doom of self-government." Comparing Kossuth and Washington as heroic figures in times of grave crises, Asbóth asked Hungarians to stand as firm with the United States as the country had stood with them in 1848.[20]

At the same time, southerners defined the revolutionary nature of their rebellion and created a national identity. Like many previous Atlantic revolutions, the southern rebellion initially embraced moderate views to avoid offending non-radicals and the international community. The Confederate government realized that states' rights and a weak central government would not work in a life and death struggle for national survival. However, the various states resisted attempts to centralize military and political affairs.[21] The Confederacy realized too late that its hope for a European intervention based on the European textile industries need for cotton was a misplaced one.[22]

---

[20] *New York Times*, May 3, 1861.

[21] For work on Confederate political development see William J. Cooper, Jr., *Jefferson Davis, American* (New York: Vintage Books, 2000); William C. Davis, *"A Government of Our Own:" The Making of the Confederacy* (Baton Rouge: Louisiana State University Press, 1994); Mark E. Neely, Jr., *Southern Rights: Political Prisoners and the Myth of Confederate Constitutionalism* (Charlottesville: University Press of Virginia, 1999); George C. Rable, *The Confederate Republic: A Revolution Against Politics* (Chapel Hill: University of North Carolina Press, 1994).

[22] For works on Confederate foreign relations see Frank L. Owsley, *King Cotton Diplomacy; Foreign Relations of the Confederate States of America* (Chicago, IL: University of Chicago Press, 1931. Reprint. Revised by Harriet C. Owsley. Chicago, IL: University of Chicago Press, 1959); Brian Schoen, *The Fragile Fabric of Union: Cotton, Federal Politics, and the Global Origins of the Civil War* (Baltimore, MD: Johns Hopkins University Press, 2009).

Furthermore, this rebellion was a new type of war, unprecedented in scale and the use of modern technology, with Atlantic-minded individuals contributing to new definitions regarding the conduct of war. The armies of William T. Sherman and Phil Sheridan devastated the Confederate countryside; both sides mobilized large sections of their population and economy to win the war. Additionally, fighting a war required more than battlefield successes, governments could not allow subversive elements to undermine the war effort. Revoking the Writ of Habeas Corpus allowed the Lincoln government to imprison opposition leaders.[23] In contrast, the Confederacy resorted to irregular warfare with guerilla bands terrorizing the trans-Mississippi region and occupied territories.[24] Guerilla warfare remained difficult to cope with; as a result, the German migrant Franz Lieber drafted General Order 100, which became known as the Lieber Code (August 24, 1863). He called for a humane treatment of occupied territories and prisoners of war. Lieber was a child of the Atlantic world. Born on March 18, 1800, in Berlin, he observed the occupation of Prussia by Napoleon's army. He embraced nationalism and joined a *Burschenschaft* (student fraternity) in college. He fought in the wars of liberation and the Greek War of Independence. His nationalist views were not appreciated and in 1826, he left for England and then the United States. Lieber accepted an appointment as professor of history and political economy at South Carolina College in 1835. In 1856, he left South Carolina for a similar position at Columbia College in New York. Lieber never wavered in his commitment to the United States; however, his son Oscar Montgomery Lieber fought and died for

[23] For works on Union politics see Michael S. Green, *Freedom, Union, and Power: Lincoln and His Party During the Civil War* (New York: Fordham University Press, 2004); Mark E. Neely, Jr., *The Union Divided: Party Conflict in the Civil War North* (Cambridge, MA: Harvard University Press, 2002).

[24] Regarding the conduct of the war see Jeremy Black, *The Age of Total War, 1860–1945* (Westport, CO: Praeger Security International, 2006); Stig Förster and Jörg Nagler, *On the Road to Total War: The American Civil War and the German Wars of Unification, 1861–1871* (Washington, DC: German Historical Institute, 1997); Mark Grimsley, *The Hard Hand of War: Union Military Policy Toward Southern Civilians, 1861–1865* (New York: Cambridge University Press, 1995); Daniel E. Sutherland, *A Savage Conflict: The Decisive Role of Guerrillas in the American Civil War* (Chapel Hill, NC: University of North Carolina Press, 2009); Daniel E. Sutherland, *The Emergence of Total War* (Abilene, TX: McWhiney Foundation Press, 1996)

the Confederacy.[25] Lieber's code provided a basis for the future regulation of warfare.

In April 1865, the rebellion in the United States ended with the surrender of General Robert E. Lee's Army of Northern Virginia, quickly followed by the assassination of President Lincoln, and the surrender of other Confederate forces. With about 800,000 soldiers and civilians dead, no other slave society sacrificed as much during the nineteenth century to end slavery. The surrender of the Confederate armies and the end of the slaveholding aristocracy hardly ended the struggle.[26] Pacification and reconciliation were difficult to achieve in the United States. In 1866, Congress asserted its authority over the reconstruction process. As a result, the South disintegrated into violence, trying to figure out race relations in a post-emancipation world.[27] Southern violence emanated from former guerrilla groups like the Knights of the White Camilla and the Ku Klux Klan. They threatened the lives and property of freedmen and their white supporters.[28] By the mid-1870s, southern white politicians had reestablished home rule and created a social system of racial separation.

The end of the rebellion in the United States meant that many soldiers for hire, like Felix Salm-Salm looked for new opportunities and they turned their attention south where a new opportunity existed. In

[25] General Orders No. 100, April 24, 1863, *The War of the Rebellion: A Compilation of the Official Records of the Union and Confederate Armies*, (Washington, DC: Government Printing Office, 1899), Series III, Volume 3, 148–164. Lieber has attracted only limited scholarly interests. Frank B. Freidel, *Francis Lieber: Nineteenth-Century Liberal* (Baton Rouge: Louisiana State University Press, 1947); Henry H. Lesesne and Charles R. Mack, *Francis Lieber and the Culture of the Mind* (Columbia: University of South Carolina Press, 2005).

[26] For studies of Reconstruction see Eric Foner, *Reconstruction: America's Unfinished Revolution, 1863–1877* (New York: Harper and Row, 1988); Scott R. Nelson, *Iron Confederacies: Southern Railways, Klan Violence, and Reconstruction* (Chapel Hill: University of North Carolina Press, 1999); Michael Perman, *The Road to Redemption: Southern Politics, 1869–1879* (Chapel Hill: University of North Carolina Press, 1984); Michael Perman, *Reunion Without Compromise; The South and Reconstruction, 1865–1868* (Cambridge, UK: Cambridge University Press, 1973).

[27] Foner, *Reconstruction*, 36, 60–62, 77–175.

[28] For works on southern violence see George C. Rable, *But There Was No Peace: The Role of Violence in the Politics of Reconstruction* (Athens: University of Georgia Press, 1984); Allen W. Trelease, *White Terror: The Ku Klux Klan Conspiracy and Southern Reconstruction* (New York: Harper and Row, 1971).

contrast, some revolutionary refugees, who had served in the US Army, benefitted from patronage positions. Wounded in the final months of the war in Florida, Alexander Asbóth received the diplomatic appointment to Argentina in October 1866. Both left a war-torn country for another. Salm-Salm mustered out of service in November 1865 and looked for an opportunity where he could put his military experiences to use. Despite having served the United States, Salm-Salm claimed he sympathized with the cause of the new Mexican emperor and decided to join the conservative-monarchical experiment in Mexico. After obtaining letters of introduction and reference, he left New York on February 20, 1866, and joined the fight as a staff officer.[29] Mexico offered both Union and Confederate veterans as well as others from the Atlantic world military opportunities as the country struggled with its search for a new political identity.

Mexico had long suffered under political instability. Many blamed the lack of a stable constitution and absence of a coherent national identity for the disastrous outcome of the war with the United States. In the early 1850s, the country still suffered from the legal and proprietary legacies of the colonial era. Especially, the preferential and isolated status of the military, which conducted itself like a state within the state, undermined Mexican political stability. The similarly aloof attitude of the CatholicChurch with its vast landholding and religious loyalty from parishioners questioned the devotion of Mexicans to the state. In 1853, Santa Anna returned from his Cuban exile, on the invitation of conservative politicians, and once more assumed the presidency. When he sold more territory to the United States, embezzled taxpayer money, and made himself dictator for life, opposition developed.[30]

---

[29] Felix Salm-Salm and Agnes Salm-Salm, Queretaro: Blätter aus meinem Tagebuch in Mexico (Stuttgart, Germany: A. Kröner, 1868), 1:2–3; Dana Coffey, *Soldier Princess: The Life and Legend of Agnes Salm-Salm in North America, 1861–1867* (College Station: Texas A&M University Press, 2002), 43–44; Robert N. White, *The Prince and the Yankee: The Tale of a Country Girl Who Became a Princess* (London, UK: I. B. Tauris, 2003), 11–13, 64–65.

[30] Will Fowler, *Santa Anna of Mexico* (Lincoln: University of Nebraska Press, 2007), 295–316; Robert L. Scheina, *Santa Anna: A Curse Upon Mexico* (Washington, DC: Brassey's, 2002), 80–81; Richard N. Sinkin, *The Mexican Reform, 1855–1876: A Study in Liberal Nation-Building* (Austin, TX: Institute of Latin American Studies, 1979), 17, 45–46, 98–100, 117–118.

In Ayutla, Guerrero, a group of opposition leaders drafted a new constitution. In 1855, the Revolution of Ayutla ousted Santa Anna and crafted a new secular, republican, and federal constitution under the leadership of Juan Alvarez and Ignaciao Comonfort. With the military, CatholicChurch, and landholders in opposition, in January 1858, civil war broke out between the Miguel Miramon government and the liberal supporters of Benito Juárez. Over the next two years, the conservatives benefitted from their close ties to the military, but the liberals controlled the customs house of Vera Cruz and thus Mexico's finances. At the end, the liberal faction emerged triumphant. With the war having depleted Mexico's treasury, the Juárez government decided to stop payment on all foreign debt in the summer of 1861.[31] The three major European creditors, Great Britain, France, and Spain, sent a military expedition to Mexico to force the honoring of the debt, but the French Emperor had ulterior motives, including the recreation of the French Empire in the Americas. Conservatives, who suffered defeat, longed for monarchical stability, had already in 1859, approached European dynasties about the Mexican throne. Napoleon was open to their proposals to recreate a Mexican Empire and to place the Habsburg Archduke Ferdinand Maximilian on Mexico's new throne.[32] Napoleon had to be careful to not reveal his plans too early.

In 1862, Napoleon III finally unleashed his overly confident army to oust the liberal government, but his troops suffered defeat before Puebla on *Cinque de Mayo*. The invasion in 1863 was more successful. Over the next years, Juárez's forces were on the defensive, but Mexicans rallied to the Constitution of 1857 as a symbol of national unity. Meanwhile,

---

[31] For studies on the Constitution of 1857 and related changes in Mexico see Jan Bazant, "The Division of Some Mexican Haciendas During the Liberal Revolution, 1856–1862," *Journal of Latin American Studies* 3 (May 1971), 25–37; Lawrence D. T. Hanson, "Voluntarios Extranjeros en los Ejércitos Liberales Mexicanos, 1854–1867," *Historia Mexicana* 37 (October 1987), 205–237; Stephen D. Morris, "Reforming the Nation: Mexican Nationalism in Context," *Journal of Latin American Studies* 31 (May 1999), 363–397; Pedro Salmerón Sanginés, *Juárez: La Rebelión Interminable* (Mexico City, Mexico: Editorial Planeta Mexicana, 2007); Sinkin, *The Mexican Reform*.

[32] For works related to the French Mexico adventures see Michele Cunningham, *Mexico and the Foreign Policy of Napoleon III* (New York: Palgrave, 2001); Hanna and Hanna, *Napoleon III and Mexico*; Jasper Ridley, *Maximilian and Juárez* (New York: Ricknor and Fields, 1992); Sinkin, *The Mexican Reform*.

Ferdinand Maximilian accepted the Mexican crown, but did not receive French guarantees that French troops would remain in Mexico and protect him. On May 21, 1864, Emperor Maximiliano stepped onto Mexican soil.[33] He refused to be a figurehead and did not implement the changes his conservative allies had hoped for, such as returning land to the CatholicChurch. Liberals resisted the invasion with guerrilla fighting, making travel between Vera Cruz and the interior hazardous. However, this was not just the second phase of a civil war; this was an Atlantic conflict.[34]

The French army had too many foreign obligations and could not devote the necessary manpower to Mexico. As a result, France looked elsewhere for soldiers. Besides deploying its foreign legion, volunteers from Belgium and Austria arrived in Mexico. Furthermore, France rented 500 Egyptian soldiers. In the United States, the arrival of African mercenaries raised concerns, especially at a time when the US government debated arming African Americans. Opposition by a variety of powers, including Great Britain, prevented additional Egyptian troops from making the journey to Mexico. Upon the conclusion of the war in Mexico, the Egyptians returned home and formed the backbone of the Egyptian army that conquered the Sudan. Historians have claimed the Mexico veterans were essential in the formation of an Egyptian nationalism. Furthermore, US veterans and even some Canadian Native Americans joined the Egyptian army at that time.[35] Finally, there were many Confederates who looked to Mexico. Jo Shelby, Sterling Price, John Magruder, Kirby Smith, and a host of others crossed the Rio Grande into Mexico and offered their services to Maximiliano. The Austro-Mexican

---

[33] Hanna and Hanna, *Napoleon III and Mexico*, 40–43, 69–74; Haslip, *The Crown of Mexico*, 241–258; Sinkin, *The Mexican Reform*, Chapter 6.

[34] Scholarship has not yet explained if Maximiliano actually sacrificed his liberal views or if he secretly maintained them. Hanna and Hanna, *Napoleon III and Mexico*, 142–143; Ridley, *Maximilian and Juárez*, 179–180; Sinkin, *The Mexican Reform*, Chapter 8.

[35] John Dunn, "Africa Invades the New World: Egypt's Mexican Adventure, 1863–1867," *War in History* 4 (1997), 27–34; Richard Leslie Hill and Peter C. Hogg, *A Black Corps D'élite: An Egyptian Sudanese Conscript Battalion with the French Army in Mexico, 1863–1867, and Its Survivors in Subsequent African History* (East Lansing: Michigan State University Press, 1995); Ridley, *Maximilian and Juárez*, 196, 213; Weaver, *The Red Atlantic*, 106–107; White, *The Prince and the Yankee*, Part 2.

government was reluctant to accept these mercenaries, unwilling to further alienate the United States.[36] Despite the amount of foreign support, the future for Maximiliano's experiment did not look promising.

In addition to the unification of Italy, Maximiliano was part of Napoleon III's Grand Design to rework the European and Latin American state system. As he planned to simplify the European political map, consolidating smaller states, he intended to place dethroned European princes on new thrones in the Americas, thus bringing stable monarchical government to the republics of the region. Napoleon had not anticipated such fierce resistance and Maximiliano's government had not provided the promised stability. Furthermore, the end of the rebellion in the United States and the start of the wars of German unification increased the diplomatic pressure on France to withdraw its armies from the Mexican quagmire. Napoleon's armies departed Mexico in the fall of 1866.[37] Within months of the French troops leaving, Juárez cornered Maximiliano in Querétaro. In the empire's final days, Felix Salm-Salm made a heroic, yet unsuccessful attempt to free the besieged emperor. On May 15, 1867, the republican army captured Maximiliano. After a swift court martial that ignored international pleas to spare the emperor's life, Maximiliano's short career as Mexican Emperor ended in front of a firing squad on June 19, 1867. With his last word, the emperor called out: "Viva Mexico, Viva la Independencia!"[38] Salm-Salm avoided the firing squad and returned to Europe, just in time for the wars of German Unification. The Mexican monarchical experiment was over, but liberal constitutionalism had not won.

With the end of the foreign occupation, Mexico hoped for peace and stability; however, the Constitution of 1857 did not last. During the war,

---

[36] Andrew F. Rolle, *The Lost Cause: The Confederate Exodus to Mexico* (Norman: University of Oklahoma Press, 1965); Daniel E. Sutherland, *The Confederate Carpetbaggers* (Baton Rouge: Louisiana State University Press, 1988).

[37] Ridley, *Maximilian and Juarez*, 244–245, 255–256. The rumor that France intended to create an independent Polish state was confirmed a couple weeks later by Bernstorff and Goltz (March 26, 3:423 and March 26, 3:427). The Herzog von Leuchtenberg was mentioned as a possible king for Poland. Werther to Bismarck, March 3, 1863, Usedom and Wilhelm I, March 27, 1863, *Die Auswärtige Politik Preussens, 1858–1871* (Oldenburg i. O., Germany: G. Stalling, 1935), 3:355, 433; Otto Pflanze, *Bismarck and the Development of Germany* (Princeton, NJ: Princeton University Press, 1963, 1973), 1:195–196.

[38] Salm-Salm and Salm-Salm, *Queretaro*, 1:175–196; Haslip, *The Crown of Mexico*, Chapter 30–31, 498; Ridley, *Maximilian and Juarez*, Chapter 25, 228–240, 277.

Maximiliano had offered José de la Cruz Porfirio Díaz Mori a command in the imperial army, but Díaz refused. Upon Juárez's reelection in 1868, Díaz sought opportunities to enhance his power and unsuccessfully rebelled against Juárez. After receiving an amnesty and getting elected to the Mexican congress in 1874, Díaz started to plot the overthrow of the Mexican constitutional government with the Plan de Tuxtepec. On May 12, 1877, he became president of Mexico and remained so for the next thirty years. A conservative-minded man overthrew the liberal institutions he created and fought for. Díaz's ascent in Mexico signaled a new age in the Atlantic world.[39] Conservative political powerbrokers usurped the accomplishments and agenda of constitutionalism and nationalism for their own benefits.

After his release from Mexican captivity, Salm-Salm returned to Prussia and military service. He returned to a region in turmoil, just like the United States and Mexico. Relations between Austria and Prussia deteriorated after Prussia had to accept the humiliation of Austria's leadership within the German Bund. In September 1862, the Prussian king, faced with a constitutional crisis over military and political reforms, called on Otto von Bismarck to assume the premiership, a consequential change in leadership.[40] In late 1863, the Schleswig-Holstein question, unsatisfactory settled in the Protocol of London of 1852, once more escalated.[41]

---

[39] Paul H. Garner, *Porfirio Díaz* (Harlow, UK: Longman, 2001); Richard B. McCornack, "Porfirio Díaz en la Frontera Texana, 1875–1877," *Historia Mexicana* 5 (January 1956), 373–410; Laurens B. Perry, *Juárez and Díaz: Machine Politics in Mexico* (DeKalb: Northern Illinois University Press, 1978).

[40] Edward Crankshaw, *Bismarck* (New York: Viking Press, 1981); Erich Eyck, *Bismarck and the German Empire* (New York: W. W. Norton, 1968); Edgar Feuchtwanger, *Bismarck* (London, UK: Routledge, 2002); George O. Kent, *Bismarck and His Times* (Carbondale: Southern Illinois University Press, 1978); Alan J. P. Taylor, *Bismarck: The Man and the Statesman* (New York: Alfred A. Knopf, 1955); D. G. Williamson, *Bismarck and Germany 1862–1890* (London, UK: Longman, 1998).

[41] William Carr, *The Origins of the Wars of German Unification* (London, UK: Longman, 1991); Werner E. Mosse, "Queen Victoria and Her Ministers in the Schleswig-Holstein Crisis 1863–1864," *English Historical Review* 78 (April 1963), 263–283; Keith A. P. Sandiford, *Great Britain and the Schleswig-Holstein Question 1848–64: A Study in Diplomacy, Politics, and Public Opinion* (Toronto, Canada: University of Toronto Press, 1975); Alexander Scharff, *Schleswig-Holstein und die Auflösung des dänischen Gesamtstaates, 1830–1864/67* (Schleswig, Germany: Gesellschaft für schleswig-holsteinische Geschichte, 1973); Lawrence D. Steefel, *The Schleswig-Holstein Question* (Cambridge, MA: Harvard University Press, 1932).

The events quickly turned violent with Prussian and Austrian troops invading Schleswig-Holstein and soundly defeating the Danish forces.[42] Unfulfilled, Bismarck prepared for the next step to bring about German unification.

Unsatisfied with the joint occupation of the duchies, the Austrians demanded a clarification of the situation, asking the German Bund to assist in the search for a solution. Bismarck used the treaty violation to provoke war. The short war brought an unexpected Prussian victory, allowing the unification of northern Germany. Over the following four years, Bismarck prepared to create a crisis with France to complete German unification.[43] He accomplished his goal in July 1870 with the outbreak of the Franco-German War. Fighting with the Prussians, Felix Salm-Salm suffered a wound at the Battle of Gravelotte that took his life on August 18, 1870.[44] In contrast, the French emperor was unable to suffer an honorable death on the battlefield and the French quickly abandoned empire and turned once again to republican government when their emperor's capture became known.[45] In their defense, the French looked to the Italian hero Garibaldi for assistance who commanded a French army in the Vosges, which included guerillas, or franc-tireur. Soldiers and populace alike were jubilant at Garibaldi's arrival.[46] Victory over France allowed Bismarck to complete German unification. On January 18, 1871, the German princes declared in the Hall of Mirrors at Versailles the German Empire with Wilhelm I of Prussia as emperor. German nationalism had finally succeeded. However, the German

---

[42] Schleiden to Smidt, August 30, 1860, 2-C.4.b.2.h.1; Schleiden to Smidt, November 25, 1864; Merck to Smidt, November 26, 1864, 2-C.4.b.2.h.1, SAB.; Carr, *Origins of the Wars of German Unification*, 64–76.

[43] Crankshaw, *Bismarck*; Eyck, *Bismarck and the German Empire*; Kent, *Bismarck and His Times*; Pflanze, *Bismarck and the Development of Germany*; Taylor, *Bismarck*; David Wetzel, *A Duel of Giants: Bismarck, Napoleon III, and the Origins of the Franco-Prussian War* (Madison: University of Wisconsin Press, 2001).

[44] Coffey, *Soldier Princess*, 86–87; White, *The Prince and the Yankee*, Chapter 13.

[45] Scholarship has not yet explored how much the guerrilla war in Mexico influenced the French decision to engage in a similar defense of their homeland. Philip M. Katz, *From Appomattox to Montmartre: Americans and the Paris Commune* (Cambridge, MA: Harvard University Press, 1998); Robert P. Tombs, *The Paris Commune, 1871* (London, UK: Longman, 1999); Roger L. Williams, *The French Revolution of 1870–1871* (New York: W. W. Norton, 1969).

[46] Garibaldi, *Garibaldi*, 2:216.

nation-state was a conservative creation forged in war.[47] In North America and Europe, new nation-states emerged in the process of war.

Where Salm-Salm died from wounds sustained at Gravelotte, Asbóth died of wounds sustained in Florida during his work as diplomatic representative of the United States in Argentina, where he tried to bring about peace between the parties of the Guerra del Paraguay. The conflict pitched the nationalism of Paraguay and its eccentric leader, Francisco Solano López Carrillo, against the developing nationalism of Brazil, Uruguay, and Argentina. The Paraguayan dictator López ruled the country in a dictatorial fashion, without the need to consult elected representatives. He relied on foreigners for military expertise. Born in 1804 in Hungary, Franz Wisner von Morgenstern arrived in Paraguay in the late 1840s. He was one of many foreigners to serve in the Paraguayan army and is credited with developing the defensive plans for Humaitá.[48] Even some of López's opponents, like the Brazilian emperor Dom Pedro II, were Europhiles. After ascending to the throne at age six, Dom Pedro formally became emperor on July 18, 1841. On May 3, 1843, he married Teresa Cristina of the Two Sicilies to gain legitimacy for the Brazilian monarchy among the European royal families. Pedro especially loved French culture and often inquired with travelers about European tastes.[49] Throughout his reign, Dom Pedro considered himself first citizen, honored the constitutional monarchy, quarreled with his ministers, and helped create a Brazilian national identity.[50]

[47] Eyck, *Bismarck and the German Empire*, 139–141, 316–323.

[48] Michael Lillis and Ronan Fanning, *The Lives of Eliza Lynch: Scandal and Courage* (Dublin, Ireland: Gill and Macmillan, 2009); James S. Saeger, *Francisco Solano López and the Ruination of Paraguay: Honor and Egocentrism* (Lanham, MD: Rowman and Littlefield, 2007); Thomas L. Whigham, *The Paraguayan War: Causes and Early Conduct* (Lincoln: University of Nebraska Press, 2002), 107–108, 176.

[49] Barman, *Citizen Emperor*, 75, 84–87, 116–119, 232–239, 275–285, also see Lilia M. Schwarcz, *The Emperor's Beard: Dom Pedro II and the Tropical Monarchy of Brazil*, trans. John Gledson (New York: Hill and Wang, 2004).

[50] For works on Brazil's nation making process see Peter M. Beattie, *The Tribute of Blood: Army, Honor, Race, and Nation in Brazil, 1864–1945* (Durham, NC: Duke University Press, 2001); Jose Murilo de Carvalho, "Political Elites and State Building: The Case of Nineteenth-Century Brazil," *Comparative Studies in Society and History* 23 (July 1982), 378–399; Darcy Riberio, *The Brazilian People: The Formation and Meaning of Brazil*, trans Gregory Rabassa (Gainesville: University Press of Florida, 1995); Eugene W. Ridings, "Interest Groups and Development: The Case of Brazil in the Nineteenth Century," *Journal of Latin American Studies* 9 (November 1977), 225–250.

The war arose out of Paraguay's territorial dilemma, being the only landlocked country in Latin America, and its desire for a self-sufficient economy. In the process of those reforms, Paraguay became rigidly centralized, a dictatorship, very modern in its extent. In 1862, after assuming power, López desired to modernize the country's army. López developed the idea of a "Greater Paraguay," which would include direct access to the sea. To achieve his goals, López allied himself with Uruguay's ruling Blanco party. However, Paraguayan armies had to cross Argentinean territory to reach Uruguay, dragging Argentina into the war. On October 16, 1864, Brazilian troops invaded Uruguay to ensure political stability and support the Colorado party. As a result, the crisis in the Rio de la Plata region escalated, the Guerra del Paraguay had started.[51]

After Paraguay's attack, Brazil and her allies soon took the offensive, repulsing the Paraguayan armies. A Brazilian naval victory near Riachuelo on the Paraná River on June 11, 1865, destroyed much of the Paraguayan navy and placed López on the defensive. By late 1865, the alliance invaded Paraguay. Under the leadership of Marshal Luís Alves de Lima e Silva, the Marquis of Caxias, the armies attacked the Paraguayan fortifications around Humaitá, which fell on July 25, 1868. As a result, Paraguay's capital at Asunción lay exposed. To prevent the capture of the capital, López threw what was left of his army against the slowly advancing Caxias.[52] On January 1, 1869, the allies occupied the Paraguayan capital. However, López and a substantial number of his soldiers remained on the run. On March 1, 1870, troops of the alliance came upon one of the last camps of the Paraguayan army, López's hiding spot. What exactly transpired during the ensuing fight remains a mystery.

---

[51] Whigham, *The Paraguayan War*, Chapters 6 and 9, 36–41, 63–69, 159–161; also see Francisco Doratioto, *Maldita Guerra: Nueva Historia de la Guerra del Paraguay* (Buenos Aires, Argentina: Emecé Editories, 2004).

[52] For other works on the war see Diego Abente, "The War of the Triple Alliance: Three Explanatory Models," *Latin American Research Review* 22 (1987), 47–69; Leslie Bethell, *The Paraguayan War, 1864–1870* (London, UK: Institute of Latin American Studies, 1996); Chris Leuchars, *To the Bitter End: Paraguay and the War of the Triple Alliance* (Westport, CT: Greenwood Press, 2002); Whigham, *The Paraguayan War*, Chapter 4, 276–281.

By the end, López was dead.[53] The Guerra del Paraguay was the result of a fierce Paraguayan nationalism centered on a dictator, creating a new nationalism in all the belligerent countries, giving rise to reforms in Brazil that eventually ended the monarchy.

Since the examples set by the Thirteen Colonies and the French Revolution, political reformers called for the creation of nation-states with constitutional governments. Their efforts met with limited success during the revolutionary upheavals in 1830 and 1848. By the 1850s, different opinions about national identities collided in conflicts in the Dano-German borderland and the Americas. As the United States, Italian, German, and Mexican lands debated their national identities and best form of government, violent conflicts became the unfortunate means to settle these questions. From the violence plagued decades emerged a conservative Italian nation-state with limited political power granted to the people, even more the new Germany centered power in the emperor and chancellor leaving the elected legislative assembly largely powerless. In Mexico, the victory of the constitutional forces that had brought about the Constitution of 1857 and won against the conservatives in the Guerra de Reforma seemed to indicate the liberal future of the country. However, even in Mexico, dictatorship soon followed the liberal victory against the French-supported conservative-monarchical experiment. While the United States claimed victory against the southern rebellion, the country turned more conservative in the aftermath of the rebellion. These were international, Atlantic conflicts. Military figures, mercenaries, and soldiers of fortune crisscross the ocean in search of opportunities, such as Salm-Salm. Others like Lieber, Asbóth, and Schurz brought European political experiences with them to the Americas and infused their intellectual baggage into these conflicts. By the 1870s, conservatives created the constitutional nation-states their opponents had tried to bring into existence for the past half-century. The movement of people from Egypt, Belgium, Ireland, and Hungary dramatically altered the events in the Americas, creating an environment significantly different from what it would have been without. The Atlantic interchange of ideas and people fostered the creation of these conservative nation-states.

---

[53] Leuchars, *To the Bitter End*, 212–216, 230, 236–237.

Bibliography

Abente, Diego. "The War of the Triple Alliance: Three Explanatory Models." *Latin American Research Review* 22 (1987): 47–69.

A'Hearn, Brian. "Could Southern Italians Cooperate? Banche Popolari in the Mezzogiorno." *Journal of Economic History* 60 (March 2000): 67–93.

Alianello, Carlo. *La Conquista del Sud: Il Risorgimento Nell'Italia Meridionale.* Milan, Italy: Rusconi, 1972.

Barman, Roderick J. *Citizen Emperor: Pedro II and the Making of Brazil, 1825–91.* Stanford, CA: Stanford University Press, 1999.

Basler, Roy P., ed. *The Collected Works of Abraham Lincoln.* New Brunswick, NJ: Rutgers University Press, 1953.

Bazant, Jan. "The Division of Some Mexican Haciendas During the Liberal Revolution, 1856–1862." *Journal of Latin American Studies* 3 (May 1971): 25–37.

Beales, Derek. *The Risorgimento and the Unification of Italy.* London, UK: George Allen and Unwin, 1971.

Beattie, Peter M. *The Tribute of Blood: Army, Honor, Race, and Nation in Brazil, 1864–1945.* Durham, NC: Duke University Press, 2001.

Bethell, Leslie. *The Paraguayan War, 1864–1870.* London, UK: Institute of Latin American Studies, 1996.

Black, Jeremy. *The Age of Total War, 1860–1945.* Westport, CO: Praeger Security International, 2006.

Brancaforte, Charlotte L., ed. *The German Forty-Eighters in the United States.* New York: Peter Lang, 1989.

Carr, William. *The Origins of the Wars of German Unification.* London, UK: Longman, 1991.

Case, Lynn M. *Franco-Italian Relations 1860–1865: The Roman Question and the Convention of September.* New York: AMS Press, 1932.

Cavanagh, Michael. *Memoirs of General Thomas Francis Meagher: Comprising the Leading Events of His Career Chronologically Arranged.* Worcester, MA: Messenger Press, 1892.

Cingari, Gaetano. *Brigantaggio, Proprietari e Contadini nel Sud: 1799–1900.* Reggio Calabria, Italy: Editori Meridionali Riuniti, 1976.

Coffey, Dana. *Soldier Princess: The Life and Legend of Agnes Salm-Salm in North America, 1861–1867.* College Station: Texas A&M University Press, 2002.

Conacher, J. B. *Britain and the Crimea, 1855–1856: Problems of War and Peace.* New York: St. Martin's Press, 1987.

Cooper, William J., Jr. *Jefferson Davis, American.* New York: Vintage Books, 2000.

Cooper, William J., Jr. *The South and the Politics of Slavery, 1828–1856.* Baton Rouge: Louisiana State University Press, 1978.

Crankshaw, Edward. *Bismarck*. New York: Viking Press, 1981.
Cunningham, Michele. *Mexico and the Foreign Policy of Napoleon III*. New York: Palgrave, 2001.
Dal Lago, Enrico. "'States of Rebellion': Civil War, Rural Unrest, and the Agrarian Question in the American South and the Italian Mezzogiorno, 1861–1865." *Comparative Studies in Society and History* 47 (April 2005): 403–432.
Davis, William C. *"A Government of Our Own:" The Making of the Confederacy*. Baton Rouge: Louisiana State University Press, 1994.
Dawsey, Cyrus B., and James Dawsey. *The Confederados: Old South Immigrants in Brazil*. Tuscaloosa: University of Alabama Press, 1995.
de Carvalho, Jose Murilo. "Political Elites and State Building: The Case of Nineteenth-Century Brazil." *Comparative Studies in Society and History* 23 (July 1982): 378–399.
De Matteo, Giovanni. *Brigantaggio e Risorgimento: Legittimisti e Briganti tra i Borbone e i Savoia*. Naples, Italy: A. Guida, 2000.
Declaration of the Immediate Causes Which Induce and Justify the Secession. Charleston, SC: Evans and Cogswell, 1860.
Delzell, Charles F., ed. *The Unification of Italy, 1859–1861: Cavour, Mazzini, or Garibaldi?* Malabar, FL: Robert E. Krieger Publishing Company, 1976.
Despatches from U.S. Ministers to Austria, National Archives. Washington, DC.
Despatches from U.S. Ministers to the Italian States, National Archives. Washington, DC.
Doratioto, Francisco. *Maldita Guerra: Nueva Historia de la Guerra del Paraguay*. Buenos Aires, Argentina: Emecé Editores, 2004.
Dunn, John. "Africa Invades the New World: Egypt's Mexican Adventure, 1863–1867." *War in History* 4 (1997): 27–34.
Evans, Charles M. *War of the Aeronauts*. Mechanicsburg, PA: Stackpole Books, 2002.
Eyck, Erich. *Bismarck and the German Empire*. New York: W. W. Norton, 1968.
Feuchtwanger, Edgar. *Bismarck*. London, UK: Routledge, 2002.
Foner, Eric. *Free Soil Free Labor Free Men: The Ideology of the Republican Party Before the Civil War*. New York: Oxford University Press, 1970.
Foner, Eric. *Reconstruction: America's Unfinished Revolution, 1863–1877*. New York: Harper and Row, 1988.
Förster, Stig, and Jörg Nagler. *On the Road to Total War: The American Civil War and the German Wars of Unification, 1861–1871*. Washington, DC: German Historical Institute, 1997.
Fowler, Will. *Santa Anna of Mexico*. Lincoln: University of Nebraska Press, 2007.
Freehling, William W. *The Road to Disunion*. 2 vols. New York: Oxford University Press, 1990, 2007.

Freidel, Frank B. *Francis Lieber: Nineteenth-Century Liberal.* Baton Rouge: Louisiana State University Press, 1947.
Fremantle, Arthur J. L. *The Fremantle Diary.* Edited by Walter Lord. New York: Capricorn Books, 1960.
Friese, Christian. *Die Auswärtige Politik Preussens, 1858–1871.* Oldenburg i. O., Germany: G. Stalling, 1935.
Garibaldi, Giuseppe. *Garibaldi: An Autobiography.* 3 vols. Edited by Alexandre Dumas. Translated by William Robson. London, UK: Routledge, Warne, and Routledge, 1861.
Garner, Paul H. *Porfirio Díaz.* Harlow, UK: Longman, 2001.
Green, Michael S. *Freedom, Union, and Power: Lincoln and His Party During the Civil War.* New York: Fordham University Press, 2004.
Griggs, William C. *The Elusive Eden: Frank McMullan's Confederate Colony in Brazil.* Austin: University of Texas Press, 1987.
Grimsley, Mark. *The Hard Hand of War: Union Military Policy Toward Southern Civilians, 1861–1865.* New York: Cambridge University Press, 1995.
Hanna, Alfred J., and Kathryn A. Hanna. *Confederate Exiles in Venezuela.* Tuscaloosa, AL: Confederate Publishing Company, 1960.
Hanson, Lawrence D. T. "Voluntarios Extranjeros en los Ejércitos Liberales Mexicanos, 1854–1867." *Historia Mexicana* 37 (October 1987): 205–237.
Harter, Eugene C. *The Lost Colony of the Confederacy.* Jackson: University Press of Mississippi, 1985.
Haslip, Joan. *The Crown of Mexico: Maximilian and His Empress Carlota.* New York: Holt, Rinehart and Winston, 1971.
Hearder, Harry. *Italy in the Age of the Risorgimento, 1790–1870.* London, UK: Longman, 1983.
Hegarty, Aidan. *John Mitchel: A Cause Too Many.* Belfast, UK: Camlane Press, 2005.
Hibbert, Christopher. *Garibaldi and His Enemies: The Clash of Arms and Personalities in the Making of Italy.* Boston, MA: Little, Brown and Company, 1965.
Hill, Richard Leslie, and Peter C. Hogg. *A Black Corps D'élite: An Egyptian Sudanese Conscript Battalion with the French Army in Mexico, 1863–1867, and Its Survivors in Subsequent African History.* East Lansing: Michigan State University Press, 1995.
Holt, Michael F. *The Rise and Fall of the American Whig Party: Jacksonian Politics and the Onset of the Civil War.* New York: Oxford University Press, 1999.
Iwańska, Alicja. *British American Loyalists in Canada and U.S. Southern Confederates in Brazil: Exiles from the United States.* Lewiston: E. Mellen Press, 1993.

Jarnagin, Laura. *A Confluence of Transatlantic Networks: Elites, Capitalism, and Confederate Migration to Brazil.* Tuscaloosa: University of Alabama Press, 2008.

Katz, Philip M. *From Appomattox to Montmartre: Americans and the Paris Commune.* Cambridge, MA: Harvard University Press, 1998.

Kent, George O. *Bismarck and His Times.* Carbondale: Southern Illinois University Press, 1978.

Lesesne, Henry H., and Charles R. Mack. *Francis Lieber and the Culture of the Mind.* Columbia: University of South Carolina Press, 2005.

Leuchars, Chris. *To the Bitter End: Paraguay and the War of the Triple Alliance.* Westport, CT: Greenwood Press, 2002.

Levine, Bruce. *The Spirit of 1848: German Immigrants, Labor Conflict, and the Coming of the Civil War.* Urbana: University of Illinois Press, 1992.

Lillis, Michael, and Ronan Fanning. *The Lives of Eliza Lynch: Scandal and Courage.* Dublin, Ireland: Gill and Macmillan, 2009.

Mack Smith, Dennis. "Cavour's Attitude to Garibaldi's Expedition to Sicily." *Cambridge Historical Journal* 9 (1949): 359–370.

Mack Smith, Dennis. *Cavour and Garibaldi, 1860: A Study in Political Conflict.* Cambridge, UK: Cambridge University Press, 1954.

Mack Smith, Dennis. *Victor Emanuel, Cavour, and the Risorgimento.* London, UK: Oxford University Press, 1971.

McCornack, Richard B. "Porfirio Díaz en la Frontera Texana, 1875–1877." *Historia Mexicana* 5 (January 1956): 373–410.

Mehrländer, Andrea. "'… ist dass nicht reiner Sclavenhandel?' Die illegale Rekrutierung deutscher Auswanderer für die Unionsarmee im amerikanischen Bürgerkrieg." *Amerikastudien* 44 (1999): 65–93.

Molfese, Franco. *Storia del Brigantaggio dopo l'Unità.* Milan, Italy: Feltrinelli, 1966.

Morris, Stephen D. "Reforming the Nation: Mexican Nationalism in Context." *Journal of Latin American Studies* 31 (May 1999): 363–397.

Mosse, Werner E. "Queen Victoria and Her Ministers in the Schleswig-Holstein Crisis 1863–1864." *English Historical Review* 78 (April 1963): 263–283.

Mosse, Werner E. *The Rise and Fall of the Crimean System, 1855–71: The Story of a Peace Settlement.* London, UK: MacMillan, 1963.

Neely, Mark E., Jr. *Southern Rights: Political Prisoners and the Myth of Confederate Constitutionalism.* Charlottesville: University Press of Virginia, 1999.

Neely, Mark E., Jr. *The Union Divided: Party Conflict in the Civil War North.* Cambridge, MA: Harvard University Press, 2002.

Nelson, Scott R. *Iron Confederacies: Southern Railways, Klan Violence, and Reconstruction.* Chapel Hill: University of North Carolina Press, 1999.

Osgood, Samuel M. *Napoleon III and the Second Empire*. Lexington, MA: D. C. Heath and Company, 1973.

Owsley, Frank L. *King Cotton Diplomacy; Foreign Relations of the Confederate States of America*. Chicago, IL: University of Chicago Press, 1931. Reprint. Revised by Harriet C. Owsley. Chicago, IL: University of Chicago Press, 1959.

Perman, Michael. *Reunion Without Compromise; The South and Reconstruction, 1865–1868*. Cambridge, UK: Cambridge University Press, 1973.

Perman, Michael. *The Road to Redemption: Southern Politics, 1869–1879*. Chapel Hill: University of North Carolina Press, 1984.

Perry, Laurens B. *Juárez and Díaz: Machine Politics in Mexico*. DeKalb: Northern Illinois University Press, 1978.

Pflanze, Otto. *Bismarck and the Development of Germany*. Princeton, NJ: Princeton University Press, 1963, 1973.

Potter, David M. *The Impending Crisis, 1848–1861*. New York: Harper Perennial, 1976.

Quinn, James. *John Mitchel*. Dublin, Ireland: University College Dublin Press, 2008.

Rable, George C. *But There Was No Peace: The Role of Violence in the Politics of Reconstruction*. Athens: University of Georgia Press, 1984.

Rable, George C. *The Confederate Republic: A Revolution Against Politics*. Chapel Hill: University of North Carolina Press, 1994.

Riall, L. J. "Liberal Policy and the Control of Public Order in Western Sicily, 1860–1862." *Historical Journal* 35 (June 1992): 345–368.

Riberio, Darcy. *The Brazilian People: The Formation and Meaning of Brazil*. Translated by Gregory Rabassa. Gainesville: University Press of Florida, 1995.

Ridings, Eugene W. "Interest Groups and Development: The Case of Brazil in the Nineteenth Century." *Journal of Latin American Studies* 9 (November 1977): 225–250.

Ridley, Jasper. *Maximilian and Juárez*. New York: Ricknor and Fields, 1992.

Rolle, Andrew F. *The Lost Cause: The Confederate Exodus to Mexico*. Norman: University of Oklahoma Press, 1965.

Romano, Valentino. *Brigantesse: Donne Guerrigliere Contro la Conquista del Sud, 1860–1870*. Naples, Italy: Controcorrente, 2007.

Rugemer, Edward B. *The Problem of Emancipation: The Caribbean Roots of the American Civil War*. Baton Rouge: Louisiana State University Press, 2008.

Saeger, James S. *Francisco Solano López and the Ruination of Paraguay: Honor and Egocentrism*. Lanham, MD: Rowman and Littlefield, 2007.

Salvadori, Massimo. *Cavour and the Unification of Italy*. Princeton, NJ: D. Van Norstrand Company, 1961.

Sandiford, Keith A. P. *Great Britain and the Schleswig-Holstein Question 1848–64: A Study in Diplomacy, Politics, and Public Opinion*. Toronto, Canada: University of Toronto Press, 1975.

Sanginés, Pedro Salmerón. *Juárez: La Rebelión Interminable*. Mexico City, Mexico: Editorial Planeta Mexicana, 2007.

Scharff, Alexander. *Schleswig-Holstein und die Auflösung des dänischen Gesamtstaates, 1830–1864/67*. Schleswig, Germany: Gesellschaft für schleswig-holsteinische Geschichte, 1973, 1980.

Scheibert, Justus. *Sieben Monate in den Rebellen Staaten während des nordamerikanischen Krieges 1863*. Wyk auf Föhr, Germany: Verlag für Amerikanistik, 1993.

Scheina, Robert L. *Santa Anna: A Curse Upon Mexico*. Washington, DC: Brassey's, 2002.

Schoen, Brian. *The Fragile Fabric of Union: Cotton, Federal Politics, and the Global Origins of the Civil War*. Baltimore, MD: Johns Hopkins University Press, 2009.

Schroeder, Paul W. *Austria, Great Britain, and the Crimean War: The Destruction of the European Concert*. Ithaca, NY: Cornell University Press, 1972.

Schwarcz, Lilia M. *The Emperor's Beard: Dom Pedro II and the Tropical Monarchy of Brazil*. Translated by John Gledson. New York: Hill and Wang, 2004.

Scirocco, Alfonso. *Garibaldi: Citizen of the World*. Translated by Allan Cameron. Princeton, NJ: Princeton University Press, 2007.

Sinkin, Richard N. *The Mexican Reform, 1855–1876: A Study in Liberal Nation-Building*. Austin, TX: Institute of Latin American Studies, 1979.

Steefel, Lawrence D. *The Schleswig-Holstein Question*. Cambridge, MA: Harvard University Press, 1932.

Sutherland, Daniel E. *A Savage Conflict: The Decisive Role of Guerrillas in the American Civil War*. Chapel Hill, NC: University of North Carolina Press, 2009.

Sutherland, Daniel E. *The Confederate Carpetbaggers*. Baton Rouge: Louisiana State University Press, 1988.

Sutherland, Daniel E. *The Emergence of Total War*. Abilene, TX: McWhiney Foundation Press, 1996.

Taylor, Alan J. P. *Bismarck: The Man and the Statesman*. New York: Alfred A. Knopf, 1955.

Tombs, Robert P. *The Paris Commune, 1871*. London, UK: Longman, 1999.

Trelease, Allen W. *White Terror: The Ku Klux Klan Conspiracy and Southern Reconstruction*. New York: Harper and Row, 1971.

Trevelyan, George M. *Garibaldi and the Thousand*. London, UK: Phoenix Press, 2001.

Vida, István Kornél. *Hungarian Émigrés in the American Civil War: A History and Biographical Dictionary.* Jefferson, NC: McFarland, 2012.

von Fritsch, Frederick Otto. *A Gallant Captain of the Civil War.* Edited by Joseph T. Butts. New York: F. Tennyson Neely, 1902.

Weaver, Jace. *The Red Atlantic: American Indigenes and the Making of the Modern World, 1000–1927.* Chapel Hill: The University of North Carolina Press, 2014.

Wetzel, David. *A Duel of Giants: Bismarck, Napoleon III, and the Origins of the Franco-Prussian War.* Madison: University of Wisconsin Press, 2001.

Whigham, Thomas L. *The Paraguayan War: Causes and Early Conduct.* Lincoln: University of Nebraska Press, 2002.

White, Robert N. *The Prince and the Yankee: The Tale of a Country Girl Who Became a Princess.* London, UK: I. B. Tauris, 2003.

Williams, Roger L. *The French Revolution of 1870–1871.* New York: W. W. Norton, 1969.

Williamson, D. G. *Bismarck and Germany 1862–1890.* London, UK: Longman, 1998.

Wittke, Carl. *Refugees of Revolution: The German Forty-Eighters in America.* Philadelphia: University of Pennsylvania Press, 1952.

Zucker, Adolph E., ed. *The Forty-Eighters: Political Refugees of the German Revolution of 1848.* New York: Columbia University Press, 1950.

CHAPTER 13

Atlantic Tourism

> If you would win confidence and respect in good society, especially in England, preserve your republican simplicity of character ... If you wish to make yourself ridiculous, the best course is to cringe to rank and wealth ... I have seen many instances, and read of more, in which prejudice and disgust have been excited against the whole American people, by this sort of conduct on the part of their representatives.[1]

The nineteenth century witnessed not only a dramatic transformation in politics, racial issues, and economics; the emergence of steam vessels and railroads created possibilities for people to travel longer distances and to see exotic parts of the world, such as the Caribbean, the Plains of the United States, or the wild animals of West Africa. Well-off individuals have always been able to travel to remote locations, but possibilities increased dramatically during the nineteenth century. In addition, travel became more affordable for individuals with lower incomes. Localized travel was common around the Atlantic, for example, a low country South Carolina planter might abandoned the unhealthy coastal plains in the summer for the cooler and healthier spas and towns in the mountains. The nineteenth century saw the emergence of a professionally organized tourism industry. The mythology people associated with the

---

[1] George P. Putnam, *The Tourist in Europe: Or, A Concise Summary of the Various Routes, Objects of Interest, &c in Great Britain, France, Switzerland, Italy, Germany, Belgium, and Holland* (New York: Wiley and Putnam, 1838), 6.

frontier, unclaimed wilderness, and the wild, savage-like native people stimulated people's imagination. Especially in the ever more restricted and urbanized Europe, people longed for an opportunity to see such a mythical region. If they had the ability and money, people traveled extensively, often for months and at times even years. Many wrote or reported their experiences to a reading audience, inviting others to go on a similar excursion, dramatically transforming travel behavior. The following chapter will illustrate some of the transformations in the emerging tourism business starting with the examples of the Marquis de La Fayette, the Brazilian Emperor Dom Pedro II, and Theodore Roosevelt. These three will illustrate some of the major themes of nineteenth-century tourism, adventurism, and the seeking out of new cultures and places. Closing the chapter will be the entrepreneurial side of tourism with the appearance of companies such as Thomas Cook, which sold tourist itineraries to customers. What once was only available to explorers and a select few was increasingly available to a wider population. Tourism tied the Atlantic world together and reshaped people's understanding of the region, enhancing their desire to see exotic places.

Before tourism could make any substantial inroads in the Atlantic world, there was a need for a transportation revolution. When the Grand Tour first started in the early 1600s, transportation networks in Europe were primitive. Even by the second half of the eighteenth century, travel was difficult, but roads improved, cross Channel ferries ran on a regular schedule, and coach services connected the ports with the interior. Once in Calais, travelers could take coach services or rent a coach themselves with regular stations arranged along the route to Paris. As travel accommodations improved, tourists continued to plan for lengthy delays as weather made the Channel crossing or road travel impossible. Eventually, the advent of steam power with railroads and steamships allowed for more secure and reliable travel.[2]

The most important literature for any aspiring tourist was the guidebook. In 1838, George Putnam published a travel guide for individuals from the United States interested in visiting Europe. In an age without an internationally agreed upon citizenship or passport system, travelers still required travel documentation. Putnam suggested approaching the State Department or the US minister in the country of arrival for

---

[2] Lynne Withey, *Grand Tours and Cooks' Tours: A History of Leisure Travel, 1750–1915* (New York: W. Morrow, 1997), 8–9, 11–12.

a passport. Even more, travel required money and considering the complicated financial channels across the Atlantic world, the easiest way to maintain sufficient travel funds was to obtain a letter of credit for a respected financial house in London or Paris, which would allow the tourist to draw money when needed not only at the specific house in London but also cooperating houses across Europe. In addition, focused on Great Britain, Putnam laid out the different benefits of taking a packet to London, Liverpool, or Le Havre. He believed Liverpool the superior option, especially if the tourist intended to visit Scotland or Ireland. He advised against the London packet, which arrived in Portsmouth and not London, and required a dull, seventy-mile overland journey by coach. Importantly, travelers should not take too much luggage, especially for excursions. Too many bags increased the danger of theft.[3] However, Europe was not the only destination people desired to visit.

Similar travel guides provided interested tourists information about North America. Wellington Williams provided one such traveler's guide in 1851. With the maze of different transportation options and independently operating railroad companies, Williams perceived the need to enlighten his readers with some details about travel distance, time, and estimated cost. For New York, Williams pointed out fourteen railroad and steamboat lines that converged in the city, such as the Hudson River Railroad, New Jersey Railroad, and Norwich and Worcester Line. In addition, he provided basic information about cost; a trip from New York to Washington was 224 miles in length, requiring about twelve and a half hours at a cost of $4.50. Furthermore, passengers arriving in the port received a beneficial list of how far certain streets were from the Battery, Exchange, and City Hall. Aware that Europeans often sought out spas for health benefits, Williams included a list of "Fashionable and Healthful Resort" in his guide. He included the most famous like the White Mountains in New Hampshire and Catskill Mountains in New York.[4]

---

[3] George P. Putnam, *The Tourist in Europe: Or, A Concise Summary of the Various Routes, Objects of Interest, &c in Great Britain, France, Switzerland, Italy, Germany, Belgium, and Holland* (New York: Wiley and Putnam, 1838), 9–10.

[4] Wellington Williams, *The Traveller's and Tourist's Guide Through the United States of America, Canada* (Philadelphia, PA: Lippincott, Grambo, 1851), 38–40, 42, 183–189; John F. Sears, *Sacred Places: American Tourist Attractions in the Nineteenth Century* (New York: Oxford University Press, 1989).

However, the list included also some lesser known and more remote springs, such as Hot Springs in Arkansas, which was 53 miles from the state capital in Little Rock. He noted, "They derive importance from the great virtue of the medicinal waters in the vicinity, and are now becoming every season more popular. The waters have been found efficacious in chronic diseases, such as scrofula, rheumatism, &c." In addition to the vast number of springs, Williams also included some other tourist spots, for example, Mount Vernon and the Tomb of George Washington. A visit could cost as much as $6, which included an hour to roam the ground at Mount Vernon. Williams noted that the "best plan ... is to take the ferry-boat from Washington to Alexandria, ... [where] a conveyance may be hired for the trip, which will cost from $3 to $4." In addition, direct steamers from Alexandria and Washington to Mount Vernon usually operated in the summer for as little as $1. He noted that entrance to the house was only possible with letters addressed to the owners, but the grounds were open.[5]

Williams built in part on the emergence of what in the United States became known as the Northern Tour, in reference to the European Grand Tour. As early as the 1790, prosperity in the United States and an improved infrastructure network created a desire for tourism. Entrepreneurs created hotels and even resorts along the route. As historian Thomas Chambers explains, "By the 1820s, prominent resorts such as Saratoga Springs, New York, and White Sulphur Springs, Virginia, emerged as destinations of choice for the national tourist class." Sightseeing and meeting people along the trip became key aspects of tourism in the United States and the creation of steamboats, canals, and eventually, railroads made tourist travel easier. By the second decade of the century, tourists could travel the Northern Tour, which started in New York and went by boat up the Hudson River, allowing visitors to see the Catskill Mountains. After visiting Saratoga Springs and Lake George, tourists traveled along the Erie Canal to marvel at Niagara Falls. The route then curved north into Lake Ontario and the St. Lawrence River Valley to allow tourists a visit to Montreal and Quebec. From French Canada, the tour returned south by way of Lake Champlain. Tourist could alter their trips to include additional locations in New England. Nevertheless, Chambers warned, "They frequently commented

---

[5] Wellington Williams, *The Traveller's and Tourist's Guide Through the United States of America, Canada* (Philadelphia, PA: Lippincott, Grambo, 1851), 196.

on bad hotels and atrocious food, cramped canal boats or lake sloops, boomtowns and rustic locals, and the general challenges of travel in an age of poor roads and improvised accommodations."[6] By the 1820, the United States developed their equivalency to the Grand Tour and were ready to welcome international tourists.

Among the thousands to travel the Atlantic, report on affairs and situation in other parts of the Atlantic world, and take advantage of the Northern Route was Gilbert du Motier, the Marquis de La Fayette. La Fayette visited the United States from July 1824 to September 1825 upon invitation by the US Congress and President James Monroe. The young French noble had supported the colonists in North America in their struggle for independence from the British mother country, gaining laurels at the Battle of Yorktown in 1781. Inspired by the events in North America, the French eventually rose in rebellion and La Fayette was on the frontlines of the French Revolution. He drafted the Declaration of the Rights of Man and of the Citizens and commanded the French National Guard. Having served two revolutions, the return of the Maquis coincided with the celebration of the country's fiftieth anniversary. On July 12, 1824, La Fayette departed Le Havre on board the US merchant ship *Cadmus*.[7] One of the most celebrated tourists of the first half of the century was on his way.

On August 15, New York came into view with the harbor littered by small vessels awaiting the illustrious guest from France. Boats approached the *Cadmus* to inquire if La Fayette was on board. Upon his arrival, La Fayette humored the celebratory spirit in the city for five days, when he took leave for Boston. As he departed New York, the city militia fired a gun salute to the former general. Two of the canons in the battery were from the siege of Yorktown, where La Fayette had fought. Even in Boston, the revolutionary heritage and La Fayette's role in the events reappeared as the citizens took him out to the Bunker Hill battlefield. The memory of the battle was still fresh on the minds of the local residents, La Fayette told the people who gathered around during his visit, "It is with deep respect that I treat this sacred ground, where the blood of the American patriots ... gloriously shed. His blood has called the two

---

[6] Thomas A. Chambers, *Memories of War: Visiting Battlegrounds and Bonefields in the Early American Republic* (Ithaca, NY: Cornell University Press, 2012), 6–8.

[7] Auguste Levasseur, *Lafayette in America, in 1824 and 1825; Or, Journal of Travels, in the United States* (New York: White, Gallaher, and White, 1829), 6.

American continents, to liberty, to republican independence; and has awakened the nations of Europe, to the necessity, and secured, I hope, for the future, the exercise of their rights."[8] Even as a tourist, La Fayette could not escape the momentous events his generation had experienced.

Besides the political, the report on his visit included a number of references, comparing the landscapes of the United States to those in Europe. As the group traveled along the Hudson, their minds wondered back to Europe and the beautiful banks of the Rhine, noting that "for one who prefers wild and virgin Nature, nothing is so beautiful as the borders of the Hudson." Upstate New York was abuzz with activity when La Fayette visited as the state busily worked on the construction on the Erie Canal. Places sprung up where none had existed before, such as Troy, New York. When La Fayette saw Troy, he exclaimed in astonishment "What! Has this city risen from the earth by enchantment?" When he visited last in 1778, Troy consisted of only "two or three little cottages." After spending his first month in New England, on September 27, La Fayette crossed into Pennsylvania. The Pennsylvania militia with 6000 men welcomed the French guest to Philadelphia. While La Fayette spent much of his time visiting various locations of significance from the revolutionary war and entertained guests, he also visited "the institutions of benevolence and public utility" in Philadelphia, including the prisons and other reform projects of the period.[9]

On October 12, La Fayette made his way to Washington, noting "We had been within the boundaries of the city half an hour, before we saw a single habitation. Being laid out on an enormous scale, it will require at least a century to complete the plan of Washington." Only a small stretch between the White House and the Capitol was occupied by homes. La Fayette likely paid little attention that first day as thousands once more welcomed him to their city. The civic spectacle of the French man's arrival at the executive mansion drew comparisons to Europe. Auguste Levasseur reported on the assembled political leaders, "All were dressed, like the President, in plain blue coats, without lace, embroidery, decorations, or any of those puerile ornaments, at which so many simpletons bend the knee in the ante chambers of the European palaces. When Lafayette entered, all the assembly arose; and the President hastening to

---

[8] Ibid., 1:8–9, 24, 39.
[9] Ibid., 1:97, 113, 133, 139.

meet him, embraced him with all the tenderness of a brother." If the audience was not yet aware of the egalitarian character of the United States, this drove home the differences between Europe and the United States. La Fayette only stayed in Washington briefly before continuing to Yorktown for the anniversary celebration.[10]

La Fayette's visit to Virginia included some of the most famous tourist stops. Upon leaving Washington for Alexandria, the French men and his party boarded a steamer. Their first stop was George Washington's estate at Mount Vernon, which had developed into a tourist attraction by the time of the Frenchmen's visit. The sight of the place forced the group to their knees, they were glad to tread the ground of Washington's estate. La Fayette faced many emotions as he revisited the site where Washington welcomed him. Washington's three nephews accompanied the group to the general's unassuming grave. Like so many before and since, La Fayette helped in the transition of Mount Vernon from home to national shrine and tourist attraction. After the short visit, the group was on their way to Yorktown. The city of the last major engagement of the conflict against Great Britain had changed little since La Fayette's departure because "its unhealthy situation offered no inducements to new inhabitants." Therefore, Levasseur noted, "Ruinous houses, blackened by fire, or marked by cannon shot; the ground covered with the remains of arms, and fragments of shells." The town still bore the visible wounds of war from four decades ago.[11]

However, La Fayette did not restrict his tourist travel to the inhabited and urban areas; he also took to the wilderness. Just like Troy had bemused the French visitors, so too did Macon, Georgia, a recently created town on the banks of the Ocmulgee River. Levasseur commented, "Macon, which is a small and handsome village, tolerably populous, did not exist eighteen months since; it has arisen from the midst of the forest as if by enchantment. It is a civilized speck lost in the yet immense domain of the original children of the soil." As the group moved deeper into the wilderness, the road disappeared, and torrential southern rains hampered their progress. There was a certain sympathy with the Muscogee people La Fayette encountered. Levasseur awkwardly lauded that the United States was removing Native people by treaty and not

[10] Ibid., 1:167, 175.
[11] Ibid., 1:175–179.

by war or extermination; therefore, "civilization is not sullied by crimes to be compared with those of Great Britain in India, but in rendering this justice to them, we, at the same time, cannot help feeling a strong interest in the fate of the unhappy Indians." As the group returned to civilization along the rivers of Alabama, the romantic landscape of the "elevated, gravelly, and oftentimes wooded shores" invited their dreams. At the same time, the realities of conflict were never far away as the Native people but also "countrymen whom political events had driven from France" illustrated.[12]

Despite the astonishing pace of innovation and expansion, the transportation revolution in the United States was not without danger as La Fayette himself discovered. On May 8, the group traveled on board a steamer on the Ohio River. Fatigued from his travel and the large body of daily correspondence, La Fayette retired early that evening. Despite the darkness of the night, the captain and pilot continued the ship's voyage undeterred. La Fayette's son expressed some concerns about the decision to not tie the vessels to the bank for the night. Around midnight a "horrible shock" awoke the party below deck. Initially, the passengers were uncertain what had happened. When the crew reached the front of the vessel, the hold was already filling with water from a snag, a rocky area. Realizing the danger, the captain order, "hasten Lafayette to my boat! Bring Lafayette to my boat." La Fayette did not realize the danger and at a relaxed pace evacuated his cabin, including a snuff box with a picture of George Washington. After some confusion, especially the whereabouts of La Fayette's son, the crew and passengers safely reached the bank of the river, abandoning the sinking vessels.[13] La Fayette was lucky, but he certainly experienced all the aspects and thrills tourists would desire in the future. His experiences became something others desired to mimic. La Fayette's recollections were part of a growing body of works about the United States and travel experiences, enticing others to go on their own adventures. His trip around the United States, especially in New England, followed the Northern Tour, which mimicked what was increasingly out of fashion in Europe: the Grand Tour.

---

[12] Ibid., 2:70–71, 75, 84.
[13] Ibid., 2:158–163.

The Grand Tour emerged as early as the sixteenth century, attracting largely British aristocratic travelers who desired to see Italy. British travelers perceived of the tour as an opportunity to overcome their cultural and historic isolation from Western continental Europe. In addition, Paris and the Mediterranean attracted tourists. As the setter of cultural standards, Paris had long attracted the interest of people as they looked to the newest styles and cultural phenomenon. Besides Paris, Italy always attracted visitors. Spain, outside of Madrid, was seen "as dull and reclusive." In addition, the crossing of the Pyrenees Mountain was difficult and facilities for tourists poorly developed. Prior to 1800, going on the Grand Tour was an expansive undertaking since "facilities for mass transport" were absent. Furthermore, crossing the Alps remained a barrier for many travelers. How to reach Italy was left to the individual tourists, some traveled through Paris and France and other along the Rhine and the St. Gotthard Pass or by way of Bavaria and the Brenner Pass. Once in Italy, Turin, Milan, Genoa, Venice, Parma, Reggio, Bologna, Naples, and Rome, all attracted tourists. Italy was at the heart of the Grand Tour, because of the close cultural connection in politics, art, and language with the ancient people who still held sway over the British educated upper classes. However, the changes in travel behavior and emergence of travel companies altered the way people experiences other countries, removing the "otherness" from the experience.[14] The existence of tourist networks allowed Europe to attract tourists, both homegrown, but also from overseas.

For many in the United States, Europe maintained a powerful attraction, especially the ancient sites. Visiting Europe offered an opportunity for professional advances by looking for subjects to write about or learn about art techniques. Historian William Stowe argues that three groups of writers used European travel for their benefit. The established writer could publish a travelogue to maintain the interest of readers and use the "abundant material provided by a European tour." The newcomer could use their visit to establish themselves and use the travelogue as their "apprentice work." Finally, there was the amateur writer of the growing middle and upper strata of society to whom a travelogue offered an opportunity to publish a book to avoid an accusation of engaging in

---

[14] Jeremy Black, *Italy and the Grand Tour* (New Haven, CT: Yale University Press, 2003), 1, 3–4, 9, 23, 34; Lynne Withey, *Grand Tours and Cooks' Tours: A History of Leisure Travel, 1750–1915* (New York: W. Morrow, 1997), 6–7.

the "sinful self-indulgence of travel." Others like Moses Ezekiel went to Europe for the study of art. Having started his education at the Virginia Military Institute in Lexington, VA and survived the devastating Battle of New Market, Ezekiel left the United States in 1867 to study art at the Preußische Akademie der Künste in Berlin. Among his over two hundred works of art is most importantly, "Virginia Mourning Her Dead," a monument dedicated to the sacrifices of his fellow cadets of the Virginia Military Institute. He refined his artistic ability traveling Europe.[15] Though only a few tourists came to Europe for study, many came to visit the sites of ancient and modern interests.

Among the politically most powerful tourists of the nineteenth century was the head of state of Brazil, Emperor Dom Pedro II. Having ascended to the throne in July 1841 after a ten-year regency, Dom Pedro faced many challenges from neighbors and political opponents. In the spring of 1871, after another cabinet shake-up, Dom Pedro decided to go on a ten-month vacation in Europe. After thirty years on the throne, he was exhausted and desired to use the vacation to energize himself but also to finally see the continent he so frequently sought to emulate. On May 25, the emperor, his wife, Teresa Cristina, and 15 members of the court embarked on a steamer to Lisbon. Despite being the emperor of an American country, Dom Pedro decided to travel incognito as "D. Pedro d'Alcàntara," but his behavior of doing "exactly what he wanted, taking not the least notice of the expenses or the inconvenience to others" was hardly incognito. Even more, on July 4, Queen Victoria greeted her fellow monarch at Windsor Castle. Just like so many tourists, Dom Pedro's schedule included sightseeing at a breakneck pace.[16]

Dom Pedro departed Lisbon for Spain and France, before heading to London in early July 1871. Historians Roderick Barman recounts the next stage of the trip, "After England came Belgium, the Rhineland, Hamburg, Berlin, Dresden, Coburg, where D. Leopoldina lay buried,

---

[15] Peter A. Nash, *The Life and Times of Moses Jacob Ezekiel: American Sculptor, Arcadian Knight* (Madison, MD: Farleigh Dickinson, 2014); William W. Stowe, *Going Abroad: European Travel in Nineteenth-Century American Culture* (Princeton, NJ: Princeton University Press, 1994), xii. Also see: Beth Lynne Lueck, Brigitte Bailey, and Lucinda L. Damon-Bach, eds., *Transatlantic Women: Nineteenth-Century American Women Writers and Great Britain* (Durham: University of New Hampshire Press, 2012).

[16] Roderick J. Barman, *Citizen Emperor: Pedro II and the Making of Brazil, 1825–91* (Stanford, CA: Stanford University Press, 1999), 236–237.

and finally Carlsbad, the Bohemian spa." After three weeks at the spas, their journey continued to Munich and Vienna, where they spent a few days with their cousin, the Habsburg ruler. Boarding a sailing vessel in Italy, they headed to Egypt on October 24. Dom Pedro was back in Rio de Janeiro by March 31, 1872. This first vacation of his reign only increased Dom Pedro's appetite for going abroad again. Only four years after his first vacation, Dom Pedro departed for his second trip overseas, this one twice the length of his previous one.[17]

In 1876, the United States celebrated its first centennial. In honor of the event, the country hosted in Philadelphia the 1876 Centennial Exposition to showcase the country's history and accomplishments. As thousands passed through the gates, one person in particular attracted attention: Dom Pedro II. Not only was this the first-ever visit of a reigning monarch to the United States, but ironically also a visit from the only head of state in the Americas where slavery still existed (the Spanish crown controlled the other). As historian Phil Roberts notes, "To many Americans, bewildered by rapid industrialization and social upheavals resulting from immigration and the fall of the institution of slavery, this first-ever visit by a royal head of state to the United States assuaged their yearnings for the stability offered by hereditary leadership confirmed in the person of an enlightened monarch." Dom Pedro drew mixed responses. He had the potential as a "hereditary head of a slaveholding nation, a Catholic, and to some degree an intellectual," to offend a vast array of people. Nevertheless, thousands greeted the emperor along his route, even if that meant getting up early in the morning.[18] A celebrity tourist could draw major crowds.

Dom Pedro's visit to the United States was all encompassing and he made sure to improve his spoken English during his voyage from Rio de Janeiro to New York. Like a modern tourist trying to see Europe in a few days, Dom Pedro's three months in the country were a mad dash to see as much as possible. Upon his arrival on April 16 in New York, he embarked by train to cross the continent, with visits planned for April 21 in Chicago, April 24, a Sunday, at the Salt Lake City Tabernacle for a religious service, and April 25 in San Francisco. The crossing of

---

[17] Ibid., 236–238, 275.

[18] Phil Roberts, "'All Americans Are Hero-Worshippers': American Observations on the First U.S. Visit by a Reigning Monarch, 1876," *Journal of the Gilded Age and Progressive Era* 7 (October 2008), 453–456, 458–460.

the continent took only six days, an illustration of the country's massive transportation innovation and how easy tourist travel was by the last quarter of the century. Like many other tourists, Dom Pedro compared San Francisco, which he called "a beautiful city," to his native country, particularly Rio de Janeiro. Like many tourists in the United States, Pedro desired to see the wild wilderness of the Western states, doing so by a circuitous route through Wyoming and Nebraska. On May 10, Dom Pedro attended the opening ceremony of the Centennial Exposition in Philadelphia, before heading to Washington to rub shoulders with the state leaders of the United States. In late May, Dom Pedro embarked on another lengthy excursion to New Orleans which he reached from St. Louis by steamer. From the Crescent City, the emperor traveled by rail to Atlanta, before closing out his vacation with a trip to New England to exchange ideas with the famous literary and scientific community.[19]

Since Dom Pedro was the first ruling monarch to visit the United States, newspaper reports frequently tried to paint him in an egalitarian light, such as the emperor carrying his own bags and paying his own bills. In addition, Dom Pedro ingratiated himself to the public with his ordinary dress, with one paper describing him as "over six-feet tall, gray whiskers and gray hair and partly bald. He dresses in plain black without any ornament at all." Dom Pedro's "common-man touches" increased his popularity among the public. Visiting the United States during an election year, Dom Pedro was cautious to avoid political issues, going so far as to avoid stopping in Chicago during the city's mayoral election. Dom Pedro's demeanor and attitude ingratiated him to the US public. When he was inducted into the American Geographical Society, a speaker summarized the country's attitude, "I am sure that no distinguished stranger ever came among us who, as the end of three months, seemed so little a stranger and so much a friend to the whole American people as Dom Pedro II of Brazil."[20]

[19] Roderick J. Barman, *Citizen Emperor: Pedro II and the Making of Brazil, 1825–91* (Stanford, CA: Stanford University Press, 1999), 276, 278–279; Phil Roberts, "'All Americans Are Hero-Worshippers': American Observations on the First U.S. Visit by a Reigning Monarch, 1876," *Journal of the Gilded Age and Progressive Era* 7 (October 2008), 457.

[20] Roderick J. Barman, *Citizen Emperor: Pedro II and the Making of Brazil, 1825–91* (Stanford, CA: Stanford University Press, 1999), 280; Phil Roberts, "'All Americans Are Hero-Worshippers': American Observations on the First U.S. Visit by a Reigning Monarch,

After concluding his visit in the United States, Dom Pedro returned to Europe for another vacation. Among the highlights of his visit was a trip to Bayreuth where he watched the opening of *Die Rheingold* and chatted with Richard Wagner. From Bavaria, Dom Pedro went to Scandinavia; by way of Denmark, Sweden, and the Finish lakes, he visited St. Petersburg, Moscow, and Nizhny-Novgorod, and Odessa. Following in the footsteps of the Vikings, Dom Pedro arrived in Constantinople on October 2. Stepping into his preferred role of scientific-minded tourist, Dom Pedro received a private tour of the ruins of Troy by Heinrich Schliemann. Having gotten a taste for ancient sites, the imperial tour continued with Athens and a visit to the Acropolis. Historian Barman recounts the remainder of the journey, "the imperial party sailed to Smyrna and on to Beirut. There followed a long slow journey, the emperor on horseback and the empress in a litter, from Beirut to Damascus, Nazareth, and Jerusalem. The Holy Land aroused in Pedro II an intensity of religious feeling not usually apparent in his writing. On his fifty-first birthday, December 2, 1876, he went to confession and took communion in the Holy Sepulcher in Jerusalem."[21] Dom Pedro fulfilled a passion by visiting the holy places of Christianity.

A pilgrimage to the Holy Land was not uncommon during the nineteenth century. Long a place for pilgrimages, the holy sites of Jewish, Christian, and Islamic religion became more accessible during the nineteenth century. The vast number of evangelical-minded Protestants in the United States, who had the wealth to afford overseas travel, determined to make a journey to Palestine. Particularly the Second Great Awakening stimulated people into traveling overseas to seek a personal and at times material connection with the holy places in Palestine. The visits prior to 1890 involved a significant culture shock to US visitors when they discovered that most of the holy sites of Christianity belonged to Muslim owners. As a result, cultural stereotypes frequently made it into accounts of their pilgrimages, including comments about "dirty and uncivilized" Arabian people or the Arab presence creating an authenticity to the region. At the same time, isolated largely from other Christian

---

1876," *Journal of the Gilded Age and Progressive Era* 7 (October 2008), 460–461, 465, 468.

[21] Roderick J. Barman, *Citizen Emperor: Pedro II and the Making of Brazil, 1825–91* (Stanford, CA: Stanford University Press, 1999), 280–282.

faiths, the eastern version of Christianity struck many US pilgrims as odd and alien. Regardless pilgrim-tourists were able to find a spiritual connection in places of religious significance.[22] Dom Pedro soon left the religious tourists behind as his trip brought him back to Europe.

After his pilgrimage, the group visited Egypt and left for Messina. In Italy, they saw Syracuse, Naples, Rome, Florence, and Venice, before revisiting some of the other European centers of power.[23] The vacation reenergized Dom Pedro, his religious views strengthened with his pilgrimage, he provided Brazil a powerful representation abroad as the emperor was not only a tourist but representative of his country. However, neither Lafayette nor Dom Pedro nor many others ventured into what many still perceived of as a graveyard for white people during the nineteenth century: Africa. The dark continent eventually by the twentieth century attracted its share of tourists.

With trains and steamships plying the Atlantic, travel was increasingly easier and traveling to distant lands less an adventure. One of the most prominent tourists of the early twentieth century was former US President Theodore Roosevelt. He departed the United States a mere nineteen days after leaving office in 1909. Reaching Mombasa in the colony of British East Africa, his party, hunting animals for the Smithsonian Institute, traveled inland to the Belgian Congo, followed the Nile to Khartoum, and departed Africa from Egypt. As a prolific hunter, Roosevelt brought many of his assumptions about the Western United States with him to Africa. He closely related what he saw in East Africa to his native West, referring to the farmsteads as ranches. He observed that East Africa would "be a country of high promise for settlers of [the] white race" and that the region reminded him of the western plains. He also carried his own racial and white supremacist views to Africa, looking at the region as perfectly suited for white settlers, "a white man's country."[24] He poetically recalled:

---

[22] Stephanie S. Rogers, *Inventing the Holy Land: American Protestant Pilgrimage to Palestine, 1865–1941* (Lanham, MD: Lexington Books, 2011), 1–4.

[23] Roderick J. Barman, *Citizen Emperor: Pedro II and the Making of Brazil, 1825–91* (Stanford, CA: Stanford University Press, 1999), 280–282.

[24] Theodore Roosevelt, *African Game Trails: An Account of the African Wanderings of an American Hunter-Naturalist* (New York: Charles Scribner's Sons, 1910), 39.

As my horse shuffled forward, under the bright, hot sunlight, across the endless flats of gently rolling slopes of brown and withered grass, I might have been on the plains anywhere, from Texas to Montana; the hills were like our Western buttes; the half-dry watercourses were fringed with trees, just as if they had been the Sandy, or the Dry, or the Beaver, or the Cottonwood, or any of the multitude of creeks that repeat these and similar names, again and again, from the Panhandle to the Saskatchewan.[25]

Besides this poetic imposition of his beloved western plains on the African wilderness, Roosevelt was in Africa as a hunting tourist. Therefore, he commented extensively on the wildlife, but the hunter-instinct clouded his writing, overshadowing his conservation-oriented environmentalist persona. For examples, he remarked on the wildebeest or gnu as "the shyest and least plentiful, but in some ways the most interesting, because of the queer streak of ferocious eccentricity." He almost complained that the animals made the hunt too easy as the "large game animals of the plains are always walking and standing in conspicuous places, and never seek to hide or take advantage of cover." However, to his satisfaction some of the other animals were shier, hiding in tall grass or bushes and wearily watching for hunters. Especially, the wildebeest drew Roosevelt's attention in that regard. He observed that the "animal will stop grazing and stand with head raised" when it sensed a threat approach.[26]

Furthermore, Roosevelt's translation of the western United States did not stop with his assumption that it was a "white man's country," he also carried the racial stereotypes of his day with him to Africa, frequently referring to the indigenous people as "savages." He derogatorily noted that "the native blacks, although many of them do fairly well in unskilled labor, are not yet competent to do the higher tasks." He, however, not only drew comparison to black populations in the United States, but also to the native people, claiming that "the natives bore no resemblance to that once offered by the presence of our tribes of horse Indians." Seeing the native people in East Africa as primarily a pastoral and agricultural people, he did observe that some were warlike, such as the Maasai. Nevertheless, Roosevelt dismissed the Maasai as "in no way [as] formidable as our Indians." Perceiving of the need to uplift

---

[25] Ibid.
[26] Ibid., 54, 58.

the native population, Roosevelt pointed to the good work performed by missionaries along his trek. He hoped that "the effort is made consistently to teach the native how to live a more comfortable, useful, and physically and morally cleanly life, not under white conditions, but under the conditions which he will actually have to face when he goes back to his people … to be in his turn a conscious or unconscious missionary for good."[27] Roosevelt translated his US experiences seamlessly into his African tourist experiences. Few could afford a safari like Roosevelt's, but tourism still transformed in the course of the century.

Tourism dramatically changed in the course of the nineteenth century altering people's perceptions about the Atlantic region. As people sought tourist adventures, local campaigners made sure visitors found adequate lodging and restaurant offerings. Like city boosters, these tourism-focused business leaders came up with flashy titles or homely locations, whether that was to create small cottage villages for tourist or by marketing the Redwoods of California as "the Switzerland of America."[28] While Europe and the United States attracted the vast majority of tourists, even the Caribbean found interested visitors. Caribbean cruises and vacations became easier and healthier in the course of the century.

Even by the 1880s, white European and North Americans continued to view the tropical parts of the Americas and Africa as a graveyard. Nevertheless, the hope among tourism boosters was to imitate in the tropics something resembling the French Riviera and attract leisure tourists.[29] In contrast to the modern perception of the Caribbean as a cruise ship paradise, nineteenth-century guests visited for the climate to improve their health. Instead of beaches, these tourists sought out the natural springs and mineral baths on the islands. On Jamaica, bath and lodging houses sprang up to cater to this audience. However, the Caribbean was slow to develop a tourist business as local governments provided generous credits to construct hotels, some 75-rooms in size.[30]

[27] Ibid., 9, 43–44, 180.

[28] Orvar Löfgren, *On Holiday: A History of Vacationing* (Berkeley: University of California Press, 1999), 3.

[29] Catherine Cocks, *Tropical Whites: The Rise of the Tourist South in the Americas* (Philadelphia: University of Pennsylvania Press, 2013), 2, 50.

[30] K. O. Laurence and Jorge Ibarra Cuesta, eds., *General History of the Caribbean: The Long Nineteenth Century: Nineteenth-Century Transformations* (London, UK: Macmillan, 2011), 146.

In addition, visitors' expectations about tropical environments were not always easy to satisfy. While local promoters worked to convince potential visitors of the benign-ness of the tropical region, they also established a system to ensure visitors did not come to settle down permanently but stayed for only a short time. Furthermore, the activist and interventionist diplomacy of the United States in the Caribbean basin after 1898 furthered tourist interests as shipping increased, especially with the opening of the Panama Canal. Commercial interests, especially banana production, formed a precursor to tourism as ships carrying freight to the United States increasingly loaded tourist passengers on their journey south.[31]

In the mid-1890s, the United Fruit Company constructed a hotel in Port Antonio on Jamaica. The hotel appealed to foreign visitors with its US management and the up-to-date interior. Despite there being other resorts on the island, the Titchfield benefitted from United Fruit's "Great White Fleet" passenger service. Furthermore, travel to resorts became easier and more luxurious as first- and second-class passengers no longer had to share a cabin with others. In addition, located on the top decks of the ships set passengers in first class apart from the rest and "reinforced their sense of exclusion and superiority." Even more, the invention of refrigeration dramatically changed the menu on board vessels and eliminated the need to carry livestock. By 1900, tourist in first class even had access to running water in their cabins.[32] Caribbean cruising was a possibility and transatlantic journeys more comfortable.

Besides the improvement in luxury travel and growth in tourism, the second half of the nineteenth century witnessed the emergence of companies devoted to help people see other parts of the world. Leading the way regarding organizing tourist trips was Thomas Cook. Cook started his travel agent career with short regional excursions for temperance organizations and Sunday school children along the network of the Midland Counties Railway, with whom he negotiated a favorable fare in return for substantial passenger numbers. While most of his clients

---

[31] Catherine Cocks, *Tropical Whites: The Rise of the Tourist South in the Americas* (Philadelphia: University of Pennsylvania Press, 2013), 4, 12, 50–51.

[32] Douglas R. Burgess, Jr., *Engines of Empire: Steamships and the Victorian Imagination* (Stanford, CA: Stanford University Press, 2016), 15; Catherine Cocks, *Tropical Whites: The Rise of the Tourist South in the Americas* (Philadelphia: University of Pennsylvania Press, 2013), 51, 55.

arranged their own hotel and food, he compiled a guidebook to help his customers. After having gotten some experiences with small excursions, Cook planned trips into Scotland, three in 1847, which were solely by rail. Importantly, Cook's travel offerings were for the less well-off working classes. The cooperation between Cook and the Midland Counties Railway worked well. Thus, when in 1851 the Great Exhibition surrounding the Crystal Palace opened, the two once again cooperated to bring workers to the event. In the end, Cook arranged excursion for 165,000 individuals, about 3% of the exhibits' visitors. Despite the large number of tickets sold, Cook failed to make any money. However, the Scotland and London excursions convinced Cook that he should expand his new tourism business.[33]

Cook's first foray into continental tourism was a trip to Paris. He struggled arranging trips with the railroads to Dover and from Calais to Paris. As a result, Cook arranged trips from Harwick to Hoek van Holland and then by rail to Paris. With the Paris trips working well for Cook, he expanded his offerings to allow workers to also experience the Grand Tour expanding into Switzerland and Italy. Taking personal control of a tour from Paris to Geneva and on to Chamonix, he made sure to arrange local hotels that did not cater for a large British audience to allow his tourists the ability to experiences a more authentic catering. Historian Lynne Withey notes that "Cook's success was his care to build upon proven strategies in expanding his business; the Swiss tours had followed the Scottish model, and the Italian tours were an extension of the Swiss experience." Despite appealing to new tourist audiences, Cook made sure to keep cost for this trips low, insuring that a "three-week tour of Paris and Switzerland should cost no more than £15 or £16."[34] Cook had established a successful tourist business and he was ready to expand.

By 1869, Cook provided tours to Holland, Belgium, France, Germany, Switzerland, Austria, Italy, and enlarged his offerings with trips to the Middle East to allow visitors access to the ancient cities and Holy Land. By the end of the century, Cook could also offer tours to Scandinavia, Spain, India, Australia, and the United States. By the time of this expansion, Cook faced in "Dean & Dawson (1871), John Frame

---

[33] Lynne Withey, *Grand Tours and Cooks' Tours: A History of Leisure Travel, 1750–1915* (New York: W. Morrow, 1997), 135–142.

[34] Ibid., 142, 150–157.

(1871), Quentin Hogg (1886), and Sir Henry Lunn (1893)" serious competition. In addition, as Cook tried to make travel more accessible for people, a concurrent push provided greater luxury as César Ritz created a luxury hotel chain and George Pullman and Georges Nagelmackers put high-class train cars into operation. Nagelmackers in 1872 founded the Compagnie Internationale des Wagons-Lite and created one of the most luxurious travel experiences in the world, the Orient Express from Paris to Constantinople. Starting operation in 1882, the line to Constantinople was not completed until 1888. Four years later, a luxury hotel awaited the Orient Express riders in Istanbul. Nagelmackers even eliminated Pullman's operation and created a monopoly on luxury train travel in Europe.[35] Tourists could travel either cheaply or in exquisite style, tourism brought the Atlantic world together.

The United States especially attracted a significant number of tourists. With the advent of steamships and lines like Cunard, Collins, Inman, the United States by the 1850s was closer than ever. While Cunard had the monopoly on safety, Collins operated the fastest steamers on the Atlantic. However, an unofficial race between Collins's *Pacific* and Cunard's *Persia* in January 1856 ended with a victory for the *Persia*, due to the *Pacific* disappearing without a trace. Historian Withey explained, "By the 1870s, 10,000-ton vessels typically crossed the Atlantic in about a week; by the 1890s, the size of the major transatlantic liners doubled again, while the time required to cross continued to drop, to as little as five days."[36] Ever larger and faster ships allowed tourists to reach their destination in greater style.

Despite Pullman failing in the European market, his luxury cars transported tourists along the transcontinental railroad lines in the United States. The luxury of the train car did not always translate into the accommodations along the way. Boosters tried to convince people in the United States to first travel domestically and see their own country, using familiar names and European reference to make their comparisons. Therefore, the Colorado Rockies became the "first cousins of the Alps," California was compared to Italy, Pikes Peak was similar to Mont Blanc, and California's Monterey had the beauty of Naples. Using opportunities to expand tourism in the West, William Jackson Palmer, the founding investor of the

---

[35] Ibid., 159–161, 175–182, 184.
[36] Ibid., 171–172.

Denver and Rio Grande Railway purchased land near the mineral springs of Manitou in the Colorado Springs area, where he constructed a luxury hotel in 1872. The town and its resort quickly became dubbed the "Saratoga of the Far West." By the 1870s, Thomas Cook and Raymond & Whitcomb competed to open the West to tourists. In 1881 Raymond & Whitcomb offered tours that lasted 44 days with stops in Chicago, Omaha, Cheyenne, Colorado Springs, Ogden, Salt Lake City, and San Francisco. The expensive $400 trip included transportation, hotels, meals, and excursions with tickets valid for ninety days, allowing guests to individualize their trip with detours into Oregon, Yosemite, and Lake Tahoe.[37] As a growing number of people could purchase everyday essentials from catalogs, so too were tourist itineraries by the end of the century available from a catalog with options for cheap, luxurious, and flexible.

While Lafayette and Roosevelt ventured into frontier regions with potentially belligerent indigenous people at the start of the nineteenth and twentieth century, respectively, Dom Pedro never witnessed such a frontier environment as he saw the cities of the United States, Europe, and the Levant. All three of them were tourists, but Dom Pedro more than the other two represented the modern nineteenth-century tourist experience. Tourism touched every part of the Atlantic world and boosters not only just desired to attract residents and businesses, but also the growing amount of tourist money available. In the course of the century, especially after 1850, tourism became available to the less well-off and with businesses like Thomas Cook, there was a possibility to purchase a ready-made itinerary to travel. Tourists desired to see the lands they read about in travel literature published by individuals like Lafayette and see the great rivers of the United States, the extensive plains of North America, the ancient sites of Europe and the Levant, as well as the major urban areas around the Atlantic region. The more adventurous minded tourists, like Roosevelt, might venture into the African or American interior to hunt large game. Tourism changed the perception of people, no longer were these exotic, faraway, impossible to reach places, but they were increasingly accessible, and even more, there was a decreasing health risk involved in visiting tropical locations. Tourism tied the Atlantic world together and reshaped people's understanding of the region, enhancing their desire to see exotic places.

[37] Ibid., 299–300.

Bibliography

Barman, Roderick J. *Citizen Emperor: Pedro II and the Making of Brazil, 1825–91*. Stanford, CA: Stanford University Press, 1999.

Black, Jeremy. *Italy and the Grand Tour*. New Haven, CT: Yale University Press, 2003.

Burgess, Douglas R., Jr., *Engines of Empire: Steamships and the Victorian Imagination*. Stanford, CA: Stanford University Press, 2016.

Chambers, Thomas A. *Memories of War: Visiting Battlegrounds and Bonefields in the Early American Republic*. Ithaca, NY: Cornell University Press, 2012.

Cocks, Catherine. *Tropical Whites: The Rise of the Tourist South in the Americas*. Philadelphia: University of Pennsylvania Press, 2013.

Laurence, K. O., and Jorge Ibarra Cuesta, eds. General History of the Caribbean: The Long Nineteenth Century: Nineteenth-Century Transformations. London, UK: Macmillan, 2011.

Levasseur, Auguste. *Lafayette in America, in 1824 and 1825; Or, Journal of Travels, in the United States*. New York: White, Gallaher, and White, 1829.

Löfgren, Orvar. *On Holiday: A History of Vacationing*. Berkeley: University of California Press, 1999.

Lueck, Beth Lynne, Brigitte Bailey, and Lucinda L. Damon-Bach, eds. *Transatlantic Women: Nineteenth-Century American Women Writers and Great Britain*. Durham: University of New Hampshire Press, 2012.

Morin, Christina, and Marguérite Christina Maria Corporaal, eds. *Traveling Irishness in the Long Nineteenth Century*. New York: Palgrave Macmillan, 2017.

Nash, Peter Adam. *The Life and Times of Moses Jacob Ezekiel: American Sculptor, Arcadian Knight*. Madison, MD: Farleigh Dickinson, 2014.

Putnam, George Palmer. *The Tourist in Europe: Or, A Concise Summary of the Various Routes, Objects of Interest, &c in Great Britain, France, Switzerland, Italy, Germany, Belgium, and Holland*. New York: Wiley and Putnam, 1838.

Roberts, Phil. "'All Americans Are Hero-Worshippers': American Observations on the First U.S. Visit by a Reigning Monarch, 1876." *Journal of the Gilded Age and Progressive Era* 7 (October 2008): 453–477.

Rogers, Stephanie Stidham. *Inventing the Holy Land: American Protestant Pilgrimage to Palestine, 1865–1941*. Lanham, MD: Lexington Books, 2011.

Roosevelt, Theodore. *African Game Trails: An Account of the African Wanderings of an American Hunter-Naturalist*. 2 vols. New York: Charles Scribner's Sons, 1910.

Sears, John F. *Sacred Places: American Tourist Attractions in the Nineteenth Century*. New York: Oxford University Press, 1989.

Stowe, William W. *Going Abroad: European Travel in Nineteenth-Century American Culture*. Princeton, NJ: Princeton University Press, 1994.

Williams, Wellington. *The Traveller's and Tourist's Guide Through the United States of America, Canada*. Philadelphia, PA: Lippincott, Grambo, 1851.

Withey, Lynne. *Grand Tours and Cooks' Tours: A History of Leisure Travel, 1750–1915*. New York: W. Morrow, 1997.

CHAPTER 14

Atlantic Financial Entanglements

Money is the god of our time and Rothschild is his prophet.[1]

These words by the German poet Christian Johann Heinrich Heine encapsulated the new financial connections of the Atlantic world during the nineteenth century. When Spain and Portugal opened the Atlantic world with their voyages of exploration and colonization, the conquistadors searched for wealth and brought masses of gold and silver from the colonies to the mother country. In the course of the colonial period, wealth tended to flow to Europe and states were reluctant to allow specie to accumulate in the Americas, even prohibiting bullion to go back into the colonies. Nevertheless, the early modern Atlantic world contained a web of financial connections. The financial ties that bound the various parts of the Atlantic region together continued after independence and into the nineteenth century. The investment by European banking houses in the emerging Latin American and North American states transformed the old colonial relationships into new economic post-colonial dependencies. In part, this was the age of informal imperial domination, but even more, the nineteenth century was the age of the Rothschilds and Baring with their respective financial empires.

The French Revolution and Napoleonic Wars dramatically altered the financial structures in Europe, shifting the financial center from

[1] Niall Ferguson, *The House of Rothschild: The World's Bankers, 1948–1999* (New York: Penguin Books, 1999), xxiv.

© The Author(s) 2019
N. Eichhorn, *Atlantic History in the Nineteenth Century*,
https://doi.org/10.1007/978-3-030-27640-9_14

Amsterdam to London. The demands for money allowed enterprising individuals to rise to positions of power. In Frankfurt, French Revolutionary ideals liberated the Jewish neighborhood from religious oppression and allowed financiers to prosper. The Rothschild family realized that the need for money by European princes to put armies in the field provided an investment opportunity. The Rothschild family members spread across the continent and engaged in a wide variety of ventures, such as investing in the Manchester textile industry, which proved high profile and risky. They helped finance the British and their allied war efforts against Napoleon. Their monetary acumen at times "stretched their credit to breaking point, sometimes losing sight altogether of their assets and liabilities." By 1815, the London house provided the British government £10 million.[2] The Napoleonic conflicts laid the basis for the Rothschilds's financial successes during the nineteenth century.

The restoration in 1815 opened a wide variety of new markets. Princes needed monetary support to reestablish their positions of power. The Rothschilds not only supported the reactionary princes, like Metternich, they also provided new states with much-needed liquidity and were willing to take risks. The bankers helped place bonds on international markets, solicit buyers, broker deals in the bullion trade, traded directly in commodities, provided financial services to private individuals, and even got involved with insurance. Spread across a number of houses around Europe, the Rothschilds operated from a much stronger basis than their peers. Besides London and Frankfurt, family scions operated houses in Paris, Vienna, and Naples. Aside from the obvious speculative ability to use price difference in the five stock markets, the houses could bail each other out in case of a localized financial crisis. By 1825, the Rothschilds were "ten times the size of their nearest rivals, Baring Brothers." The London branch of the Rothschilds alone had £1.14 million of capital available; the Baring Brother's banking house had only £490,000.[3] However, the Rothschilds were not as impervious as their wealth appeared.

Like any financial institution involved in a variety of high-risk ventures, the Rothschilds suffered their fair share of setbacks. When the

---

[2] Ibid., xxii–xxiii.

[3] Ferguson, *House of Rothschild*, xxiii–xxv; Philip Ziegler, *The Sixth Great Power: A History of One of the Greatest of All Banking Families, the House of Barings, 1762–1929* (New York: Alfred A. Knopf, 1988), 96.

bank issued bonds for the Spanish and Portuguese governments, political instability caused a default by these governments and much embarrassment for the bankers. Attempts to gain a financial foothold in the United States also failed due to the decentralized character of the financial system in the country. By the 1840s, like many banking houses, the Rothschilds branched out into railroads. Despite their desire to avoid a deeper commitment with railroad management, they eventually had to get more involved. The boom of railroad construction increased the financial status of the Rothschild houses, allowing the branch in Paris to overtake London as the most profitable and wealthy. However, by the 1850s, countries increasingly tried to place their bonds without a financial middleman, left-leaning workers' rights organization attacked the bank's financing of exploitative railroad business, and the illusion of being able to prevent political instability came crumbling down.[4]

By the middle of the nineteenth century, the Rothschilds established with August Belmont an agent in New York, whom they reluctantly granted extensive powers to operate and engage in financial ventures. To the Rothschilds, Brazil was the most important market in the Americas. In 1851, after getting involved in the war between Argentina and Uruguay, Brazil needed a loan of £1.04 million. The bankers also helped with additional monetary needs for infrastructure projects, such as railroad construction. As historian Niall Ferguson indicates, Brazil and the London Rothschilds had "an exceptionally monogamous financial relationship … which, between 1852 and 1914, generated bond issues worth no less than £142 million." However, the Rothschilds remained committed heavily to the European continent and helped a wide variety of states issue bonds. They had their hand in the financing of German and Italian unification and the attempt of returning to great power status in Spain.[5] The Rothschilds remained a financial power broker throughout the nineteenth century, but their financial monopoly and power did not last like Baring who with great success jumped on the new opportunities in the Americas.

Having started the post-Napoleonic era with a substantial loan for the French government, Baring Brothers was cautious and marred with personal insecurities about the future of the house. Independence in Latin

---

[4] Ferguson, *House of Rothschild*, xxviii–xxx.
[5] Ibid., 65, 68, 74–80, 100–105.

America and the financial needs of those states offered Baring an opportunity. After failing in Chile, Baring was able to help place a £1 million loan for Buenos Aires which the city needed for infrastructure improvements. Long term, the loan was devastating since Argentina defaulted on its interest payments in 1828. Similar trouble materialized in Mexico. Investment returns in Latin America were promising, but the risks were high as Baring discovered, and until 1851, there was very little government support to collect debts. By 1830, Baring had increased its position despite some of these setbacks in the Americas and grown its Bishopsgate operation to a formidable staff of 30, compared to the 50 at Rothschild and 10–15 at other banking houses. These clerks faced an onslaught of visitors from the United States and other countries, somewhere between 100 and 150 at any given time, who desired Baring's financial support.[6]

In 1829, Thomas Baring visited the United States. The house could follow the Rothschild example and appoint an agent to take care of the Baring business. But Baring worried of the damage an unreliable agent could cause especially considering that it still took weeks for instructions to cross the Atlantic. Despite these concerns, Baring appointed Thomas W. Ward as the banking house's agent in the United States on January 1, 1830. His duties included, "select the individuals and houses with which Baring should do business, to assess their credit-worthiness, probe their weaknesses, gauge their honesty, secure information on their bank balances." Ward was an ardent promoter for more Baring involvement in the country. However, British investors were reluctant until the late 1840s when it came to invest in the Americas. Therefore, Baring maintained a diverse investment portfolio. By 1858, Baring's supported the governments of "Russia, Norway, Austria, the United States, Chile, Buenos Aires, New Granada, Canada, Nova Scotia, New Brunswick, and Australia."[7] Baring had an Atlantic reach, and with the Rothschilds, they carved up the Atlantic world into individual spheres of influence, just like the imperial powers of the era did politically.

Baring continued undeterred with investments in North America. The bank helped issue millions in bonds and loans. Latin America remained a volatile terrain. Argentina and Uruguay were the primary focal points of Baring finances. However, the banking house also floated

---

[6] Ziegler, *Sixth Great Power*, 101, 103, 127, 143.
[7] Ibid., 143–145, 155–156, 164.

loans for Chile and Venezuela and even cautiously entered Rothschilds' Brazil territory. During an 1889 visit, John Baring was impressed with the opportunities available in Argentina and how little the local people seemed to care. He commented, "There really is no limit to the riches of the republic ... The bribery and corruption is really quite awful." However, Baring had overextended. Faced with too many outstanding liabilities, Baring faced the danger of closing down in bankruptcy. Rothschild, the Bank of England, and the British government had to help Baring untangle from their Atlantic overextension.[8] Despite their setbacks, Baring and Rothschilds were the Atlantic world's bankers during the nineteenth century, helping foster an intertwined Atlantic financial network.

Nothing illustrates the Atlantic world's financial entanglement better than economic crisis. In 1837, the Atlantic monetary system suffered its first major crisis of the century. The young United States had economically grown at a phenomenal rate in the first three decades of the nineteenth century and foreign investors took advantage of the high rates of return for bonds and stocks issued in the United States. In 1830, Edmond Jean Forstall, a New Orleans merchant, visited Great Britain to tap into the deep pockets of British financial houses to expand his cotton trade business, shipping the white fiber to Liverpool. Forstall was lucky in that he made contact with Francis Baring. The relationship between Forstall and Baring grew, and by 1835, Baring was heavily invested in New Orleans banks, mostly on Forstall's recommendation, contributing to the existence of sixteen banks with a capital of $46 million by 1837. Despite the growing banking network in the United States and the establishment of a semi-national bank in the Bank of the United States, larger transactions were still done in pound sterling and not dollars.[9] Independent for sixty years, the United States still remained intimately connected with the British financial systems.

The 1830s witnessed some significant financial changes. President Andrew Jackson and the Bank of the United States were at loggerheads over the financial power of the unelected bank directory. At the same time, Jackson forced the French government to provide indemnities

[8] Ibid., 207–266.

[9] Jessica M. Lepler, *The Many Panics of 1837: People, Politics, and the Creation of a Transatlantic Financial Crisis* (New York: Cambridge University Press, 2013), 8–9, 11, 15, 17.

for loses suffered during the Napoleonic War, adding additional gold to the coffers of the US government. Distrusted banks and paper currency, Jackson's government decided to focus on gold. At the same time, Mexican silver was flowing in greater number into the United States since Chinese merchants increasingly refused the new Mexican coins, distrusting the coin's value with its new emblems. Despite the growing desire to use metallic currency, the United States remained decentralized, much to the nightmare of banking houses like Baring and Rothschilds.[10] These complications undermined a key aspect of the Atlantic financial system: trust.

Much of the transatlantic financial system relied on trust and banking houses honored notes promising payment based on that confidence. As historian Jessica Lepler notes, "A single failed bill could not destroy the transatlantic financial system, but many unfulfilled promises could. Confidence was valuable in part because it was vulnerable." Just like the United States relied on paper money, so did Great Britain, where an increasingly large number of banks populated the landscape, issuing their own paper money for circulation. The directors of the Bank of England, which controlled the country's gold reserves, were in the dark on the amount of paper money in circulation. The Bank of England had an obligation to maintain financial stability, even if that meant hurting the country's trade. The financial interrelationship and fiscal worries raised problems. In 1835, Forstall tried to place another bank bond with Baring Brothers, but there was no interest.[11]

On August 2, 1836, Nathan Mayer Rothschild died. His death coincided with growing anxiety about investments in the US market and the entangled web of banking. The perception reverberated through the European financial markets and a lack of confidence set in. These misconceptions caused a chain reaction, "By August 1836, the English directors of both private financial institutions … and quasi-public institutions … put in motion policies designed to protect themselves from the financial crisis they predicted based on intelligence interpreted out of context." When the Bank of England refused to discount bills

---

[10] Ibid., 21–22.
[11] Ibid., 29–30, 39–41.

of exchange from the United States, financial troubles were on the horizon.[12]

Just as Martin Van Buren took the oath of office in Washington, on March 4, 1837, the directors of the Bank of England determined that the collapse of the US financial houses, caused by a policy refusing to honor bills of exchange, was not acceptable and that the bank had to provide financial support. The hope for stability was misplaced, only four days later, the Louisiana cotton growers, speculators, and creditors realized that the market was collapsing around them and news of the financial panic quickly spread through the news and trade channels of the Atlantic world. With New Orleans houses suspending payment and Rothschilds withdrawing credit, on March 17, J. L. and S. Joseph & Co. closed its doors in New York. The uncertainty left many unsure if any mercantile papers still had value.[13] An Atlantic financial panic was on hand.

The initial news of the growing panic left bankers, like Rothschilds, troubled about how to proceed. August Belmont received orders to proceed to Cuba, where Rothschilds assumed opportunities were more profitable than in the United States. However, Belmont suggested profiting from the devalued stocks, hoping for a speedy recovery and rising prices to make a decent profit. Rothschilds had little control over Belmont actions and collecting all the debt owed to Rothschilds in New York alone was a daunting undertaking. In the end, only the Bank of England had the resources to bail out struggling financial houses and stabilize the economy. As the crisis deepened, banks in New York faced a run on their resources and emptying vaults. Suspending payment in specie was the only viable option to stay afloat. Banks in other parts of the country followed suit to retain liquidity and avoid bankruptcy.[14] Years passed before the financial systems had recovered from the events of 1837. However, what had started over cotton speculation and miscalculation in New Orleans quickly escalated into an Atlantic wide economic crisis, and the Bank of England had to bail out the domestic as well as the US financial system.

---

[12] Ibid., 43, 46–47, 50–51, 55, 57.
[13] Ibid., 102–103, 110, 130.
[14] Ibid., 134–135, 172–173, 209.

Despite the setbacks, bankers like Baring and Rothschilds "were the architects of nearly every facet of the Atlantic economy." These bankers had a disproportionate influence on trade and politics. They helped place massive loans. Europeans saw many opportunities in the Americas and bought bonds issued by governments in the Americas. By 1861, the indebtedness of the United States was to 90% in foreign hands. In the preceding decade, US bonds were extremely popular in Europe and even "house[s] not known for [their] risk-taking in American securities" like Rothschilds decided to make investments. Furthermore, US bonds found buyers in France and the German states.[15]

By the 1850s, infrastructure projects demanded significant amounts of money. Especially, in the United States, railroad construction required large financial outlays before any income could be generated. However, as historian Jay Sexton notes, "American capital funded the majority of railroads construction … , foreign investment was crucial to the construction of several significant lines." Investment in the Americas, even the United States, was a risky undertaking. In the 1840s, nine US states defaulted on interest payments to foreign creditors and Mississippi, Arkansas, and Florida repudiated their state debts entirely, not increasing investor confidence. Worse, the financial collapse of the Ohio Life Insurance and Trust Company in August 1857 had a massive ripple effect across the Atlantic world, just like the events of 1837. With the value of US securities decreasing, firms from Glasgow, London, and Hamburg which had invested in North America failed. Interest in US bonds was at a low point by the end of the 1850s.[16]

By 1871, the United States hoped that financial stability had improved, and Europe was once more ready for a loan. To place the new bond issue, the Treasury approached five banking houses in London, Baring Brothers, Rothschild, Morton, Rose and Co., Jay Cooke and Co., and J. S. Morgan and Co. Especially Morton, Rose and Co. was a relatively unknown house, whereas Jay Cooke was a well-known Republican party supporter in the United States. Even with the transatlantic cable, the Treasury in Washington, DC, had difficulty coordinating five banks in London. Interest in the new bond was limited. Rothschilds and Baring pulled out when the Treasury added a sixth bank to the

---

[15] Jay Sexton, *Debtor Diplomacy: Finance and American Foreign Relations in the Civil War Era, 1837–1873* (Oxford, UK: Clarendon Press, 2005), 12–13.

[16] Ibid., 56–57, 60, 70, 76–77.

consortium and seemed willing to even let a Russian banking house in on the profits. Ironically, most of the banks purchasing US bonds in the issue were from the United States and had to meet requirements "to hold federal bonds as reserve." Yet, the presence of Jay Cooke proved a problem as the bank collapsed not two years later causing the Panic of 1873.[17] Even by the end of the century, the Americas remained a dangerous investment option.

Throughout most of the nineteenth century, when it came to financial matters, Great Britain and its many banking houses remained the leading Atlantic financier, with a diverse investment portfolio. Between Spanish-American Independence in 1825 and the outbreak of the Great War in 1914, Great Britain was the largest foreign investor in Latin America. The region accounted for about 20% of the British foreign investment by the time of the Great War. The British investment portfolio changed over the course of the century. Irving Stone asserts that "By 1865 British long-term investment in Latin American reached nearly £81 million, of which three-fourth consisted of government loans." Over time, investment shifted to financially support projects like railroad construction and management, public utilities, and "financial enterprises." Despite investments also moving into other parts of the world, the Atlantic region remained a focal point. Britain invested heavily in foreign countries, but increasingly also in "newly settled countries, including the white settled colonies."[18]

In the course of the nineteenth century, British investment in Latin America grew from a modest £24.6 million in 1825 to £1.18 billion at the time of the Great War. Whereas in 1825, most of the money, 84%, was invested in government loans, by 1913, the portfolio was far more diverse. Only 37.8% of British capital remained in government loans. An almost equal amount of money, 34.3%, was tied up in railroad companies. The remainder spread over financial enterprises, raw materials, industrial projects, and shipping business. Similarly, the number of countries British investors gave money to grew in number. In 1825, Mexico received 35.4% of Great Britain's foreign investment in

---

[17] Ibid., 217–219.

[18] Peter J. Cain and Anthony G. Hopkins, *British Imperialism: Innovation and Expansion, 1688–1914* (London, UK: Longman, 2000), 163; Irving Stone, "British Direct and Portfolio Investment in Latin America Before 1914," *Journal of Economic History* 37 (September 1977), 692.

Latin America. About 29.3% were invested in Colombia. Brazil, Chile, and Peru received the other third of British Latin America investment. By 1913, Mexico remained an important investment partner, but only accounted for 11.2%. In contrast, Argentina steadily increased its share of the British investment portfolio in Latin American to account for 40.7%. Also outdoing Mexico was Brazil, which accounted for 21%. Both countries prominence was due to the Baring and Rothschilds, respectively. The rest of Latin America accounted for the remaining roughly 25%, with Ecuador, Bolivia, Paraguay, and Venezuela having the smallest share. At times, the investment portfolios were even more entangled since British investors bought shares in Latin American companies that were owned by individuals from the United States.[19]

By the later part of the nineteenth century, Great Britain faced increasing competition in the Latin American monetary markets. Just like in Africa, where there was a scramble for land, Peter Cain and Anthony Hopkins see a similar scramble for financial opportunities taking place in South America. There was always the fear that just like during the Mexico incident in the 1860s, a foreign creditor might take advantage of internal differences in a Latin American country and expand its empire into the region. By the end of the century, the United States was an active player in both trade and investment. More concerning was "Germany made a bid for informal influence by mounting an export drive consisting of manufacturers, military aid, and settlers backed by the Deutsche Ueberseeische Bank, which aimed at freeing German trade from its dependence on British finance." Even the French, through Crédit Mobilier and Banque de Paris et des Pays Bas, made its influence felt in Latin America.[20] Even if formal empire returning to Latin America over financial entanglement was unlikely, the intertwined financial networks created interdependencies and rivalries that held the potential to cause conflict.

Over the course of the nineteenth century, Great Britain never surrendered its position as the world's premier financier. According to Sidney Pollard, Great Britain provided $20 billion to the world in investments, making up 44% of the investments. The next largest investor in the world was unsurprisingly France with $9 billion or 19.9%.

---

[19] Stone, "British Direct and Portfolio Investment," 694–695, 702.

[20] Cain and Hopkins, *British Imperialism*, 250.

Having played hardly any role around the middle of the century, Germany had quickly emerged as an international power with an investment portfolio of $5.8 billion or 12.8%. The United States by 1914 had gained some international role, but still only accounted for 7.8% of the overseas investments.[21] Pollard does not break down the areas of the world where investments were located, but it is safe to assume that well over 50% were tied up in the Atlantic world.

As the European powers developed colonial empires in Africa, investment opportunities increased. Britain had a significant interest in the diamond and gold mines in South Africa. At the same time, less well-off states like the Transvaal required financial support. In 1892, Rothschilds received permission to place a loan of £2.5 million for Transvaal. The loan and its potential for political control was a gateway to gain a foothold in the Transvaal and slowly draw the region into the British sphere of influence. At the same time, as the imperial realm stretched, Cain and Hopkins claim that "the region still deserved its zero-credit-rating: African states were in no position to attract foreign capital." However, the foreign office did not enjoy the support of a banking institution like with the China trade since the "states in the west and east of the continent were unable to fund sizeable foreign loans."[22] Nevertheless, finance could function as a precursor to empire.

In the end, Baring and Rothschilds were the financial barons of the nineteenth century and helped, with the intertwined financial webs they created, to maintain the vibrant Atlantic community of old. They facilitated investment opportunities in the Americas and eventually Africa, allowing infrastructure projects to proceed and to further bring the Atlantic world together. However, not all was gold in this ever-transforming Atlantic world. The close ties in Atlantic finance meant that events in New Orleans or Vienna could cause dramatic ripple effects and that a financial crisis was no longer localized. Atlantic financial connections throughout the century contributed to a vibrant Atlantic community.

---

[21] Sidney Pollard, "Capital Exports, 1870–1914: Harmful or Beneficial?" *Economic History Review* 38 (November 1985), 492. Some of Pollards and Stone's findings about the growth of British overseas investment are also confirmed by Cain and Hopkins, *British Imperialism*, 161, 207.

[22] Cain and Hopkins, *British Imperialism*, 322, 326, 328, 330.

Bibliography

Cain, Peter J., and Anthony G. Hopkins. *British Imperialism: Innovation and Expansion, 1688–1914.* London, UK: Longman, 2000.

Ferguson, Niall. *The House of Rothschild: The World's Bankers, 1948–1999.* New York: Penguin Books, 1999.

Lepler, Jessica M. *The Many Panics of 1837: People, Politics, and the Creation of a Transatlantic Financial Crisis.* New York: Cambridge University Press, 2013.

Myers, Philip E. *Caution and Cooperation: The American Civil War in British-American Relations.* Kent, OH: Kent State University Press, 2008.

Pollard, Sidney. "Capital Exports, 1870–1914: Harmful or Beneficial?" *Economic History Review* 38 (November 1985): 489–514.

Sexton, Jay. *Debtor Diplomacy: Finance and American Foreign Relations in the Civil War Era, 1837–1873.* Oxford, UK: Clarendon Press, 2005.

Stone, Irving. "British Direct and Portfolio Investment in Latin America Before 1914." *Journal of Economic History* 37 (September 1977): 690–722.

Ziegler, Philip. *The Sixth Great Power: A History of One of the Greatest of All Banking Families, the House of Barings, 1762–1929.* New York: Alfred A. Knopf, 1988.

CHAPTER 15

Industrial Reform, Progressivism, and Socialism

> The working men have no country. We cannot take from them what they have not got. Since the proletariat must first of all acquire political supremacy, must rise to be the leading class of the nation, must constitute itself the nation, it is so far, itself national, though not in the bourgeois sense of the word.[1]

The nineteenth century was an era of ideologues whose ideas and writings dramatically changed the human condition, political relationships, and economic theories. Intellectual figures, like Giuseppe Mazzini, laid out arguments for national identities and constitutional government, and others like Joseph Ernest Renan provided problematic foundations for race theory. Arguably, no other nineteenth-century figure altered the world more than Karl Marx with his theories on economic dislocation, class conflict, and socio-political revolution. Published in 1848, the Communist Manifesto, co-authored with Friedrich Engels, laid the foundation for a revolutionary revision on the political left and the modern industrial society. Marx's ideology was nothing new, communist (the notion of the communal ownership of the means of production) and socialist (state control of the means of production and some of the means of transportation) thought had long attracted adherents as the Atlantic world faced the growing trend of modern industrial social organization,

---

[1] Karl Marx and Friedrich Engels, *Communist Manifesto* (1848), online at https://www.marxists.org/archive/marx/works/1848/communist-manifesto/index.htm.

work conditions, and crowded urban living quarters. However, where communists and socialists called for social or economic change, Marx called for not only a social and economic, but also politically revolution, embracing violence to bring about his new workers utopia. These new radical writings circulated freely in the Atlantic world, putting fears of revolution in the mind of property owners and industrialist, worrying about their workers. As strikes multiply, the Paris Commune in 1870/1871 brought a full-scale communist experiment, and uncertainties only increased to the point that state authority had to step in to assist in the fight against rowdy workers. Even more, as anarchism laced these new movements, states became subject to anti-government terrorism. After mid-century, Marxist reform ideas, but also less radical one, like Social Democracy, Progressivism, and trade unionism, circulated widely around the Atlantic world. As workers looked to these radical ideas for help and inspiration as they faced the dredges of modern industrial society, so too did modern capitalists, industrialists, and property owners share ideas on how to combat the new radicalism of the working classes. The late nineteenth century was a contested period as working and industrial interest clashed and influenced each other around the Atlantic world.

During the last six decades of the early modern Atlantic world, technological advances changed all aspects of production. The steam engine revolutionized manufacturing, no longer relying on water or wind, liberated industry. Steam engines drove power looms, dramatically increasing productivity for spinning and weaving in the textile industry. Steam engines were not only stationary, they allowed for a transportation revolution. By putting engines in ships and on rails, transportation became faster and more reliable. Because of the need for boilers and rails, iron making increased dramatically. All these new tools allowed for machinery that could produce precision-made parts. Industrialization and the breakdown of manufacturing steps created an increasingly unskilled working class, easily replaced and endangered by unsafe conditions in the factory. Reactions to this alienation ranged from the creation of trade union and in Great Britain to the emergence of the Luddite movement, which destroyed machinery.[2] The industrial revolution created dislocation and people searched for ways to cope with these changes.

---

[2] For general works on the Industrial Revolution, see Lenard R. Berlanstein, ed., *The Industrial Revolution and Work in Nineteenth-Century Europe* (London, UK: Routledge, 1992); David S. Landes, *The Unbound Prometheus: Technological Change and Industrial*

The emergence of a working class, pulling the leavers and participating in small steps along the assembly line in the production process, and the creation of a self-conscious working class, which Marx required for his revolution, were two very different things. Time was needed before a self-consciousness working class emerged from the dislocated mass of industrial workers. Between 1780 and 1832, the workers in the most industrialized country, Great Britain, started to develop such a consciousness. Workers had agency in the creation of their identity as they suffered under dismal working conditions, slum-like housing, and poverty-inducing wages. "Between 1780 and 1832 most English working people came to feel an identity of interests as between themselves, and as against other men whose interests are different from (and usually opposed to) theirs," explained working-class historian E. P. Thompson. However, it was not just the working class that grew more conscious and aggravated about their status, women too wondered about their role in society and especially working women partook in the process of defining a working-class identity.[3] This new working-class identity was increasingly at odds with the evolving nation-state identities and capitalist economic systems embraced by states around the Atlantic world.

Aware of the situation in Great Britain, many countries, that aspired to modern industrialism, desired to avoid the social upheaval they saw in British industrial cities. As a result, in Massachusetts in the United States, Lowell's textile barons decided to use single women as workers and to construct a landscaped industrial town with parks and green spaces to be different and prevent social turmoil. The Lowell Mill Girls were a major social experiment, but by the 1830s, the need for increased industrial output, mass immigration, and cost factors altered the situation. Dismissing British social problems, Lowell's industrialist turned to

---

Development in Western Europe from 1750 to the Present (Cambridge, UK: Cambridge University Press, 1969); Charles More, *Understanding the Industrial Revolution* (London, UK: Routledge, 2000). For the Luddites see Brian Bailey, *The Luddite Rebellion* (New York: New York University Press, 1998).

[3] Anna Clark, *The Struggle for the Breeches: Gender and the Making of the British Working Class* (Berkeley: University of California Press, 1997); F. K. Donnelly, "Ideology and Early English Working-Class History: Edward Thompson and His Critics," *Social History* 1 (May 1976), 219–238; Edward P. Thompson, *The Making of the English Working Class* (1980. London, UK: Penguin Books, 2013), 11.

the same techniques their British counterparts used with similar results.[4] Working-class experiences were remarkably analogous during the nineteenth century and grew more so as the century progressed.

The desire to bring about social change, be that a socialist approach to involve the government in the work of manufacturing or communist allowing the workers of a factory to run the facility on their own, was an outgrowth of the French Revolution. Neither Great Britain nor Germany had an intellectual tradition that embraced social reform measures. After 1830, socialism transformed from an idea into a movement that looked to the events of the 1790s for inspiration. The French Revolution suggested a total overhauling of society, not dissimilar from what socialists demanded from an activist government. A wide variety of groups emerged, including the religious-infused socialism of Saint-Simon and primitive forms of communism.[5] The growth of radical-left ideologies was primarily a North Atlantic phenomenon, mirroring industrial development in the same region.

However, the French were not alone in providing philosophical underpinnings and experiments for socialism and communism. The Welsh-born Robert Owen started his own communist experiment in 1799 when he and a partner purchased a New Lanark textile mill. Employing 2000 workers, Owen wanted the mill to operate on a higher moral and social plain. Many of the workers were from the lowest levels of society and Owen determined to provide for his workers. As New Lanark matured, Owen considered expanding his philosophy into a countryside environment. In 1825, Owen tried his ideas with the colony at New Harmony, Indiana. In the United States, his vision fell on deaf ears and within two years the project was economically dead. Individualism and the desire to own land were too strong in North America.[6] Communalism was one of the many avenues residents in the

---

[4] Thomas Dublin, *Women at Work: The Transformation of Work and Community in Lowell, Massachusetts, 1826–1860* (New York: Columbia University Press, 1979); Patrick M. Malone, *Waterpower in Lowell: Engineering and Industry in Nineteenth-Century America* (Baltimore, MD: Johns Hopkins University Press, 2009).

[5] George Lichtheim, *Marxism: An Historical and Critical Study* (New York: Columbia University Press, 1982), 22, 24–25.

[6] For works on Robert Owen's Atlantic work, see Robert A. Davis and Frank O'Hagan, *Robert Owen* (London, UK: Bloomsbury, 2014), ix, xiii, 59–61, 191–222; John F. C. Harrison, *Robert Owen and the Owenites in Britain and America: The Quest for the New Moral World* (London, UK: Routledge, 1969), 31, 90, 126–138, 151.

Atlantic world tried to cope with during the changing economic environment of the industrializing nineteenth century.

By the 1840s, the field of left-leaning philosophers grew even more crowded as new voices emerged, especially in France. Reformers debated the role of government in society. Refining socialism, Louis Blanc called for a greater involvement of the government to benefit the workers. He suggested universal suffrage in order for the working classes to gain a voice in government. Furthermore, a cooperative spirit would help every member of society improve his or her condition. Some French radicals even suggested anarchical systems of government, seeing the state as the problem and not solution to social and economic ills. Among these proto-anarchists was Pierre-Joseph Proudhon. States helped exploit workers in a capitalist society. When Proudhon called out property theft, he alienated many wealthy members of society.[7] The political landscape grew vastly more complex during the first decades of the nineteenth century.

By 1848, Marx and Engels altered the dynamics of radical-left ideology with their powerful, influential, and revolutionary theories. Despite not having an impact on the events of 1848, the program provided by the two authors in the Manifesto of the Communist Party offered a historical dialectic to show how the bourgeoisie and proletariat engaged in an epic struggle. While the former controlled everything, the latter were at the mercy of the ruling middling sort. Marx and Engels provided a detailed program for their new ideology. The communists demanded the end of private property and the stranglehold of the bourgeoisie over finances. They asked the state to take a role in banking, transportation, and communication to prevent abuses by private, profit seekers. In order for workers to overcome their poverty, education needed to be free. The program aimed to end the distinction of class within society. However, there was more to Marx and Engels's program than just a liberation of workers.[8]

---

[7] Richard T. Ely, *French and German Socialism in Modern Times* (London, UK: Trübner, 1883), 108–142; Pamela Pilbeam, *French Socialists Before Marx: Workers, Women and the Social Question in France* (Montreal, Canada: McGill-Queen's University Press, 2000), 144–147, 157, 187.

[8] Marx and Engels, *Communist Manifesto*.

Marx and Engels faced a society in transition. Industrialization arrived on the European continent taking many different forms from the factory style mimicking of the British system in the German states to the trade-focus in France. The uprooting of modern industrialization caused hardship for working families and undermined their well-being. The lack of change created disillusionment. In the words of Émile Zola in Germinal, "Étienne's hopes were raised again; he finally came to believe that a third month of resistance would bring about the downfall of the monster, crouching sluggish and bloated out there in its liar, in the hidden depths of its tabernacle."[9] To many of these reformers, the bourgeoisie was the enemy of the working classes. By the middle of the century, as government and elites created nation-states and political reforms, many workers demanded improvements of working conditions and started to develop their own separate identities.

The cause of the workers was a universal one according to Marx and Engels and not restricted to any one country. They wrote, "In short, the Communists everywhere support every revolutionary movement against the existing social and political order of things." In another place, the authors established, "In the national struggles of the proletarians of the different countries, they point out and bring to the front the common interests of the entire proletariat, independently of all nationality." Because the movement was international, Marx and Engels called on "Working Men of All Countries, Unite!" While in 1848, the ideas were too new and working-class consciousness still developing, Marx and Engels worked tirelessly over the next decades to bring their movement to fruition.[10]

On September 28, 1864, at St. Martin's Hall in London a large number of delegates from European working-class organizations and parties, including Karl Marx, Pierre-Joseph Proudhon, and Louis Auguste Blanqui, came together to form a new organization to promote their views on an international level. The organization centered in London with a governing committee of 21 members. In his opening remarks, Marx explained the situation, "It is a great fact that the

---

[9] Mark Traugott, *The French Worker: Autobiographies from the Early Industrial Era* (Berkeley: University of California Press, 1993), 1–46; Émile Zola, *Germinal*, trans. Peter Collier (Oxford, UK: Oxford University Press, 2008), 380.

[10] Marx and Engels, *Communist Manifesto*.

misery of the working masses has not diminished from 1848 to 1864, and yet this period is unrivaled for the development of its industry and the growth of its commerce." After recounting the challenges faced by workers, including child labor, Marx concluded with a question, "If the emancipation of the working classes requires their fraternal concurrence, how are they to fulfill that great mission with a foreign policy in pursuit of criminal designs, playing upon national prejudices, and squandering in piratical wars the people's blood and treasure?" He concluded with the all too famous call for the workers around the world to unite and fight against their oppressors.[11] The International Workingmen's Association or First International was born.

For the next twelve years, the leaders of the European socialist, communist, Marxist, Social Democratic, trade union, and anarchist organizations worked within the framework of the First International to provide a cohesive program for political, economic, and social change. A good illustration of this cooperative spirit is the 1871 composition by Eugène Pottier, a member of the ParisCommune. He serenaded L'Internationale. While the anthem lamented the oppressed status of the workers and asks them to take liberating action, Pottier also included an important refrain. Every stanza ended with "C'est la lutte finale | Groupons-nous, et demain | L'Internationale | Sera le genre humain." The refrain called on the people to come together for the final struggle, which would allow the International to govern humanity. The anthem provided a rallying cry to the recently formed organization. However, internal conflict between the French and German leaders undermined the International's ability to bring about change.[12] The organizations brought together in the International were never capable of working jointly, but their work sent shock waves around the Atlantic world, similar to the slaves in the Americas seeking emancipation after Saint-Domingue. The cause of the workers gained attention and raised fears after the events of the Paris Commune.

---

[11] Henryk Katz, *The Emancipation of Labour: A History of the First International* (London, UK: Greenwood Press, 1992), 1–20; Karl Marx, "Inaugural Address of the International Working Men's Association," reprinted in *Inaugural Address and Provisional Rules of the International Working Men's Association*, marxists.org.

[12] Donny Gluckstein, *The Paris Commune: A Revolutionary Democracy* (London, UK: Bookmarks, 2006), 235.

During the war with the German states, the French Emperor Napoleon III suffered captivity after the Battle of Sedan and the French political elite decided to remove him from power. However fearful that the National Assembly would restore monarchy and that the disarming of the mostly working-class populated national guard would leave the lower strata of society exposed and at the mercy of conservative elements, workers in the major urban areas of France resisted the disbandment order of the national guard. In Paris, the removal of their canons on March 18, 1871, sparked violence. Within a week, the revolutionaries in Paris organized elections that populated the government of the Commune. The Commune government included a diverse group of radicals such as Jacobins, Proudhonists, and Blanquistes, who at least could agree on social reform measures such as a 10-hour workday and no more government support for religion. On May 21, the government sent troops to suppress the Commune, which started *la semaine sanglante*, "bloody week." After barricade fighting, pushing the Communards back street by street, and the burning of many public buildings, including Tuileries Palace, 20,000 Communards lay dead in an act of state vengeance.[13]

The Paris Commune, its radical socio-political experiment, and the violence associated with the Communards sent ripples across the Atlantic. In the United States, the newspaper media covered the events in great detail, wondering about the meaning of the fateful events in Paris. To labor organizers, the Commune served as a reminder that work remained before the US republic lived up to its political promises for workers. However, with terrible and unsafe working conditions and falling wages, workers struck in 1877 unsettling the country as never before. The image of the Commune served as a reminder for the middle and upper classes of how dangerous working-class agitation was, just like Saint-Domingue had for slaveholders. Henceforth, labor organizers had to illustrate to the bosses that their intentions were not to recreate the Commune with their agitation for higher wages and better working conditions. After 1877, only foreign-born workers continued to celebrate the Paris Commune as a historically significant event. Events like the

---

[13] For works on the Paris Commune, see Carolyn J. Eichner, *Surmounting the Barricades: Women in the Paris Commune* (Bloomington: Indiana University Press, 2004); Alistair Horne, *The Fall of Paris: The Siege and the Commune 1870–71* (London, UK: MacMillan, 1965); Robert P. Tombs, *The Paris Commune, 1871* (London, UK: Longman, 1999).

Haymarket bombing created anxieties about another Paris Commune in the making.[14] Just like the French Revolution's reign of terror and the slave rebellion in Saint-Domingue eighty years earlier had unsettled the Atlantic world, so too did the Paris Commune.

The ParisCommune and the emergence of the First International illustrate that by the 1870s, new identities defined people in the Atlantic world. With the nation-state experiments largely concluded and such states in existence, individuals looked to class as an additional identifier. Having participated in the 1848 uprising in Schleswig-Holstein and representing the mercantile city of Bremen in the United States during the rebellion of the southern states, Rudolph M. Schleiden was back in Europe by the time of German unification and noticed the shift from liberal nationalism to international socialism. From 1867 to 1873, Schleiden defended the right of the duchies of Schleswig-Holstein, assisted veterans of the First Schleswig-Holstein War, and criticized Prussian policies in regard to the duchies within the political framework of the North German Parliament and the German Reichstag. In 1873, he was running for reelection. His liberal-nationalist record suddenly stood for nothing anymore. Neither did his support for the Augustenburg candidacy or the many other topics he had spoken out for in the Reichstag.[15]

By 1873, the new Germany suffered from questions of loyalty as Bismarck provoked an anti-Catholic crusade during the *Kulturkampf*. Later, Bismarck's wrath focused on the expanding parties on the left, which he tried to fight with his anti-socialist laws. The new Germany also dealt with the uprooting nature of industrialization. As these new issues arose, Schleiden faced a powerful challenge from the left in his home district of Altona, a trade port on the Elbe. The ideals of the first half of the nineteenth-century Atlantic world no longer held true and Schleiden represented one of the many who did not adjust.[16] A liberal-nationalist,

---

[14] Katz, *From Appomattox to Montmartre*, 184–185.

[15] Schleiden to Rösing, July 7, 1873, Schleiden to Rösing, January 15, 1874, *Rheinromantik and Civil War*, 196, 200–201; Schleiden also recorded the incident in his diary: July 1, 1873, pp. 19–20, book 25, LBSH.

[16] Schleiden to Rösing, July 7, 1873, Schleiden to Rösing, January 15, 1874, *Rheinromantik and Civil War*, 196, 200–201; Schleiden also recorded the incident in his diary: July 1, 1873, pp. 19–20, book 25, LBSH; Eyck, *Bismarck and the German Empire*, 202–210, 236–243.

who earned his laurels in the mid-nineteenth century's revolutions, he had to make room for the new leaders of the working class and their ideologies, which would grow in influence during the last quarter of the nineteenth century.

What Schleiden faced in the new Germany was an outgrowth of Marxist thought, a new form of socialism. Two competing parties vied for working-class votes in the German states at the time of Schleiden's defeat, the Social Democratic Workers' Party of Germany (SDAP) and the General German Workers' Association (ADAV). Created in Eisenach in 1869, Wilhelm Liebknecht and August Bebel's brainchild, the SDAP, embraced Marxist thought, but also promoted the activities of labor unions. The organization called for a "freier Volkstaat," which allowed for private enterprise and a larger role of the state with unions protecting workers against capitalist extremes. Similar in orientation was Ferdinand Lassalle's ADAV, which aimed to protect the workers from exploitative industrial and capitalist practices, but desired to remain within the bounds of politics. Both groups abhorred Marx's revolutionary overthrow of the established order. In 1875, representative of the SDAP and ADAV met at Gotha to talk about a merger of the two parties. Having suffered frequent government monitoring, the two groups decided to bridge their ideological difference, especially the right to strike, and form the Socialist Worker's Party of Germany (SAPD).[17]

The unified SAPD's program, or Gotha Program, demanded the implementation of universal suffrage, freedom of association, limiting the hours per workday, and health protection for the workers. Under Otto von Bismarck's Anti-Socialist Laws of 1878, the SAPD was banned, styled an enemy of the state. Nevertheless, interest in the party grew, and once the ban expired in 1890, the SAPD reemerged on the political landscape as the Social Democratic Party of Germany (SPD), becoming the largest party in the German Reichstag by 1912. Despite his failure to alter working-class political allegiances, Bismarck implemented a wide-ranging reform package to benefit workers, which laid

---

[17] Ralf Hoffrogge, *Sozialismus und Arbeiterbewegung in Deutschland: Von den Anfängen bis 1914* (Stuttgart, Germany: Schmetterling Verlag, 2011); Arno Klönne, *Die deutsche Arbeiterbewegung: Geschichte, Ziele, Wirkungen* (Düsseldorf, Germany: Diederichs, 1980); Detlef Lehnert, *Sozialdemokratie zwischen Protestbewegung und Regierungspartei 1848 bis 1983* (Frankfurt am Main, Germany: Suhrkamp, 1983).

the foundation for another vast exchange of ideas in the last decades of the nineteenth and early twentieth centuries.[18]

By 1900, reformers in the North Atlantic world could build on centuries of established ties and interactions. Industrialized societies around the Atlantic shared a similar set of experiences and challenges. However, the Atlantic exchange of ideas was still, like during the early Atlantic world, a largely one-directional exchange, with knowledge flowing from Europe to the Americas, primarily the industrialized United States. European universities, considered among the best in the world, witnessed their fair share of students from the Americas. Compared to the expansive and gentry-dominated British elite universities, German universities were public and easily accessible. Former students maintain their relationships once they returned home and worked hard to bring the experiences, and they had enjoyed to their home country. In the United States, graduates of German universities were responsible for the introduction of modernized curriculums and seminar-style classes at universities.[19] However, the intellectual baggage also included social reforms to alleviate the suffering of an urban, industrial proletariat.

Reformers around the Atlantic world witnessed the desolate state of their industrialized societies and called for changes. They could look at each other's experiences for inspiration. However, Europe was the testing ground for reforms and the United States tried to copy as best as possible the accomplishments of urban, social, economic, and political reformers. Bismarck and Napoleon III first experimented with social insurance programs. Bismarck's insurance funds provided for people during sickness, injury, or retirement. In France, *sociétés mutuels* served a similar insurance purpose. Even British politicians realized that social reform measures and to provide for the people were the future and could help deal with working-class radicalism. Across the Atlantic

---

[18] Edgar J. Feuchtwanger, *Imperial Germany: 1850–1918* (London, UK: Routledge, 2005), 108–111, 153–154; Georg Fulberth and Jürgen Harrer, *Die Deutsche Sozialdemokratie, 1890–1933* (Darmstadt, Germany: Luchterhand, 1974); Alex Hall, *Scandal, Sensation and Social Democracy: The SPD Press and Wilhelmine Germany, 1890–1940* (Cambridge, UK: Cambridge University Press, 1977); Gerhard A. Ritter, *Die Arbeiterbewegung im Wilhelminischen Reich: Die sozialdemokratische Partei und die freien Gewerkschaften 1890–1900* (Berlin-Dahlem, Germany: Colloquium Verlag, 1959).

[19] Daniel T. Rodgers, *Atlantic Crossings: Social Politics in a Progressive Age* (Cambridge, MA: Harvard University Press, 2000), 85

region, reformers did not last long in government. In the United States, Progressives represented only minorities within the established party system with little success as a standalone political organization. Georges Clemenceau's reform government in 1906 only lasted months, consumed by labor strikes. A new wave of social reform legislation in Germany lasted from 1905 until 1911. Nevertheless, reformers looked to each other's accomplishments for inspiration, but unfortunately, some only looked at the finished product and how best to copy it, instead of the long process to accomplish the reform measure.[20]

Reformers took special interest in the improvements of the urban landscape. Cities were in great need of work considering many neighborhoods remained garbage-infested slums, especially in the working-class parts. The Préfet de la Seine Georges Eugène Haussmann set the standard for urban renewal in the 1850s. Like many cities at the time, Paris had dramatically grown in size and its infrastructure was unable to cope with the mass of people. During Napoleon III reign, Paris became a massive construction site. The city received a significant update to its water system but more importantly, Haussmann leveled hundreds of buildings and constructed eighty kilometers of new roads. Having purchased the structures they erased caused significant expenditures for the city, but the construction of new, uniform-looking buildings and the sale of apartments allowed Haussmann to recover most of the costs. Furthermore, Haussmann simplified the road network across the Ile de la Cite and improved transportation between the city and the rest of France. Finally, inspired by London's Hyde Park, Haussmann added the Bois de Boulogne and Bois de Vincennes as well as Parc des Buttes-Chaumout and Montsouris to increase the amount of green space around the city. Haussmann set the standard for urban redevelopment.[21] City planners around the Atlantic looked to Paris for decades to accomplish a fraction of what Haussmann accomplished.

Few cities could implement such a large redevelopment project like Haussmann had done. However, governments with autocratic aspiration had a much easier time doing so than democracies. As a result, Porfirio Díaz looked to Paris when he contemplated the redesign of Mexico City. Just liked Paris, Díaz ordered the redesign of the urban core of the city.

[20] Ibid., 54, 57, 72.
[21] Ibid., 166–167.

Already before Díaz, Mexico City embraced Haussmann like changes. When Maximiliano arrived in Mexico, he suggested the creation of the Pasco de la Reforma, mimicking Paris's grand boulevard, the Champs-Elysées. Besides Mexico City, Chicago also contemplated a reenvisioning of the urban landscape like Paris. According to Tyler Stovall, "Paris [was] the ultimate example of the modern world city." With architect Daniel Burnham, Chicago eventually received an urban plan, similar to what Haussmann had done in Paris. However, for lack of money Chicago never fully implemented Burnham's plan, only the White City of the World Colombian Exposition of 1893 served as a reminder of what Chicago ought to have been.[22] Urban landscapes remained a primary focus for reformers to bring positive change to society.

European visitors found the cities in the United States appalling, and they reeked with dirt and garbage. Whereas European reformers actively pursued urban reform measures, including utility supplies, reforms in US cities operated largely in theory. Cities in the United States looked to the public transit systems in Europe for inspiration and desired to implement streetcar routes. However, cities did not plan their franchising well and left private companies with extensive freedoms. Only a handful of cities in the United States, in contrast to Europe, owned the transportation lines running in their city. US reformers noticed that urban planning was infused with social design, which they perceived went against the individualistic nature of the country.[23] Nevertheless, reform ideas continued to crisscross the Atlantic, but implementation in the Americas was more difficult as systems of government diverged dramatically between the two sides of the ocean.

Besides urban reforms, reformers also took inspiration from what were early forms of welfare politics. States finally determined to provide assistance to the poor through public relief. Among the first relief measures to cross the Atlantic was the British poor law system. The United States never developed the same political efforts for poor relief and relied on mutual assistance, which suffered from "social and political

---

[22] Michael Johns, *The City of Mexico in the Age of Díaz* (Austin: University of Texas Press, 1997); Tyler Stovall, *Transnational France: The Modern History of a Universal Nation* (Boulder, CO: Westview, 2015), 133; Jeremy Tambling, "City-Theory and Writing, in Paris and Chicago: Space, Gender, Ethnicity," in *The Palgrave Handbook of Literature and the City*, ed. Jeremy Tambling (London, UK: Palgrave Macmillan, 2017), 6.

[23] Rodgers, *Atlantic Crossings*, 127, 131, 133, 144–147, 152, 165.

fragmentation." Even when the state took a role, providing insurance to the less well-off, state leaders like Bismarck, did not desire to turn the state into a "giant insurance company." Over time more and more people benefitted from Bismarck's sickness, accident, old age, and invalidity insurances. By 1914, almost all Germans were covered by these government-sponsored insurance programs.[24] These programs like so many other reforms were supposed to undermine the appeal of working-class radicalism but failed to do so as working-class identity politics grew in the last quarter of the century.

Despite the predominately North Atlantic interchange of reform ideas, Marxist influence extended into Latin America during the nineteenth century. As Latin America started the process of industrialization, trade unions emerged to protect workers' rights. As a result, Marxist ideas appeared, but they never had the same impact in Latin America. The region was predominately agricultural, and only about 10–15% of the population worked in industry. These factors made it difficult to organize the population and its allegiance to Catholicism created additional hurdles against Marxism. Nevertheless, agro-businesses like sugarcane cutting, banana picking, meatpacking, and mining did see the organization of workers into trade unions. The emergence of these early industries at the turn of the twentieth century allowed Marxism to move out of the intellectual debate circles of the salon. Working people eventually benefitted from Marxist ideas as their protest helped improve the lot of these exploited people.[25] If North Atlantic business communities and political elites worried about radicalism among the workers, Latin Americans should worry as well.

The brand of leftist ideology that reached Latin America's working classes heavily depended on the immigrant group populating the state. Especially, Spanish and Italian migrants were likely to bring with them not Marxist thought but some form of anarchism influenced by Mikhail Alexandrovich Bakunin. In contrast to most trade unions, which only required leadership approval for strikes, anarchists desired a democratic approach to strikes with rank and file approval. Realizing the economic difference, anarchists understood the need for both industrial and agricultural reforms. Whereas Marx expelled anarchists from the First

[24] Ibid., 211, 220, 222–224.
[25] Howard J. Wiarda, *The Soul of Latin America: The Cultural and Political Tradition* (New Haven, CT: Yale University Press, 2001), 212–213, 219.

International, in Latin America, anarchist exercised a significant influence on Marxist organizations. As a result, labor relationships in Latin America were far more antagonistic and violent. As their influence grew, anarchist played a significant role in the Mexican Revolution of the 1910s and the Cuban independence movement in the 1890s. Anarchism emerged as early as the 1870s in Argentina and Uruguay.[26] Marxism had made an appearance in Latin America, but it was an altered version infused with anarchist ideal, carried to the Americas in the mind of many southern European immigrants. The Atlantic exchange of revolutionary ideas continued with reforms and working-class radicalism crisscrossing the ocean to influence each other and transform the experiences of everybody in the region.

When slaves violently challenged their status of bondage in Saint-Domingue during the 1790s, their efforts sent ripples through the entire Atlantic world, creating fears among planters about their bodily survival and the economic well-being of the slave. Similarly, when workers in Paris determined to self-govern and embrace left-leaning policies, they created a new nightmare for elite property owners and the political establishment that had worked hard to create coherent nation-states. However, by the middle of the nineteenth century, identifying with a nation was no longer sufficient for an increasingly self-conscious working class that saw itself oppressed and in need of liberation. The philosophical development of communism, socialism, Marxism, Anarchism, and various other left-leaning ideologies was primarily a European affair starting as early as French Revolution. These ideas travelled with people around the Atlantic world, influencing labor leaders from Buenos Aires to Chicago. The opposition relied on a vibrant Atlantic network of their own to bring about political, social, economic, and urban reforms to address working-class demands. The Atlantic world was a testing ground for new ideas and promoters exchanged them freely along the lines of communication. Where the early nineteenth century witnessed a vibrant intellectual exchange to promote nation-state and constitutional government, the late nineteenth century transformed with new working-class radical idea and reforms freely exchanged across the Atlantic.

---

[26] Ibid., 219–221.

Bibliography

Bailey, Brian. *The Luddite Rebellion.* New York: New York University Press, 1998.

Berlanstein, Lenard R., ed. *The Industrial Revolution and Work in Nineteenth-Century Europe.* London, UK: Routledge, 1992.

Clark, Anna. *The Struggle for the Breeches: Gender and the Making of the British Working Class.* Berkeley: University of California Press, 1997.

Davis, Robert A., and Frank O'Hagan. *Robert Owen.* London, UK: Bloomsbury, 2014.

Donnelly, F. K. "Ideology and Early English Working-Class History: Edward Thompson and His Critics." *Social History* 1 (May 1976): 219–238.

Dublin, Thomas. *Women at Work: The Transformation of Work and Community in Lowell, Massachusetts, 1826–1860.* New York: Columbia University Press, 1979.

Eichner, Carolyn J. *Surmounting the Barricades: Women in the Paris Commune.* Bloomington: Indiana University Press, 2004.

Ely, Richard T. *French and German Socialism in Modern Times.* London, UK: Trübner, 1883.

Eyck, Erich. *Bismarck and the German Empire.* New York: W. W. Norton, 1968.

Feuchtwanger, Edgar J. *Imperial Germany: 1850–1918.* London, UK: Routledge, 2005.

Fülberth, Georg, and Jürgen Harrer. *Die Deutsche Sozialdemokratie, 1890–1933.* Darmstadt, Germany: Luchterhand, 1974.

Gluckstein, Donny. *The Paris Commune: A Revolutionary Democracy.* London, UK: Bookmarks, 2006.

Hall, Alex. *Scandal, Sensation and Social Democracy: The SPD Press and Wilhelmine Germany, 1890–1940.* Cambridge, UK: Cambridge University Press, 1977.

Harrison, John F. C. *Robert Owen and the Owenites in Britain and America: The Quest for the New Moral World.* London, UK: Routledge, 1969.

Hoffrogge, Ralf. *Sozialismus und Arbeiterbewegung in Deutschland: Von den Anfängen bis 1914.* Stuttgart, Germany: Schmetterling Verlag, 2011.

Horne, Alistair. *The Fall of Paris: The Siege and the Commune 1870–71.* London, UK: MacMillan, 1965.

Johns, Michael. *The City of Mexico in the Age of Díaz.* Austin: University of Texas Press, 1997.

Katz, Philip M. *From Appomattox to Montmartre: Americans and the Paris Commune.* Cambridge, MA: Harvard University Press, 1998.

Klönne, Arno. *Die deutsche Arbeiterbewegung: Geschichte, Ziele, Wirkungen.* Düsseldorf, Germany: Diederichs, 1980.

Landes, David S. *The Unbound Prometheus: Technological Change and Industrial Development in Western Europe from 1750 to the Present.* Cambridge, UK: Cambridge University Press, 1969.

Lehnert, Detlef. *Sozialdemokratie zwischen Protestbewegung und Regierungspartei 1848 bis 1983.* Frankfurt am Main, Germany: Suhrkamp, 1983.

Lichtheim, George. *Marxism: An Historical and Critical Study.* New York: Columbia University Press, 1982.

Malone, Patrick M. *Waterpower in Lowell: Engineering and Industry in Nineteenth-Century America.* Baltimore, MD: Johns Hopkins University Press, 2009.

Marx, Karl, and Friedrich Engels. *Communist Manifesto.* 1848. https://www.marxists.org.

More, Charles. *Understanding the Industrial Revolution.* London, UK: Routledge, 2000.

Pilbeam, Pamela M. *French Socialists Before Marx: Workers, Women and the Social Question in France.* Montreal, Canada: McGill-Queen's University Press, 2000.

Ritter, Gerhard A. *Die Arbeiterbewegung im Wilhelminischen Reich: Die sozialdemokratische Partei und die freien Gewerkschaften 1890–1900.* Berlin-Dahlem, Germany: Colloquium Verlag, 1959.

Rodgers, Daniel T. *Atlantic Crossings: Social Politics in a Progressive Age.* Cambridge, MA: Harvard University Press, 2000.

Schleiden Papers. Landesbibliothek Schleswig-Holstein. Kiel, Germany.

Schleiden, Rudolf, Johannes Rösing, and Clara von Ammon. *Rheinromantik und Civil War: Im diplomatischen Dienst in den Vereinigten Staaten von Amerika: Briefe von Rudolph Schleiden, Johannes Rösing und Clara von Ammon aus den Jahren 1862–1874.* Edited by Norbert Klatt. Göttingen: Klatt, 2003.

Stovall, Tyler. *Transnational France: The Modern History of a Universal Nation.* Boulder, CO: Westview, 2015.

Tambling, Jeremy, ed. *The Palgrave Handbook of Literature and the City.* London, UK: Palgrave Macmillan, 2017.

Thompson, Edward P. *The Making of the English Working Class.* 1980. London, UK: Penguin Books, 2013.

Tombs, Robert P. *The Paris Commune, 1871.* London, UK: Longman, 1999.

Traugott, Mark. *The French Worker: Autobiographies from the Early Industrial Era.* Berkeley: University of California Press, 1993.

Wiarda, Howard J. *The Soul of Latin America: The Cultural and Political Tradition.* New Haven, CT: Yale University Press, 2001.

Zola, Émile. *Germinal.* Translated by Peter Collier. Oxford, UK: Oxford University Press, 2008.

CHAPTER 16

A New Atlantic World

> During this delay time was given me for reflection and gradually as my eyes wandered over the crowded waterway with its myriads of crafts of every description, from the quaint channel fishing-boat to the mammoth East India trader and ocean steamer, topped by the flags of all nations and hailing from every accessible part of the known world, carrying the productions of every clime and laden with every commodity, … The fight I had brought with me across the broad Atlantic was such a strange and curious one that I naturally wondered whether, after all trouble, time and expense it had cost me, this pioneer cargo of Nebraska goods would be marketable.[1]

By the time of the Great War, the Atlantic world was a different place from over a century ago. Explorers, settlers, travelers, revolutionaries, and ideologues created new interconnected Atlantic worlds and brought myths about various regions to a wide variety of people. Among the greatest mythologies of the late nineteenth century was the US West and nobody perpetuated this myth better and more permanently than William Frederick Cody. Cody brought something never seen before, but much anticipated and desired, to Europe when he penned the words above. His Wild West Show had a major impact on the United States. Cody sought out any opportunity to present his innovative form

---

[1] William F. Cody, *The Wild West in England*, ed. Frank Christianson (Lincoln: University of Nebraska Press, 2012), 25.

© The Author(s) 2019
N. Eichhorn, *Atlantic History in the Nineteenth Century*,
https://doi.org/10.1007/978-3-030-27640-9_16

of entertainment. Thus, in 1893, when Chicago illustrated its desire to become equivalent to Paris with its massive urban renewal by hosting the World's Columbian Exposition, or better known as the White City, showing its embrace of ancient architectural styles, Cody's show came to perform. Some visitors never reached the exposition area with its elaborate landscaping and structures, getting detoured by Cody who had pitched his tents right outside the doors of the World's Columbian Exposition. Buffalo Bill's Wild West Show: Congress of Rough Riders of the World was a unique new show presented to the Chicago audiences.[2] The Wild West Show showcased the mythology of the US West and encapsulated the nineteenth-century Atlantic world, building on the century long efforts to form coherent states, attract tourists, and deal with question of race and empire.

Buffalo Bill's Wild West Show presented and fostered the mythologies of the western plains. Cody made a point to use Native Americans in his show, paying them well and allowing them to practice their own traditional ways and religion, which was far better than their status on reservation land, where missionaries wearily opposed the continuation of traditional religious ceremonies. With experienced helpers, Cody choreographed an exciting performance for guests, including stage coach chases, bison hunts, and a Native American attack on a settler's cabin fended off by a bunch of wild cowboys. Organized according to the standards of modern circuses like Barnum and Bailey, the show grew into an efficient machine that traveled the country and the North Atlantic world.[3]

What premiered in Chicago was a new show, an Atlantic show. The Congress of Rough Riders of the World broadened Cody's appeal to bring more immigrants to the show. He still attracted those fascinated by the nostalgia of the old west, but there was a new crowd of respectable middle-class citizens who could draw lessons from the old west for their modern urban residence. More importantly, the Congress of Rough Riders of the World included not only Native people and cowboys, but also Russian Cossacks, Turkish riders, English and German cavalry soldiers, and finally Gauchos from the Argentinian pampas. However,

[2] Louis S. Warren, *Buffalo Bill's America: Warren Cody and the Wild West Show* (New York: Vintage Books, 2007), 419–420.

[3] Joe Dobrow, *Pioneers of Promotion: How Press Agents for Buffalo Bill, P. T. Barnum, and the World's Columbian Exposition Created Modern Marketing* (Norman: University of Oklahoma Press, 2018); Warren, *Buffalo Bill's America*, 229.

Cody only had real Gauchos with him from 1893 to 1895; afterward he used imposters, actors. Eventually, even some of his cowboys were actors who worked for the growing entertainment industry. With barbwire fences, real cowboys, just like Gauchos, had gone extinct as herding animals in the western plains was no longer needed.[4] Buffalo Bill's Wild West Show was a microcosm of the Atlantic world. Tourists traveled the Atlantic world seeking to learn about other cultures and experience firsthand the wild frontier regions; Cody brought these places and its people to them for an easy ride by streetcar or even walk away.

Even more, the show reminded people of the new imperialism of the late nineteenth century confirming white-Eurocentric assumption of how much indigenous people were an obstacle to the advances of European civilization. The Congress of Rough Riders continued to evolve as international events change public attitudes and imperial clashes arose between British forces and Boer settlers in South Africa. In 1901, Cody signed a contingent of Boer to address the popularity of the Boer in the United States during the conflict. He had no problem putting British and Boer cavalrymen on stage to foster his image as a peacemaker, an image in dramatic contrast to his antics after the defeat of George A. Custer at Little Big Horn when he traveled west to avenge the fallen Custer, taking the scalp of an indigenous warrior.[5] Even so, no black Africans joined the cast, Cody had assembled an eclectic group that represented the various groups and regions of the late nineteenth century Atlantic world and the myths associated with the various frontiers regions.

However, Cody's impact on the Atlantic world grew even larger than the cast of his show. In March 1887, Cody departed New York for his first European tour. Participating in the show and crossing the ocean were 90 Lakota, 200 horses, and 18 bison. The show was a rousing success and performed in front of royalty, including Queen Victory, and layperson alike. Buffalo Bill's show spent a third of its lifespan overseas touring Europe. In 1889, Cody and his cast were in Paris for the opening of the Exposition Universelle, which included the unveiling and opening of the Eiffel Tower. Besides Paris, the shows visited Spain, Italy, Austria, and Germany, performing before hundreds of thousands of interested individuals who wished to see the exotic and mythical West of

---

[4] Warren, *Buffalo Bill's America*, 401, 421–425.
[5] Ibid., 427–428.

the United States, they had read about in travel literature and fiction stories. Cody returned in 1902 for another five-year tour.[6] The Wild West Show left a permanent impact on Europe and its perception of the US West. People did not have to travel as tourists into the US West; instead, they could watch it visualized at home, confirming their views.

By 1906, Native American and cowboys from the United States were a typical fare in German circuses. In 1912, Sarrasani created a new show, Sarrasanis-Wild-West-Show, which included Lakota from the Pine Ridge Reservation, the same reservation where Cody recruited his Native performers. Europeans took a keen interest in Native Americans, treating them at times like exotic commodities. Especially, Native men attracted attention and were even sought after for some intimate meetings. At the same time, Native Americans were given a great amount of respect from the European population. For example, Standing Bear, a Minneconju, suffered an injury during the 1889 Buffalo Bill's Wild West Show visit to Vienna and stayed behind to recover. He eventually married his nurse, Louise Rieneck, and the couple moved to Pine Ridge Reservation where they raised their children.[7] However, Lakota were not the only indigenous people of interest appearing in European entertainment.

In 1907, Carl Hagenbeck in Hamburg presented at his zoological gardens not only a cage-less animal experience, but also human beings. In what became known as *Völkerschaustellung* (exhibition of peoples), indigenous people became curiosities just like animals. Hagenbeck had put Africans on display for the first time in 1874 to address contemporary desires in show business and among the visiting public. Putting indigenous people on display for white European amusement was not a new development. Already in 1501, Eskimos had made an appearance in Bristol and Brazilian natives in Rouen, France, in the 1550s. African indigenous people attracted significant attention at the end of the nineteenth century and early twentieth century at international exhibitions and in zoological gardens.[8] Where Africans had long shed the chains of

---

[6] Ibid., 282, 297.

[7] Ibid., 354, 390–396, 406,

[8] Anne Dreesbach, *Gezähmte Wilde: Die Zurschaustellung "Exotischer" Menschen in Deutschland 1870–1940* (Frankfurt am Main, Germany: Campus, 2005), 14; Bernth Lindfors, *Africans on Stage: Studies in Ethnological Show Business* (Bloomington: Indiana University Press, 1999), vii; Robert W. Rydell and Rob Kroes, *Buffalo Bill in Bologna: The Americanization of the World, 1869–1922* (Chicago, IL: University of Chicago Press, 2013), 115.

slavery, the new entertainment industry literally put them in cages for the amusement of white Europeans in the North Atlantic states.

The works of Charles Darwin and African explorers stimulated white European fascination in Africa and its inhabitants. Some like Theodore Roosevelt went to Africa to hunt, while others went to explore the remaining obscure and unknown parts of the continent. To others even, Africans were closely associated with animals and considered a missing link between humans and apes in the evolutionary chain. As Bernth Lindfors writes, "This 'animality' of Africans was the feature thought to set them apart from the more rational varieties of the human species. So when the unusual African specimens began to be displayed publicly in Europe and the United State, emphasis often was placed on their kinship with animals." In the worst of cases, like Ota Benga, Africans were placed in cages in zoos. With the high demand by zoological gardens, there were not enough Africans willing to degrade themselves as caged animals. Enterprising Afro-Americans stepped in fill the void as faux Africans. Lindfor concludes, "Africans were again denigrated, humiliated, dehumanized, and exploited. Transported across the seas, employed in demeaning jobs, blacks labored largely for the benefits of whites and were rewarded mostly with contempt."[9] There had been many transformations in the nineteenth-century Atlantic world; however, for African people little had changed over the past one hundred years.

During the nineteenth century, the early modern Atlantic world community transformed as new technology eased the transfer of people, good, and ideas, but an Atlantic community persisted. The early modern predecessor created unique experiences that existed because the various parts of the Atlantic region were intimately connected. Local experiences would not have been the same without their interaction within the Atlantic network. In the course of the nineteenth century, various localities transformed because they were part of a set of Atlantic networks. Without the intellectual, mercantile, migratory, tourist, and investment ties that connected the various parts of the Atlantic region, experiences would have been very different. Africa, without returning freedmen and women, without the removal of people into slavery, without European imperial designs, and without the altered trade patterns following the end of the slave trade would have been a dramatically different continent. Independent Mexico would have been dramatically different had it not been for the imperial

---

[9] Lindfors, *Africans on Stage*, viii–x.

designs of the United States and France as well as the long road to create a constitutionally governed Mexican nation-state. The pampas of Argentina and agricultural regions of Chile would have languished as undeveloped frontier much longer had it not been for the trade in hides and migration patterns of the nineteenth century as well as the desire to put the region to economic use by removing the indigenous population. The Atlantic world remained a profoundly interconnected world.

Nobody better represented the many shared experiences of the nineteenth-century Atlantic world then Giuseppe Garibaldi or Henry Williams. This Italian seafarer ventured into the Atlantic as a mariner, but he more so left his mark as a revolutionary. After the failure of the Italian uprising in the 1830s, he tried his luck in South America, assisting Brazilian provincial separatism and Uruguayan republicanism. He helped in the defining of state identities by participating in local and national conflicts. Failing to help bring about an Italian nation-state, Garibaldi briefly came to North America, returned to Italy and assisted in the final push to oust the hated Austrians. Once more, the US nation-state and eventually France called on the revolutionary hero to assist in their own struggles. Garibaldi was something of a mercenary of national liberation and showcased how much people in the nineteenth century crisscrossed the Atlantic. He was truly a nineteenth-century Atlantic world revolutionary nationalist.

Similarly, Williams was a Trinidadian lawyer who also fostered national identity politics. However, he supported a new movement against the exploitation of Africans and the imperial occupation of the continent by bringing into existence the Pan-African Movement. Leaving his native Trinidad for first the United States, then Canada, and finally London to become a lawyer, Williams faced many obstacles. Concerned with the treatment of Africans and the exploitation of the continent, Williams helped create the African Association. He crisscrossed the Atlantic in his pursuits to bring equal justice, freedom, and respect to his fellow Africans and Afro-Americans, and he embraced politics to further his cause. Just like Garibaldi, Williams extensively travelled in the Atlantic region to promote notions of African equality and rights against imperial oppressors. He was an Atlantic reformer.

However, besides the desires to end imperial oppression and create constitutional nation-states, the nineteenth-century Atlantic world continued to struggle with legacies of colonialism. The various imperial powers had pushed indigenous people off their lands, advanced the settlement frontiers, and had worked to explore the interiors. The vastness of Africa remained unknown at the start of the nineteenth century, but explores quickly changed that. In the course of the century, the struggles started in colonial times between indigenous people and frontier settlers continued unabated and increased in brutality as new weapons technology had a devastating impact.

The Age of Revolutions had dramatically transformed the Atlantic world with independence movements in the Americas significantly reducing in size the European colonial empires. Furthermore, revolutionary change gave way to a new age of industry and nationalism. Ideas continued to follow the established Atlantic patterns and allowed the various people and states around the ocean to liberally exchange perspectives and share experiences. The region transitioned from one form of bound labor into another that was supposedly superior where workers labored at low wages in factories under abysmal conditions, giving rise to working-class extremist identities. States developed identities and went to war to enlarge their territories with neighbors, indigenous people, and themselves. The need for reform was felt everywhere as the century progressed. From 1789 to 1914, the Atlantic world dramatically transformed as new means of transportation and communication allowed revolutionaries, migrants, merchants, settlers, and tourists to crisscross the ocean, share their experiences, and bring new ideas into other parts of the Atlantic world, contributing to a vibrant community that left every part of the region a uniquely different and continuously changing place.

Bibliography

Cody, William F. *The Wild West in England.* Edited by Frank Christianson. Lincoln: University of Nebraska Press, 2012.
Dobrow, Joe. *Pioneers of Promotion: How Press Agents for Buffalo Bill, P. T. Barnum, and the World's Columbian Exposition Created Modern Marketing.* Norman: University of Oklahoma Press, 2018.
Dreesbach, Anne. *Gezähmte Wilde: Die Zurschaustellung "Exotischer" Menschen in Deutschland 1870–1940.* Frankfurt am Main, Germany: Campus, 2005.
Lindfors, Bernth. *Africans on Stage: Studies in Ethnological Show Business.* Bloomington: Indiana University Press, 1999.
Rydell, Robert W., and Rob Kroes. *Buffalo Bill in Bologna: The Americanization of the World, 1869–1922.* Chicago, IL: University of Chicago Press, 2013.
Warren, Louis S. *Buffalo Bill's America: Warren Cody and the Wild West Show.* New York: Vintage Books, 2007.

Index

A
Africa, 5, 6, 15, 16, 22, 25, 106, 108, 109, 112, 114, 125, 135, 136, 141–143, 145, 146, 149, 153, 165, 173, 174, 246, 247, 271, 273
African Association, 180, 182, 183, 272
Algeria, 164, 165
American Colonization Society, 112–114
Antwerp, 17
Apache, 152
Argentina, 22, 23, 28, 43–50, 97, 154, 204, 205, 239, 240, 246, 263, 272
Asbóth, Alexander, 195
Ashanti War, 145, 153
Austria, 30, 31, 41, 62, 187–190, 200, 203, 240, 269

B
Balboa, Vasco Núñez de, 143
Bank of England, 241–243
Barbados, 145, 179

Baring Brothers, 237–242, 244, 247
Belgium, 16, 25, 43–50, 63, 146, 187, 200
Belmont, August, 239, 243
Bendixen, Georg Laué Julius, 1–3
Bismarck, Otto von, 173, 202, 203, 257–259, 262
Boer, 150, 151, 153, 269
Boston, 37, 38, 125
Brazil, 4, 21–23, 26, 30, 40–51, 64, 88, 89, 96, 98, 107, 133–135, 204–206, 239, 241, 246
Bremen, Hanseatic City of, 16, 17, 19–21, 23, 26, 35, 36, 39, 41–44, 47, 51, 257
British Empire, 17, 123, 128, 136, 154
British Parliament, 78–80, 106, 128, 173, 257

C
Caillié, René, 146
Calhoun, John C., 67, 191
California, 1–3, 26, 40, 150, 151, 167, 168

Canada, 5, 23, 24, 43–50, 114, 172, 173, 240
Cape Colony, 21, 23, 150, 153
Cape Town, 182
Caribbean, 5, 46, 51, 114, 127, 129, 160, 163, 166–168
Carr, John, 110
Castilla, Ramón, 25, 130, 131, 133
Catholic Church, 63, 78, 79, 82, 170, 198–200, 257
Cavour, Camillo, 187–189
Céspedes, Carlos Manuel, 134
Cetshwayo, 153
Charleston, 39, 132, 192
Charles X, 82, 83, 164, 165
Chicago, 142, 225, 226, 234, 261, 263, 268
Chile, 1, 5, 22, 23, 26, 27, 43–50, 90, 128, 147, 155, 163, 164, 240, 241, 246, 272
Chincha Islands, 163
Cleburne, Patrick, 194
Cody, William Frederick, 267–270
Colombia, 27, 42–50, 90, 129, 168, 240, 246
Colombo, Cristoforo, 143
Confederate States of America, 29, 30, 132, 147, 192–197
Constantinople, 227, 233
Cook, Thomas, 216, 231–234
Costa Rica, 27
Cotton, 135, 165, 195, 241, 243
Crazy Horse, 152
Cuba, 5, 16, 41–51, 107, 133, 134, 159, 166–169, 243
Cuban Libre, 169
Cunard, 19, 30, 37, 38, 40
Custer, George Armstrong, 152

D
Darwin, Charles, 147, 271

de La Fayette, Marquis, 216, 219
Dom Pedro II, 88, 96, 216, 224–226
Dublin, 79

E
Egypt, 62, 147
Erie Canal, 218, 220

F
Fichte, Johann Gottlieb, 55, 56
France, 16, 42–51, 62, 82–84, 90, 98, 136, 147, 160, 187, 199–201, 203, 244, 246, 253, 254, 256, 259, 260, 270, 272
French Revolution, 61, 80, 82, 84, 85, 237, 252, 257

G
Garibaldi, Giuseppe, 95–100, 188–190, 203, 272
Garrison, William Lloyd, 125, 126
Grand Tour, 216, 218, 219, 222, 223, 232
Grant, Ulysses S., 162
Great Britain, 4, 5, 16–18, 20, 21, 23, 24, 28, 29, 31, 36–51, 62, 68, 79, 80, 83, 89, 98, 106, 107, 114, 123, 126–128, 131, 133, 136, 143, 147, 150, 153, 154, 163, 170–173, 187, 199, 200, 238, 240–242, 245–247, 250–252, 254, 259, 261, 269
Great Salt Lake, 144, 150
Greece, 61, 62
Guatemala, 25, 28
Guerra Carlista, 166
Guerra de los Diez Años, 134
Guerra del Paraguay, 154, 204–206
Guerra de Reforma, 165

H
Habsburg Family, 30, 199
Haiti, 41, 43–50, 160, 161
Hamburg, 1, 2, 19–22, 31, 41, 244, 270
Haussmann Paris, 260, 261
Hungary, 30, 31, 41, 86, 87, 167, 193, 195, 204

I
Ireland, 16, 31, 38, 68, 79, 126, 171, 194
Irish Republican Brotherhood/Fenians, 171, 172
Italy, 31, 41, 43, 44, 47, 48, 68, 95, 98, 99, 188–190, 203, 269, 272

J
Jackson, Andrew, 30, 67, 87, 241, 242
Jerusalem, 227
Jesuits, 90
Juárez, Benito, 199, 201, 202

L
La Amistad, 16, 17
Lagos, 136
Lakota, 143, 151, 152, 269, 270
Lamartine, Alphonse Marie Louis de Prat de, 84
Latin America, 23, 27, 28, 31, 46, 51, 61, 88–90, 128–130, 142, 143, 147, 168, 202, 205, 237, 239, 240, 245, 246, 262
Le Havre, 17
Liberia, 110, 113, 114
Lieber, Franz, 196
Lincoln, Abraham, 130, 132, 133, 190–192, 197
Liverpool, 17, 37, 241
Livingstone, David, 146
London, 27, 28, 63, 110, 126, 146, 171, 173, 202, 238, 239, 244, 254, 260
López, Francisco Solano, 204–206
López, Narciso, 60, 90, 166, 167, 205
Louisiana, 131, 243
Louis-Philippe, 74, 83, 89, 165

M
Macdonald, John A., 172, 173
Mapuche, 155
Marx, Karl, 249–251, 253–255, 258, 262
Marxist, 250, 255, 258, 262, 263
Massachusetts, 125, 126, 192
Maximiliano, Ferdinand Maximilian, 199–202, 261
Mazzini, Giuseppe, 56, 57, 95–99, 188, 189, 249
Meagher, Thomas Francis, 27, 194
Mexico, 27–30, 41, 43–50, 59, 60, 128, 129, 142, 162, 163, 165, 186, 198–203, 240, 242, 245, 246, 260, 263, 271
Mitchel, John, 108, 193, 194
Mormons, 149–151
Morocco, 161–163
Mount Vernon, 218, 221

N
Nagelmacker, Georges, 233
Netherlands, 5, 41–50, 63, 150, 154, 164
New Brunswick, 40, 172, 240
New Orleans, 39, 60, 146, 226, 241, 243, 247
New York, 17, 22, 36–40, 75, 108, 114, 126, 146, 149, 169, 172, 196, 198, 217–220, 225, 239, 243, 269
Nicaragua, 40, 168

Norddeutscher Lloyd, 19
Northern Tour, 218, 222

O
O'Connell, Daniel, 78, 79
O'Donnell, Leopoldo, 162
Olshausen, Theodor, 24, 25
Owen, Robert, 252

P
Palestine, 227
Pampas, 154
Pan-African Conference, 181, 182
Panama, 168
Paris, 17, 28, 45, 46, 67, 82, 83, 169, 238, 239, 255–257, 260, 263, 268, 269
Paris Commune, 255–257
Patagonia, 154
Pedro, Dom, 89, 96, 134, 204
Peru, 27, 41, 43–50, 108, 129–131, 147, 163, 164, 246
Philadelphia, 126, 220, 225, 226
Piedmont-Sardinia, 95, 96, 187, 189
Portugal, 237
Proudhon, Pierre-Joseph, 253, 254
Prussia, 41, 196, 202, 203
Puerto Rico, 5, 41, 169
Pullman, George, 233
Putnam, George, 215–217

R
Raymond & Whitcomb, 234
Renan, Ernest, 67
Rio de Janeiro, 40, 96, 111, 135, 225, 226
Rio de la Plata, 28, 89, 98, 205
Rio Grande do Sul, 61, 97
Roca, Alejo Julio Argentino, 154

Roosevelt, Theodore, 216, 228–230, 234, 271
Rosas, Juan Manuel de, 28, 154
Rothschild, House of, 237–244, 246, 247
Russwurm, John Brown, 113, 114

S
Saint Domingue, 255, 256, 263
Salm-Salm, Felix, 201, 202
San Francisco, 1, 2, 145, 150
Santana, Pedro, 161
Santo Domingo, 160, 161, 170
Savannah, 39
Schleiden, Rudolph M., 39, 257
Schlesinger, Louis A., 167
Schleswig-Holstein, 24, 64, 202, 257
Schurz, Carl, 193
Second Great Awakening, 88
Sheridan, Phillip H., 152, 196
Sherman, William T., 196
Sierra Leone, 106, 110, 112
Sitting Bull, 152
Slavery, 4, 5, 16–18, 23, 25, 30, 36, 61, 106–110, 112, 114, 125–136, 174, 191–194, 197, 204, 255, 263, 271
Sokoto, 135, 136
Sokoto Caliphate, 135, 136
South Carolina, 40, 67, 127, 132, 191, 196
Spain, 4, 27, 28, 31, 41, 43–50, 62, 63, 133, 134, 147, 155, 159–167, 169, 170, 199, 237, 239, 269
Stanley, Henry Morton, 146
Sylvester Williams, Henry, 179

T
Timbuktu, 145

INDEX

Trinidad, 110, 179, 183, 272
Tucker, John R., 147, 148, 163
Turner, Frederick Jackson, 142

U

United Fruit Company, 231
United States, 17–24, 26–30, 38–51, 79, 88, 106–108, 112, 113, 126, 127, 129, 131, 133, 136, 141, 144, 147, 151, 153, 163, 164, 166–172, 186, 192–198, 200, 201, 239–244, 246, 247, 251, 252, 256, 257, 259, 261, 267, 269, 270, 272
Uruguay, 97–100, 188, 204, 205, 239, 240, 263
U.S. Civil War, 257

V

Valparaiso, 1, 2, 26, 147, 164
Vanderbilt, Cornelius, 40
Venezuela, 42–50, 166, 170, 241, 246
Vera Cruz, 199, 200

W

Walker, William, 167
War of 1898, 169
Wertheman, Arturo/Arthur Werthemann, 147
Williams, Wellington, 217, 218

Z

Zulu, 143, 151, 153